Me and Bobby D.
A MEMOIR

by
Steve Karmen

Published by Hal Leonard Corporation
7777 West Bluemound Road
P.O. Box 13819
Milwaukee, WI 53213, USA

Trade Book Division Editorial Offices:
151 West 46th Street, 8th Floor
New York, NY 10036

Gay Haven Supper Club photos by Leo Fiedor used by permission of Mrs. Helen Fiedor

Visit Hal Leonard online at **www.halleonard.com**

Library of Congress Cataloging-in-Publication Data

Karmen, Steve.
  Me and Bobby D. : a memoir / by Steve Karmen.-- 1st ed.
    p. cm.
Includes index.
  ISBN 0-634-04876-7
  1. Karmen, Steve. 2. Composers--United States--Biography. 3. Darin,
Bobby. I. Title.
  ML410.K1878A3 2003
  781.64'092--dc21

                    2002155715

Printed in the Canada
First Edition

10 9 8 7 6 5 4 3 2 1

Table of Contents

To Nancy

Thank You!

"I need a favor, please..."

"Is this clear...?

"What do you think about...?"

"Will you give me your opinion...?" (The old joke: "You want my opinion? *You're drunk*. I want a second opinion; *Okay, you're ugly, too!*")

I wish to express deep appreciation to my state-of-the-art friends who were willing to read, and then offer constructive commentary as this effort took shape.

Ken and Patsy Olshan graciously became my first-call sounding board. Their generosity of time helped this book grow.

My unconditional pals, Chuck Balis, David Heacock, Kenny Karen, Larry Karmen, Buddy Polatsch, David Saperstein, Julie Schwartz and Geoffrey Wharton provided the endless encouragement I needed along the way.

Joyce Myrus urged me to think like an eighteen-year old again—*yeah, that's how we really talked back then*—and to tell the story not only as I remembered it, but as I felt it as well.

Susan Grushkin, Bryan Hurley, Michael Jacobs, Dr. Abbe Karmen (PhD), Dr. Mel Karmen (PhD), Lisa Karmen, Elinor Lipman, Dr. Ron Odrich (clarinet player/DDS), Lee Perlman, Pauline Pinto, Ed Rak, Linda Riefberg and Debbie Slevin were unfailing in their honesty and support.

I am indebted to Pam Bernstein, Liza Dawson, Tad Lathrop, Peter Rubie, Jane Rosenman, Carole and Lyle Stuart, and Robert Youdelman for their invaluable professional guidance; and to Keith Mardak, Mary Vandenberg and John Cerullo, of Hal Leonard Publications for their confidence in my writing.

Special thanks to my daughter, Carrie Karmen Curro, who designed the photo layouts. Carrie always made me laugh when she asked: "Is that really you, Dad? Wow, you looked so *cool!*"

Nancy Coyne, to whom this book is dedicated, taught me to trust the process. Her caring became the motivation to do my best work. Nancy is my glass-half-full. This book is infinitely better for her loving presence in my life.

For me, the neon marquee is still flickering out there

somewhere in the forgotten mist. My *Brigadoon*. Maybe I'll be reading the entertainment section of *The Times* and spot an ad that uses that same fifties-style typeset, and I'll suddenly feel the old buzz and start searching for our names. Sometimes, I catch a whiff of something that reminds me of that unique, impersonal, stale, beery nightclub smell, and I'm back there in an instant, back to an innocent time before concert tours, before theaters-in-the-round, before stadium-sized audiences and roadies and strobe lights and theatrical smoke effects, before customized sound systems and amplified everything, back when the world was still mono.

I've kept a scrapbook of my career—you know, *for the grandchildren*—and about twenty years ago, as I was doing a periodic update, I thought that the story of how I got into the music business might make a good novel. So I sat down at my brand new word processor and wrote it. When I finished, it occurred to me that it wasn't really a novel at all, but an idea that could work well as a Broadway *musical*. After all, I am a composer and lyricist—why not try to develop it for the stage? So I did—libretto, thirty-plus songs, the works. Then, when I started to have *book* problems with the *musical*—the curse, I've discovered, of all such projects— I decided to go back to the source material, my novel, to learn where I had gone astray. *I've always wanted to take another pass at that thing,* I said to myself, trying to justify the continuing obsession that telling this story had clearly become. And then, after I'd rewritten the *novel*—and hopefully learned how to solve the problems with the *musical*—some very dear and trusted friends read it, and ever so tactfully suggested that I had one more step left: the big one; the one where you don't hide in the fiction, but the one wherein you tell the truth. That is how this memoir came to be.

For legal reasons, I've changed a few people's names and altered identities. Others characters are amalgams of the many show business types I've encountered in my travels. For the record, Club Temptation was actually a nightclub called The Gay Haven Supper Club. But since *Club Temptation* was the title of my novel, my musical, and the non-ending metaphor for what that period of time has meant in my life, that name has become more real to me than the actual name of any club ever was.

And, of course, the unforgettable friend of my youth, Bobby Darin, was real, too; just not yet the Bobby Darin of "Mack The Knife" fame, who ruled the record charts for a time in his life, who later married movie-star Sandra Dee, and who wanted to become a legend before he was twenty-five. This is his story as well as mine.

What you are about to read has been nothing more than a few sentences in other books. What really happened was the first great adventure of my life.

November 1972. TWA Flight 711. Lucky seven-eleven: the gambler's flight to Las Vegas. Smiling Jack's Crosby baritone crooned out our flight plan: *...an on-time landing at McCarron Field in four-hours-and-twenty minutes, blue skies all the way, buh-buh-buh-boo, no turbulence, settle back, relaaaax, and enjoy.* Yeah, sure. My stomach was an acid pit. Amazing. After all these years, just talking to him on the phone had given me the runs.

I eased back into my first-class seat. *Something to drink before lunch?* What d' ya got that stops churning? Pepto-Bismol on the rocks? Maybe I'd feel better after a drink or two or eight. No, booze would only blur the edge, and this time *I* needed the edge. That was *my* flight plan: clean, crisp, clear, sharp, in control. Coffee, black. Right-right.

There'd been a "Hollywood" tone in his voice. I hadn't heard it in a long time. A con? Absolutely. Well, maybe not; give him the benefit. Respect? *I'd certainly earned it,* I thought, desperate to puff up my surprisingly fragile ego. My music was being heard daily on radio and TV by millions of people; the jingles I'd written for Budweiser and Pontiac and Hershey and Wrigley Spearmint Gum and Nationwide Insurance were as popular and familiar in American culture as some of the hit songs. I'd already won five CLIO Awards—the Oscars of the advertising industry. I was considered one of the top composers in the business. By any standard I was a success; and best of all, I'd made it on my own! *Sure-sure, Karmen, bang away, you can pound your chest as hard as you like, but it won't help you here.* No, respect for anyone, particularly someone from his past, was never high up on Bobby's list. Beneath the forced humor he was clearly maneuvering for position. And he hadn't forgotten how to push my buttons.

"I'm Mr. Darin's driver," the uniformed chauffeur said, meeting me at the gate. Unexpected. A nice touch. Still the maker of grand gestures, just to remind me of who he was—no, who he had become—and that out here, at least, it was his deck.

But you knew my flight info. Why didn't you come out and meet me yourself? Were you too busy? That would have been class-class. We could've hung out at the pool, shot the shit about the old days, reconnect, have a few laughs...

No! Gotta watch those expectations. This is all *business.* Professional—that's what our relationship is now. Wait a minute: what *relationship?* One phone call in sixteen years doesn't make a relationship.

At the registration desk, there was a message in his lumpy scrawl: "Dinner show, 8:00 PM., see Victor, don't eat. We'll dine backstage between shows." *Yeah, Bobby, I've always wanted to "dine" backstage. The big time.* When the pretty room clerk asked for my credit card, I smiled—no comp. Why did I even expect one? Even a grand gesture has its limits. I checked in, and killed the rest of the afternoon in the casino, making an appropriate contribution to the Desert Inn's bottom line—after all, the headliner might suddenly appear just to count my chips.

I'd brought my best custom-made suit, a brand new hand-made Sulka shirt, and three silk ties to choose from—no narry-Larry's or wide-Clyde's, just straight down the middle perfect, conservative, accomplished, assured, confident.

Bullshit! Nothing felt or looked good enough. Was he this nervous about seeing me? Not likely. When Bobby went after something, he was never nervous.

By seven forty-five, I had been dressed for half an hour—way too soon. I paced, I watched TV, I brushed my teeth, I paced some more, I went to the bathroom twice. At ten-to, I went down to the show room and announced myself to Victor, who blandly led me to the center-most booth, the house table, the star's table, his table, set for one, another nice touch.

The room was only half full, about four hundred, eating, drinking, noisily awaiting the show. Not bad for a Monday, but not great either. Not like the days of his hits, when he was breaking records everywhere. But he hadn't had a hit in a long time. Maybe he was playing out an old contract. *Yeah, you must really be in a bind to reach all the way back for me.*

This was the new Vegas crowd, women in light, summery dresses, skirts and blouses, nothing serious. Some men wore jackets, even a few ties, but most were in open shirts, jeans, cowboy hats—dressing down, the new casual, farmers-on-a-bus-tour, the white-socks-and-brown-shoes-from-Omaha. You could go almost anywhere today without a tie or jacket, another reminder of how different things used to be.

A waiter appeared. I ordered a Coke.

Come on, Steve, let it go, enjoy this moment. You have nothing to fear any more. What's past is done. Finished. History. He's just Bobby Cassotto, your old friend from high school.

But the glitz and power of the room were all pulsing out a different message: he's *Bobby Darin*, the household name, the *Star*. Who was I kidding? The butterflies were for good reason. This was a command performance. Mine.

At eight o'clock, the lights dimmed in respect for casino promptness. The Oakies rustled with anticipation. The show-curtain billowed up to reveal the orchestra *Variety* had described as one of the largest ever to accompany any act in Vegas. Half a house or not, he still had clout. The production number was huge: at least twenty dancers. I tried guessing which girls were plastic, but it didn't help. *What the hell am I doing in Las Vegas? I could have graciously been too busy. Nah, that would have been too easy. Besides, he's too smart—he knew I'd come.*

The comic was one of the hot kids from the Carson Show, and he got big laughs, and there were moments when I almost started to enjoy myself. But then he would say something that would remind me of where I was, and then *bam*, back to reality. Now I just wanted to get it over with and go home.

Finally, after an overture of all his hits, the room went black. There was a long, low timpani roll. A single spotlight illuminated the microphone that rose dramatically up out of the floor.

Suddenly, the drums stopped.

There was an instant of absolute silence.

And at precisely the right moment, with no intro, and with the impeccable timing and self-assurance he was famous for, he simply stepped into the light. Moses had parted the Red Sea for the eight o'clock show. They roared.

A chill shot through me. *Dear God, why am I here, ripping open old scars...*

Part One

NEW YORK CITY
April 1956

Chapter 1

"WANNA BE IN A BAND?"

Around the world, momentous events were happening that would change the course of human history.

In the Middle East, Egyptian President Nasser was mobilizing his armies for war against Israel, and British Prime Minister Winston Churchill was waving his cigar, mumbling that if hostilities occurred, then *Her Majesty's Government would have no choice but to come to the aid of that tiny new-born nation.* (I don't do a good Churchill—Bobby did a great Churchill.)

At home, it was an election year. President Eisenhower was fully recovered from his recent heart attack, and healthy enough to run for a second term. He was undecided, though, about keeping Richard Nixon as his running mate. The Democrats were squabbling about whether to re-nominate Adlai Stevenson, loser to Ike four years ago, or to present a fresh ticket of Senator Estes Kefauver—star of the popular Congressional hearings on labor racketeering—for President, and Senator John F. Kennedy for vice-president. Kefauver-Kennedy sounded good, but there was intense debate about whether Kennedy would help or hurt the ticket. Should a Catholic be a heartbeat away from the Presidency? Would he support the Constitution, or answer to the Pope? In either case, Ike looked unbeatable— people weren't going to vote against a guy who'd just had a coronary.

In the West Bronx, spring had brought the locals back to the benches across the street from our apartment building, with daily arguments about the new baseball season. Will the Yankees win again? Manager Casey Stengel thinks so, if Mickey Mantle's battered knees hold up, and Whitey Ford has another good year. And who's better: Mickey, Willie or *Da Duke? An' how 'bout dose rotten Dodgers, treatening to move to L.A.? Dey had some noive!*

Of course, absolutely none of this mattered in my life.

Gene Vincent's "Be Bop A Lula" was moving up with a bullet on the *Billboard* charts. Carl Perkins's "Blue Suede Shoes" had made top ten, joining The Platters' "Great Pretender," and Frankie Lymon's "Why Do Fools Fall In Love?" It was the dawn of rock 'n' roll, and Columbia Records had just announced they would no longer use the old 78 rpm lacquer format, but would release all new singles only on vinyl 45s. The big band era was teetering on the brink of Elvis Presley, with effects being felt everywhere—particularly in the nightclub business, where Fats Domino was booked in to headline at the Copacabana during prom time with Chuck Berry to follow. Guitar sales were skyrocketing—I had just bought one, wanting to be a part of the new music. Folk songs were battling rock for chart space, and Harry Belafonte, my idol, shirt open to his twin-circled belt buckle, was breaking records at the Waldorf Astoria's Empire Room, and getting big air play with "Mama Look A Boo Boo," a novelty calypso song that Bobby wanted to try in the act. These things were *significant!*

But while I was watching Ted Steele's "Teen Bandstand," listening to Alan Freed and Murray the K on the radio, and devouring the music business trade papers—*Variety, Backstage, Billboard,* and *Cashbox*—my parents were reading *The New York Times* and worrying that Ike's military background would inspire him to dispatch a few battalions out somewhere just to prove he could still do it. I had recently fulfilled the legal obligation of my eighteenth birthday by registering at the Selective Service office. If things got hot, I would surely be drafted. My only hope for a deferment, the second-overriding obsession of all boys my age, was to stay in college—students were exempt from military service. If I could stick it out for four years, a bachelor's degree might lead to the continuing safety of medical school, where I could follow in my big brother's footsteps, learn to save mankind from crotch-itch and athletes foot, and by then be too old for the draft, and most importantly, cured of the show-biz bug.

Arthur, seven years my senior, was (fanfare, please) *my-son-the-doctor,* the fulfillment of my parent's hopes and dreams. Diligent, studious, and hard working, he was everything a good son should be. I, on the other hand, was (don't get up) *my-other-son-the-bum, the fledgling musician who was wasting his life slamming on that rotten guitar all day long, and grunting around the house in that stupid West-Indian accent!*

I had tried, but calculus and chemistry and Roman history seemed hopelessly irrelevant, especially when that time could be better spent practicing finger-picking and writing songs. By the end of that first painful month at NYU, I was cutting classes regularly. Then, one day, I just stopped going altogether.

Admitting the dreadful deed to my parents, however, had required much more courage than I possessed. I never felt rebellious. I just wanted to do something I loved: to make music. So, in order to delay the inevitable explosion, I had continued the charade of being a student, inventing fictitious class schedules, and pretending to leave for school early in the morning—but instead, hiding out around the corner until my parents went to work, then doubling back to play my guitar or just spend the day listening to records. The longer they believed I was still in college, the more chance I believed there was for something positive to jump-start my career.

It was not to be. A few short weeks after I quit, the meticulously grinding wheels of organized education did me in. A letter arrived, addressed to my parents from the Dean of Freshmen Students, saying that, "Your son, Stephen Karmen, has attended classes an insufficient number of times to qualify for final exams, and in accordance with University policy has be given an F in all subjects, and put on academic probation..."

"So what are you going to do now, Mr. Big Shot?" my mother had yelled, waving the envelope at me.

"I want to see if I can make it as an entertainer."

"Our kind of people are not entertainers!"

"What kind of people are *our kind of people?*"

"Not entertainers!"

"Bobby's going to try and make it, and I want to try too."

"Your smart-aleck friend quits school, now *you* quit. When will you ever think for *yourself*, you mindless sheep?"

I tried to be calm. "I do think for myself, Ma. I don't belong in the medical profession any more than you belong with the Rockettes."

"Maybe he's right," Pop said.

Deep down, I believed my father was an ally, though he rarely showed open support, and certainly never in front of my mother. But Pop had a special look in his eyes when I played my guitar, or sang—a look that I read as approval. I liked to think I was taking the kind of step forward that he might have dreamed of for himself, and that I was raking the embers of some long-buried spirit of adventure. If he could cross half the world to live in the Land of Opportunity, why, then his son could be in show business, or at least give it a try. Yes, I wanted desperately to believe that. "I know you understand, Pop. I want to be a musician, a song-writer, a singer. Bobby's doing it..."

She was on a roll. "He's a mindless bum, too! Do you ever open a book? No! Do you ever spend a minute studying? No! Just banging on the piano and yelling with that guitar."

"I was singing, Ma, not yelling."

"Do you know what the neighbors think of you?"

"I don't care what the neighbors think."

She never heard me. "Do you know what the whole family thinks of you? You're a bum! Who goes out at eleven o'clock at night? Burglars, and robbers, and my son! Do you know how many times Mrs. Raymond-downstairs has complained about your screaming, and jumping on the ceiling, blasting music all day while her husband is trying to sleep?"

Mr. Raymond-*downstairs* worked at some dumb night job—I didn't know what—but whatever it was, his lifestyle was playing havoc with my music. "I have to rehearse *somewhere!* I'm not asking for your permission. I don't need *anybody's* permission. I would just like to think you were on my side."

"So, what can we do?" Pop, ever the referee, pleaded. "Kill him? Murder him? So, maybe school *isn't* for him. Arthur says if he tries it, maybe he'll get it out of his system." My brother's words were always treated as gospel. "Now, *please*, let's end this argument."

But it didn't end. In the months that followed, the mood at home became one of mourning. Any passive tolerance for my musical antics vanished completely. Now, deep hurt and anguish filled their eyes whenever I entered the room. I was officially *a dropout!* No one in our entire family had ever dropped out of *anything*. Abandoning my formal education flew in the face of everything my parents knew. We were a sprawling clan of *professional* people—the damn word haunted my existence. No Karmen child ever dared even *dream* of becoming a fireman or a policeman or a cowboy or a farmer, and most certainly not an entertainer. I wasn't born in a trunk in the Princess Theater in Pocatello, Idaho. There were no ex-vaudevillians hanging around to teach me the buck-and-wing. My rela-tives were accountants, electrical engineers, garment manufacturers, maternity-wear salesmen, furriers, and bookkeepers. One uncle ran a luncheonette—a definite cultural rung below the rest, but even *his* trade earned passing grades because he went to work early and put in long hours, giving him the appearance, at least, of a semi-professional man. (Uncle Jack could slice corned beef so thin that you could see through it—a tangible talent—and the occasional free sandwiches he gave to the family didn't hurt his *professional* standing, either.) My cousins were all either *in* college, or had already graduated with degrees in something respectable. And my revered brother—*Hallelujah!*— had attained the pinnacle of pinnacles, becoming the first doctor, and everyone's pride and joy.

We were a middle-class Jewish family living in a predominately Irish-Catholic neighborhood in the West Bronx. My most powerful childhood memories are ones of fear. Fear that Arthur might not get into medical school. My parents were convinced that only small quotas of Jews were admitted to these ultimate bastions of higher learning. Fear that our Catholic neighbors would find ways to take advantage of us and abuse us—a fear not unfounded when the toughs from the next block occasionally took sport by beating up on the few *Christ-killers* in my building when they could catch us. (Sometimes, in response to my frantic ringing of the lobby bell, Arthur, who was six-feet-four, and Pop, who was short but immigrant-tough, would come charging down the stairs to frighten away the hordes of attacking Huns.) Fear that our Jewish neighbors would think less of us because we didn't keep a kosher home—the main reason we never invited anyone into our apartment. (In fact, until I was eleven years old, I naively believed we ate *sturgeon* and eggs every morning for breakfast. It was only after I'd gone to a friend's apartment one weekend that I learned that the sturgeon of my innocence was really forbidden bacon under a nom-de-traif.) Fear that demanded we make the once-a-year, face-saving journey to schul to show our observance of the high-holy days, passing through non-Jewish neighborhoods, risking yet more beatings. Fear so deeply rooted it dictated that the only way to survive in a world of non-stop anti-Semitism was to become an educated *professional* man.

So strong was my parent's commitment to Arthur's education, that in the years before he was accepted to medical school, we lived in silence. Tip-toe-and-whisper was the order of the day, every day. The higher his education, the more restrictions. We cowered in the kitchen when he was at home studying, taking care to walk and talk softly and not clatter dishes. Our radio was rarely on. Even listening to Jack Benny or Fred Allen with headphones on a crystal set was ruled out because I laughed too loudly. (Our sleeping arrangements had my parents in the single bedroom of our apartment, Arthur in the living room on a pull-out cot, while I slept on a daybed in the kitchen alcove next to the stove.)

For his part, Arthur simply shut us out, barricading himself in the living room, hanging a quilt over the door to muffle any utterance we might issue by mistake. When we inherited my grandfather's TV set, it was placed where none of us could watch, in Arthur's living room, as a ready reward during a study break. But Arthur didn't watch; he really studied. Things got so bad during final-exam weeks that we were not permitted to flush during the night for fear of disturbing the slumbering Einstein.

My mother's shining moment came when Arthur received his first acceptance to medical school. Someone clearly had a sense of drama, because at seven AM on Thanksgiving morning, 1949, a Special Delivery letter arrived from the Medical School of Mt. Sinai Hospital granting Arthur entrance to the next phase of his pre-ordained life. He would later be accepted by three other schools, finally attending New York University Medical School on academic scholarship. But nothing came close to the thrill and sheer joy my parents experienced on that Thanksgiving morning. Four years later, when he graduated, with honors, finally *Doctor* Karmen, the entire family gathered to witness the ceremony—uncles, aunts, cousins, anyone who could walk. He was close to the top of his class, and *cum laude* followed his name on the program. He had missed *magna cum laude* by only a few points. Someone must have flushed when they were not supposed to.

How the Muse of Music managed to sneak into our stifling study-hall apartment when my mother wasn't looking and to save me from all this *professionalism*, I'll never quite understand. (I've always regarded my talent as a gift from a higher power. For this story, I've called it a Muse.) But one day, when I was about nine, there she was—and I know she's a *she*—arms open wide, inviting me into her magical realm, offering me a sense of individuality and expression I had never been allowed before. Her gift of music became my first real love.

It began with a recorder, a small, wooden, flute-like instrument that Arthur had brought home—a requirement of his high school music class (he never played it). Almost at once, I found I could produce notes by blowing softly into it while covering the holes with my small fingers.

My parents considered the squeaking merely a passing annoyance, but a few weeks after figuring out how the recorder worked, and wanting to show off to anyone who would pay attention, I convinced my fourth grade teacher to let me present a radio show to my classmates. It was the first time my Muse of Music would go head-to-head up against the Muse of Education.

Instead of doing my homework, I spent a few hours with my imagination scribbling out a "Lone Ranger" script, imitating the style of that popular adventure program. The idea was for others students to act out the parts I had written, while I provided the musical background on the recorder: the opening and closing themes, the Indian signals, the ominous long-tones before the bank robbery, even the sound effect of horses (by slapping my hands on my knees). Playing the opening strains of the *William Tell Overture* on the recorder was easy enough; and if my lips dried up, I reasoned, I could always whistle the part.

Unknown to me, however, on the day of the performance, my teacher, Miss Brennan—who always wore the same blue polka-dotted dress every single day—had invited our school principal to sit in and witness this exhibition of budding talent. Charles L. Klein was a tall bully who was born frowning, and who doled out punishment by roughly jabbing his finger into the chest of any student caught bending his rules. When Mr. Klein entered the room just before show time and took his place along the side of the desks, reeking discipline, arms folded, the bulldog furrows of his brow deep enough to hide a number-two pencil, I choked. Blowing too hard on the recorder gets you nothing. Zip. No sound. Only air. My backup whistle abandoned me, too. My musical cues were inaudible. Now, terrified in the presence of authority, I urged my unrehearsed actors into continuing without me. After the Lone Ranger and Tonto had finally caught the bad guys, put them in jail, and then rode off into the sunset accompanied by my weakly-patting sweaty hands and my most forlorn whistle, Mr. Klein broke the applause-less silence by summoning me to the front of the room; not for praise, but to remind me that school was a place to *learn* (finger, finger in my chest) and to not waste time on *nonsense* (finger, finger!). The only good thing that happened that day was that no one reported the events to my parents.

My Muse, however, was undeterred. Like all Jewish boys approaching bar mitzvah age, I was required to attend Hebrew School to learn the portion of the Torah that I would recite on my thirteenth birthday. The classes were taught by a young rabbi named David Zucker, whose personal form of discipline was to rap distracted students on their knuckles with his peacekeeper ruler.

Initially, I liked Hebrew School. The singsong rhythms of the prayers came easily, and my clear voice hovered above my classmates as we chanted. I was a good student—so good, that at the end of my first year I was presented with the prize for being the best in my class. The award certificate was accompanied by a little plastic radio, which my parents allowed to be plugged in on a shelf in the kitchen over my bed.

One day the prize radio exploded—literally going *boom!*— showering little pieces of plastic all over my bed and on to the kitchen floor. It seems that the volume had been turned so low to accommodate Arthur's studying requirements that my parents thought it was off. When the tubes overheated and shattered, I think my Muse was sending a message not to push things too far too fast.

Next, I discovered how to play Pop's mandolin, a relic from the old country that he took out occasionally to attempt a Russian folk song—the only melody he knew. By picking away at the double strings, I figured out how to make a chord, and could then accompany myself when I sang.

Then I brought our old second-hand upright piano back to life, and began imitating the songs I'd heard on the radio (only, of course, when Arthur wasn't studying). The piano had been purchased before I was born with hopes that Arthur might show interest (he didn't), and had stood un-played in our living room for years, nothing more than a repository for the doilies my mother knitted each silent night. The first song I ever wrote was inspired by one of the older neighborhood girls, Marilyn Kroft. I was ten. I called it "Symphony For Marilyn" (what else?), and took great pains to write it out, using my own form of invented musical notation. My parents hardly noticed my effort, and sadly, I never got to play it for Marilyn—she moved away. But at a holiday gathering that year, one of my uncles agreed to listen patiently while I played it for him, providing for me the first-ever, family praise of my musical abilities.

When you have a Muse in your corner, you can't go wrong. When I was eleven, She convinced my cousin Larry that he would have more fun playing basketball than playing the alto saxophone, and his discarded instrument was offered to me. It took a major negotiation for Pop to convince my mother that there would be no horn blowing in the house while Arthur studied, and when the glorious instrument arrived, he asked one of our neighbors—an ex-musician named

Jerry—to show me how to set it up. Jerry was a big, friendly man with enormous lips, puckered and full. He was in the umbrella business now, but Mom equated his big lips to his experiences with the saxophone, and warned me not to blow too hard or I might become deformed. Jerry showed me that saxophone fingerings were similar to those of the recorder, and by the end of that first day, I had mastered "Auld Lang Syne," and given my mother a migraine headache.

The next week, Pop found a music teacher so I could take lessons. But when music so thoroughly captured my imagination and I began spending all my free time practicing (and not studying), my grades began to fall off, and the lessons were stopped. Still, I kept on playing, concentrating on what I had been taught in those few lessons. I would practice in the bathroom when no one was home, the notes bouncing off the tile until there was nothing left in the world but me and my music. Practicing was a way of shutting out everything else. When I brought my new instrument to play at a seventh-grade show-and-tell class, one of the teachers suggested that I apply to Music and Art High School, to further develop my obvious abilities. But even though I filed an application and was accepted at Music and Art, my parents would have none of it. Instead, when the time came, they insisted that I follow my brother's footsteps (of course) and go to the elite Bronx High School of Science, in order to acquire the foundation for a *professional* career. (Bronx Science graduates more future doctors, physicists, biologists, nuclear engineers, and top business types than any other City school. Science kids are considered super-smart: you have to pass a test to get in.) And though it was not obvious to me at that moment, I'm certain my Muse had a hand in this, too.

Three memorable things happened as I entered high school.

First, Arthur moved out to live at Bellevue Hospital as part of his medical school training, and the living room became my bedroom. Now I could make music without interrupting his educational process. Then, because she no longer had my brother to wait on hand and foot, my mother took a job as the bookkeeper for my uncle Ben, the electrical engineer, out in Freeport, Long Island, and her four-hour daily commute meant that our apartment would be empty each afternoon after school and an even more conducive place to practice.

And on that most important day of all, I met Walden Robert Cassotto.

Bobby had also wanted to go to Music and Art High School, but because he was neither a musician nor an artist, couldn't get in; so he went for the best education available in the New York City public school system, took the test, and was accepted at Bronx Science. Before his heathen storm had come crashing into my parched world, I was just another straight-ahead kid with an undeveloped gift, filled with teenage uncertainty, only hiding in my music. It was going to take a good strong kick in the ass to seriously change my life's direction. Bobby Cassotto was that kick.

I had just given another unaccompanied saxophone recital to another bored student assembly, when he stopped me on the stairway.

"Hey, you, with the curly hair. Wanna be in a band? Come on, we'll have some fun. We've got drums—that's me—electric guitar, trumpet, and piano. We're looking for a sax. We're all here at Science."

"You a soph?" I asked cautiously.

"Junior."

"Well, I'm kind of...you know, just learning."

"Yeah, I heard," he winked mischievously.

"Was it *that* bad?"

"No, of course not," he smiled warmly. "Hey, if it was bad, would I ask you to join the band?"

"Well, I don't read too well, and..."

"So what? Come on, we're *all* learners too. I can't read much either. Don't worry, you'll be in good company."

"When do you practice?"

"It's hard after school 'cause I work, but we try for weekends. Saturdays, sometimes Sundays, at Eddie's house; he's the pianist. I got a piano at home too; when my mom feels okay we practice there. Come on, say yes."

There was a spirit about him I felt I could trust. We shook hands, and exchanged phone numbers.

Our first rehearsal was more noise than music as we began to learn about each other. I was hesitant and poor at sight-reading, but could play a piece of music after I'd heard it a few times. Dick Behrke, our trumpet player, was a better reader, and I started to follow his lead and phrasing as we developed a musical bond. Guitarist Walter Raim had his amplifier cranked up so loudly that at first it was a battle just to tell if he was even playing the right chords. Bobby, I discovered, had admitted the truth: he couldn't read drum music at all, but could keep pretty good time, and would follow changes when told what to do. Eddie Ocasio, the pianist and the only one who could actually sight-read any music put in front of him, was our immediate choice to become leader of the band.

We all chipped in so Eddie could go downtown to the music district on 48th Street and buy some combo-orks. These easy-to-play arrangements of current hit songs were ready-made for small bands of different sizes. In a few weeks we were able to play three songs from beginning to end. But how would we know if we were any good? Eddie's parents were always nodding along approvingly while we practiced—something my parents would never have done—but still they were biased, we thought. It was time for the validation of strangers. Bobby's brilliant idea was to call people on the telephone, randomly picking names from the Bronx phone book, and then admit the truth: "Hello, I'm a drummer in a new band, and we need someone to tell us how our music sounds. Would you mind listening for a few minutes while we play something for you over the phone? Gee, thanks! Hang on, here it comes!" Then he would dash back to his drums and we would begin. One of our better tunes was Irving Berlin's "You're Just In Love," from the Broadway show *Call Me Madam*. We were particularly together during the duet part where the saxophone plays "You Don't Need Analyzing," and the trumpet plays "I Hear Music And There's No One There." But, more often than not, when we had finished playing, the party on the other end had already hung up. Once in a while someone stuck it out to tell us that we were "wonderful." Could they hear the drums? "Not really, the guitar was too loud." Could they hear the sax? "Not really, the phone was too close to the drums." But it didn't matter. We began to believe in ourselves. All we had to do was convince someone else.

We had been rehearsing for about two months, when Eddie breathlessly informed us that he had talked the teacher in charge of the recreation hall at Science into letting our band augment the jukebox at one of the weekly after-school dance sessions in the gym, where, normally, the kids would dance only to records. We wouldn't be paid, of course, but it would be *for experience*, and our first working job. "Ten tunes is all we need to know," Eddie said. "We can always play them twice: a couple of lindies, a rumba, a mambo, twelve-bar blues. Does anybody know a Charleston...?"

"What's a Charleston?"

"...And something slow, with lots of piano solos, so we can stretch for time if we have to."

"Yeah, right, and drum solos," Bobby added.

"Yeah, and guitar solos..."

"And trumpet solos..."

"And sax solos..."

"*And*, if we do well," Eddie said triumphantly, "it's ninety-nine percent definite that we'll be the band at the Junior Prom! And for *that* job, we'll get paid!"

I cut my last chemistry class to set up early. We opened with a fox-trot, "I'm In The Mood For Love," with lots of trumpet/sax duet, and a long piano solo, definitely a hold-her-close type song.

No one danced. When the song ended, there was no applause.

"Turn on the juke box," somebody yelled, "play 'Comes Along Love'."

"Let's do 'Business in F'," Dick said, "the harmony'll get 'em."

The harmony didn't get 'em.

"Let's try the mambo."

Our instruments sounded hollow in the vast gymnasium, so different from the small confines of Eddie's apartment. Any sense of melody was lost up in the rafters among the ropes and basketball hoops. We tried playing louder, but volume didn't help. Still, no one danced.

"Can you play 'P.S. I Love You'?" someone asked.

We didn't know it.

"Can you play 'The Number Mambo'?"

We didn't know that either.

"Turn on the juke box!"

"Let's do 'Saints,' Bobby," Eddie ordered, desperation in his voice. It was our best tune—up-tempo Dixieland, lots of solos, and a big sing-along with Bobby leading the way. We had planned it as our closing number, but it was clear that if we didn't win the crowd quickly, we would be closing sooner than we had planned. With visions of a stethoscope around my neck instead of a saxophone, I moved the microphone over to the drums.

"Hey, come on over here, everybody!" Bobby shouted. "Gather 'round! That's right, even you folks in the corner. We're going to do a song that needs all your help." He broke into the drum solo intro.

"Oh, when the Saints

Go marching in,"

"Come on, everybody, sing with us!" Bobby yelled, as we joined him in harmony.

"Oh, when the Saints go marching in,

Oh, I want to be in that number

When the Saints go marching in."

At first, only girls came over, shyly, in groups of three or four. But then, a few boys joined them. Bobby was in rare form. "That's it! Come on, sing along with us."

"Oh, when the Saints..."

"Drum solo!" he called, and he was off, gyrating to the rhythm like Gene Krupa, pounding wildly on his tom-tom and cowbell, his hair flying in all directions. Then, he introduced each of us in turn to take our solos. By this time, he had all the kids clapping along.

We had won them over.

No, Bobby had won them over.

"What are we going to play *now* for a closer?" I asked excitedly, during our first break.

"We'll play it *again*," Bobby said, proudly, "and they'll love it again!"

While Eddie was our musical leader, Bobby quickly

became our main attraction. His junior-year shop project was to build a special microphone stand so he could drum and sing at the same time, and we began practicing songs that featured his voice, with the rest of us singing background. These vocal numbers—songs like "Wimoweh, The Lion Sleeps Tonight" and "You Call Everybody Darling"—became an important part of our little band's material.

Bobby found a place to buy used white dinner jackets for five bucks each, and we shortly earned back our investment by sharing the twenty-five dollar fee we earned as the band at the Junior Prom.

We rehearsed steadily through the winter months. As our confidence grew, our band enjoyed the glow of playing at every weekly student assembly, and at the after-school dance sessions in the gym. Lunch hour was a daily opportunity to gather in the dining room for an impromptu jam session. Study halls were spent listening to records on headphones in the library, nodding along silently to Duke Ellington, and Benny Goodman's 1938 Carnegie Hall Jazz Concert. We felt different from the other students, proud *musicians* in the midst of all those intellectual science types.

In the spring, Eddie wrote letters to some of the Catskill Mountain resorts that advertised in the *New York Post*, inquiring about summer band jobs (Catskill hotels, especially the smaller ones, were notorious for their frugality, and there was the very real possibility that one of them might hire a beginner band). Two hotels answered, and dates were set for the owners to hear us play.

Our first audition took place at New York's Nola Studios, a building filled with large rehearsal rooms that rented by the hour. We were scheduled for four PM. When we arrived, dressed in our white dinner jackets, three other bands were milling around in the hallway, their instruments all set up and ready to play. We learned that everyone had been told to be there at four PM.

As each group was called into the room, we waited with the others, listening attentively through the closed door, whispering amongst ourselves, trying to get a feel for what the owners liked. Each band had a vocalist and played short versions of the current Top 40 songs, some of which we knew but many of which we didn't. At five-thirty, it was our turn.

The owners were seated at a long table in front of a large bandstand. "We're running late. Play a mambo," yelled one of the unsmiling faces as we rushed to set up. They stopped us almost as soon as we began. "Okay, play a fox-trot...a lindy...a samba...a rumba...a tango...okay, read the music on the bandstands."

"What's the tempo?" Eddie asked.

"Bright four," the grumpy owner called, as if we should have known.

The music had no title. The signature was jammed with sharps. Out of the corner of my mouth I asked Dick what key it was. He wasn't sure. Eddie kicked it off. After eight bars, Bobby and I were lost. The owner stood and waved us to stop. "You kiddies ever cut a show before?"

The single most important measure of a competent resort band was its ability to "cut a show"—to sight-read the background music for the entertainment that was booked at the hotels each weekend. Unfortunately, this absolutely essential requirement was our most glaring weakness. "No," Eddie answered with as much confidence as he could muster, "but we just need a few minutes to work it out. We also do some wonderful vocal numbers. Would you like to hear..."

"You mean you can't *read*? How the hell do you expect to cut the show?"

"We've only been together for a few months," Eddie said, trying to ignore our failure. "But, would you like to hear..."

"Call us next year," the owner laughed, for the enjoyment of the others at the big table, "when you're out of diapers. Who else is out in the hall?"

A week later, the results were the same at our second audition. Our inability to cut the show had cost us both jobs.

Then we got lucky.

Bobby had been dating a girl in his English class whose mother fancied herself as a booking agent. After attending one of our practice sessions, she convinced the owner of Hotel Sunnyland, a small resort in Parksville, New York, to let us work over the Memorial Day weekend for free. Fortunately, there was no show to cut, and we were able to win the job with our youthful smiles and enthusiasm. Our pay would be ten dollars a week, each, plus room and board, and we agreed to pay the "agent" a fifteen percent commission on our weekly earnings for the entire summer. (Because I was under sixteen, I needed my parent's permission to work.

It was only after much pleading that they agreed to sign my Department of Labor working papers, rationalizing that it was just for a summer job.)

But on the July 4th weekend, we learned the hard way that youthful smiles and enthusiasm can only go so far. When it came time to cut the holiday show, we absolutely butchered the first act we played: a Latin dance team named Ramon and Maria. At rehearsal, we couldn't read their complicated notes and key changes. Bobby's drumming couldn't keep up with the frantic tempos that Ramon demanded. Show time was a train wreck. Numbers that began fast slowed quickly. Ramon kept dancing, seething at Bobby through clenched teeth, hissing "fasta, fasta!" Backstage, after the show, Maria had crucified us in machine-gun Spanish, and when they finally stomped out, Ramon had yelled, purposely loud enough for all the guests to hear: "Chew are no-sing but a bunch of inept musical morons."

When word got back to the booking agent about how bad the band was at Hotel Sunnyland, for the rest of the season all the performers brought along their own piano player who cut the show alone, while we just sat there on the bandstand watching, humiliated, branded before the world as rank-amateurs, and only allowed to play bow music at the end of each act.

But we were city kids in the country for our first summer vacation, and while we practiced every day to improve our musical skills, we were also determined to have fun.

And I was about to have my first serious contact with Cassotto's insatiable need for conquest.

Bobby was sixteen months older than I, but when it came to experience with girls, he was years ahead. He had been de-virginized when he was fourteen, and in that category, was easily the most knowledgeable member of our band. He went out with a whole different kind of girl than I knew—girls from his neighborhood that he called "Fast Frannie," "Easy Esther," and "Bango Betty" (Bobby had a nickname for everybody): girls who let him do anything he wanted with them. Bobby had a "need-to-be-mothered" aura, and there was always some girl readily susceptible to it.

As soon as our summer began, he went into action. Hotel Sunnyland had a day camp where kids were left while their parents were off doing grown-up things. One of the counselors, a well-built eighteen-year old named Sue Ellen Berger, had quickly fallen for our drummer's charm. After work each night, they would disappear into the darkness for a few hours while we would all wait up to hear the enthralling descriptions of the romance under the stars that only got better and better. (With Bobby, there was never any question of exaggeration—you always knew that what he described had actually happened).

After a few nights, he returned with the news that he and Sue Ellen had "done it" on a blanket behind the tennis courts.

But then, less than a week later—amazingly—he informed us that he was bored. *Bored*, we asked? How could anyone be *bored* getting laid each night? But, likening himself to a jungle animal in need of fresh meat, Bobby said he had found a new challenge.

"Gentlemen of the orchestra," he began, "your drummer needs a big favor: Big Suzy is getting very possessive and asking for commitments that I am not prepared to make. Besides, I think there's a shot with one of the guests. But I need some time. Which lucky member of Local 802 would like to take her off my hands? I will share any advice I can offer."

We were all still on the desperately-needing-help list, and knew that any technical input from Bobby was definitely worth exploring. In the true spirit of democracy, we drew straws—and I won.

My own encounters with girls up until that time was less than minimal—the stuff of quick gropes and hopeful dreams. The girls in my building were all *good* girls, BTNA types (big talk, no action); at least to me they were. And whenever I met someone new at school or on a band job, any hallway necking or dry-humping on the couch when her parents weren't home always ended far short of the ultimate when they'd stop me with lines like "I'm not that kind of girl," or "I'm saving it 'til I get married."

"This is a lock-fuck if you do it right," Bobby tutored in front of my jealous bandmates, "and it's gonna be great-*great*! I'm gonna teach you everything you have to know. Your biggest problem will be to get her mind off *me*, of course; something that will be very difficult, of course-of course."

"Of course-of course," we all agreed, sitting on the edges of our beds, listening to the chief.

"Now," he continued, "it's all a matter of attitude. Here's what you gotta do: make eyes at her, smile at her a lot, you know, open the door for her, that kind of shit. She'll love you, Curley; you're tall and skinny. She loves variety, trust me."

"B...but, I don't know what to do! I mean, what do I *do*?"

"*You* may not know what to do, but she doesn't *know* that you don't know what to do. Take your time. With women, timing is everything. *Everything*! She'll never suspect that you don't know anything if your show confidence. Confidence is *everything*! Whenever you get nervous, keep repeating in your mind: 'timing and confidence, timing and confidence...'"

"Okay, I'll try. 'Timing and confidence...'"

"Timing and confidence, timing and confidence" my parroting bandmates chimed in.

"Shut up," I said.

"Okay, you start by giving her some crushers, with lots of tongue. Take your time. *Liiiinger* a lot. Then whisper in her ear, say that she makes you feel *soooOO* excited. Then slowly, *sloooowly*, put your hand on her jugs, and massage 'em gently. If she pushes you away—but she won't—take your time, and start all over again. Keep the routine going. Then, slowly, *sloooowly*, put her hand on your pecker, *slowly*—don't rush! If she won't keep it there, start again, 'til she feels comfortable. Then, help her with the zipper. Say, 'I wanna be *insiiiiide youuuUU*, I wanna be *insiiiiide youuuUU!*' Wait 'til she starts breathing heavy—that's always a sign that they're getting hot and ready. Remember, 'timing and confidence, timing and confidence!'"

My Greek chorus wouldn't quit. "Timing and confidence, timing and confidence."

"Will you please shut up?" I begged again.

Bobby waved them off. "Just keep saying 'I want to be *insiiiide youuuUU!*' and that you're '*burrrsting!*' Guaranteed, she'll go fucking crazy!" Then, he became deadly serious. "Now, pay attention, here's the important part..."

"Jesus, what they hell was all of the rest of it?" I asked.

"Quiet! No ad-libbing! Be as convincing as possible. This is the moment of truth. You look directly into her eyes—don't look away!—and kiss her, and then say in your most bar mitzvah serious, 'this is my first time.' I'm telling you, she'll love it! She's gonna say the same thing to you, *guaranteed*! Make like you really believe her. I mean, she's gonna love it! Then lie back, Jack, and let her do you! Ya got it?"

I took a deep breath. "I'll try my best."

"How 'bout we draw straws again," Walter said. "He'll never handle it."

"No, I can do it," I insisted.

"Come on, he'll blow it for all of us."

"No, he won't," Bobby said with finality, cutting off any further objections. "Let's root *for* him, not against him." Then he turned to me. "You're gonna do great-*great*!"

After weeding out the parts of his sage advice I wasn't sure I could handle, in the next days I made my move. First, I delivered a message to Sue Ellen that Bobby was sick with a cold and was in bed resting. He confirmed the story by rubbing makeup around his eyes, and blowing his nose a lot while we were working. Then, after mucho winking and smiling, when I felt the right moment was at hand, I casually suggested to Sue Ellen that maybe we might casually get together one casual night after work, just to have a casual drink and, "*you know*...get to know each other."

On our next night off, and with the rest of the band silently nodding encouragement, I convinced a puzzled Sue Ellen to take the bus with me into town to split a pizza. I thought I would be able to handle her better if she had a little buzz, so I ordered seven-and-sevens for both of us. Unfortunately, she only sipped hers, blabbing away about anything and everything, while I nervously guzzled three.

On the ride back, she didn't stop me when I held her hand. *Timing and confidence, timing and confidence…*

It was a quarter-mile dirt road from the bus stop back to the hotel. I suggested we walk the *scenic* way, through the bushes behind the tennis courts, romantically observing that it would be pretty there in the moon light.

What she didn't know was that I had hidden a blanket there that afternoon, and that Bobby had rehearsed me in a story about how *lucky I was to find it after it had been stolen.*

As we walked, talking about schools and other unrelated subjects, every few steps I would pause, mechanically take her in my arms, and kiss her. She didn't stop me, but kept her body at a safe distance so I couldn't really plant any crushers.

When we got to my planned place, I used the lucky blanket story, quickly spread it out, then sat down and beckoned her to sit next to me.

I guess I should have picked a different spot than the one Bobby had been bringing her to. I don't know why I didn't think of that before.

"Why do you want to sit *here?*" she asked, squinting suspiciously, towering over me, hands on her wide hips, "in *this* particular place? What did Bobby Cassotto tell you about me?"

"N...nothing. Nothing at all," I said, trying to be casual and convincing. *Timing and confidence, timing and confidence...*

"Don't lie to me! Tell me what he said. I *insist!*"

"Nothing," I pleaded. "Why would he say anything? About what? We never talk to each other about *anything.*"

"Steve Karmen, it's time to go back!" she said angrily, turning and stomping off down the dark road toward the hotel.

Struggling with the damp blanket, I chased after her, begging, trying to temper her rage with fast talk. It wasn't fast enough. She went straight to her cabin, and slammed the door in my face. When I got back to our room, my failure was obvious.

"Well?" Bobby asked, pretending to be hopeful. But I knew he knew.

"Nah, nothing happened. I kissed her a couple of times, but she wouldn't let me touch her. Nothing."

"It's okay," he said, comforting me in front of the others. "It's all experience. Ya did good tonight even though you don't think you did. Timing is everything. Tonight, it wasn't together. But it will be. It's coming. Guaranteed-*guaranteed!*"

By mid-summer, bad weather had killed off what little business there had been, and our band was fired. Faced with the potential disgrace of having to come home before the end of the season, Bobby talked Sunnyland's owner into letting us stay on through Labor Day by working for free in return for room and board. (I didn't tell this detail to my parents until after the summer.)

Our agent, however, gave us a hard time. She still insisted on receiving her fifteen-percent commission based on the value of our room and board. It sounded ridiculous when she said, "If you don't pay me, you'll never work in this business again," but as a naïve fifteen-year old, I took the threat seriously.

When I revealed the situation to Pop, he pointed out, without mincing words, that "no one, under any circumstances in the world, could ever curtail the future of his young son." He said he'd handle it, and after one phone call, the threats stopped. Bobby stopped dating her daughter, too.

In the fall, when school began again, and with our summer experience at the top of our band's resume, Eddie was able to book jobs at sweet sixteen parties, local social events, and at all the school dances. We worked almost every weekend, which allowed me to earn enough money not to have to ask my parents for an allowance.

We soon moved up in price—Eddie now charged *fifty* dollars for four hours of our music. We even got to play at someone's wedding—our first exposure to a serious drinking crowd. There were the usual rounds of family toasts, and as the evening wore on, the father of the bride decided to loosen us up as well by placing a few pitchers of beer on the bandstand. Neither Bobby nor Eddie drank, but Walter, Dick, and I dared a few glasses each. It didn't add anything to our repertoire, but certainly made it a little less painful when the Best Man insisted on playing Bobby's drums and another drunk honked into my saxophone.

Being able to make music also gave me the cache to compete for girls with the other boys in my building. I was never very athletic, like Barry, who ran on the Science High School track team (I loved to race Barry to the bus stop—I never beat him, but came close enough to make him worry); or Roger, who was good at baseball (my parents never allowed me to play baseball—"What? And risk getting hit in the head with a bat?"); or Howie, who was strong enough to play football (Howie had his front two teeth knocked out in a game one day, confirming to my parents their wisdom against all sports in general). But I learned that a piano and a guitar are like magnets. Whenever I played, girls seemed to magically appear—to sway to my rhythms and giggle amongst themselves in a language only they understood. Having this special ability leveled my social playing field a whole lot.

By spring, with our sight-reading skills not much improved, a malaise settled in on our five-piece orchestra. My bandmates were all scheduled to graduate in June, and the feelings of unrestrained joy we had shared together at the beginning were coming to an end. Instead of trying to please each other musically, we were now five experts with five different opinions about everything. Rehearsals, when everyone could attend, became charged with not-so-subtle commentary: "Your harmony is too loud," "your pitch is under," "the tempo is dragging." Soon, even choosing new songs required a majority vote. I liked playing Dixieland, which I felt didn't require great reading skills and allowed more freedom to roam around musically. Dick leaned towards cool jazz, for the trumpet a more introverted style—something that seemed to suit his quiet personality. Bobby, of course, wanted to do songs that featured *him*. Walter waffled between us, but as long as he had an amplifier, his approach sounded pretty much the same anyway. I had been bringing Pop's mandolin to our jobs, to add a change of color when we sang backup for Bobby, who loved the new sound. This didn't sit well with the others.

We went through hotel-audition season again, with the same results as the previous year. The only place that would offer us a job was Hotel Sunnyland—this time with the added responsibility of running the soda concession each afternoon. I guess the owner figured that he could fire us anytime the bookings got slow, and that we would stay on and play for free again.

With my own graduation now less than a year away, my parents turned up the heat and insisted that the fun days were over. "You have to earn some real income for college, and this music business must stop," they declared. I gave in and took a job running the office of the same summer camp, Camp Roosevelt, where Arthur had worked when he was in high school saving for his college tuition. What my parents didn't know was that Camp Roosevelt was just a few miles from Hotel Sunnyland, and that I spent every free minute there making music with my friends.

As I began my senior year, Bobby entered Hunter College, in the Bronx, hoping to use their drama department as a stepping-stone to the next level of his development. Then Dick announced that he was fed up with our lack of progress, and left to join another band that could actually read music. We discussed trying to find another trumpet player, but we were smart enough to know that we couldn't compete with real musicians. When Walter bailed out too, deciding to give his full attention to earning his college degree in music, Eddie finally admitted his plan to become a doctor (*Hallelujah* for his parents), saying he could no longer take time away from his studies to rehearse.

Bobby and I were left on our own.

Recognizing that our weak reading skills would prevent us from getting into another band, Bobby encouraged me to buy a guitar to expand our potential as an act. "You can play anything you set your mind to," he said, "*Anything!*" And one Saturday morning, he accompanied me to the shop of John D'Angelico, a famous guitar maker. It must have seemed odd to the other customers to hear Bobby singing as I tried different acoustic instruments, but when he finally found one in my price range that sounded right to his ear, I bought it. From then on I carried it everywhere. My parents saw the thirty-dollar investment as another step toward my ultimate ruin, but now Bobby and I had the goal of becoming an "act," and not merely remaining as background musicians.

Having the guitar made us self-contained. We became a traveling sideshow. If we went to the beach, I would bring it along, and we would sit on the sand while Bobby would lead all our friends in song. On weekends, whether working or not, we would meet at Vinnie's, a local Italian restaurant in the Bronx and, as expected, Bobby would sit at the old piano and I on a barstool next to him—hunched over my guitar, strumming, completely focused on the glory of the sounds we made together—and we would play and sing until closing time, with everyone circled around to listen.

We developed a comfortable set routine, always beginning with his piano songs, instrumentals like "In The Mood," that he played with fumbling fingers, but well enough. Then he would sing "Five-Foot Two, Eyes Of Blue," or "You Must Have Been A Beautiful Baby," while I faked any chords I didn't know. When it would be my turn, I would sing some folk tunes—"Jimmy Crack Corn" or "On Top Of Old Smokey"—and then we would trade choruses on the calypso songs that we'd learned from the records we listened to over and over again at his apartment. I enjoyed singing harmony parts, while he played the set of bongos he'd purchased from a pawnshop. And we'd go back and forth like that, neither one of us ever getting tired.

Thanks to Harry Belafonte, calypso was hot, and we found that other bands would hire us—not to play sax and drums any more, but to do our little novelty show, our folk act, during their breaks.

Even attending separate schools couldn't stop us: if Bobby found a new song he wanted to try, I'd get the sheet music or the record, and we'd learn it after school or on the weekend.

The incredible experience of singing together in perfect sync, of instinctively knowing at a glance without a word being spoken or necessary what the other was thinking and about to do, opened up a whole new set of emotions for me, of literally heart-pounding pleasure. The act became our passion, and I felt very comfortable as Bobby's accompanist, adding my thin tenor harmony to his rich baritone.

By the time I had graduated from high school and tried unsuccessfully to attend NYU, Bobby had quit Hunter College to devote all his energies to the music business—making rounds and looking for a show business manager.

It seemed only natural to follow his lead.

Chapter 2

"THE PHONE CALL"

On the street, George Scheck was considered a good manager: someone who could open a door with just a phone call. One rung under the heavies, like Bullets Durgum, who managed Jackie Gleason, and Milton Blackstone, who handled Eddie Fisher, George produced "Startime Kids," a local TV show in New York that featured young performers. George came on very slick about what was going on in the business, and had an office and rehearsal studio at 1697 Broadway. Always on the hunt for new talent, he'd listened to Bobby's vocal demos, was impressed with his voice and songwriting ability, and agreed to handle him.

"Everything starts with a record deal," George had said, and we spent a solid month reviewing and choosing material, then rehearsing the same four songs over and over until he felt we were ready to audition for record companies. Bobby had written two of them; the others were folk tunes we had been doing in our act. Decca Records liked Bobby's sound immediately and signed him to a contract.

Our first record date had just taken place. On the session Decca had added two additional guitarists, a bass player, and a drummer, and Bobby and I had taught them our music as we went along. After we had completed our prepared material, Milt Gabler, Decca's A&R man, surprised us by asking Bobby to record an additional song—to cover a fast rising hit by a new British artist named Lonnie Donnegan. We were unprepared and nervous as they put the sheet music in front of us.

Making a cover-record was a common industry practice. Hoping to latch on to the popularity of new hit songs released by small labels, the major labels—RCA, Capitol, Columbia, Mercury, and Decca—would often quickly record their own versions of the song with their own artists—*covering* the record—and then try to out-clout the small label through their more powerful and well-established distribution systems. Pat Boone's career had gotten a big boost when he covered Little Richard's "Long Tall Sally" and "Tutti Fruitti." Without telling us, Decca had decided to make Bobby's first release a song everyone was already listening to.

In the next hour we learned and recorded "Rock Island Line," a cute, up-tempo folk song with simple chords, a narrative opening, and lots of repetitive choruses. Bobby's performance had wowed Gabler, and now Decca was preparing to make a big promotional push to catch the Lonnie Donnegan record.

The following morning, Bobby called, bursting with news. "George just played 'Rock Island Line' for the guys at William Morris, and they set up an audition with the producers of 'Stage Show' at five o'clock *today*! Just 'Rock Island Line.' 'Stage Show!' Curleywig! Big time TV! And I don't need nobody 'cept you pickin' chicken! If they like us, we're on *this Saturday night*! Do you hear me right? *Network TV, Sat-ur-day Night!* Meet me at George's at three-thirty; we'll run it a few times. Jeez, I hope I remember the words. Why the hell couldn't it be something simple like 'I love you, I need you, I want to fuck you.' Never mind. Wear a tie!"

"Stage Show" was a musical variety program that featured the Tommy and Jimmy Dorsey Orchestra and the June Taylor Dancers. It had the eight o'clock slot on CBS, just before Jackie Gleason's "The Honeymooners," and was considered the most important TV show for new acts. (Gleason's company produced "Stage Show"). Each week there was a featured spot for a singer with a new record. Last week, a young rocker from Memphis, Elvis Presley, had knocked America on its collective crew cut. Acts would *kill* to be on "Stage Show."

Jackie Gleason's production offices were in the Park Sheraton Hotel. We were led into a small room jammed with staff members, who were to be our audience. As soon as everyone was ready, George introduced Bobby, and then nodded for me to begin. My first chord brought rapt attention. Bobby took out a small card, and began to sing, glancing occasionally at the lyrics. When it was over, there was no reaction.

"What's with the cue card?" producer Jack Philbin asked.

"I just wanted to be sure of the words," Bobby said defensively.

"Come on, *sing it!* Fake the words. I want to see if you can move. You can learn the words after you have a hit."

That got a big laugh.

George glared daggers. "*Move!*" he growled, then squinted that I begin again.

This time Bobby fixed his gaze on a cute young secretary with turrets like a battleship. He worked to her and to the other women in the room. It was as if he were willing them to like him. He rolled his shoulders to accent words, and did a little soft shoe in the breaks. Pretty soon he had them all clapping and swaying along with him. When we finished, there was a burst of applause. Most importantly, George looked pleased.

Then, there was that moment of absolute panic. "Does he need the guitar player for the show?" Philbin had asked. "Tony Mattola's with the band."

But George had come to my rescue. "Yes, he needs the guitar player. He can sit with the orchestra."

Nothing beat the wink and numero-uno smile that Bobby had flashed at me at that moment.

At the "Stage Show" dress rehearsal on Saturday afternoon, I was given a band jacket and positioned on a stool just behind Tommy and Jimmy Dorsey, to be ready to accompany Bobby, who was the first guest. The show opened with the June Taylor Dancers, the most famous chorus line on TV (known particularly for their precision steps that were seen from an overhead camera). As Tommy Dorsey was about to kick off their dance arrangement, Jimmy Dorsey stopped him, and coyly leaned over to examine my thirty-dollar guitar. Then he asked, loudly enough for the whole band to hear: "Hey, kid, want a part to play along?" My face went crimson. Not sure if I should take him seriously, I declined, saying softly that I'd prefer to just listen. "That's okay, kid," he said, evoking a laugh from the band. "You just sit there and listen." And for the next eight minutes, I sat close enough to Tommy and Jimmy Dorsey to hear them breathe; lifted by their fantastic music. Later that night, during the actual show, right after Bobby sang "Rock Island Line," the Dorsey brothers announced the first commercial. I leaned in as close as I could, flashing my toothiest smile, hoping to be seen by the national audience. But the camera angle had been too tight, and my TV debut would have to wait for another time.

For our young act, the weeks and months devoted to rehearsals,
meetings, and auditions were all a joyous part of the process. To my parents, playing on a recording session and appearing on television hadn't made a dent. Each inch of progress was met with more pressure to return to college. Truthfully, even though things were really beginning to happen, there were occasional frightening moments when I actually considered it. Only Bobby's relentless optimism

sustained me through these dark lapses in dedication. On the Tuesday night after "Stage Show," the phone rang. Mom was washing dishes while Pop dried and put away—their standard routine.

Bobby never said hello, assuming that whomever he called would automatically recognize his voice. "This is it, Curley," he announced, dramatically. "It's Club T, Detroit!"

Club Temptation was a five-hundred-seat showroom out in the heartland; one of a network of small nightclubs around the country that booked acts—mostly comedians, dancers and singers—for a week or two. Not a top room, like the Copa in New York, the Chez Paree in Chicago, the Coconut Grove in L.A., or one of the great hotels on the Vegas strip (those ultimate goals of every performer), Club T was a minor-league joint that catered to local tastes, where an act could break in, experiment, make mistakes, learn, and begin again. Almost anyone who had ever made it in show business had paid their dues by working in a Club Temptation-type room at some early stage of their careers.

Although this moment was not completely unexpected, and more a part of the inevitable evolution of things, actually hearing Bobby's words made me suddenly lightheaded and flushed. "D...Detroit?"

He was doing John Wayne, one of his better imitations. "*That's right, Pilgrim, George just called. The Morris Office came through. We fly out Sunday night, Pilgrim, open Monday for two—not one—but two whole weeks.*" Then, "Ready? This is it! Official-OFFICIAL! Ya comin'?" Then, pleading, "Come on, ya *gotta* come!"

Behind me, all activity stopped, as though some unerring parental radar had told them who was on the phone and what this evil was all about. Now, Pop refolded his towel and sat at the table, cleaning his reading glasses, pretending to get involved with the newspaper, while my mother stayed at her post, reducing the water to a silent trickle, sudzing in slow motion, her antenna on full scan.

Bobby and I were always on the phone, plotting and planning the act. But when my parents were home I spoke softly, to the point, with no ad-libs. Our phone was centrally located in the foyer of our apartment, and conversations could be overheard in every room. (During the War, Pop's role as our building's air-raid warden had provided us with the priority to get a much-sought-after telephone. Part of the deal was to allow phone-less neighbors to receive emergency calls in our apartment. When Pop suggested that we apply for a longer cord so people might speak privately in another room, my mother had vetoed the idea: "a short cord means a short call," she'd ruled, and a now easily-available extension phone was still considered an unnecessary luxury.)

"You didn't have to ask, but official-OFFICIAL, of course, I'll come."

Bobby knew what was going on. "What do you think they'll say?" he asked, his voice hushed as if they could hear him, too.

I slid down to the floor. "Don't know."

"Does it matter?"

"Well..."

"I know-I know."

"No, it really doesn't."

But it really *did* matter. A big part of me was terrified.

He was doing Cary Grant. "*Sunday-Sunday, Judy-Judy! Can you believe it, Judy? We're off to Detroit, Judy!*" Then, on fire with energy, he began reciting as if he had worked it all out years ago: "We'll wear dark suits and light ties, and no arguments! If we had tuxes, *that's* what we'd wear. Case closed." (I had wanted to wear open shirts, like Belafonte, but this part was his decision). "I'll get some makeup and show you how to use it. How about this for a running order? Open with 'Timber!' for drama; then 'Jamaica Farewell,' or maybe 'Limbo'; then 'Rock Island Line' third—good place for a record tune; then you come up, and we'll do 'Man Smart' together, split choruses; then off for a bow; then 'Scarlet Ribbons,' in a pin-spot, just guitar and voice, no band—we'll kill 'em!—then 'Limbo,' or 'Jamaica' in this slot; then close with 'Jump Down,' together, trading verses, with the whole band wailin' behind us. It makes sense, doesn't it? Seven tunes, twenty minutes. It has balance, it has build, it has pace. I think it really holds up. What do you think?"

I was frozen. "There's...a band?"

"There is," he said, matter-of-factly.

My heart was racing. "What'll we do? We have no parts. We'll work alone, right? We don't need the band, right?"

We had *always* worked alone. On "Stage Show," the only members of the Dorsey band who had accompanied us were the bass and drums, and they had used the music parts from the recording session.

"No, we can't work alone," he said sharply. "Those days are gone. They're expecting a class act, and that means we have to use the band. It would look pretty dumb if they just sat there, wouldn't it? No, we have to have charts..." (He had that certain tone in his voice.) "And...well...seeing how it's only *Tuesday*...and we don't have to leave 'til Sunday...I was wondering what I could do to help you write 'em out."

I was usually able to anticipate where his head was going, but this stopped me cold. "You want *me* to arrange the act? You're crazy. I'm not an arranger; you know that. What about George?" If we ever needed band arrangements, I had expected George to provide them—most managers advanced money for this part in the beginning.

Bobby was adamant. "No, he won't pay. Or can't. Or whatever. Doesn't matter. You have to do it." He paused. "I'll help you."

But we both knew he couldn't help me. While I had mastered the simple guitar chords necessary to play our folk act, I knew nothing of orchestrating and arranging. And Bobby was just as untrained, still unable to read or write music at all.

"How big is the band?" I asked cautiously.

"Fifteen strings, eight brass, five reeds, rhythm. You know, just like the Dorsey Band."

"*What?!* You're kidding! Please? Please tell me you're kidding!"

"*Of course, I'm kidding, old man. Mortimer Kidding here, old chap. And you're whom? WHOOOM did yew say you were, old shoe?*" He was doing Ronald Coleman. Thank God! Now I knew he was kidding. "*Aah, it's a fah, fah, better club...it's a fah, fah, better booking...it's a fff...five piece band.*"

"Horns? We've never worked with horns before. N...never horns! No, there's absolutely no time to write horn parts!"

Bobby's way of asking for something never included the possibility of refusal. "And better make 'em for nine men—we'll probably be going to other clubs after Detroit."

"Bob, I'm serious. Full band charts are impossible. I can't handle it."

"I had a girl who said that to me once. Come on, you can do anything. Okay, how about just for the five?"

"Bobby, I'm not an arranger!"

"*Please*, Curley, somebody's got to do it. The natural person is you. You know our material better than anybody in the world. You can write a lead sheet."

"A lead sheet is not a band arrangement."

"Seven tunes for five men."

"I'm telling you I *can't*. There's no time."

His voice became hard and demanding. This was the only Bobby Darin I didn't like, when he became unreasonable—which was not too often—only when there was something he wanted immediately that he couldn't have immediately. "Steve, I have no choice. We don't have money for charts, and we have to walk in with something. If you're coming with me, then you *have* to do it."

Now the intense quiet on the other end of the phone matched the pin-drop atmosphere in the kitchen. He was pissed off. I could tell. "Suppose...we just have chord parts," I offered quickly, desperate to satisfy. "I...guess I could do some kind of rhythm charts by the weekend, kind of a road map. Would that be all right?"

His voice brightened instantly. "All right? Yeah! Sure! That would be great! GREAT! Hey, just as long as we walk in with something, I can talk the riffs down with the horns, and you can sketch 'em out later, right? A road map for seven tunes. Anything else, we'll fake. We're the best fakers in the world, right?"

"Yeah-yeah, right-right," I said, resigned, eager to change the subject. "What else did George say?"

He took a deep breath. "Well, there's an option on the contract. It's really two *one-week* jobs, but he says it's automatic. It's there just in case we're terrible. We might be green, but we're not terrible, right?"

"Right."

"And Detroit's a great record town, so we'll be doing lots of promotion. And with your ol' guitar, podner, we can do things *live*, right on the air!"

"On the radio? Wow!"

"Unbelievable, isn't it? Last week TV, this week radio, next week, who knows!"

"Incredible!"

Buoyed by his contagious enthusiasm, I had almost forgotten where I was. But a rattling dish, like a face-full of ice water, shocked me back to reality. It was time to get some solid ammunition for the confrontation to come. "I hate to raise the delicate subject, but...how much are we making?"

"Okay, Steve, here's the plan." Whenever he wore his businessman's hat, Bobby abandoned my instant nicknames—Curley, Goldie-lox, Moptop, Brillo-ball, Ringlets, Stretch, Skinny, and Picker, to list just a few, were all good for lighter moments of camaraderie. This was business—*show* business—a subject he regarded with the most serious attention to detail. "George'll lay out the airfare and deduct it later, fifty-six bucks, round-trip, each. We're staying at a hotel called the Wolverine, three bucks a night, each." He paused. "It's three-hundred a week."

"Each?"

"No, for both."

"Is that good?" I asked, knowing it wasn't.

"It stinks. It's first-time-out money, but that's what the job pays. Ready for this? They also get an option for two more weeks within a year at the same money, and then two more weeks *next* year at better bread. That's in case the record takes off."

"Sounds fair. They're booking us now, that's what counts."

"That's what George said, too. So...I thought that if you could bring a few bucks, Mama's gonna get something together, and we'll share expenses 'til we get paid. Whatever's left after everything, we split fifty-fifty. Okay?"

Until this night we had never discussed any kind of formal business arrangement, always dividing everything we had earned equally. But I recognized that the record deal with Decca was strictly in his own name, as was his management contract with George. On "Stage Show," he had kept the performer's fee and paid all the commissions himself, while I was paid along with the band through the musicians union.

"I'll bring whatever I can," I said. "Are you nervous?"

"Nah. Oh, well, yeah, a little. But you know what they say: *a little nervous is good.* Do you realize what's happening, Curley? We're in *show business!* Somebody recognized me on the street today, from 'Stage Show!' And who knows where we'll go from here. George says there'll be other clubs, in Cleveland, Indianapolis." His voice dropped to a whisper. "Nina wanted Charlie to come along, get this, as my *road manager*, can you believe that? 'He ain't working anyway,' she says."

Nina, the Burly Barracuda, the female Ralph Kramden, was Bobby's older sister, married to Charlie Maffia (that really was his name), a sometimes mechanic, sometimes garbage truck driver, and oft-times unemployed civilian. Bobby lived with them, their two daughters, Veevee and Vanna, and his widowed mother, Polly, first, in the tenement apartments in the South Bronx just beneath the Triboro Bridge, and most recently in the City-subsidized project buildings on Delancy Street on the lower East side of Manhattan. Bobby hated every place he lived, and swore that if he could make it in show business, he would never go back to the repressive conditions in which he had grown up.

Bobby's father had died some years earlier, and Bobby never talked about him— except once. We were sharing our dreams for the future on the subway ride home from a Saturday night club date. It was a rare, unguarded moment.

"Recognition is what it's all about, Picker. Life is a fight for recognition, more than for money, which of course helps a lot, but it's more important to leave something for society and be recognized for it. That's what counts."

"Yeah, scientists do it all the time."

"Yeah, but that's no fun. Ya gotta have *fun!* A hundred years from now people are going to remember Frank Sinatra for his music, for his personal style, for his impact on the scene. Nobody's going to remember who the President was, but they'll remember the songs that people sang. Music lasts forever. That can only happen in the entertainment business."

"Do you really think you can make it big?"

"Why not? Guys are having hit records every day. All you need is the right piece of material and a few breaks. That's how it starts, you know."

"Yeah."

He paused. "My father got recognition. A different kind. He paid the price for failure. And everybody knew it."

I didn't know anyone who had lost a parent. "What happened?"

He hesitated, then looked right into my eyes. "Promise you won't tell anyone?"

"Of course not."

"Ever."

"Never."

He looked away. "He died in prison."

"No!"

"Yeah. Nina won't tell me the whole story; I think she's afraid. And Momma breaks up when she starts to talk about him. He owed money to somebody, and didn't pay up. Gambling, something, I don't know. He thought he could tough 'em out, but somebody set him up and he was arrested. Then, one day, Mama got the call. They made him an example for the rest of the neighborhood."

"Wow."

"Yeah. So you gotta get to the point where nobody can touch you, Curley. It's the only place you'll ever be safe, where they can't touch you. Capice?"

"I think so."

But I wasn't sure.

He never spoke of his father again.

Now, he was doing Charlie. "*I could drive the car for youse, take care of youse luggage, get youse stuff, hang around when youse needed something, ya know? Ya know what I mean?* Charlie's a little short on gray matter," he added. "He has no concept of what it costs to travel. All they really want anyway is for me to get rich so I can take care of them. They don't understand about the rest of it. I told George never to tell them how much money I make. They hear one number; they think it's automatic every week. Nina heard five-hundred for 'Stage Show,' she went out and ordered a color TV. She's got a big surprise coming if she thinks I'm gonna pay for it! Jesus, I don't mind helping out, but she's got it spent before I make it! I finally have my first taste of something right happening, and all of a sudden, my career is public property. So, just for the record, Strumbum, realistically, I don't think we'll have much left when it's over."

"Hey, so what's new about that?"

"Yeah, that's what I say. It's the next step, that's what counts. It's going to be fabulous! It's going to be fabulous for *you*, too."

"I know. I can't wait."

"No, I mean really...*FABULOUS!*"

I knew exactly where he was going. "Oh, I really hope so."

"This is when it's all gonna come together for you, Picker. Everything! There's a chorus line at the club, dancing babies with beautiful bouncing boobies. And who knows who we'll meet at a radio station or at a hop? Hey, Harry, we're going to the hop! I'm telling you, man, they're gonna name a car after you!"

I couldn't help but laugh out loud. "Go easy, coach."

"It's guaranteed-*guaranteed!*"

"Well, I've heard that before, but I sure hope you're right."

"*Hey, Stevila,*" he said, with a Yiddish accent, "*dun't fehget: vhen it heppens, ya hoid it here foist!* Now, when will you begin to write?"

Once again I refocused, this time on the huge job before me. "Right away. Tonight. But there is something you can do: I don't have enough music paper for the whole act. Go to Wedo's tomorrow, get about two hundred pages. I'll pay you back."

"No, this is on me, and no arguments."

"That's not necessary..."

"No, on *me*, and no more talk!"

"Okay. Get a hundred-fifty doubles, twelve stave, and fifty more with title space. I'll print your name on top, in case the band forgets. By the way, will it still be Darin?"

"Cute-cute."

Bobby was always experimenting with new names, ones that sounded more "showbiz." To date, he'd been Bobby Cassotto, Bobby Walden, Robert Walden, Walden Roberts, Bobby Titan, and most recently, Bobby Darin, the name he'd used for the record. (Bobby Titan was a knee-jerk reaction to a club-date agent who had teased him about being too short. George killed that one fast).

"Tell me about the band," I asked.

"Tenor, trumpet, piano, bass, drums."

"Think they'll be able to handle our kind of music?"

"If they can't, you can, my Millard, although, as I said before, I would not like to."

I was pleased that he compared me to Millard Thomas, Belafonte's guitarist. "I hope they're a better band than we were. What are we going to do if they're like *that*? Remember what Ramon called us? 'Chew inept musical morons!'"

"Ah, we were just kids," Bobby said. "No one could be that bad."

"Oh yeah? What'll we do if the drummer plays like you did, huh?"

"And the sax player like *you*? Come on, Steve, this band has played other acts before. I'm sure they can read anything. *And*, as I recall, *you* couldn't read that syncopated shit either! Quick, how many sharps in G flat?"

"F...four," I guessed.

"There are no *sharps* in G *flat*, dummy."

"Oh, so what."

"Sharps and flats are just details, Curley," he said warmly. "The important thing is to keep the band happy. Then they'll play better for us. How about if I bring the paper by tomorrow, after dinner? Got enough 'til then?"

"I guess so."

"I really appreciate this, Steve, you know that. I couldn't do it without you. And while I don't want to be pushy, if you can finish by Friday afternoon, maybe we can run the act for George, before he goes home?"

"No promises, but I'll do my best."

"I know you will."

I paused for a moment. "I couldn't do it without you either, Bob. I want you to know that."

"Hey, didn't I tell you we'd bust out? It's happening, Curley! It's really starting to happen!"

"Believe me, I know it."

"Go to it. I'll see you tomorrow," he said, hanging up.

He was right. It *was* happening. Now all I had to do was break the news.

But I couldn't. "I'm...going for a walk," I said, grabbing my jacket, struggling with a damn twisted sleeve.

"What's going on?" my mother asked in a tone so deadly I knew she already knew.

"I've got to clear my head."

She pressed in. "Was that Bobby? What did he want?"

"N...nothing, just...nothing." I stopped. They'd heard most of it anyway, and if I didn't tell them something now, they'd surely be waiting up when I came back. I wanted so much to sound confident, but there was an uncontrollable tremor in my voice. "Look, I have a ton of writing to do, and...well, I'm going to Detroit, on Sunday, with Bobby, for two weeks, to work in a club..."

"What!!?"

"...but don't worry," I added hastily. "I'll be all right. I'll tell you all about it tomorrow. Just not tonight."

"Why not tonight?" she shot back. "We're your *parents*! We have a right to know what you're doing with you life!"

But something inside me refused to allow this moment to be ruined by yet another argument with yet another unacceptable explanation. "I...I...I'm sorry, I can't discuss it now."

Instantly, I was through the door, ignoring the elevator, bounding down the five flights of stairs and out into the night, running, floating, gulping cold air, exhilarated by the arrival of my day of deliverance, my pulse hammering in my ears, my head swirling with images of the magnificent journey that lay before me. All the hard work and planning that had gone into building the act these last months was finally paying off.

It wasn't a dream anymore!

I was going on the road!

Chapter 3

"SOUNDS LIKE A DIVE TO ME"

"Do they have *sidewalks*...in Detroit?" my mother asked, dripping sarcasm.

"Of course, they do," Pop said, playing along. "That's where they build cars. If there are roads and highways, there have to be sidewalks."

It was the next night. We were waiting for Bobby to bring the music paper; I was fielding questions about the unpopular reality. I fully expected him to show up tomorrow, sometime around mid-day, probably an hour or two after I had run out. "Lateness is a virtue," he had often said, "one of the eccentricities necessary to becoming a star." It wasn't unusual to call his home when he hadn't appeared for an appointment, only to find him still in bed.

"The club's not really in Detroit," I explained patiently. "It's in Dearborn, Michigan. Like the Bronx to Manhattan."

"Did you finish today?" she asked, eying the music papers, rulers, pens, and ink spread out all over the kitchen table.

"Only three. I have to do the whole act."

"You getting paid for this?"

"No, I'm just doing it."

She gave Pop the all-knowing look. "See?"

"It's more for the experience than the money, Ma. I'm doing it to help Bobby."

"Go, apologize to the dean. Maybe he'll take you back."

"Ma, if I went back, I'd have to take all those subjects again, and I'm just not going to do that. Please try to accept that *this* is what I want to do."

"Do we have any relatives in Detroit? Near Detroit?"

"Let's not look for relatives, okay? Everything'll be fine. I'll call, and I'll write."

"Give us a signal," she ordered. "Call collect, person-to-person, for Arthur. If we want to talk, we'll accept the call. At least let us hear the sound of your voice so we'll know you're alive!"

Before going off to work that first summer at Hotel Sunnyland, I had been tutored in the time-honored method of letting parents know that their traveling offspring had reached their destination safely without being abducted by little green men from Mars. By placing person-to-person collect calls to *Arthur* Karmen (while identifying myself as *Steve* Karmen), my mother could skillfully transmit bits of information at the expense of the phone company. "It's raining now, so Arthur is not home. Call back in an hour," she would say. "I'm going to rehearsal now, and can't call back," I would say, and we would talk our little code until the operator finally prodded us to finish, when I would leave my phone number. I don't know if we ever really fooled anyone with this insanity, but at least it pleased my parents when I did it.

Pop sipped his instant coffee. "What kind of a name is Club Temptation? It sounds like a dive to me."

"It's not a dive, Pop. It's one of the major nightclubs on the tour. All the record acts work there. It's a top place, so don't worry."

"Don't tell us not to worry! What are you going to do 'til you get paid? Do you get something in advance?"

"No, Ma, I wish it was like that, but...well...I was hoping that...well, maybe that you could lend me some money, just until I get home, of course. I'll pay you back out of my pay, you know that."

"Explain, please, Mr. Musician, how do you expect to pay back if you not making anything?"

Pop raised his hand. "Stop. We'll give you some money. We'll send you off the right way."

She glared at him, but turned back to the dishes. Maybe Pop had talked it over with her already. Then, under her breath, she said, "Don't tell Bobby, or he'll take it away from you."

I ignored this cheap shot. "Please, I'd like to get back to work. For the last time, don't worry. I can take care of myself."

Of all the reasons my mother could voice, the one she would never dare was her biggest: Bobby was Italian, a *goy*—not Jewish—and therefore never to be believed or trusted. But I had learned that in the liberal world of music, people were judged on their talent, not their religion or color. We weren't the *Jew* and the *Italian*; we were the *act*, and that's all that counted.

Pop lowered his voice. "Remember...behave yourself like a gentleman...if you know what I mean."

"Oh, don't talk disgusting in this house!" she snapped.

It was agonizing. "I will, Pop, I will."

Saved by the lobby buzzer.

"Is that him?" Pop asked.

"Probably."

Mom pushed the talkback button. "Who is it?

An Irish brogue crackled through the tiny speaker. *"This is officer Moynahan, farty-third precinct. D'ya have a son named Steaphan?"* He was doing Pat O'Brien. I went back to work.

Pop said, "Maybe it's really a cop."

"Answer, Ma."

Caught up in the moment, she said, "Yes? I have a son named Steve."

His response was pure Groucho. *"Well, tell him he's under arrest for impoisenating a musician, then say the secret woid that'll open the door."*

"Told you."

She buzzed him into the lobby, and waited, listening for the elevator.

"Hi! Mrs. Karmen, Mr. Karmen," he said flashing his best numero-uno, startling her with a kiss on the cheek, while pumping Pop's hand.

Bobby was five-feet nine, with intense dark eyes, a wiry build, and soft, wavy, brown hair, the kind that flicked with a nod. Secretly, I wanted hair like that. Guys with loose hair had a freer look, cooler, and I wanted that look. Unfortunately, my six-foot skinny frame was topped off with a kinky, dirty-blonde, brillo-mop that just wouldn't flick. Sometimes, to try, I would let it grow, but no matter how long, it would just flap in huge uneven hunks until my mother's nagging drove me to get the haircut I was grateful for anyway. (I had also worn glasses since I was six years old, but, of course, never when we performed, or on a date. I thought I looked better without them.)

"Come on in," I called. "Want something to drink?"

"Yes, please come in," Pop said, grandly. "Have a cup of coffee. Tell us about the job."

Mom was tersely polite. "Would you like coffee, Bobby?"

"That'll be great, Mrs. K., if it's not too much trouble." He plopped a large package in front of me. "There's enough paper here for a symphony."

"Not this week, star."

"How's it comin'?"

"It's comin'. I never knew how long these songs were until I started to write them out."

"I know they'll be great. They look great."

"I'm using a special copying pen. See how the lines get thicker when I press harder?"

"I got some extra ink too, in case you run out. The guy at Wedo's said it's the kind all the top arrangers use."

That made me feel a little better. I moved the music to one side to make room.

"Excited?" Pop asked, as we all squeezed around the table.

"It's the real beginning, Mr. K. I can feel it. 'Stage Show' was the kickoff."

Mom poured coffee. "You know, Bobby, you looked older on television. Your face looked fuller."

"That's just the CBS televising system. They say it makes you look heavier than on NBC, or ABC."

"Did anyone notice that you had the words written on your hand?" she asked.

"'Rock Island Line' has a complicated lyric, Mrs. K. I just learned it a few days ago. Truthfully, even though we've been practicing it, I needed a little insurance."

"It wouldn't matter even if he had read off a piece of paper," Pop said. "He gave a great performance."

"Thanks, Mr. K. I appreciate your honesty. Fortunately, not too many people caught it. Only eagle-eyes like you. Did you see your son on the tube?"

"I thought I did," Pop said, "but he was so far in the background I wasn't sure."

"How does your family feel about all this?" my mother asked.

Bobby winked at me. "This is the start of the dream, Mrs. K.," he began passionately. "If we're good—and we're going to be *great-GREAT!*—there'll be more work, and better deals. It's called paying dues. Everybody has to start somewhere, right? For us, this is it. It's the perfect first job; we can't get hurt. We're not headlining, so we're not responsible for business." Then, he added, clearly for my benefit: "My family is very happy 'cause they know it's something I want very much to do."

Mom got up to wash dishes again. Bobby took the cue. "Now, I really have to go. Don't want to keep your young genius from his writing." He thumbed through the finished music. "Think you'll make rehearsal?"

"Don't worry, I'll make it,"

"We'll talk before, for sure-for sure. Call me if you need anything."

Mom shook her finger. "Don't forget to call your mother when you get there. Mothers worry, you know!"

"I will. And I'll take care of Curley here, too."

"Hey, I'll take care of *you*."

"You'll take care of each other," Pop smiled.

He was everything I wasn't: independent, cocky, a street kid with big smarts, constantly on the lookout for any opportunity that might improve his station in life. In a world of carbons, Bobby Darin was an unpredictable original, bubbling with talent and imagination, bursting with self-confidence, a whirlwind determined to make it all the way to the top in show business by singing, dancing, acting, writing songs, playing instruments, doing imitations, doing *anything* that might possibly help him get there.

His ideas were revolutionary.

I had been taught to *count the change*, that money was to be spent only on necessities, and that anything left over was to be squirreled away as a hedge against the certain disasters that would surely befall tomorrow.

Cassotto's head was completely different. Bobby viewed money strictly as a tool to be turned back into the pursuit of his dreams. He saved nothing. If he wanted something that cost more than he had, he bought it anyway and always found a way to work it out. He had the moxie to pull off even the most far-fetched schemes. If he said something was worthwhile, I accepted it without question or reservation.

Bobby brought a magical list of firsts into my life.

He was the first of my friends to own his own car: a two-hundred-dollar, beat-up maroon coup he called Hotel Dodge, because it improved his sex life so much. The glove box was usually crammed with crumpled, unpaid parking tickets that he claimed were his rebellion against the establishment. Bobby also proudly claimed to be the recipient of the first-ever speeding ticket issued in the Brooklyn Battery Tunnel.

He was the first to have his shirts custom-made, conning a newly established tailor into cutting them one at a time instead of the standard four-shirt minimum. When I had saved enough money, he brought me to Maurice, proudly introducing me as his "musical partner" who needed that "special look that only Maurice could provide"—of course, one shirt at a time.

He was the first to have his hair cut in the elegant privacy of the small barbershop in the Warwick Hotel, where Joe LaBianca was second chair to Rudy of the Warwick—famous for cutting the showbiz who's-who in town. Convincing me to give up my thirty-five-cent visits to Dennis's walk-in-window-shop in the Bronx, and reminding me that the expected tip was five bucks, we scheduled biweekly appointments with Joe—Rudy was always solidly booked with his regulars—and quietly waited for each other, eavesdropping on the chit-chat between Rudy and Perry Como, Walter Cronkite, Ralph Edwards, Ed Sullivan, or whichever big star was in the first chair.

Bobby included me in everything he did, encouraged me when no one else would, and became my whole world rolled into one joyous, scrappy pal; someone my own age to whom I could turn for advice and laughter when there was nothing to laugh about at home.

We weren't poor, not *poor*-poor, but we lived tight to the vest anyway.

We managed on what Pop alone earned. My mother shopped with the ration stamps that were standard issue during the war. We shook bottles of plain milk to distribute the cream rather than pay the few cents more for homogenized. We never went on vacation except as the guests of relatives who had rented a bungalow somewhere for the summer. We never went out to dinner, and we didn't own a car—something other neighbors did. Pop bought his first car only after Arthur had graduated from medical school. My parents simply gave up any luxury in their own life style for the long-range goal of Arthur's education.

My father, the eldest son of eight children, was born in Russia, in 1899. He had immigrated to America with his parents in 1912, joining the great exodus of Jews from the persecution that was strangling Eastern Europe at the turn of the century. My great-grandparents had been killed by Cossack soldiers on a road somewhere between Minsk and Pinsk. (I have an old sepia photograph of them dressed as though central casting had sent them to audition for *Fiddler On The Roof*). At family gatherings, my aunts and uncles would often tell stories about Bordyonka, the town in the Ukraine that was once their childhood home. It was not quite "Oh, I Wish I Were In The Land Of Cotton," but they were certainly happy that their new roots were in America.

Pop learned to speak English, got a job, went to school at night, earned a college degree, and ultimately became a United States citizen. He always took his responsibilities quite seriously, and later, when his father became crippled with arthritis, Pop became the defacto head of the family.

My mother, also the daughter of Russian immigrants, was born in New York City in 1907. As the middle child sheltered between two brothers, she was doted on by her parents and given a college education at a time when women were rarely encouraged to reach that high. She won several awards for scholastic excellence, and after hearing my uncles describe how their household had to be pin-drop quiet when she studied, I began to understand the strict guidelines that surrounded Arthur's academic life.

My parents met on the lower East side of Manhattan, and their attraction was immediate. He, the believer in a strong work ethic, could provide the solid sense of security she wanted; she, in return, gave him the step-up that an educated, native-born American could add to the life of an accented immigrant. They were married in 1928. It was a time of daring, when other ambitious young men were starting their own businesses. But during the first year of their marriage, my mother's father died suddenly of a heart attack, and it again fell to Pop to be the steadying hand in yet another family. A year later, when the Great Depression came crashing down on America, to make ends meet my parents gave up their own apartment and moved in with my widowed grandmother and her sons.

Pop was destined to kept his dreams on the back burner. "A steady job is more important than taking risks," he often said, primarily for my mother's benefit, and later for mine. For his entire professional career he had worked for the City of New York as a civil engineer. Under the protection of the Civil Service system— by law, City employees could not be fired—he was certain of an income during uncertain times, and, most of all, of pleasing my mother.

I loved him dearly. He was a man of deep honor and commitment. When he took on a job, he saw it through, down to the last detail. He had endless patience— something he used with great generosity by devoting many evenings to tutoring the other kids in my building so that they might pass their final exams in trigonometry or algebra. He was good at math—good at anything he studied— and he loved to read. I think his respect for education grew out of an acknowledgement that he had been given a chance for a better life in America, and that that chance should not be wasted.

Pop loved to fish. One year someone in the New York City Watershed Department offered him an old, wooden, round-bottom rowboat that had been abandoned on Titicus reservoir in northern Westchester County. If he wanted to fix it up, it was his, for free. On the next several weekends, he and Arthur took the two-hour, bus-and-train ride up to Purdys, New York, to repair the old boat and make it usable. I was too young to go along for the caulking process, but when it was water-worthy, Pop would take me fishing, too; always displaying his trademark patience when unraveling the tangled mess I made of my fishing line. With chopped-egg sandwiches my mother prepared jammed into an old army knapsack, these are the comforting memories of my childhood, sitting in that boat, fishing with my father. I believe that Pop did his best to treat us equally, but I don't think my mother could control her favoritism toward my brother.

The irony is that it was my mother who introduced me to show business. When I was eight, nine, and ten, during those blistering New York City summers, she would take me to matinee performances at the Windsor Theatre on East Fordham Road (one of the few air-conditioned buildings in the Bronx), to see the stock company versions of the hit Broadway shows of that time. Holding my hand, we watched Eddie Foy in *High Button Shoes*, Sylvia Sidney in *Detective Story*, and Gertrude Berg and Menasha Skulnick in *Molly And Me* (the show in which Mr. Skulnick, a star of the Yiddish theatre, uttered the famous line often used in tough labor negotiations: "I don't work here, I'm only the manager."). Later, when *South Pacific* opened on Broadway, and cheap balcony tickets became available in the second year of the run, we took the subway to Manhattan, and I witnessed Mary Martin "Wash That Man Right Out Of (Her) Hair." They even took me to the City Center Opera, to see *La Traviata*, *Carmen*, and *Aida*. But that's where they lost me. I wanted my lyrics in English, and with a harder backbeat.

Of the three people who shaped my young world, I felt least connected to my brother. When you're a child, a seven-year age difference is immense. Arthur had several boyhood friends his own age who lived in our building, and they were all always off in their own world somewhere—a world I was not permitted to enter. Even when we fished, Arthur was in another place, in another boat, under another tree. I desperately wanted a buddy, someone I could complain to about the silence, about my parent's narrow point of view, about the restrictions; someone who might support my music and make me feel like part of a family rather than distanced from it. Then I gradually came to realize that he resented my music, something he saw as coming too easily to me—success without studying—and that he was on their side. After all, the rules were enforced for his benefit.

But Arthur had a unique sense of humor, that very special kind that has been reserved only for doctors who think they're as funny as Buddy Hackett.

During World War II, the government issued gas masks to many residents, frightening-looking devices with wide, plastic eyeholes and a long snout for filtering out any poisonous substances that might be used on us in an attack. They made the wearer look like a giant bug. No self-respecting gas would want to be in the same room with one of these masks. One day, when I was five years old, and quietly taking care of my own business while sitting on the toilet, Arthur, wearing the hideous gas mask over his face, and screaming a blood-curdling cry, threw open the bathroom door and created in, one shocking instant, a new definition of "having the shit scared out of you."

Sleeping in the kitchen, and being gently awakening by the warm, homey smells of sizzling eggs and browning toast may sound cozy, but whenever I overslept, it was usually Arthur who provided my reveille, by holding a kitchen sponge over my head, and squeezing drops of water into my ears.

I cannot recall one significant exchange of brotherly dialogue, not about sports, not about girls, not about the weather, not about anything. He never said goodbye to me when he left for school or acknowledged me when he came home.

It was clear that Arthur could not provide what I needed.

Bobby could.

And did.

Now, I was pumped and ready.

Now, I had a *new* brother, one who understood what music meant to me. One who could help me and guide me in the direction *I* wanted to go.

Chapter 4

"YOU CAN COUNT ON ME, GEORGE"

"DAAAAAAAAAAAAAAAAAAAA-YOH!!!"

I sang, reaching back to de roots of me island heritage for de guttural sound of a banana picka.

"DAAAAAAAA-AAAAAAAAAA-AAAAAAAAA- YOH!!!"

I smashed a violent chord on my guitar. Belafonte never did it better! On cue, the banging started; Mr. Raymond-downstairs commented that my only island roots were with Uncle Morris, in Cedarhurst.

It was late Friday morning, the last weekday before the glorious Sunday. I was practicing, running the act, letting off steam, working through the tunes we were going to use and some that I just enjoyed singing myself.

I finished the last chart after midnight. Becoming an arranger in three days had certainly taught me a lot of respect for real arrangers. Simply counting out the correct number of bars and indicating proper starts and stops were more than I had ever put on paper before. And, because I had wanted our book to look as professional as possible, I had copied in ink, without first making a pencil-score to guide me. That meant that every time I made a mistake, I had to redo an entire page. My fingers were sore from holding the pen, but I had done it. We were ready for the road.

My pajama top was open, tied tight to my stomach by the knotted bottom, twisted into a ball just below my navel. My guitar hung around my neck. Oh, Harry, eat your heart out!

"DAYLIGHT COME, AND ME WAN GO HOOOOOOOME!"

Bang, bang, bang, bang. If only he kept better time.

"DAY!!!"

"ME SAY DAY!

ME SAY DAY!

ME SAY DAAAA-AA-AAAAAAAAAA-YOOOOOO-OOOOOOO!!!"

Another chord. More banging. I hunched over, planting my bare feet apart in my most animal-like crouch.

"DAYLIGHT COME AND ME WAN GO HOOOOME!"

I waited for the banging to stop, then sat down and started strumming, beating time with my foot.

"COME MISTER TALLYMAN, TALLY ME BANANA..."

This time his response was accompanied by muffled shouting. "Well, I have to practice *somewhere*!!!" I yelled at the rug.

I got up and paced the room. *You're Goddamn right! I have to practice somewhere!* I sat again and tried strumming softly, but I was bursting with pent-up energy. Before I knew it, I was singing at performance pitch, pounding my heel on the floor while Mr. Raymond's broom clanged against his radiator pipe. I stopped, and the banging stopped. "I hope plaster drops on your head, you tone-deaf moron!" I said, loudly enough for me to hear, but not quite loud enough for the music critic downstairs. Mr. Raymond was a very large man, and with my hours, I might meet him coming home some morning. Why risk an unnecessary confrontation?

I packed my guitar and put on Sinatra's latest album. "You make me feel so you-uuunnnng," I moaned along, holding my arms out in the same flying position as Frank on the album cover. I needed a hat. I cranked up the volume, glided to the hall closet, and put on one of Pop's fedoras. "You make me feel like spring has spruuuunnnng..." I was floating through the apartment, singing along with Frank, eating up the adoring glances of the imaginary audience when the banging started again. Act Two. But this time it wasn't my foot that was shaking the room and ruining Mr. Raymond's morning. It was the pulsating rhythm of the great Nelson Riddle arrangement blasting out of the phonograph, bass control turned to maximum. I lowered the volume. The banging stopped. *I'll practice tonight when you're eating breakfast! Maybe you'll puke!*

I showered, and while I was shaving, the phone rang. "Steve? This is George Scheck."

"Oh, Hi, George! How is everything?"

"Everything is fine, Steve. I'm calling to thank you for all the effort you're putting out on Bobby's behalf."

I always tried to speak respectfully to George. "It's my pleasure, George."

George was in his mid-forties and had an annoyingly smooth, foggy-satin voice that concealed a hard, tough business attitude. Though I thought that everything he had done for Bobby and the act so far had been really fantastic, one thing had raised an instinctive flag of caution within me: George had put his name on Bobby's record as co-author of the original songs, and had also kept the publishing rights for his own company. When I questioned Bobby about this, he shrugged it off as the price beginners pay to land a good manager. When my parents asked about it, I gave them the same answer. After checking around and hearing similar stories from other songwriters, I accepted it. But it didn't seem fair. I guess I got that instinct from my mother—she didn't trust George either, even though he was Jewish.

I had only been in his inner-sanctum office once, but I pictured him there now, sitting at his big desk, gesturing with his ever-present cigar, the wall behind him covered with framed autographed pictures of top entertainers: *To George Scheck...from Jack E. Leonard; To George Scheck...from Danny Thomas; To George Scheck...from Sophie Tucker; To George Scheck...from Dean Martin and Jerry Lewis; To George Scheck...from Milton Berle.* George made quite an impression in the midst of all those major stars.

His tone was fatherly. "Now, Steve, you know that my commission and the commission to the Morris Office comes off the top, and that I have to be responsible for how Bobby spends the rest of his money."

That wasn't technically true: *nobody* could ever tell Bobby how to spend his money. "Of course, George."

"And it's my job to see that he doesn't waste it on things he doesn't need. What I mean exactly is that his family is very concerned, and simple economics says that Bobby should go to Detroit alone, to save whatever is left over for his family. You know, his mother hasn't been well, and they can use the money."

I broke a cold sweat. Was he withdrawing the job?

"But I'm letting him take you along because he says that it will make him comfortable. And I'm willing to let him incur the extra expense of another person, the airfare, hotel, and food money, because he says that you're the only one who knows his music, and he wants you to be with him the first time he goes on the road."

"I'm glad about that," I said, relieved, silently catching my breath.

"I want you to make every effort to help Bobby, Steve. He's counting on you."

"I'll do everything I can, George."

"It very important that nothing *harmful* happens to his career at this early stage. What I mean exactly is that you should do everything possible to make him come off as the star."

"You can count on me, George."

"I'm glad we understand each other, Steve."

"Yes, we do, George. Absolutely, George."

"You can give my office number to your parents, in case they want to call me while you're gone."

"Thanks, George."

"One more thing: if anyone asks, he's *nineteen*. It's better for the kids who buy records to think he's still a teenager."

"No problem, George."

"Don't forget our little conversation, Steve."

"I won't, George."

"Good luck, Steve."

"Thanks, George."

I finished dressing, gulped down some orange juice, and wondered why George thought I needed a pep talk. Maybe he's nervous about the job, too.

Ah, but who cares if he's nervous. I'm going to Detroit! That's all that counts!

Bobby was tense. "Are you sure the charts are the same routine as we just did?" he asked after our second complete run-through of everything. We were working out in front of the big mirrors in George's rehearsal studio. Even though we had done these tunes a hundred times before, with less than two days to go, he was looking at them with a new eye.

"Exactly. I checked each part and played along with it. It's the act."

"I just want to be certain. I wouldn't have asked you to do all that work if I could afford a real arranger...not that you're not a real arranger, Steve, but you know what I mean, someone like Nelson Riddle, who's been doing it for a long time, who can write for brass and strings."

"Don't worry, I'll be able to write down whatever the horns play. If I have any questions, I'll just ask the band. What time will George be here?"

"He's not coming. But I talked the act down with him. Some last minute meeting at MGM with Connie."

"Was she around?" I asked hopefully.

"Yeah, but I couldn't get near her. You know."

"Yeah, I know."

Connie Francis, a seventeen-year old girl-singer, was George's main act. She had gained her first recognition in the cast of George's "Startime Kids" TV show. Connie hadn't had a chart record yet (*Who's Sorry Now?* was still a few years off), but everyone knew that one day soon she'd become a big star. She recorded for MGM Records and had a wonderful voice and a cute, bouncy personality—absolutely perfect for the teenage record market. All she needed was the right song. Connie was sweet, naive, and immature—the image of the pure, wholesome American girl. She and Bobby had met at George's office while we were rehearsing the act. It didn't take long for the Bronx street kid to flip for the innocence of the small-town New Jersey sweetheart and to capture her with his swagger and bravado. Connie would take the bus to New York for auditions, and then she and Bobby would go to the movies, hold hands in the hallway, or just sit and have coffee somewhere, gazing into each other's eyes for hours on end.

But when Connie's tough, ever-vigilant father George Franconero (Connie's real name) got wind that his daughter was romantically interested in an entertainer, particularly one with no money, he forbade Connie from seeing Bobby socially. To make sure that never happened, "Papa" began to accompany Connie to New York, and for Bobby to even be alone with her at George's office was no easy feat. Sometimes, when we were all in the building, I would occupy her father with small talk while she and Bobby stole a few private moments in the rehearsal studio. George Scheck knew what was going on but said nothing, not wanting to anger Mr. Franconero, thereby putting himself in the position of having to choose between Connie and Bobby. Secretly, I liked Connie, too. She had a perfect heart-shaped mouth, a perfect smile, a perfect hourglass figure, perfect hair, and she moved like an angel. Connie was my first star, and I had a crush on her, too. But of course, I kept any thoughts in that category completely to myself.

"What did George think?" I asked, back to business.

Bobby shrugged. "Same old story: too much folk, not enough pop."

"Want to rehearse a few pops? I can fake along. I'm sure the piano player can carry 'em."

"No. I'm committed. Everybody's doing pop. We're gonna be different. Folk is the answer. But *classy* folk, unique, distinctive, individual."

"Let me ask you something: how come George has never come to see us work in front of a live audience—never in all the time you've known him? I've been with you everywhere, and he's never been anywhere."

"He's busy," Bobby answered defensively, "but he's not unaware. He says he's gonna lay out money when we get back so I can have a big band book written."

"That's great. By the way, I think you should know that he called me this morning."

"I know. I was there."

I was surprised. "You were?"

"Yeah. I came in early. Nina called him and wanted him to read me the riot act about bringing money home. Ready for this? She tried to get him to take commission *after* all the expenses, but he wouldn't budge."

"Sounds like my mother."

"That's why he gave you the big speech about me traveling with someone. Those are bucks that he feels I could be keeping."

I began to check my guitar tuning. "That's what he said to me, too."

"But there was never any question in my mind about you coming with me, and that's what I told him. You know my music better than anyone. And in the end, it's my decision, not his."

"You could probably get by without a guitar on most of the songs, except the calypsos and 'Rock Island.'"

"Hey, Brillo-ball, relax. Don't you want to come?"

"Well, actually I was thinking of going back into brain surgery. But if you twist my arm, I'll postpone it for a while. Oh! Ouch! Stop twisting!"

"When my price goes up, I'll be able to take care of everybody."

"Then let's run the act again. The better it is, the better we'll be."

"No. Let's practice a bow."

"What do you mean?"

"What it's all about, Dumb-curl. *Le raison d'etre.* After we absolutely destroy 'em, they're going to be screaming, stomping their feet, jumping up and down, throwing roses in our path. We have to be prepared to acknowledge the adulation of the crowd."

"How do you propose to do that, O Great Caesar?"

"Stand next to me," he ordered.

I obeyed, watching in the mirror.

"Bow from the waist. No, don't look in the mirror, Jughead! Look at your shoes. When you get to the low point, count to three, then rise slowly to full height, then turn and walk off. Let's try it from the end of 'Man Smart.' Sing!

Smarter than the man in

Ev…'ry…Way!"

"Now, down for a bow, together! One, two, three, that's it! Then up, then turn together, now walk off. When we get to *off*—wherever *off* is—turn quickly. No, turn *downstage*, then back for a last bow. This is a one-down, count one, then up and off. And this time, no coming back, even if they tear the joint apart! Always leave 'em wanting more."

We rehearsed the bow a few times, and not knowing what the stage would be like, we practiced walking off to both sides. "Enough-enough," he said. "We're ready-we're ready."

It was nice to hear that at least one of us thought so.

On Broadway, Lindy's was the hang-out for the established. On

Seventh Avenue, the rendezvous for the hopeful was Hansen's. Located at the corner of 51st Street, everyday, seven days a week, songwriters, song-pluggers, musicians, dancers, actors, singers, comedians, and most every other showbiz type wandered in and out, catching up with what was going on. A door in back led to the lobby of 1650 Broadway, which along with the Brill Building down the street, made up the hub of the music business—Tin Pan Alley. The Roxy Theatre, diagonally across the street, and Radio City Music Hall, a short block away, each had four shows a day, five on weekends, with big orchestras and full casts; so Hansen's was always busy.

Mr. Hansen—no one knew his first name—was a jowly, baldish man in his fifties who spoke with a European accent. He was always in the store, day and night, never giving any indication of having a family life.

"Mr. H., I need your help," Bobby began as we strutted in. "I need makeup for two people, for Steve and me. You know The Curls, don't you?"

I smiled, and nodded.

"I seen him before. Vat kind you vant?"

"Albolene, grease, and powder to last two people two weeks."

"Albolene? Okay. Powder? Okay. Grease? You playing a theatre vit a lot uf lights? Grease is only for bright lights. Maybe a pencake."

"Trust the pro, Mr. Hansen. I know all about makeup. Studied it in college. Grease is perfect if you powder it down right." He lowered his voice. "Can I owe you 'til we get back? Two weeks? Promise."

Mr. Hansen eyed him warily. "I'm going to trust you. You haf an honest face so I'll help you cover it up. Just don't stiff me ven you become a bik star. I vork hard for my business. It ain't a charity."

"I'll pay you back. I promise. And can I put some dinner on that tab, too, if you don't mind?" Bobby asked, flashing his winning smiling. "I'll have the special of the day, whatever it is."

"Me too," I said quickly.

Mr. Hansen glanced at me.

"Oh, I'm paying cash. Thanks anyway."

"Your food is always so good, so wholesome, so enjoyable, so delicious..."

"Enough!" he commanded. "Save the baloney. It's goulash. Sit down. I'll bring ven ready." He turned to the counterman. "Two goulash."

"And two milks," Bobby said graciously.

"And two milks."

We joined Woody Harris and Freddy Sharp at one of the rear booths.

Woody Harris was an eccentric, old-time songwriter who'd had a few hits in the forties, and though he was from another generation, his longevity earned him respect from ours. Woody didn't have his own office. One of the publishers in 1650 let him use a desk, but more than any other place, Hansen's was his home. Tall, emaciated, stooped, with heavy, horn-rimmed glasses that were never clean, he could have been anywhere from forty to sixty—it was impossible to tell. His hands were huge, and his dirty-nailed fingers carried the stains of many cigarettes. Woody always wore his topcoat and porkpie hat; I never saw him without that outfit. He and Bobby were always gabbing about writing songs together, but so far, neither had pushed it to the point of getting serious.

Freddy Sharp was one of us, a folksinger-type brought up in Chicago—that other metropolitan breeding ground for city boys who sang about cotton balls and mule whippings. His material leaned more toward comedy than folk, but since he played guitar, and everyone was singing calypso, Freddy had become one of the open-shirt crowd. With a square face and black wavy hair, at twenty-six he was the voice of experience, constantly boasting of his accomplishments, ready to let you know that he knew everything about everything. But there was always a tinge of jealousy in what he said. Recently, he had been bragging about the record deal he was about to sign with Capitol, but when he'd heard that Bobby had signed with Decca, Freddy's future label had changed to RCA, Belafonte's label, so we were never sure where the truth was. Bobby enjoyed jousting with Freddy because he was competition. Bobby was "The New," and he wanted Freddy to know it.

"George got me Detroit, Woodman," Bobby said, sliding in next to Freddy. "Club Temptation. Open Monday."

I sat next to Woody, who was eating noisily. "That's terrific," he rasped between swallows. "Do promotion. Detroit's a good record town, see the deejays, do their shows. You can help your record a lot in Detroit."

"As much as I can," Bobby said. " Decca's promised a big push job on 'Rock Island Line.'"

"What're you doin' in the act?" Freddy asked.

"Folk, calypso, things like that. Steve's coming with me."

"Must be making good bread."

"Enough for two people," Bobby lied. "And the reaction to 'Stage Show' helped."

"Yeah, I heard you were on. I played Club T last year. It's a big room…small band. They rush tempos. A comic, maybe a stripper…

Bobby winked at me. "A stripper? Now that sounds interesting."

"Must we be subjected to another dinnertime sex parade?" Woody groused, his nostrils flaring. "If you guys were that good, you wouldn't have to talk about it."

"Eat your porridge, papa bear," Bobby said.

"Where ya staying?" asked Freddy.

"The Wolverine."

"It's not the Waldorf, but all the acts stay there. Workin' open shirts?"

"Wrong, Sharps. Dark suits. If I had a tux, that's what I'd wear. We're going to look *different*. Open-shirt is like everybody else."

"Suit yourself."

"Clever-clever."

"This is your first club, right?" Freddy asked.

"Right."

"Pay attention. I'm going to give you some advice that you'll thank me for for the rest of your lives: don't let anyone change your act. Everybody from the owner to the bartender is an expert. Giving advice is the national disease. Smile politely, but in one ear and out your ass."

Woody nodded between chews. "On this subject, I concur. The heart of creativity is the ability to resist other people's opinions."

Bobby asked, "How do they pay, cash or check?"

"Doesn't matter. Most clubs'll cash your check for you. If they don't, get to the bank right away. You never know when it might be made of Goodyear. Take a tip: save the best movie for the end of the week. That way you'll have something to look forward to. 'An' be good to the band an' they'll be good to you' is what my Pappy always said," Freddy drawled. "And take care of the maitre d'. He can make or break your show by where he puts a loud drunk."

I was making mental notes of everything.

Woody burped and wiped his mouth. "It would be nice to sit down for an afternoon, Mr. Darin, and maybe try a tune together, if you ever find the time."

"When I get back, Woods, I promise. Mr. Hansen! Coffee for the table, please. And put it on my check."

"Ah, the last of the big spenders!" Woody said, eyes bulging gaily. "Have a wonderful time. I wish I was going with you."

Barbara Thau, the girl who lived next door, was the only neighbor to offer any kind of real encouragement when she learned that I was going to Detroit to be in show business. The Thaus were one of the few other Jewish families in the building and our parents were good friends—they could literally see and talk to each other across the dumbwaiter shaft that separated our kitchens. On Saturday afternoon, Barbara rang our bell to offer her wish that I become as successful as Eddie Fisher.

Barbara was my age, and in grade school she had been the first kid on the block to do anything musical—she formed an Eddie Fisher Fan Club, and she ate, lived and breathed Eddie Fisher, and had driven everyone crazy with it. I was particularly disturbed that Eddie Fisher, and not me, had captured Barbara's pubescent attention just as she was beginning to pop up and out. Now, any fantasies I had of using *her* for my de-virginization, or even just to cop an occasional feel, had been drowned in jealously as *Oh My Papa* and *Dungaree Doll* came drifting across the dumbwaiter. Inflamed with teenage envy, I became quite vocal about my dislike of Eddie Fisher. Sometimes, when we'd meet in the elevator, I would whisper things like "Eddie Fisher is a fag," or "Eddie Fisher sings flat," or "Eddie Fisher can't keep time," and this would make Barbara go absolutely nuts. So this first mention of Eddie Fisher and me in the same sentence was a real boost to my morale.

But Barbara's kindness was insufficient armor to protect me from the onslaught I received as my parents drove me through a misty rain to LaGuardia Airport. My mother felt compelled to prepare me for everything in life that a young man should know when he leaves home for the first time.

"Don't forget to wash your socks."

"I'll wear the same pair for two weeks."

"Be careful with your money."

"I'll let the desk clerk hold my cash."

"Don't let your guitar out of your sight."

"I'll sleep with it in my bed."

"Don't eat junk."

"Pizza for breakfast, lasagna for lunch, spaghetti for dinner."

"If you're such a smart-aleck, why don't you go back to school?"

That stopped me.

Initially, Mom didn't want to come along, probably suspecting that seeing me off would lend some sort of tacit approval to my irresponsibility. But when she found out that Bobby's mother was going to be there, she changed her mind. This would be the first time our families would meet, and I knew she was curious.

Between her constant warnings that he watch the road, Pop would flash me a quick smile, his eyebrows raised in excited anticipation. I felt he was genuinely happy for me. *I'm doing it for both of us, Pop,* I thought. *For both of us.*

The signs for Capital Airlines led to a long row of barracks-like buildings that were far removed from the main terminal. Since none of us had ever been to an airport before, it seemed quite a sleazy place—a Quonset hut, more like *Back To Bataan* than a major New York airport. But, sure enough, it was really Capitol Airlines. Hand-printed cards asked apologies while new facilities were being built. Pop dropped us off and then went to park the car. Mom's guard was up.

A skycap approached—a gruff man, ruffled, scowling. "Where are you all goin' to?"

"To Detroit, on Capital 242," I smiled.

"Checkin' the gee-tar?"

"Oh, no sir, it stays with me."

He crayoned some scribbles on a tag and attached it to my suitcase. "This way," he motioned with his head, roughly hoisting the bag, as we followed inside.

"I'm traveling with Bobby Darin on flight 242," I said proudly to the agent, assuming that the whole world had watched "Stage Show." "He has my ticket."

"Name, please?"

"Karmen. Steve Karmen."

The agent scanned her passenger list. "Thank you, Mr. Karmen. Your reservation is in order. Is Mr. Dorin here?"

I ignored the miscue. "He'll be here soon."

The skycap was standing next to me, too close, staring dully at my face, waiting for a tip. I pulled out a dollar.

My mother's arm shot out. "That's too much money for one bag," she said, snatching the bill, thrusting him a quarter that somehow appeared in her hand. Before I could protest, the skycap was gone.

Giving me back the bill, she warned, "You have to be careful about how you spend your money, and that starts now."

"I'll hold your bag until Mr. Dorin comes with your ticket," the agent smiled, amused by this parental interplay. "Boarding is in thirty minutes."

"Darin."

"What?"

"Darin, not Dorin."

She looked at the list again. "Oh, yes, Darin. Sorry."

Pop came in, and we stood across from the counter, watching and waiting. When Bobby arrived, protectively guiding his mother through the narrow terminal, he was strutting like John Garfield, his raincoat flowing open like Errol Flynn's cape, his hair bouncing with each step. When he spotted us he winked, and smiled broadly. I felt better just seeing him. Sister Nina waddled behind.

Tommy handed our tickets to the agent. The same skycap had carried his bag, and Bobby smoothly palmed him a buck. My mother just shook her head.

"I was getting worried," I whispered so only he could hear.

"Never fear, Kemosabe, the Lone Ranger will always be here. Charlie had to stop for gas." He introduced everyone, and we gathered near the boarding gate.

"This certainly is a big day," Pop said, breaking the ice.

"Mrs. Cassotto, what's your opinion about the boys working for such little money?"

"Ma!"

She ignored me, jutting her chin out. "I just want to know what Bobby's mother thinks about all this!"

Polly Cassotto was a frail woman, with thinning gray hair, unfortunately sick with asthma. The illness made her seem quite old. She had recently been in the hospital, and Bobby was constantly worried about her health. Sometimes, I felt a little envious of how completely this kindly old lady believed in her son.

"Whatever Bobby decides to do, I know he'll do the right thing," she answered softly. "He's a good boy, and he's trying hard."

Nina barreled in. "Of course, we want him to be able to bring more money *home*. And we'd like that to happen *soon*. So behave yourself and eat properly, young man. Going on the road is one thing, behaving like a loon is another!"

"Exactly my feelings," Mom added stiffly.

"It's a broken record," I whispered. Bobby nodded his agreement.

"Hiya, kid," Charlie called, waving, shuffling through the doorway. "Great to see you, and good luck. Hi, everybody, I'm Charlie."

Charlie Maffia was a big, crude, outgoing teddy bear, unshaven and wearing an old canvas jacket over a t-shirt. I could sense my mother's revulsion. What a contrast to my father, who always wore a white shirt and tie wherever he went.

Charlie shook my hand, then Pop's, then did a half-bow to Mom. "Nervous, kid?"

"A little."

"I'll bet," he laughed, clapping me broadly on the shoulder. "Bobby couldn't sleep at all last night. Hey, you're going on the road! The first job, the first flight, the first everything. Well, maybe not the first *everything*, but you know what I mean, ha ha! I told Bobby that as soon as things get rolling, I'm ready to travel with him, you know, to look after him, to be his road manager."

"Those are dreams for the future, Charlie," Bobby said rather harshly, "for the *future*," he emphasized.

Charlie retreated. "I just want to help."

"Bobby won't forget his family when he becomes a big star," Nina warned, with ominous certainty.

Bobby hugged his mother. "You better know it!"

Gratefully, our flight was announced. We separated into family groups. I looked at my parents for a speechless moment. There were no words that could make sense now, anyway. Would their emotions be the same if I were leaving for an out-of-town college? They might have had more pride, but in two weeks I would be a different person, and they knew it, too. Pop gave me a bear hug. "Good luck, my son. Don't forget, keep your spirits up."

Mom kissed my cheek. "Please take care of yourself," she said sincerely, actually looking sad, like she might cry.

After more kisses and hugs and handshakes all around, I followed Bobby out into the rain and across the slickened concrete to the plane. We each paused at the top of the boarding ramp for a dramatic wave, just like in the movies. I couldn't tell if anyone was still there.

"We're off to the big time!" he called to the New York skyline before ducking into the cabin.

"Off to the big time," I echoed.

The stewardess wanted to check my guitar, but I assured her that I could keep it safely out of the way, between my legs. We could always work without clothes if they lost our luggage, I reasoned, but never without the guitar. And it would be a catastrophe if they smashed it.

Our seats were in the next-to-last row. Bobby squeezed in near the window. As we pushed back from the gate, the noise of the engines got louder. When we taxied out into the night, the whole plane began to shake.

"Can you see the ground?" I asked, peering over his shoulder. "Do you think we're flying yet? Are we in the air?"

He peered out the window. "I can't see anything, but I don't think we've left yet." But he wasn't sure. "Let's sing something. Let's run the act," he said nervously.

"Do you think we can? I mean, this is an airplane, not a rehearsal hall."

"*Take out your ol' git, buckaroo,*" said Gabby Hayes. "Let's run 'Jump Down.'"

I unpacked the guitar and began to strum, leaning close to hear him. It was impossible. A few people turned their heads at the distraction, but we were totally drowned out, even to each other. Every time the shrieking engines changed pitch, we stopped singing to see if we had moved.

Suddenly, with the mightiest roar yet, the plane charged down the runway. I was thrust back into my seat. The sound was deafening. This was the real thing. Bobby pressed his face to the glass trying to see where we were going. Quickly, I packed up the guitar, double checked the locks, and jammed the case protectively between my knees.

I leaned on his shoulder, looking out. We could not have been closer in that moment. "Good luck, Bobby."

"Yeah, good luck, Steve," he said, reaching back, squeezing my hand.

"The very best," I said, hugging his back.

The runway lights flashed by and became twinkling memories as we lifted off the ground.

Belle, Steve, Hyman, and Arthur Karmen, 1940

The Doctor-to-Be
and his kid brother

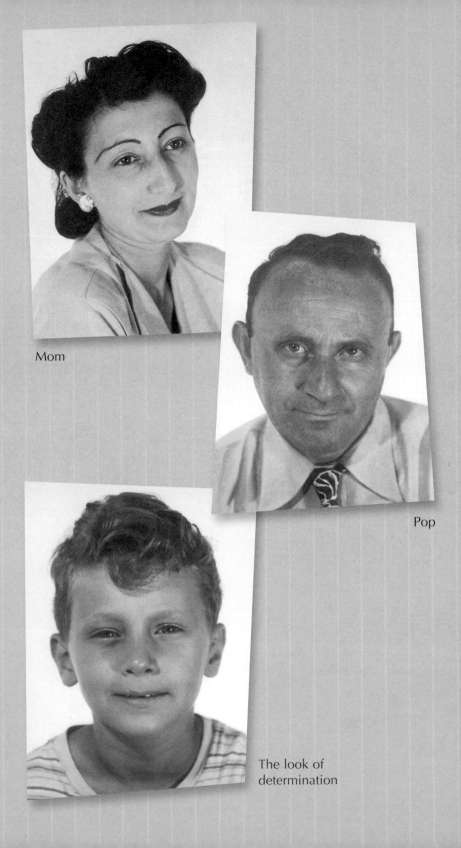

Mom

Pop

The look of
determination

The Best Memories of My Childhood

Pop, Arthur, Harry Thau
(our neighbor),
Barbara Thau, and
the Composer-To-Be

A big catch and
the fixed-up boat

Eddie Ocasio and His Orchestra

At the Bronx High School of Science —
Eddie, Bobby, Walter, Steve, Dick

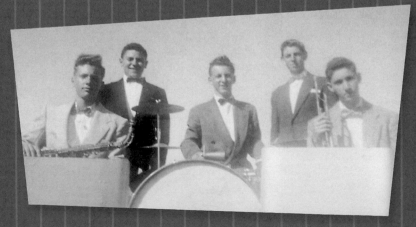

At Hotel Sunnyland — Steve, Eddie, Bobby, Walter, Dick

The Skinny Saxophone Player and the
Leader of the Band, Eddie Ocasio

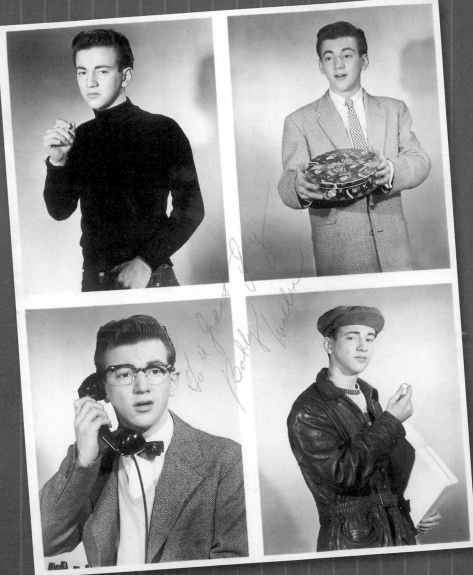

Bobby's first acting composite
signed "To A Great Guy, Bobby Walden"

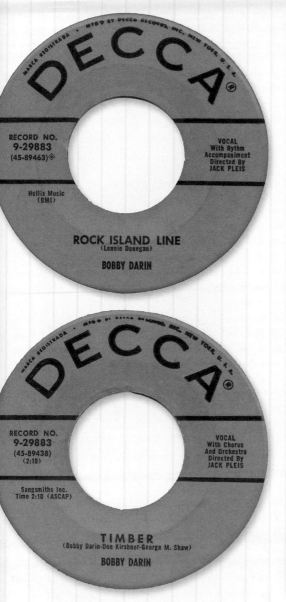

The first record, and the first ad for the Club

Opening night — "Jump Down, Spin Around"

Part Two

DETROIT

1956

Chapter 5

"WHO DID YOUR BOOK?"

I have often thought of the unspeakable courage it must have taken for my father to leave his homeland as boy of twelve, to travel across Europe with his parents on the worst possible of trains, and then make the twenty-one-day crossing of the Atlantic, steerage class, to come to America. I can only imagine the awe he felt when his ship passed the Statue of Liberty. When I visited the Lady in the Harbor up close on a high school field trip, it gave me chills thinking what it must have meant to my Dad.

Arriving in Detroit after my first airplane flight certainly did not stack up against an immigrant's journey, but as naïve as it sounds, I was just as in awe. And because I am my mother's son, a small part of me did wonder if the Detroit airport would really be hay-seedy, befitting a pioneer settlement with questionable sidewalks out in the great wilderness beyond the Hudson River. Yeah-yeah, sure-sure. Innocence breeds one hell of an imagination.

When we landed, it was right into the big time. Willowrun Airport was a brightly lit terminal, much cleaner and more modern than LaGuardia, bustling with people even at this late hour, and either a six-dollar bus ride—each—or an eighteen-dollar taxi to downtown.

"We're entitled to the best we can afford," Bobby said, leaving no room for discussion. "At least 'til the gelt runs out." I was too exhausted to argue with the hole this extravagance shot in my projected budget. All I could think of were wrong chords and other potential musical embarrassments that might be caused by my charts.

Our driver had been thoroughly unimpressed when Bobby bragged that we were entertainers here to perform at Club Temptation. We were his "last freakin' fare," he'd grumbled, "and our freakin' plane was the last freakin' flight of the whole freakin' night that he had waited two freakin' hours for," and he just wanted to get home.

It was raining. We had each settled into personal thoughts, hardly speaking, just staring out our own fogged-up windows, hypnotized by the squishing tires and the steady rhythm of the wipers. Beyond the rain, the sleepy landscape seemed nothing at all like the Bronx. Bleak pastures stretched on forever, flat and forbidding—probably farms, but it was too dark to tell. If I hadn't been so bleary-eyed tired, I would have probably been scared. "What the hell are we doing in Detroit?" Bobby had muttered when we stepped off the plane. There was something quite profound in his words: what the hell was I doing here? I'm supposed to be in college, a good son, on my way to a career as a *professional* man.

The Wolverine Hotel was on Elizabeth Street, one block from Woodward Avenue, a wide boulevard that looked a lot like the Grand Concourse—the main divider between East and West Bronx—except that here both sides of the street were lined with stores and office buildings instead of tenements. Across from the entrance, a row of one-story, boarded-up shops stood in various states of demolition; behind them, outlined in the murky night sky, were the cranes of a construction site. The air smelled of crushed concrete. A huge sign announced the future home of Woodward Plaza.

Bobby paid the driver. "Someday, this'll be a big limo, Curls," he said without a smile.

I had often fantasized about a moment like this: checking into a hotel accompanied by a luscious, willing lady whom I was about to ravish, and gallantly registering as Mr. and Mrs. John Smith. But tonight, as we lugged our bags into the lobby, I was glad Cassotto was taking care of business.

"I'm Mr. Darin, this is Mr. Karmen. Reservations have been made for a double room."

The desk clerk, a grumpy man wearing a baggy, gray cardigan, was reading a magazine. "Fill out a card," he pointed, not looking up. "How long?"

Bobby winked at me. "*Two* weeks."

"You fill one out, too," the clerk said, pointing at me, still not looking up. "Was there a deposit?"

"Certainly. From George Scheck Management."

"Who?"

"Scheck. George Scheck."

The lobby was as seedy as Freddy Sharp had described: a few oversized armchairs scattered about the dingy marble floor, splotchy plaster in places where the grimy flowered wallpaper had peeled away. A porter was mopping up next to the shuttered newsstand; each time he moved his pail, the scraping sound echoed off the high ceiling. The whole place reeked of ammonia, like a subway bathroom. In one corner, next to the darkened coffee shop, a flickering neon arrow buzzed the way downstairs to the Polynesian Room.

"Great, huh?" Bobby said.

Clearly annoyed at the young punks who had interrupted his reading, the clerk shifted out of his chair and flipped through the reservation tabs. "Got no Scheck."

"No, I'm Darin, he's Karmen."

"Oh, yeah, here you are. You're okay. Forty-two-dollar deposit received. Let's see, two beds, six-dollar rate, 407 'll be good—corner room, very quiet, all that. Elevator man'll help with your bags."

"Thanks. We'll manage," Bobby said.

"Hey, wait a minute! You can't play that thing in the room, you know," the clerk sneered, pointing his bony finger at my thing.

"Oh, I won't," I assured him. "I won't."

"Whatta dump! Whatta dump!" Bette Davis said, opening the door to room 407.

"I think it's a palace."

There were two beds separated by a night table. A single bureau stood on the opposite wall next to a plain wooden chair. The windows were covered with half-drawn shades—one had a string, the other didn't. The tan rug was worn next to each bed and around the closet and bathroom doorways. The walls were bare. No pictures, no wallpaper, just paint. Had other entertainers trod this frayed carpet? Hookers? Johns? Doctors? No, not doctors. This was way below doctors.

"It's nice to know that things can only get better from here," he said. When we played at Hotel Sunnyland, our five-piece kid-band had all bunked together in one huge attic. This was the first time I would be sharing a room with only one other person. Bobby offered to flip for the bed.

"No, you pick it," I said. He chose the one near the door.

We divided the closet and the dresser, designating the bottom drawer as a communal laundry. The window in the bathroom had been painted shut many times over. "If you hang your suit on the shower rack and run hot water, the steam'll take the wrinkles out. Of course, don't hang your suit *in* the shower, or you'll slosh when you wear it."

"Now?"

"Tomorrow, before rehearsal. That way they'll look pressed when we come back."

I took ten dollars from my wallet. "Here's my half of the taxi."

He frowned, and stopped unpacking. "Steve, if you're going to keep track of every dime we spend, become an accountant. Forget it. We'll work it out at the end of the week."

"I just thought we'd keep it straight."

"When have we ever *not* been straight? Don't be like Nina, always talking money. The goal is the show, not the cost of the cab that gets us there."

"Agreed."

"And one more thing: when George calls, let me talk. It only creates confusion for him to have to repeat things. If you have anything to say to him, let me do it."

"Sure, but I want to know what's going on, okay? Just keep me posted, okay?"

"Don't worry, Jellybean, I will." We put our empty suitcases in the closet. "Hungry?" he asked.

"Yeah! Our first road meal! Spaghetti with red clams!" Bobby had taught me all about Italian food. I ate it every chance I got. The closest thing to spaghetti sauce in my mother's kitchen was cottage cheese laced with ketchup.

"Call up. Let's find a Vinny's."

There was no dial on the phone. I tapped the lever a few times. There was a deafening click followed by a clamor of clanking and phone-dropping on the other end. "Just a minute, be patient!" barked a testy male voice. It was the desk clerk, doing double duty. I must have interrupted his magazine reading again. "Now, what number do you want?"

"Is there any place in the neighborhood to get some good Italian food?" I asked politely.

"Coffee shop closed at nine."

"Anything else around?"

"Try the Bagel. Open all night."

I covered the mouthpiece. "Wanna eat bagels? There's nothing else."

"Too heavy. If we can't get spaghetti, let's go to bed. Truthfully, I'm beat. It's been a long day. Wait! Ask if there's room service."

"Is there any room service?"

"You kidding?" the voice snickered.

I covered the mouthpiece again. "Nothin' from nothin'."

"Cancel."

"Right."

Before I could sign off, there was another ear-bursting click, then no one. For a moment, neither of us spoke. When our eyes met, he cracked a sleepy smile. "Ta da! The road!"

"Yeah, the road. Let's sack out, to be fresh for tomorrow. I'm going to take a shower. Wanna go first?"

"*No, you go*," said a weary Groucho. "*And don't take it too far. I wanna use it after you.*"

Later, in the darkened room, I apologized. "Sorry about that money business. It's force of habit."

"Ah, that's okay. I'm just jumpy about the opening. You struck a nerve."

"It's gonna be great, Bob. I can feel it."

"Yeah, me too."

"Good night, Star."

"Good night, Gracie. Big day coming."

"You're telling me?!"

"*Tomorrow is another day.*"

"Thanks, Scarlet."

"Shut up already."

"Up yours."

After a few minutes, he went into the bathroom, took a prescription bottle from his travel kit, swallowed a pill, and then got back into bed.

"You okay?"

"Vitamins. Sleep good, Curley."

"You too, B.D."

The first blast literally shook my bed. Squinting at my

watch, I remembered where I was, and then poked my head under the shade to see what the hell could have shaken the building like that. Across the street, a wispy puff of dirt was billowing up from a huge yard of pockmarked earth. Almost immediately there was another dull concussion.

It was eight AM, still raining, but the inclement weather hadn't stopped work at the future home of Woodward Plaza. Derricks were hissing and grinding, dragging wide pieces of metal meshing, preparing for the next dynamiting. "That bastard was full of shit about a quiet room," I said to the ball of blankets that was Bobby. "They're building a stadium under our window."

The blankets grunted as we were whumped again. "Crowds breaking down the door to hear the act. Go back to sleep."

Sleep was impossible. Bobby was restless, too. We pulled on yesterday's clothes and headed downstairs. The coffee shop was crowded with cheap suits. We sat at the counter. The waitress didn't appreciate our clam sauce order, so we each settled for three eggs, over; double bacon, double OJ, and coffee. Bobby went out to the newsstand and brought back the *Detroit Free Press*.

"Listen to this: 'The Birth of a Pearl. Presenting the Lovely Arlene in a Fantasy of a Sea Nymph heading a New All-Star Show.' That must be us—the new *all-star* show."

"Maybe it's still last week's ad," I said, hopeful for some kind of billing.

"Maybe it's a typo, who knows. I wonder if Arlene is really that lovely." Then he added, "Sweet Jesus, listen to *this*: 'Bowling Banquet Accommodations.' We're gonna be singing to *bowlers!*"

The breakfast check was huge. At this rate our cash might not last out the week. But I kept this financial concern to myself.

Back in the room, I was suddenly very tired. When Bobby phoned for a 12:30 wake-up call, a woman answered; the grump must have finished his magazine.

Rehearsal was scheduled for two o'clock. We allowed

an hour for the ride. Twenty minutes later we were in front of a long, low building that looked like a Grand Union supermarket. I expected the neighborhood to be something like downtown, where concrete dominated everything. Instead, there were trees, garden apartments, and private homes on the next block. We were in the country, the 'burbs. Beyond the parking lot were a few small stores, a dry cleaner, a hairdresser, and an electrical repair shop.

A long iron canopy stretching to the curb covered the entrance. The doorway was shrouded with heavy canvas weather protectors.

"Hey, wow! Look at that!" Bobby whistled, pointing to the marquee, while I paid the fare (my turn).

MICKEY'S CLUB TEMPTATION
THE BIRTH OF A PEARL
LIZ CARLETON
CLIPPER DANIEL
BOBBY DARIN
THE CUTIES

"Well, at least we know we're expected. Next time around, it'll be top billing, Curley. The singer *always* closes the show. Maybe they haven't learned that yet in the Boonies."

I tried the door. Locked. There were no windows. I knocked. Nothing. "Are you sure George said two?"

"Yeah. Somebody'll come by soon," he said, glancing nervously up and down the street. "How do you like the big time so far?"

I was glad not to be the only one with the shakes. "Beats college. Maybe we should eat something. I'll bet there's a deli somewhere close."

"You're consistent, my friend. No, we stay put 'til someone shows."

"Right."

"I couldn't eat now anyway," he said. "I've got the runs."

"Me too."

"Okay, let's not mull too much. We're gonna be great-great!"

"Right-right!"

We huddled in the doorway, watching traffic. The chilly drizzle continued. I wondered if the weather would affect our opening night crowd.

"Let's run the act," Bobby said.

"In the *street*?"

"Sure. Why not? There's nothing else to do."

"Okay. Why not."

I unpacked my guitar, facing the wall so that it wouldn't get wet, and began to strum. Bobby softly droned the lyrics. A passing car filled with girls applauded as they waited for the light to change. "Hey, come back tonight! We neeeeeed you!" he yelled, as we all laughed and waved.

At last! Recognition!

At a quarter to three, a pasty-faced man wearing a wrinkled rain-coat shuffled up to the door. "You the new act?"

"Hooray! The troops have arrived! I'm Bobby Darin, this is Steve Karmen."

"Larry Cutter. Drummer."

"Great!" I said.

Larry wore round, wire-rimmed glasses, and moved like a jazz musician, bopping his head up and down, effortlessly shifting a toothpick from one corner of his mouth to the other. He was in his twenties, and I was relieved that our drummer wasn't some middle-aged club-date musician. A young, hip band would understand our music. "We'll start in about half an hour," he grooved, unlocking the door. "We switched rehearsal time. The sax player teaches school. They scheduled some kind of last minute parents' conference or something. No one knew where to reach you guys. Wait a minute; I'll hit the lights. Where're you coming from?"

"New York," Bobby answered, as we followed into the darkness.

Club Temptation wasn't the first nightclub I'd ever been in. Sometimes, after our band jobs, we would go to a gin mill on Seventy-eighth Street—imaginatively named the Club 78—to sit in with the solo guitar player, Big Chucky, and learn what it was like to interact with an audience and sing to drunks.

And, with the power of the *schmeer*—ten bucks to the doorman and twenty to the maitre d' (we split it)—Bobby was able to get us in to see Frank Sinatra's midnight show on closing night at the Copa. He had instructed me to dress *old*, and not look anyone in the eye because I was under age. We were seated with four strangers at a small table way back in Siberia. That was my first time watching a big star in a major venue, and what an incredible, unforgettable night it was! For Bobby, it was a defining moment. The Copacabana stage was actually the dance floor directly in front of the band. Some of the audience sat at floor level—if they were lucky enough to get a table there—while the rest were a few steps up on the balcony that surrounded the entire room. When the Copa Girls (eight tall, gorgeous dancers wearing their famous Copa Bonnets) opened the show, we couldn't even see their legs over the heads in the packed room. Comedian Joey Bishop followed, and during his act, waiters kept going out on the floor, placing new ringside tables in front of the *old* ringside tables, seating new parties in front of people who thought *they* had ringside tables. Talk about knowing somebody who knows somebody! As his working area got smaller and smaller, Joey Bishop joked about a man on line outside, who couldn't get a table, asking the maitre d': "If President Eisenhower showed up, would *he* get a table?" "Why, of course," answered the maitre d'. "Well, he's not coming," the guy says, "I'll take *his* table!" The crowd loved it. Then Sammy Davis, Jr. arrived, and Joey introduced him to a roaring ovation. Sammy was starring on Broadway in *Mr. Wonderful*, and had a table reserved for every midnight show of Frank's engagement. Finally, with the room shuddering with celebrity excitement, the lights dimmed, and Frank's drummer began that all-familiar, high-hat rhythm: *Tsss, Ts-Ts-Tssss, Ts-Ts-Tssss, Ts-Ts-Tssss*. The band broke into the unison opening notes of the theme from The Man With The Golden Arm, Frank's latest hit movie: *BA DA DA DA DAP! Ts-Ts-Tssss, Ts-Ts-Tssss, Ts-Ts-Tssss, BA DA DA DA DAP!* Four bars later it was bedlam—the crowd on their feet, cheering, screaming—as Frank, with no introduction whatsoever, coolly walked down the few steps to the dance floor, wearing the most elegantly tailored tuxedo in the history of tuxedos, a raincoat casually thrown over one shoulder, and a wideband fedora set at a rakish angle on his head. It was the album cover, *live!* There was no doubt in anyone's mind that Frank had just come from the boudoir of some fabulous *broad* he had just vanquished. Smiling and bowing graciously, he handed the hat and coat to the bandleader, toasted the audience with the glass of booze that was waiting on the piano (Jack Daniels, of course), took a healthy sip, and paused until everyone was seated. "You Make Me Feel So Young" was his opener. Bobby's eyes were as intensely wide and focused as everyone else's in that room as Frank sang every great song he had ever recorded. But the highlight of this performance of highlights was "One For My Baby, One More For The Road." Seated on a bar stool, lit only by a pin spot, accompanied by just the piano, and holding a Lucky Strike in one hand and a glass in the other, Frank was every man who'd ever had his heart broken; and we all became jilted lovers with torches to be drowned. For three minutes, eight hundred people didn't breathe. Later, when the show ended, we both left in stunned, respectful silence. That was Bobby's first exposure to the public adulation he wanted desperately for himself. From that moment on, he wanted to be everything Frank. I did too.

What a difference now: we had just walked into Bowling Banquet Accommodations!

Mickey's Club Temptation was divided into two sections: a long bar near the front door where customers could watch the show through a glass partition, and a large showroom filled with tables that were now topped with inverted cane chairs. Three long, red-carpeted walkways broke the pattern of the black-and-white-checkered linoleum. The dank air smelled of stale beer and cigarettes. We followed Larry to the stage. It was much bigger than any we had ever worked on before.

"Who did your book?" Larry asked, probably the first question that all drummers always ask a new act about their musical arrangements.

I had blabitis. "I did. Er...we just have chord sheets. We haven't done the act with a band yet—I mean a band that's not *our own*, of course. Bobby and I used to play in a dance band, in high school, but, of course, they never played *this* book, of course. The only other *real* band that we've worked with was last Saturday, on "Stage Show," with Tommy and Jimmy Dorsey (I expected this to impress him—it didn't). They were great! Did you see the show?"

"No. What show was that?"

"Stage Show," Bobby repeated, checking out the ceiling lights. "On CBS? Right before Gleason?"

"I was working."

"Is there a spot light?" Bobby asked, looking towards the back of the room.

"Yeah. See Sharon, in the photo lab."

"You been here long?"

Larry reached behind his drum kit and threw a few switches, lighting the stage. "Eight months. I was on the road with Benny for a year." Musicians were always bragging about how they played with Woody or Dizzy or Sammy or Benny.

"Goodman?" I asked respectfully, wanting to win him over.

"Right."

"Wow, that's *great*! He's *great*! What a *great* band!"

"What'd you say your name was?"

"Steve. Steve Karmen."

"Steve, when you pass out the parts, pass out the alto book. Len plays tenor, but he'll transpose." I guess Larry hadn't been listening to me.

In arrangements for full saxophone sections, the alto sax part is traditionally written as the first part. Even when the chart is played by a small band, the alto still plays the lead. In our case it didn't make a difference.

"Oh, we don't have an alto book," I said, trying to sound professional. "But I thought if the horns heard our act a few times, they could ad-lib in the appropriate places. We usually work without accompaniment. Except me, I mean. I'm the accompaniment, of course. That's why I didn't write a full book, only chord charts. But they'll be easy," I added confidently.

"Okay. Not my department. Talk to Tiny. He's the leader."

Bobby was busy measuring the stage, but not missing a thing. "What's the show schedule?"

Larry picked up a handful of drumsticks and began loosening his wrists. "First show goes at eight. Second's supposed to go at midnight, but during the week we start early. John—he's the maitre d'—wants to keep the crowd so one show ends and kind of glides into the next; maybe a couple of quick dances in between."

"Do you know the other acts?"

"Oh, yeah. They've all been here before: girl-singer, comic, stripper, line'll open, you'll go on after the comic, stripper'll close."

Bobby sounded concerned. "There's another singer on the show? What kind of material does she do?"

"Standards. They like her here."

I nodded confidently to Bobby. "Oh, standards. That's great! We sure are different from her. We do folk songs, like Harry."

"James?"

"No. Belafonte."

Bobby shushed me with his hands.

"Oh, yeah. Calypso. 'Ma-til-dah! Ma-til-dah!' That what you fellas do?"

"Not that particular one," Bobby replied, "but we do 'Man Smart,' 'Hold 'em Joe.' Know them?"

"No, but whatever it is, keep it clean. Lots of social clubs come in here. Don't get dirty. John'll have your asses." He pointed toward backstage. "You share the left dressing room with us and the comic. The girls are on the other side of the dark-room. Now, excuse me fellas, but I don't get a chance to play full-out at home, you know, neighbors and all, so I come in a little early on rehearsal days to work out." And without further warning, Larry lashed into a pounding drum-solo, complete with crunching cymbal crashes and flashy stick technique—the ulti-mate sign of a hip drummer. The sudden sound in the quiet room startled me, and I jumped back. But Bobby bravely stood his ground, listening, nodding along, continuing the task of winning over the band.

To play our act, I imagined the kind of young musicians we knew in New York: goateed jazz types, stooped groovers that plucked big bass fiddles, sax men and trumpeters who bravely carried their instruments in unprotected vinyl bags, Birdland characters, players seriously dedicated to making new sounds and—most of all—aware of the new music.

When the rest of the Club T band arrived, they were anything but.

Tiny Simpson, the leader, was a tall, hulking, very fat man in his mid-forties, at least four hundred pounds, who defied the chilled air by wearing only a flowered short-sleeved shirt. His head was a crew-cut melon; his face spotted with broken blood vessels. There was a huge wart on one side of his nose.

"You the act?" he asked, maneuvering his string bass up on to the stage, blubbery flesh flapping from his armpits. He sounded like Rocky Marciano, with a high-pitched kid's voice that didn't at all match his immense bulk.

"Right," Bobby said brightly, extending his hand.

"Ready in a minute," Tiny puffed, ignoring the hand. "Everybody's outside."

"Sure, take your time," I added politely.

Tiny glanced at me, but said nothing. A shiver of fear shot up my spine.

Len Walters was the saxophone player. I knew immediately that he was the schoolteacher. In his fifties, paunchy, wearing a business suit and frameless bifo-cals, he had a stern look of authority—more math professor than musician.

Teddy Frosh, the trumpet player, looked like Señor Wences—small, Latino, with a black pencil-mustache and the most awful-looking toupee of stiff bristles plastered straight back. At first I thought it was a leather cap, but as he warmed up, blowing his cheeks out like Dizzy Gillespie, the rug pulled back from his sideburns and I knew for sure it was a serious piece.

Artie Maxwell, the round-shouldered pianist, looked most like a musician: tall, bony-thin, about thirty with hollow, spacey eyes and sallow skin. When he talked, his slender hand nervously pushed loose hair away from his eyes. He seemed to be off on a trip somewhere.

An eternity passed as we watched them set up. Finally Tiny said, "Okay. Where's your book?"

"Coming right up," Bobby said, taking charge while I distributed the folders. On each, I had printed BOBBY DARIN in large, red letters.

Ruffling through the pages, Tiny announced to no one in particular, "I've got the guitar book."

I cleared my throat. "Er...no, that's correct. Everyone has the same parts. Just chords. I thought that you could add something where necessary. I'll show you as we rehearse."

Suddenly, I realized the absurdity of it all. How could I have ever believed that my childish scribbles would be acceptable to this professional orchestra? They were going to laugh us out of the room!

As I ducked down to pick up my guitar, out of the corner of my eye I saw Tiny give Len one of those *What-the-hell-is-this-shit, get-a-load-of-these-amateurs* looks.

"You want me to ad-lib my part?" Artie asked, brushing his locks.

"That's right," Bobby said easily. "I'll show you exactly what I want as we go through everything. We open with 'Timber.'" He nodded to me.

I strummed the opening chord.

Tiny held up his hand. "Hey, wait a minute, fella. Just a minute, okay? Hold it right there. Don't forget who's leading this band, okay?"

"Sorry," I said softly.

"I'll tell you when to begin, fella, so just cool it. There are other acts too, you know." He was looking out into the dimly lit showroom. "Y'all set, honey?" We turned to see whom he was talking to. "And since your book is so...*complicated*, first, we're going to run down the girl singer so we can get her out. We've played her before. It's mostly a talk-through. Ready Liz? Come on up here, honey," he called. "I figured you wouldn't mind."

I figured we had no choice. Actually, I was grateful for the reprieve.

"Hey, no problem," Bobby answered easily.

My attention had been so intent on the band that I hadn't noticed Liz Carleton standing a few tables back in the showroom, unpacking her music books. She had long blonde hair and wore a dark, form-fitting business suit.

"*Hello there*," ventured Laurence Olivier, sauntering over to the edge of the stage. "I'm Bobby Darin."

"Hi, Liz Carleton." Her voice was breathy, like Marilyn Monroe.

"That's Steve Karmen," he motioned with his head in my direction.

"Hi!" I waved.

Mr. Suave was checking her out. "You certainly may rehearse first, if you wish."

"Thanks. The only hair appointment I could get was at four o'clock." She looked about thirty. Her eyelashes fluttered when she spoke.

Clark Gable tested the water. "*Sheems fine to me, my dear.*"

Liz smiled. "That's because it's dark in here, Charmer."

I wanted the opportunity to inspect another act's book. "May I help pass out your music?"

"Why, thank you." She was wearing lots of makeup and perfume.

"Nice folders," Bobby said appreciatively, not looking at the folders. "Where'd you find them?"

"A music store in Cleveland special ordered them for me."

I examined the leatherette binders. "Expensive?"

"Five dollars each. They include the case when you order more than ten."

"How big is your book?" Groucho asked, not interested in the size of her book. But he wasn't making a dent.

"Fifteen," she said.

Wow! Seventy-five bucks just for folders!

"Do you get a chance to use a big band often?" he asked.

"At county fairs, one-nighters, but mostly, no. It's usually only five or six men. Excuse me, please," she said briskly, ending the banter, "and thanks again."

"Have a good rehearsal," Burt Lancaster squinted.

We headed to a rear table to watch—and to regroup.

"Anything new?" Tiny squeaked, sifting through his folder.

When she picked up the microphone, Liz's personality changed completely. Now, all business, even her voice was different as she gave instructions with the aplomb and authority of someone who had conducted rehearsals many times before.

"Yes, a ballad. I only have sheet music. But I thought that Artie could ad-lib behind me—we'll use it second show. Everything else, you've played before. It's all in order. Open with 'From This Moment,' watch the intro, keep it going 'til I reach the mike. Tempo is like this: uh, uh, uh, uh..."

"Good, let's begin at the top, please. Everybody ready? One, two, three, and..."

> *"From this moment on...*
> *You and I, babe...*
> *We'll be ridin' high, babe..."*

Bobby nudged me—it was a forties-sounding arrangement. He seemed relieved.

Tiny waved the band to a halt. "Got it. We know this one. Next?"

"'Que Será.' The opening is al-fresco on the piano, waltz feel, and then..."

"I remember. Let's take it from the coda...and...arpeggio, and...one-and-a-two..."

> *"Que será, será....*
> *Whatever will be, will be...*
> *The future's not ours to see..."*

"Told you they'd read," Bobby said, as Liz ran through "Day In And Day Out." The band sounded together even though Liz's musical style was dated.

"Our charts will just take a little explaining," I said, wanting to convince myself as well.

Bobby nodded. "Tiny's a little strange, no?"

"Yeah."

"Always look out for fat guys, or guys with one arm, or cripples, or people with deformities. They always have an ax to grind."

"Right."

We listened as Liz rehearsed. "Too much makeup," he said.

"Right."

"Too much perfume."

"Nah, it was great!"

When Liz stretched her arms, her open jacket blossomed up against her full chest. "Nice-nice."

"Right-right," I said. "Think she's married?"

"Not. No ring."

"Oh."

"If they're married, they advertise. Check her finger. See? Zippo. She's not."

"Oh."

"Ever think about banging something like that, killer?"

"No. Well, sure, yeah, but no. I mean, she's too old. I don't know...she's...a grown woman."

"That's major league, pal. Looks like a great ride. You know what they say about a well-played piano. Why don't you take a shot at that?"

"You're incredible, you know. Why don't *you* take a shot at that?"

"Not my type."

"They're *all* your type, Cassotto."

"True, true. But this one's yours."

"That's ridiculous..." Yet, for a preposterous instant I wondered. "Do you really think that I would stand a shot with...her?"

"She's not married, or at least plays it that way, maybe even staying at our hotel. Who knows?" he chuckled. "How do you like the big time so far?"

This time, Liz stopped the band. "We'll close with 'You're Nobody' after bows, start easy, then sock it home."

Tiny took over. "Let's do eight bars...one, two, three, drum solo!"

> *"You're nobody 'til somebody loves you!*
> *Come on and find yourself somebody to love!"*

Liz nodded approvingly. "That was just great, Tiny. Thanks, guys. And thanks to you, too," she called out to us. Her entire rehearsal had taken ten minutes.

"All right, fellas, you're up," Tiny called. Then he whispered to Liz, just loudly enough to be heard on the open mike, "Folk act—no charts."

Bobby headed for the stage. I was right behind. "You sounded great," he said.

I picked up my guitar. "Yeah, *great!* Your charts were *great!*"

"Where are you coming from?" she asked, really not caring, now back to her breathy voice.

I was blabbing again. "New York. That's our home. We...Bobby was on 'Stage Show' last week. Did you see it?"

"What's 'Stage Show?'"

Bobby said, "Before 'The Honeymooners?'"

"Oh. No. I rarely get a chance to watch television. I'm usually working. But that's wonderful for you."

Bobby helped with her coat, winking at me from behind her back. I ignored him.

"See you tonight. Thanks for letting me go before you," she whispered, leaving through the wings.

For an arranger, hearing his work for the first time is a moment of holy judgment. In the studio-recording world, where the best musicians are available, the arranger decides exactly what he wants to hear, and then hires exactly that number of players to deliver the sound. The arranger is king, and the players know it. No matter how bad, unmusical, or sloppy an orchestration might be, studio musicians are guaranteed to *love* it. Negative comments are non-existent—every smart musician knows that *loving* and *smiling* go a long way towards ensuring future employment.

But in the nightclub world, particularly in the smaller clubs, the band is the boss. The players have nothing to prove and no one to impress; they've already got the job. Club bands play different acts each week, with different books written by all different levels of arrangers. Preparing charts for a nightclub performer is a unique talent: the same arrangement must sound good when played by a large band as well as a small one. As part of the opening night ordeal, an act must endure its first review from the band, and this jury can be brutal. Often, the individual music parts are smeared with penciled corrections and snide comments left by the previous band—messages within the brotherhood. (And, God forbid that during rehearsal the trumpet player should lean over and whisper something to the saxophone player; though it might only be a comment about a baseball score, this obvious act of secrecy can strike fear into the heart of an insecure act who assumes it to be a hushed criticism of their book.) It takes an individual with great self-confidence and a firm self-esteem to not crumble under a band's withering verdict. As both the arranger *and* the act, I had neither.

"Okay, okay, let's go fellas," Tiny ordered, testily. "This is not break time. What's up first?"

"'Timber' is first," I said firmly, stepping right up to the plate. "You'll find the act in order. 'Timber' is up first. It begins with a guitar chord." I took a step back and strummed.

Tiny waggled his hand. "Hoooold it. Slow down, fellas. What do we play you on with?"

"Nothing," Bobby stated simply. "We come on cold."

"No play-ons? How does that work?"

"Easy. Whoever does the intros will just say my name and I'll walk on. It'll be dramatic."

"Dramatic?" The pitch of Tiny's voice was rising. "*Dramatic?* You'll die. Take my word, I wouldn't steer you wrong. It's a long walk. These people don't applaud when acts come out. We'll play you on with 'Fine And Dandy,'" he said, ending the discussion. "Fine And Dandy" was the old chestnut that every band used for acts that didn't have their own special bow music written for them. "It'll be better," he nodded, with certainty. Besides, John'll make you put play-ons in after the first show just to keep it alive. Save yourself a confrontation."

"Hey, Tiny, relax. No one is going to *make* me do anything. Silence is dramatic. It's theatrical. It'll work great. Now, lets run it from the top..."

"Maybe we should try it his way," I whispered. "Maybe he knows."

"No!" he hissed, "our opening will work. We come on cold, as planned! Now let's run it."

Tiny wouldn't quit. "Everyone mark 'Fine And Dandy.' We'll stop before he gets to the mike so he can get...*dramatic.*"

Bobby fought back. "Tiny, I won't waste time on this. I'm coming on cold. That's it. There's no debate. When you do an act, you do it your way. This is my act—you do it my way. Okay? Now, instead of yakking about how we walk on, let's play the damn music!" He clapped for attention. "Everybody ready?" He nodded for my strum.

They began weakly, without enthusiasm. I began frantically, strumming as hard and as loudly as I could, shaking my head crazily up and down, pumping my foot on the floor. Mr. Raymond-downstairs would've gone berserk. It was time for the first chord change. The band didn't change.

Tiny stopped. "What bar you at?"

I was beginning to sweat. "It's the first time at letter B...or is it C? I...I'm not sure." I looked over at his part. "Letter C," I called out to everyone. "C, C."

"Si," Larry said softly, in a Mexican accent.

"Si," Teddy answered, picking up on the old Jack Benny-Mel Blank routine.

Larry: "Cy."

Teddy: "Sue"

Artie: "Sew."

"Enough!" Tiny barked. "Don't start! We have too much to do."

"Uhh...my part doesn't have letters," Artie called, his fog lifting momentarily.

Tiny's blood vessels were bulging. "Has anyone played this chart before?"

"Well...er...no. I just finished it."

"Well, it's *wrong*." He turned to the band. "This should be *cut-time*. Everybody mark *cut-time*."

Bobby stood close to the bandstand and spoke softly, with respect. "Tiny, how about helping us out? You're right, it's the first time I've ever used these charts. They need your expertise. I know they'll work if you help us. Can we try it again? At cut-time? Please?" He stepped back. "Gimme the chord, Steve."

I strummed.

It took twenty minutes to find and fix four more errors in our opener.

"How many tunes do you fellas do?" Tiny asked, crankily fingering the folder.

"Four, then bows—*your* bow music, Tiny, if you don't mind—then three, then off."

Tiny leaned his bass up against the piano. "Okay, we only have another half-hour for rehearsal, so let's take a fast pee-break, then slug through the rest."

Bobby waited until they had all walked off. "Why are they having so much trouble? What's different from what we've been working on? It should sound better with them playing, but it doesn't. It just drags. It's empty."

I tried to be practical. "Well, first of all, it's only bass and drums. And we've never played this particular song with a band before, until this very moment. These guys are just not used to our material. You heard Liz's act; that's what they know. They've never even *heard* our kind of stuff before. But don't worry, they'll get into it."

"Jesus, they just plotz along. Coming on right is *so important*! These guys sound like *undertakers*. Do the rest of the charts have to be *cut-time*? Tell me now so I can tell them."

"Damn it, I don't know! I never heard of *cut-time* before! Look...everything'll be all right. We'll work it out. The chords are there. If I don't know the right language, they'll fix it. They fixed 'Timber,' didn't they?"

"Yeah, but it was like pulling teeth!"

"Oh, pull this! They'll get it! The more they play it, the better they'll be. They just have to grow into it."

"I hope you're right," he muttered.

I checked my tuning, avoiding more chatter. "I'm right-I'm right." I prayed that I was right.

When they returned from the pee-break, we rehearsed "Jamaica Farewell." Nuclear Physics would have been easier. Everything sounded the same—thin and monotonous. Then we got to "Rock Island Line."

"How about adding something to the ending," Bobby said to Len and Teddy, "to fill it out?"

Tiny continued the war. "*I'm* the leader, kid, talk to me."

"My name is Bobby," he bristled.

"Okay...*Bobby*...what did you have in mind?"

"Something like *ON THE ROCK*...bap bap bap bap bap...*ISLAND*...bap bap bap... *LINE*...badap bap bap bap badap!"

"What's your name again?" Tiny asked.

"Steve."

"Okay, Steve. Play it."

We repeated the ending while they all listened.

"Let me think about it. We have to get a little more familiar with your material before we can add our 'bap-a-daps.' Let's move on! It's getting dark. Next tune."

"Sure you don't want to try something now?" Bobby asked, a little deflated.

"No. Everyone turn pages!"

Bobby gave in. "*Ooookay, mih felloh Trinidadians*," he said with renewed enthusiasm, "*let's get 'appy and pahform 'Man Smart,' to close up de first half of our sho. Can you play de paht on de floot, man?*"

Tiny interpreted. "Len, you got your flute?"

"Yeah, flute would be GREAT!" I said, hoping for a touch of Belafonte authenticity.

"No. Sorry. In the shop 'til Wednesday. But don't worry. I'll follow on sax."

Tiny was rushing us along. "Okay, okay, let's just do it,"

I began the intro. When Larry joined in, his feel for calypso was awful.

Bobby stopped them. "Hey guys," he pleaded, "this is *calypso*, not a rumba. Listen to the Curley-head play the rhythm. It's not hard."

I strummed the intro, changing chords in the best tradition of Lord Kitchener. But when they joined in, it was still rumba-land. The saxophone sounded ridiculous—completely out of place. Bobby waved us to a halt again, and then walked over to the drums. "May I show you, please?"

"You belong to the union, man? Hey, Tiny, if he doesn't have a union card, do I have to let him play my drums?"

Tiny was steaming. "You gonna teach Larry how to play?"

"Of course not, I just..."

"Okay, okay, do it."

When Larry wouldn't move over, Bobby knelt next to the drum set. "Come on, Steve. Let's show 'em." I strummed as he tapped on the snare with his fingers.

Larry was a wise-ass. "You'll never be heard if you play with your fingers."

"You're going to play it with *sticks*, Larry. But that's the feel I want. Can you write that rhythm down so you're able to play it? See? It's calypso."

"I don't think I have to write it down," Larry sassed. "I actually think I can remember it."

We began again.

"You've got it!" I called to everyone, nodding, smiling broadly at Bobby. But it was still a rumba, and we both knew it. It was just pointless to argue.

Tiny's leg was twitching. "Look guys, rehearsal time is over. Some of us would like to see our families for dinner. Write down a running order. We'll have a fast talk-through before the first show."

"Talk-through?" Bobby exploded. "Wait a minute! We haven't finished yet. There are three more tunes. You can't just leave..."

Tiny cut him off. "You've had more than an hour. Rehearsal is over. There's nothing for the band to play anyway. It's only Larry and me. You other fellas can cut out."

"No!" Bobby yelled sharply. Everyone stopped. "I want you to ad-lib parts in these tunes. How are you going to know what to play if we don't rehearse?"

For a minute, I thought they would all stay. Fat chance.

"I told you we'll review everything again before show time," Tiny said in a tone that left no room for doubt. "After we hear your tunes a few times, maybe we'll be able to add something."

"I don't want you to add just *something*. I want to discuss it, and work it out, and *rehearse* it. That's what rehearsal is for."

"Don't tell *me* what rehearsal is for, fella! Rehearsal is for rehearsing what's on the *paper*. There ain't no notes for anybody except bass and drums, and they ain't even notes, just chords. No saxophone notes, no trumpet notes, no piano notes, no rhythm figures, nothing. They have nothing to play, they don't have to stay."

"Nice rhyme, Tiny," Artie said under his breath.

"Go home, fellas," Tiny ordered. Len and Teddy continued to pack.

Bobby was sizzling, realizing that they were actually going to leave. "What did I do wrong, Tiny? I'd like to know what I did wrong."

"You don't listen to advice."

"Advice? Your advice is to do everything *your* way. You never considered that I might be right. You haven't given my way a fair chance."

"You'll get your fair chance tonight," Tiny said, putting his bass down, closing the book. "And at the risk of having my advice thrown back in my face *again*, if you do all of your tunes with just a rhythm section, it's right into the toilet. I'm not shitting you. This ain't some beatnik folk joint—this is *Detroit*! Do you know any big ballads? How about 'Prisoner Of Love,' or 'As Time Goes By.' They'll love 'As Time Goes By.' The whole band can play on that."

Bobby just stared at him.

"Well, think about it," he grunted, plodding off backstage.

On their way out, Teddy and Len stopped to tell us not to worry. Since they had nothing to play, their consolation didn't help much. Artie said nothing. Tiny had said everything.

Larry was our buddy again. "Don't be too upset, guys. Tiny's got a hard-on for folk music. He's the union delegate. He thinks this whole folk thing is going to put musicians out of work. But he's right—your book'll be a piece of cake once we get to know it."

Bobby wasn't buying it. "That's hard to believe. He fought me all the way. He's very negative and also very wrong. And he quit before we were finished."

"Don't worry. If you look bad, we look bad. We don't want to look bad, right? I've got a feel for your groove now. It'll come together. But he's got a point about your material. You don't know this joint. I'd feel better if you had big tits and a tight ass."

Riding back to the hotel, the old adage about "bad rehearsal, good show" kept popping through my mind. Yet, I couldn't imagine how the shambles we had just experienced was going to lead to a good show. In a few hours we would be facing our first nightclub audience practically unprepared. My charts were nothing more than a barely useable guide. The fullness I had expected from the addition of other instruments never happened. Bass and drums were just bass and drums, nothing more. It was a painful lesson.

I knew Bobby was disappointed, too. "If the tempos are steady, it'll be all right," he said. "Just keep the tempos steady."

"Right. I'll lean into my mike."

"Yeah. Jesus, I wish you were a better arranger." He immediately frowned an apology. "Well, you know what I mean. If we could only have worked out something for the horns to play, that would have helped. Now we just sound dumb."

"Bobby, our kind of music has it's *own* sound. It doesn't include saxophones and trumpets and pianos, at least not as basic instruments. Folk is a *guitar* sound, calypso is a *guitar* sound. Too bad there's not another guitar in the band. That would help. But since it's only rhythm and me, let's make *that* our sound. We've done it alone before. Let's be optimistic."

"When that big tub grew up, he was the kid on the block that nobody liked, and now he's getting even. What the hell are we going to do after the first bow? We didn't rehearse *anything*! How do you like that bag of bullshit, leaving in the middle of rehearsal? That was very unprofessional, *very* unprofessional."

"After the bow, how about if we come back with 'Scarlet Ribbons?' then 'Limbo,' and let's close with 'Man Smart.' At least they've played it. I'll talk over 'Jump Down' with Tiny. We can use it to close the first half. Sound okay?"

He just nodded.

"These cabs are costing us a fortune," I said absently, wanting to change the subject. "Maybe we ought to think about taking a bus to the club."

This was *absolutely* the wrong thing to say at this moment. He blew. "Holy shit! Instead of worrying about the *fucking* cab fare, how about worrying about the *fucking* show? Jesus, Steve, where's your *fucking* head? Don't start that fucking money shit now, okay? Jesus *Fucking* Christ, that's all I fucking need!"

The driver was watching us in his rear-view mirror. I turned away and looked out my window. "Sorry. I meant...maybe later in the week, maybe...I...was just making conversation."

He eyed me, then the guitar case between us. "You're a duet, Karmen, you know that? What if we want to take some action back to the hotel? There's no room in here. Why don't you leave your guitar in the dressing room? No one'll take it. Ask the guys in the band what they do with their instruments."

We rode the rest of the way in silence.

I spent a long time under the shower, trying unsuccessfully to puke up the knot in my stomach. He had counted on me and I had let him down. I had embarrassed him in front of professional musicians. They must think that we're the worst hicks to ever walk into that place, and it was all my fault.

His shower ran for a long time, too. When he came out, he apologized. "I know you worked hard on those arrangements, Curley. Sorry about what I said. It's nerves."

"Forget it."

"Just hang in close and guide them. That's all they need—guidance."

"Right. You know, something? Sometimes you're a real prick, Cassotto, you know that?"

"Yeah-yeah."

"I really did work hard on those charts. They're gonna do the job if we give 'em a chance."

"I know-I know."

I began to dress. "What do you think of the room?" I asked, trying to buck up my spirits.

"It's big, but we'll handle it. If it fills up on the weekends like Larry says, with that low ceiling, *Marone*, the applause is gonna sound great!"

"If we get any."

"Come on, Steve! You know we're gonna kill 'em, don't you? We just have to get it together with the band."

"Now look who's trying to convince who!"

"Guitarraro, did you see the pictures of the Pearl in the lobby? I've decided: she's gets the first shot at me."

"Good luck. Make sure that she doesn't have a big shark watching over her." I paused, searching for a little fantasy. "Do you really think I have a shot with Liz?"

"Sure-sure."

"W...what would she want with someone my age? It just seems so unlikely."

"Listen, wrinklebrain, she's exactly what you need. She's yours. I'm going Pearl diving."

"Okay-okay. If we're gonna eat, we should go now. It's not good to eat too close to the show."

"Yeah, veal parmigiana, with spaghetti marinara," he drooled. "We didn't have that for breakfast, did we?"

"Breakfast was a year ago. Who remembers? It's been a long day."

"Yeah," he said with a knowing nod, "and it's only just beginning."

Chapter 6

"I RUN A TIGHT SHOW"

There was no activity in front of the club when we pulled up, no people coming or going, not even a doorman. Inside was just as bad: two customers at the bar—men, factory types, beering, watching TV—and only four small groups in the showroom, eating dinner. The band was playing society music, ancient and boring. Their brittle sound echoed through the empty room. No one was dancing. Artie's piano playing was very cocktaily—the Dearborn Liberace, with lots of arpeggios. Teddy cracked and splatted high notes. Len sounded like the whole Guy Lombardo saxophone section, dripping with sweet vibrato. *Ugh!* They were all dressed in dark blue suits except Tiny, who wore a huge, tan dinner jacket. He looked like a blimp in an army tent.

"At least they play fox-trots together," Bobby muttered. "That's hopeful."

"Yeah, maybe we're lucky we don't have a horn book. Just imagine what these guys'd do to those Nelson Riddle charts you're going to pay all that money for."

"Enough-enough. You made your point."

A tall, slim, well-dressed man in his fifties was leaning on the partition that separated the bar from the showroom. "John DiCicci," he said, as we approached, not moving off the wall. "How was your trip?" He had tight, humorless lips, and a nose that looked like it had been flattened by somebody's fist. His silvered hair was pomaded straight back.

Bobby extended his hand. "Great, John, just great. Meet Steve Karmen."

"Hi," I smiled.

John seemed awfully grim for someone who greeted people in a nightclub. "How's your record doin'?"

"Moving up all the time," Bobby said.

"Hope so. We don't normally run more than three acts, but the Morris office's got the hots for you. They told Mickey you're gonna have a hit. How was rehearsal?"

"Some more time might have helped."

"I heard. That's what they all want, pally. Sometimes, you gotta make do." He tapped his watch. "I run a tight show. I want my acts here an hour before show time. I don't like to worry. Discount is twenty-five percent on food, forty at the bar." He squinted at Bobby. "You gonna do record promo?"

"Oh, absolutely. Decca's setting up a whole tour."

"Good. It'll help business," he said, dismissing us, walking into the bar.

I smiled at everyone in sight as we headed backstage. Bobby waved to the band. Teddy was the only one who nodded. The rest of them just kept playing, following us with their eyes. Pushed up against the center of the bandstand was a giant clamshell, large enough to hold a human body.

"Must be Pearl's house," Bobby said. "Don't take too long getting to your mike."

"Right."

A short, stocky man wearing a black rubber apron was limping around in the darkroom that separated the dressing rooms.

"Hi, I'm Bobby Darin."

"Steve Karmen."

"Andy Raffles," the photographer said. "You dress next door."

Bela Lugosi crinkled his bushy eyebrows. "*Yes, ve know. You zee, ve are going to change our garments in the room next to your la-bor-a-tory, zo you'd better be careful not to have too many experiments going on, or there vill be bats in your belfry.*"

"Listen, guys," Andy said. "I'm responsible for what goes on back here, so keep the place clean, okay? Don't write on the walls. No noise during the shows. See Sharon about the spot if you want somethin' special, but don't get too technical—she's only the assistant in the lab. At the end of the week, I'll take your pictures—eight-by-tens. Only charge you my cost. You won't find a better deal anywhere. Glossy paper. The works."

"*Thank you viddy much. I'm sure that's a definite bargain, a definitly definite bargain,*" Barry Fitzgerald answered.

"You do imitations? John said you was singers."

"Rrrright. It's time to get dressed, Steve. See you later, Andy," Bobby said quickly, leading me away, letting his eyes go cockeyed in comment. "The farmers here are weird!" he whispered. "*WEIRD!*"

The men's dressing room was barely big enough to accommodate two people: a counter with a few chairs in front of a makeup mirror, and a small sink streaked with rust and only one faucet. The walls were made of unpainted plasterboard with the framing nails still exposed. The coats of the band members hung on big metal hooks; their empty instrument cases cluttered the floor beneath a shallow bench. There was a portable coat rack bearing the inscription FOR ACTS ONLY scratched into the old metal. Bobby pushed to one side the garment bag that was hanging on it and hung his own bag in the middle. I moved the rack into a corner so we had more room to maneuver. I tried the mirror switch; most of the lights were burned out.

"Hey, Andy!" Bobby yelled. "Are there any spare bulbs?"

"In the carton under the counter."

I replaced the burned-outs; half of the new bulbs were duds. We spread out our combs, brushes, towels, and toothpaste, each staking claim to territory.

"Clipper Daniel, my parents named me," said the man standing in the doorway. "Don't tell me, let me guess: you're Bobby, and you're Darin. Would have known you anywhere. Welcome to the show business capital of Dearborn, Michigan."

"I'm Bobby. Meet Steve Karmen." We all shook hands.

Clipper was in his late thirties, round but not fat, and had a high forehead of tightly curled red hair and a shiny freckled face. He looked a little like Bozo the Clown. "Now gentlemen, in my capacity as MC, is there anything special you'd like me to say when I introduce you?" He punctuated every short phrase with a jabbing hand move.

"Just say that I was on 'Stage Show' last Saturday, and that I record for Decca. Anything else is up to you."

"What's 'Stage Show'?"

Bobby looked at me. "It's a disease."

"'Stage Show' is a disease?"

"On before Jackie Gleason? 'The Honeymooners?' Saturday night? CBS?"

"Nah, hardly ever watch the boob tube—see too many boobs in here. Only kidding-only kidding. If you think of anything else you want me to say, like immigration is after you, or you recently got out of prison, just ask. Of course that doesn't mean you're going to get it, but…it never hurts to ask. Only kidding." Clipper moved the garment bag back to the middle of the rack. "Damn cleaning people. You never find your things where you leave them."

"Blame me," Bobby said. "Sorry."

Clipper opened the bag, and took out his tuxedo. "I'll jump into my superman suit now, and leave the room to you. More than two people in here violates the fire laws. Tried a gang-bang one time; got so warm that the gang never showed. Only kidding-only kidding."

"Nice tux," Bobby said.

"Thanks. Rolled a headwaiter in Pittsburgh. On a warm night you can smell linguine. Where are you coming from? Wait! Let me guess. Texas. They crossed a male Texan with another male Texan. You know what they got? A very cross Texan."

"New York," Bobby answered.

Clipper dressed nervously. "Well, don't lose your sense of humor. These are really nice people…when they're sleeping. Have you met Johnny D? Detroit's Godzilla?"

"Yeah. You've been here before, right?"

"Oh, yes. Unfortunately, yes. Only kidding. A few months ago. Then a few months before that. In fact, I was on my way to the Sands, in Vegas, when John called last week and pleaded with me to fill in for Billy Falbo, who got sick and cancelled. So I called Jack Entratter and begged out, as a favor to an old enemy. Yes, I've been here before. The experience of a lifetime, one of the highlights of my multifaceted career."

"Anything special we should know?"

"Yes. Never sit directly on the toilet seat; always spread out paper. Only kidding-only kidding. Nah, just do your stuff. Then *duck!*" Finally, he was dressed. "I'm going out to count the house. I work on commission, you know. Very special deal:

if I'm not funny, I get an immediate commission back to Korea. Ta ta, comrades," he waved, and was gone.

Grateful silence returned to the room. "I hope he's funnier on stage," Bobby said.

"Gee, I thought he was really great; *only kidding-only kidding.* Now, how about showing me the makeup before anybody else comes back here to make us laugh, *only kidding.*"

"Good idea. Very timely." He dumped the contents of the Hansen's bag on to the counter. "First, you use albolene as a base. Use plenty. If you don't, you can't take the makeup off. You really can, but it takes so much rubbing that your skin'll come off with it. Go easy on the grease. If you use too much, *chor punim es gon to look Spanitch, meng.* And if you don't powder good, the reflection'll blind the first three rows."

"Do we take it off between shows?"

"Nah, too much trouble. Just keep it powdered down, it'll last the whole night. Now, put some on two fingers and spread it around in your palm like this..."

We were halfway through makeup when the band took a break. Tiny and Larry came in to follow along while I played through "Jump Down." I gave them the running order I had written on a dinner napkin.

Clipper's description was correct; it got very warm very quickly with Tiny huffing in all the oxygen. The open door didn't help much. This time I was grateful when rehearsal ended.

Chapter 7

"MAYBE IT'S BECAUSE IT'S MONDAY"

Our first mistake was that we were fully dressed and made up before the show started. At exactly eight o'clock, we watched through the open doorway as the dancers came out of their dressing room to line up. There were eight of them; their brilliant costumes brightened the drab hallway as, oblivious to us, they continued to adjust their stockings and primp their outfits.

All these scantily clad ladies gathered in one spot was impossible to resist; Bobby went to the doorway, brimming with the Darin charm. "Hi girls! Break a leg-break a leg! No, certainly not that one. That's too *beautiful* to break. Good show, girls. Hi, I'm Bobby Darin. Good show-good show! Hi there! Hi!"

A few smiled back. Most ignored him.

Suddenly, the stage went black. There was a fanfare, then a drum roll. I stood next to Bobby, watching, checking out the dancers as Tiny's squeaky voice announced the acts.

"Good evening, ladies and gentlemen, Mickey's Club Temptation is proud to present our first show of the evening." He was conducting the band with his right hand and reading from a small card in his left. "Opening tonight, The Club T Cuties!" A chord, *da dah!* "...songbird Liz Carleton!" Another chord, a key higher, *da dah!* "...our master of laughter, comedy star Clipper Daniel!" Da dahhhh! still higher, while Larry rolled harder. "...direct from New York, Decca recording artist Bobby Darin!" *Da daahhhh!* Bobby winked at me. "...and STARRING...," *da da da da daaaaaaaahhhh!* "Arlene Stevens!...The Birth...of a Pearl!" *DA DAAAAAH!*

Larry switched to his floor tom-tom, intensifying the next exciting moment. "...and NOW, ladies and gentlemen, to open our show, HERE COME THE CUTIES!!!"

The overhead lights burst on, and out they pranced, taps pounding up the three wooden steps that led to the stage, their wondrous perfumed vapor trailing behind them. The band was racing through "Keep Your Sunnyside Up." We both dashed to the blackout curtain that separated the wings from the stage. I huddled behind Bobby, amazed and wide-eyed, as every "Up! Up!" was matched by a crotch-revealing kick.

"MMMMMMmmmmm, look at that!" he groaned, leaning out a little more.

"Oh, *wow!*"

"Oooo, hurt me–*HURT ME!!!*"

Someone had crayoned a huge arrow on the wall between the showroom and the wings, pointing to a tiny peephole. I squinted through to look at the audience. All the tables on the far right side were empty. In the distance, there were a few more customers at the bar.

At center ringside, seven men—lugs, a construction crew—were eating, drinking, and noisily eyeballing the dancers. The man closest to the stage was wearing horn-rimmed glasses, thick as coke bottles, and a ridiculous-looking red fez with a giant tassel that bounced as he bobbed along with the music. Across from Fez, the stage lights glared off the crew-cut skull of a three hundred pound, leather-jacketed Gestapo Colonel. Fat Heinrich was so big that his ass hung over the side of his chair. None of the others wore ties. I tried to read their faces; they all looked insensitive and uncaring. I shuddered at the thought of what their reaction might be to our classy folk act.

Seated at tables further back were four older couples. There were no young faces.

"Check out the crowd," I whispered, as we exchanged places.

"Mondays must be a slow night in Dearborn," he said.

When "Sunnyside Up" ended, we swapped places again. There was a strange sound mixing in with the thin applause. Like children in kindergarten banging on toy building blocks, the audience was banging on their tables with the Club T knocker, a dowel stick topped with a wooden ball. Instead of using both hands to acknowledge an act, it could with only one. Maybe management thought that people would drink more this way.

Bobby shook his head. "It's 'Romper Room.'"

Larry leaned back, and deftly flipped a few switches with his drumstick. Artie began a tinkling pattern high up on the keys. The dancers stood frozen in soft, blue light, looking sensuously delicious, their breasts pushed up and out by their extra-tight costumes. Each was wearing a diamond tiara and long sparkly earrings. Earrings, however, were absolutely not the objects of the audience's attention. The bounce-to-the-ounce was incredible. One by one, the Cuties began undulating around the stage, swaying, grinding, bumping, and humping in slow motion in front of wide-eyed Fez and company.

Everyone in the room was just staring. I glanced back at Bobby. He was hypnotized, too. I wondered if Larry was putting us on about keeping the show clean. Maybe the line does a mass strip, a preliminary before the main event. Maybe just their tops. Show business is *wonderful*!

But my fantasy-fueled imagery exploded with a loud cymbal crash as Larry flipped more switches, flooding the stage in bright pink. A spinner on the main spotlight sent little stars cresting off everything. The band segued to a cancan. The girls squealed with excitement as they formed a straight line across the stage. Then, each girl in turn performed a little solo while the others watched, screeching and clapping. When they locked arms and began kicking, I recognized it as the same big-closer step that the June Taylor Dancers had used on "Stage Show."

Fez's tassel was flapping furiously while the other tables knockered along. The line had certainly woken the joint up—all except for Herr Heinrich, who was still expressionless, sitting stiffly at attention, cemented in one position, but following with his eyes.

Suddenly, Larry hissed at us, motioning with his head that we stand back from the steps. Just as the Cuties were kicking their final circle around the stage, Fez's hand shot out, clutching, just barely missing one of the dancers who jumped back, stumbled, and caught her balance at the last instant by grabbing the girl next to her. Fez's table cheered as the line completed their exit.

We pressed back into the wall as eight panting, sweating, fully-endowed fillies came thundering by, inches from our faces. I decided then that there was nothing in the world quite as beautiful as an almost-naked dancer trying to catch her breath.

"If that pig tries it again, I'm going to kick his eyes out!" the attacked dancer said viciously, as they headed back on to take a long, circular, dancing bow.

"Ladies and gentlemen, The Club T Cuties!" Tiny's voice distorted into the microphone, "The CUTIES!!!"

Off they came again, past our appreciative glances, this time bounding away into their dressing room.

"Great-GREAT!" Bobby applauded. "Super show-SUPER show! Loved it- LOVED IT!"

Everyone ignored him except the last dancer, who smiled as she ran by. "Hi! Gotta change. Good luck tonight."

"Thanks," we both called, but she was gone.

"Nice teeth," Bobby said.

Clipper was standing behind us. "This boy needs a doctor if all he noticed was her teeth."

"And now, ladies and gentlemen," Tiny continued, "our master of ceremonies…"

"For what I am about to receive, I am truly undeserving," Clipper said, on his way up the stairs before Tiny had finished his intro.

"…the comedy star of our show, back by popular demand, Clipper DANIEL!"

By the time the band had started "There's No Business Like Show Business," Clipper had already reached the microphone, eliminating any need for welcoming applause, of which, of course, there was none. He waved them off.

"Good evening-good evening, ladies and gentlemen. Welcome-welcome.

There once was a butcher named Sutton,

Whose wife was a glutton for mutton,

He snuck up behind her,

Pushed her into the grinder,

No Sutton, no glutton, no mutton, no nuttin'."

Fez groaned.

"I was right! No nuttin'!"

Larry hit a rim shot. *Ba-dum-chick!*

"Okay. *The madam of a whorehouse opens up the door, and sees a guy in a wheelchair. 'What're you doin' here?' she says. 'You got no arms, you got no legs...' He says, 'I rang the bell, didn't I?'*"

This time, Fez's whole table groaned.

"Only kidding-only kidding. Okay. *Two guys are getting dressed in a locker room, and one of them is putting on ladies panties. The other guy says, 'Hey, how long you been wearing those things?' And the first guy says, 'Since my wife found 'em in the glove compartment!'*"

Larry hit another rim shot. There was another groan. Artie played an arpeggio, and Clipper drifted into a Danny Kaye-style piece of special material: "It's my job to make you laugh, and if I make you laugh, well I've done my job."

As we listened to the hum of Clipper's voice, Bobby paced the hallway. It was warm and my stomach was doing flip-flops, but I stayed in the dressing room— there was only room for one pacer.

Liz Carleton came out of the girls' dressing room seeming quite relaxed for an opening night. She was wearing a low-cut gown and her hair was all glittery and fluffy.

"Good luck, Bobby and..."

"Steve."

"Good luck, Steve." She was using her breathy voice.

"Thanks. You too."

"Nerves?"

"No..." Bobby said, "well, I guess a little. It's natural before a show."

Liz was all smiles. "You'll be great."

"You've worked here before, haven't you?" I asked.

"Yes, a few times."

"This is our first club job. What do you do about guys like that front table?"

Bobby stopped pacing. "I can deal with guys like that, Steve," he snapped.

"Oh, just ignore them. Work to another part of the room. They're harmless. Might be for Arlene. I worked with her in Windsor. She does big business, mostly men."

Clipper's song ended to skimpy applause. "I'm next," she said.

I had expected him to be on much longer.

"Message from Garcia!" a voice yelled from the back of the club.

I peeked through the hole, but couldn't see who it was.

"That's John," Liz said, glancing in the small mirror nailed next to the stage entrance. "It's his little code for when he thinks you're on too long. He thinks it cute."

"He better not try that when I'm on," Bobby said.

"He won't. Don't worry. He only does it to comedians."

Clipper wasn't on a roll. "And now ladies and gentlemen, as you can see, I'm very funny, but not much of a singer."

"Yeah, right!" John again.

Fez nodded his agreement. Clipper was frowning. "That bad? Really, really, REALLY that bad?"

The whole table was nodding.

"Well, we're going to fix that right now, because it's time for you to all welcome a real singer, and a real sweetheart. So get your knockers ready, guys...hey, that didn't sound right, did it? Only kidding-only kidding. And now, ladies and gentlemen, here she is! Let's give a warm, Club T welcome to the songbird stylings of..." He waved for a drum roll. "Miss...Liz...Carleton!!!"

Liz popped a numero-uno and walked on to the strains of "From This Moment On," passing downstage of Clipper, who bowed graciously to her.

"Asshole audience," he said, stepping into the wings. "Drunks, idiots, and mental defectives; that's all they get here. I don't know why I agreed to come back. Try and do something intelligent, it goes right over their heads. Why don't you guys relax? She'll do about twenty minutes, then I do another half."

"Another *half?*" Bobby asked in disbelief.

"Yeah, John gets his jollies by watching comedians die."

"Jesus, I'm glad you told us. We can use the time to fix our makeup."

"I'll be in the house in case a fire starts. Maybe I'll start one. Did you hear the one about the two nightclub owners who meet on the street? One says 'Hey, I hear your club burned down.' The other says, 'Shhh, *tomorrow* night!'"

I forced a laugh as Clipper disappeared into the showroom. Bobby closed the dressing room door. "Steve, I can handle any audience. You know that. Why are you asking *her* for advice?"

"I had to say something. We were all standing around, you know."

"Just let me handle it."

"Sure-sure. I'm nervous, that's all."

We took off our jackets and loosened our ties. I followed as he put tissues between his neck and shirt collar. "It's too late to take it off and put on fresh," he said. "Just powder down so we don't glow too much. Damn it, sweat makes it streak. I should have known about the time. From now on, we'll make up when Liz goes on and save ourselves the repair job."

"Our minds were on other things," I said quietly.

He opened the door. "Yeah, but I should have known."

I was antsy. I re-tuned. Bobby threw practice smiles at the mirror.

"Wanna go out and see what it looks like from the front?" I asked. "It's too nerve-racking just waiting."

"No," he said. "You go. But don't go far."

The club was still practically empty. Some of the Cuties were seated along the side wall, wearing jackets over their costumes. Two others were in the bar talking with customers, not paying attention. I stood unnoticed in a corner.

Liz sang like a lot of singers from the swing era who were trying to sound hip, and her familiar material made up for any lack of original style. Her smile was convincing as she roamed the stage with the hand mike, working to another part of the room, avoiding the long table down front. But, since there were hardly any people in that part of the room, to me, she looked kind of ridiculous.

Fez's gang was mostly oblivious to the show, loudly laughing at their own jokes, offering non-attentive applause between her songs. Their behavior was becoming annoying to other customers.

Liz began "Getting To Know You."

"Come on over here, baby" Fez yapped, "I'd like to get to know *you*, too!"

John was leaning against the rear wall, arms folded. One of the dancers caught his attention. Jaw set, he shook his head slowly, but didn't move.

> "You are precisely,
> My cup of tea…"

"And you're my scotch and soda," Fez gushed, tinkling his ice, really cooking now, encouraged by his cronies' laughter. I wondered how long John would allow this rudeness to continue. It was getting harder to hear Liz above it all. Finally, John un-folded, un-leaned, and ambled down the empty aisle. When he reached the table of loudmouths he tapped Fez sharply on the shoulder. Fez shot up like a reprimanded schoolboy as John leaned over and whispered something to him. Fez quickly shushed the others.

But as John walked back out of earshot, Fez sassed something to Heinrich that broke the whole table up again. They were impossible.

Liz was into her Patti Page medley when Clipper came out of the bar, heading backstage. I waited a moment, then followed. In the dressing room, he was combing his hair, talking to Bobby.

"Never let an audience throw you. Do you think that after all my years in show business, I'd be afraid to venture out to face that bunch of seething animals? People don't scare me. I *love* people. Fear not, my young friends. I've done it all before. Besides, it's much less strenuous than manual labor—there's no heavy lifting. Remember him? Manuel Labor? He was a migrant grape picker." Bobby said nothing. "Hey, only kidding. Holy cow, you're as bad as they are!"

When Liz reached her big finish, she bowed, and headed off. The band was into "There's No Business Like Show Business." Clipper ran on and grabbed the microphone. "Liz Carleton, ladies and gentlemen! LIZ CARLETON!!!"

"Tough room," she said in the wings, dabbing her damp forehead with a tissue, "especially that front group. I'm glad it's over."

Clipper jumped in with both feet. "Where are you guys from?" he asked Fez's group.

"Hamtrameck," challenged one of the goons.

"Oh, yes, Hamtrameck. I spent a week there one day. Yes, Hamtrameck, the birthplace of the donut hole. That's where they say 'incredible' instead of 'no shit'. Only kidding-only kidding."

"Only not very funny," Fez said to Heinrich. Their whole table laughed.

"Listen, fellas," Clipper said seriously, "I have a show to do, and I know that you good people want to hear it. So do me a favor: go easy. Let's all have a good time." This brought scattered applause from the other tables. "See? Everybody wants you to have a good time. Even the band. How 'bout a big round of appreciation for Tiny Simpson and the Club Temptation Orchestra! Our wonderful band just came back from a long engagement on the road—they were paving potholes on the interstate." A few laughs gave Clipper more confidence. "And while you're putting 'em together, how about a hand for John DiCicci, our maitre d-d-d-dee. Wave a claw at the folks, John. When I came in tonight, I asked John what he was serving. He said, 'Five-to-ten for manslaughter.' John was called for jury duty last week—they found him guilty! John's so smart, when he was in school, they asked him to spell Mississippi, and he asked, 'which one, the river or the state?'"

"That's a pro," Liz said, as Clipper regained control. "I'm going to change so I can watch you. Good luck again." Bobby resumed pacing.

"What are you going to do if the Fez keeps shpritzing?"

"I told you not to worry about him, Steve. That's my job. You just worry about keeping the band together. That's your job."

"Sure." The topic needed changing. "When do you think Pearl gets into her shell? What's her name?"

"Arlene," he said blankly. Then he started to come around. "She gets in when the show starts and takes naps. She's in there now."

"No, she goes in when the club opens."

"No, she lives in there. Tiny feeds her three times a day. If she's in there while we're on, I'm going to jump in and play with her oyster."

Clipper zipped through his laugh-less act. I wanted to go to the bathroom, but there wasn't time. My fingers were trembling.

"Did he say the monkey bit was his last hunk?" Bobby asked. "Is this it?"

"I think so."

He took a deep breath and checked the mirror one last time. "*Are you ready, my curly haired guitararro?*" asked Ronald Coleman. "*Are you ready to meet our destiny?*"

My stomach was churning as we stepped into the wings. "Ready as I'll ever be."

The band was into "Fine and Dandy." Clipper came off for a fast bow. "They're screaming for you guys, ripping the joint apart," he said, crossing his eyes, then running back out.

"Ladies and germs, if any of you were home last Saturday evening—and if you were, why weren't you here?—and you happened to be watching 'Stage Show,' that mecca of TV entertainment, you might have seen the start of the career of a bright new up-and-coming singing star. He's the sensation of the nation for the new generation..."

"Good luck, Bobby," I gulped.

"You too, Curls" he said, flexing his cheeks in and out.

"... so let's hear a big Club T welcome... for YOUNG...BOBBY...DARIN!!!"

I followed him up the stairs as he led the way for both of us on to the stage.

Chapter 8

"STRUMMING AS HARD AS I COULD"

Tiny was right. Without walk-on music, all we heard were our own footsteps. Len and Teddy just sat there, expressionless, instruments on their laps, watching. Artie was watching too, but more through us than at us. Tiny was squatting forward on his stool, arms wrapped around his bass, his beady eyes inspecting us, waiting for something to happen.

I smiled right past them all, and quickly circled around the shell to my position at the far end of the bandstand. Bobby went down front and center. Any scant knocker noise ended well before we were in place. The room was deathly quiet.

The audience had stopped eating to look us over, but there was no feeling of excitement coming from them, no smiles to greet us, wanting us to do well, no real interest in the fact that we were about to sing our hearts out for their entertainment. Just passive puzzlement on middle-aged faces, and hostility from the ringside table of men so close they were literally at Bobby's feet.

I searched the room for any sign of friendliness that I could go to if things got rough.

Nothing.

Switching to my most attentive, concentrating, accompanist face, I waited as Bobby set his legs apart, clenched his fists like a prize fighter, and replaced his numero-uno with his most intense Robert Mitchum.

The hour-and-a-half wait had taken its toll. Bobby's face was glowing, simonized, and I knew mine must look the same. Worse, under the harsh lights, the make-up was actually much darker than it seemed in the poorly lit dressing room. We were two greased-up Indians in mohair suits. Not quite *The Jazz Singer*, but definitely in the neighborhood.

Our opener was an homage to the travails of an Arkansas lumberjack and his obstinate mule. Bobby and I both thought it would be a sure attention-getter. I strummed the downbeat chord.

It was inaudible. I had assumed that my mike would be on. It wasn't. Tiny's revenge? Maybe. I quickly flicked the switch, generating a shrill, ear-shattering whistle.

"Jeez!" Tiny snorted, grunting down under the piano, twisting a knob until there was silence.

Bobby, who had been holding his pose through all of this, turned slowly to me, still Robert Mitchum, and nodded that I begin again.

I played the chord.

"*HOLLER, TIIIIIMBER!*"

Ca-chunk-a-chunk.

Not together.

"*HOLLER, TIIIIIMBER!*"

My strum was the only sound. This time they didn't play at all!

"*LORD, DAT TIMBER GOT TO ROO-OOO-OOO-OOOLLLLL!*"

I started the tempo, but I was still alone. I glanced at Tiny and Larry, indicating with my eyes that, if they were not too busy doing other things, this might be an appropriate time for them to join me. I prayed they would follow the chart.

I tried to concentrate completely on Bobby, my vision drilling into his back, wanting to add anything I could to the intensity of the serious lyric. But out of the corner of my eye I could see the audience, now no longer watching but back to chewing, only half looking up at the histrionics on stage.

All except Heinrich: his two red, whiskey-fired coals were following Bobby's every move.

I played harder.

"*HOLLER, TIIIIIMBER!*" Bobby wailed, flaying the air with his fists as we neared the ending. He was moving with so much body-English that Heinrich's eyes actually blinked.

"*LORD, DAT TIMBER GOT TO ROO-OOO-OOO-OOOLLLLL!*"

Finishing the song with one mighty, shuddering, guttural grunt of, "*NUGGGGGG!!!*" Bobby remained rigid, arms locked in full extension, holding his most ferocious mule-whipper expression, triumphant, waiting for the dramatic, ovation-winning blackout we had planned that never came because we had both forgotten to tell anyone about it!

The audience was now completely attentive again.

Still trying to maintain the dignity of my ending strum, I hissed at Larry through clenched teeth. "Blackout-*BLACKOUT!*" When he finally realized what I was saying, our drummer/lighting man jerked around, and flipped all the switches down at once.

But the main spotlight was still on, flooding Bobby in harsh white light. After a silence that lasted an eternity, he uncoiled, stepped back, and took a slight, dramatic bow. "Thank you," he said forcefully.

At that instant, Sharon must have also gotten the idea of the whole thing because the spotlight went out, plunging the entire room into black, except for the neon exit sign that glowed eerily off Bobby's glistening face.

There was no applause.

Not a sound.

Larry turned the lights back on.

Still no applause.

Only knives, forks, and renewed chewing.

Mercifully, someone in back began to clap. A few customers joined in, mostly knockers.

Tiny, his mouth twisted into an I-told-you-so smirk, arrogantly flipped his music to our next song.

Bobby did a fast head bow, and motioned that I begin "Jamaica Farewell."

> "*Down the way,*
> *Where the nights are gay*
> *And the sun shines daily on the mountain top...*"

As we got deeper into the song it became apparent that Tiny was right again. There was no variety in our sound; everything was guitar, bass, and drums. With each successive chorus, there was a perceptible loss of audience attention. People were talking, creating a distracting buzz in the room. Where Liz's music at least had the colors and volume that trumpet, saxophone, and piano added, we were only a droning rhythm section.

When this gentle calypso ended, with it's soft delicate chord, again there was no applause. Two of our most dramatic songs had gone right into the crapper.

Again, Bobby showed his teeth, and then said firmly, "Thank you very much."

Again, someone in the back started the applause.

Without waiting, I began the introduction to "Rock Island Line," and held my breath. When we reached the spot where the bass and drums were to join in, the unseen applause-leader started clapping along. Immediately, he was joined by other clappers in back. It was John. Maybe he had ordered the Cuties to help out. Maybe they sensed we were struggling.

Customers started using their knockers, maybe they had been waiting for something to happen. Their tapping sounded like brapping machine guns, but when Bobby began to clap with them, rocking his shoulders up and down to generate enthusiasm, he came alive for the first time.

Larry started to ad-lib little drum fills, and for an instant, a groove was developing between the song and the band.

But he was rushing, which made everyone play faster. I tried to motion to him to be steady, but my line-of-sight was blocked by Len and Teddy who were now standing, oblivious to me, happily clapping along. I was strumming as hard as I could, swaying from side to side, trying to rein in the cantering beat. The knockers were winning—our folk song was becoming a polka!

Tiny must have been reading my mind, because when we reached the last eight bars, he whispered sharply, bringing the band to instant attention. "Polka! Two, three, and..."

And all of a sudden the horns and piano came in, blaring an om-pah-pah ending that fit *exactly* with the rhythm and chords of "Rock Island Line." It was amazing: it sounded just like an arrangement made especially for the song, except, of course, that it was a polka. The rhythm and drive surprised me completely. When we all miraculously ended together, the applause was the best yet.

"Sing that one again," John called from the dark, evoking a big laugh.

Bobby agreed, hanging on with his fingernails to the small piece of audience connection. "*Okay, Curley, let's do it again for the people,*" he said in his best Al Jolson. "*They ain't heard nothin' yet! That was only rehearsal! Let's take it from the chorus!*"

"Sing it! Joly boy!" one of the goons at Fez's table yelled.

"Mammy! Mammy!" yapped another.

Quickly switching from Jolson to Groucho, Bobby stooped over, raised his eyebrows, and began gliding around the stage, microphone in one hand, flicking an imaginary cigar with the other. "*Say the secret woid and the duck will come down.*" Fez laughed. "*Tonight's secret woid is…Screw! So why don't you go to your DeSoto-Plymouth dealer and tell him to…screw!*" He aimed the next line directly at Fez. "*Tell 'em Groucho sentcha!*"

Everybody in the room laughed and then applauded.

Now he was Bing Crosby. "*Yes, sir, right here on the Rock Island Line, with John Scott Trotter and his orchestra, we got lots and lots of my famous Minute Maid Orange Juice, right here-right here; chug, chug, chug, chug-a-chug.*"

More clapping.

This time when the band joined in again for their polka-style ending, the fuller applause was much more the reaction we had hoped for.

Bobby looked at me, and then caught a deep breath. I did the same. We had broken through. He nodded a "thank you" to the band. Tiny's face was granite.

"And now, ladies and gentlemen, I want to introduce my very best friend in the whole world, my accompanist, Steve Karmen. Come on down here, Curley." A few people knockered as I crossed the stage, pearlies flashing, strumming the intro to "Jump Down."

"Jump Down, Spin Around" was another hit folk song we had borrowed from Harry Belafonte, doctoring the lyrics to suit our own version. Bobby began snapping his fingers, and the audience immediately started clapping again. Our up-tempos were certainly getting a better reaction than the dramatic stuff.

I began the vocal, singing in my most non-authentic country twang.

"I know a gal up on a hill
She won't do it, but her sister will."

Bobby answered, picking the hayseed out from between his teeth.

"Let me tell you something, Mister,
I'd rather be with that little girl's sister."

"So would I," yelled Fez, as his table laughed.

"So would I?" Bobby frowned, breaking out of the song, looking at me. "Did we rehearse with him this afternoon?"

"I don't think so," I smiled. "I didn't see him."

Another man at Fez's table called out, "Weeeee know where Walter was this afternoon, don't we, Walter? *Rehearsing!*"

This broke up everyone, including the band. "Walter was on 'The Rockalocky Railroad Line," slurred another.

"Choo, Choo, Walter!" came yet another shpritz.

"Gotta jump down, spin around
Pick a bale of cotton,
Gotta jump down, spin around,
Pick a bale a day…"

As the heckling got stronger, what seemed funny to everyone else was becoming a great concern to me. When it came time for the next chord change, my fears were confirmed. With all the ad-libbing and fooling around, the band was lost. It would have been easy to find our places if there were horn parts, but with just bass and drums, there was no landmark.

I looked back at Tiny; he was shrugging at Larry.

Suddenly, a thin man in a baggy suit jumped up from Fez's table and began dancing, twisting around in circles, and singing, "Jump down...jump down...turning around...spinning...around..."

Instantly, the audience's attention was on the twirling drunk. From the back of the club, John rushed down the aisle.

We were nearing our big finish, singing with all our might. But no one was watching us.

"Pick…a…bale…a…
DAAAAAAAAAAAAAY!"

We ended.

Tiny and Larry were still playing, lost.

Down for a bow. Count one, two, three, and up. Turn together, step, step.

Our movement startled Len, who like everyone else had been watching the Twirler. When he realized what we were doing, he shouted to the rest of the band, jamming his saxophone into his mouth. "Bows! Two, three, fuffff…!" And without ending "Jump Down," they did an immediate segue into "Fine and Dandy."

At the exact moment that we reached our turnaround point, John reached the drunk who, oblivious to everyone, was still rotating, lost in his own spinning rhythm. Grabbing the Twirler's shoulders, John yanked him around and roughly planted him down in his chair.

The audience was applauding.

Unfortunately, Twirler thought the applause was for him. Now inspired, he rose again and did a little herky-jerky bow—first to John, who was still standing next to him, then to the rest of his table, then to the rest of the room, and then, thoroughly confused, to the empty chairs behind him. John pushed him down again. "Don't do that, understand?" he threatened, loud enough for us to hear on stage.

People at close tables were getting ready to move out of the way of possible violence.

Meanwhile, Bobby and I had returned to our performance positions, and the band had concluded "Fine And Dandy."

When Twirler realized that the whole room was watching him, he crumbled. "Oh, I'm sorry, I'm really sorry," he swallowed, embarrassed, looking to his colleagues for refuge. Then he turned to the stage, eyes pleading to Bobby. "I'm really sorry, *really* sorry," he said, hanging his head, staring at the floor, leaning on the table for balance.

"Come on, everybody, let's give him a big hand," Bobby said. "Maybe we can get him an audition with the Cuties."

Twirler nodded weakly, then slid back down into his chair. John went back to his post.

Bobby waited for complete silence. "I'd like to sing a ballad for you, and I hope you enjoy it." He finally had everyone's attention.

As I began the quiet fingerpicking intro to "Scarlet Ribbons" (another Belafonte hit), Bobby stepped back, casually took out his breast-pocket handkerchief, and wiped his brow, producing a large, glaring, flesh-colored smear on his forehead. He glanced at the handkerchief, folded the brown stain to the inside, and put it back in his pocket. Then he took his most tender-ballad pose.

Larry flipped the lights to the same deep blue as the dancers had used. The spotlight iris'd down to a pin spot. It was very pretty, very still, and very dramatic.

> "*I peeked in,*
> *To say goodnight*
> *And then I heard*
> *My child in prayer,*
>
> '*And for me,*
> *Some scarlet ribbons,*
> *Scarlet ribbons,*
> *For my hair.*'"

I closed my eyes, lost in the music, trying to put every part of my being into the sensitive song.

The audience was hanging on every word; it was perfect.

Then there was a loud crash as a chair fell over.

"Oh shit!" someone yelled.

Trying desperately not to break the mood, I squinted into the darkness.

Twirler was standing again, but not twirling, or bowing. Instead, he was leaning with both hands on his table, puking streams of Club T dinner over everything.

Someone gasped, "Quick! Let's get him to the can!"

The smell reached me an instant later. I almost gagged.

Bobby kept singing, concentrating, focusing on some imaginary spot out in the bar, fighting for the audience's attention, trying not to acknowledge the mayhem taking place at his feet.

> *"All the stores*
> *Were closed and shuttered,*
> *All the streets*
> *Were dark and bare."*

Supported by Heinrich and another man, Twirler lurched up the aisle, still heaving, as John angrily stiff-armed him in the direction of the bathroom.

> *"In our town,*
> *No Scarlet ribbons,*
> *Scarlet ribbons*
> *For her hair."*

Three waitresses rushed down the aisle in front of us. Pushing the men in Fez's group to one side, two of them quickly stripped and re-set the table, while the third threw heavy cloths on the floor to cover the barf (this was clearly a routine they had been through before). Bobby could have dropped his pants at this moment and no one would have noticed.

> *"If I live*
> *To be one hundred,*
> *I will never know*
> *From where…"*

When the men were all seated again, looking blankly at each other, Bobby stopped singing, held his hand out for me to pause, and then spoke to Fez. "I think I know a *really* good use for that hat...*SIR!*"

This got a huge laugh, and a burst of applause.

He began again.

> *"Came those lovely*
> *Scarlet ribbons,*
> *Scarlet ribbons*
> *For…her…hair."*

This time, probably more out of pity than anything else, the audience applauded Bobby's bravery under fire.

"Limbo" was a calypso song Bobby had written about an American who visits Trinidad and learns a new dance. But on a Monday night in Dearborn, Michigan, Larry's drumming kept us well north of the islands. Len's saxophone loudly ad-libbed in all the wrong places, stepping on key lyrics. The audience appeared distracted and uninterested—like people who had just survived a major ordeal and needed a rest (which, unfortunately, was the case). During the song, the ashen-looking Twirler returned to his table and again waved apologetically to Bobby, who nodded. Although we all ended together, the applause was back to tepid.

As I began the introduction to our closer, "Man Smart," all attention was again drawn away from us as John led a new party of eight to the ringside table next to Fez.

The lady who sat in front was an absolute knockout. She had long brown hair, a beautiful young face, big sensuous eyes, and a superb figure packed into a very revealing, black dress. The Grand Canyon shuddered each time she moved. From his vantage point, Bobby was able to look right down into her cleavage, and she knew it. Even from my distant spot beyond the clamshell, it was hard to turn away from this positively magnetic sight. The other women at the table were attractive, but definitely not in the same league.

The men were rough, hardened, all business, the type that never smiles. They wore tight-fitting dark suits, dark shirts, dark ties—gangsters in the flesh. In comparison, Fez's party was a bunch of Boy Scouts.

The addition of this group to the room completely changed the tone of Bobby's performance. In the spill of the stage lights, Cleavage couldn't help but be part of the show. She slowly crossed her legs and smiled at him, allowing her dress to slip a little further up her thigh, almost to the top of her stockings.

Bobby was off and running. "Hi, folks! Welcome!"

"Where's a waitress?" snarled one of the other women in a nasal voice. "I wanna drink."

"Shhh, be quiet, Cheryl," Cleavage whispered. "The show is on."

"Hey, you're cute," Cheryl called to Bobby.

"He's good, too," the now-very-friendly Fez said brightly, tilting back on his chair, tassel bopping.

One of the gorillas twitched.

Fez tilted back down.

"I'm going to sing a song for you, ma'am, and for all of the other ladies in the room, that I know you're going to identify with. Come on up here again, Goldilocks."

I strummed to center stage, trying my best not to look down into her dress. With her back to the gorilla seated next to her and her long Veronica Lake hair blocking off any side view, no one could see Cleavage's eyes except the band and me as she glanced back and forth from Bobby's face to his crotch, smiling, teasing, challenging him.

In response, he was cool, playing key lines of the song to the other women at her table, looking at everyone else in the room *except* her. Only once did he make eye contact, followed by a quick instinctive flick down.

But once was enough. Now, her gorilla was checking *him* out, too. I kept staring directly at Bobby, trying my best to keep his concentration on the lyric.

"Wanna eat, Monica?" the gorilla asked loudly enough to make his point, never taking his eyes off Bobby.

She fluffed him. "Later, Carlo."

Still focused on Bobby, Carlo leaned back, and then said, "Sure, let's have a few drinks first. Arlene's on next. We'll eat between shows." Then he raised his hand and snapped for a waitress. The crack of his fingers rang through the room.

When we reached the last chorus, again, the horns and piano entered, this attempt at calypso sounding more like Desi Arnaz than Harry Belafonte. But now that they had found a formula, their addition lifted us to a big ending.

It was over. We had done the act. I couldn't tell if the audience was applauding or not, because the band was really blowing when they played us off with "Fine and Dandy." I guess they were glad it was over, too. We executed our bow, and I went down the steps first, staying behind while Bobby leaned out for a last wave.

Standing silently the wings, listening for applause that had already died, I looked at Bobby, expecting him to say something profound that we could recall years from now when talking about this historic night. But any sense of completion evaporated as I watched his lips tighten, and his eyes lose their stage sparkle. "Let's talk," he said, frowning, clenching his teeth. "Let's change, and let's talk."

Just as we turned toward our dressing room, the entire club, including the wings, was plunged into complete darkness. Larry began a tom-tom roll.

As my eyes got accustomed to the blackness, I saw the door to the girl's dressing room open. It was dark in there, too. She must have one hell of a contract to black-out the whole building like this. I sensed her sliding by close to me. I couldn't see her face.

"Hi, I'm Bobby," he whispered.

"Hi," I said, even softer, "I'm Steve."

"Back the fuck off, boys, or I'll cut your balls off!" she said in a razor-like voice that left no doubt that she would do it.

Without another word, she paused on the top step, daintily stepped out of her bedroom slippers, and then tiptoed out onto the darkened stage. Silhouetted only by the exit sign, wearing a flimsy, see-through robe, she opened the clamshell, climbed in, and closed the top, dropping her robe at the very last instant. A hushed silence gripped the entire building. The drum roll intensified.

"Ladies and gentlemen," Tiny said, trying to sound deep and sexy, "the STAR of our show...Mickey's Club Temptation is PROUD to present...The One...The Only...Miss Arlene Stevens...THE BIRTH...OF A PEARL!!!"

There was no applause. Everyone's attention was focused on the shell. Larry switched on the deep blue lights as Len cut loose with a long clarinet wail and Artie played underwater-sounding music. I huddled back, as far out of sight as I could, watching, wide-eyed in amazement at the incredible scene unfolding before me. The spotlight was creating a watery effect over the entire stage as the shell slowly opened. Then up and out came the unbelievably sensational body of Arlene Stevens; a sea nymph caressing her waist-long golden hair with a diamond comb, wearing nothing but two seashell pasties and a coral g-string, and writhing with a movement that put the Cuties back in the minors. A naked woman with a body straight out of my wildest fantasy was dancing not fifteen feet in front of me. Her breasts were magnificent!

As Arlene slithered oh so slowly away from the shell, the tom-tom became a pulsing beat. The band eased into "Temptation," the relentless anthem of strip-dom. I glanced at Fez's table. Every wide eyeball was riveted to her fluid drive. The rest of the gawky audience was frozen at attention, too; even the gorillas and their molls.

"Holy shit, look at that!" I whispered, leaning out to get a better view.

"No, let's talk," Bobby said curtly. "We can watch another show."

"Come on, just a little..."

I looked at him. His eyes held an expression I had never seen before.

"This is business, Steve," he ordered, heading for the dressing room.

Chapter 9

"THEY NEVER SAW ANYTHING LIKE US"

He motioned for me to close the door.

At this moment, what was happening on stage was of no importance. It was time for truth. We had bombed, terribly. Not so much in audience response—because there wasn't much of an audience—but in the intent of our material. What we did just didn't work. Nothing really grabbed them or even felt good. Maybe working with a band for the first time had thrown us. If it hadn't been for John's clapping, there wouldn't have been any reaction at all. We were out of our element—city boys in the sticks, folk-pretenders, and everyone surely knew it. I had done my absolute best on the charts and in our performance as well, but it just wasn't enough. I felt like shit.

Bobby stripped off his soaked jacket and stared into the mirror, examining his streaked face. His eyes were hollow, distant, sobered, beaten. His tone was lifeless. "Well, *that* was the big time, Steve. How do you like it so far?"

I didn't answer. I couldn't. I didn't know what to say.

He sat down. "Okay. Post mortem. Let's run through it. Walking on cold will work, I know it will. Tiny doesn't know shit. I'll get more familiar with the stage and it'll work. It's a question of attitude. Do you think they'll ever get the opening of 'Timber' together?"

I nodded. "After they learn it."

"'Jamaica' was deadly. I don't know what to say about that. The chewing was louder than the band."

"I'll play harder. Want me to sing some harmony?"

"No, that's not the problem. It's the sameness of sound. Maybe Tiny was right. Move closer to the mike. Use it! That's what it's for." He paused. "The band has to play much softer during the talk part of 'Rock Island.' Direct 'em! That's your job. I was almost shouting. They've got to be much, *much* softer. And the tempo rushed. It was a goddamn railroad train! How do you like those knockers? It was a hundred drummers to one."

"That's why it sped up. Do you think you could get 'em taken off the tables during the show?"

"Fat chance. Use your guitar as a baton. Wave time at Larry. Can't you see him from where you're standing?"

"Not always. He's blocked by Tiny and the shell." I hung my wet jacket on a hangar. There were huge perspiration stains around the armpits of my shirt.

"Okay, I'll try snapping my fingers. Maybe that'll help. Amazing. 'Jump Down' was the best tune. Isn't that something? The one we didn't rehearse felt the best. It even got that asshole up dancing. *That* was something, wasn't it?" He paused. "But you've got to come up *faster*. You took a country mile. Too long-too long."

"It felt slow when I did it."

"'Scarlet Ribbons' will work with a different audience. I'm not worried about that tune—we know it works. *Jesus*, how about that wino? I've heard of negative comments, but throwing up is a bit much."

"Unbelievable!"

"The sax in 'Limbo' was awful. I gotta tell him not to play. Maybe we should do it second slot. Keep things moving early."

"Right."

"And how do you like that fucking John, seating that table in the middle of the act? Right at fucking ringside! I'm going to talk to him about *that*. At least he could have waited until we finished."

"Do you think you could ask for no service while we're on?"

"*We* may want quiet, but *he* wants to sell booze. 'Man Smart' was good, though. But I almost lost my concentration. Did you see the set on the chick in black? Eh, *Marone*! Yum! What beauties!" He was starting to sound like himself again.

"Yeah, wonderful," I said without enthusiasm.

"Okay, let's think positive. It's only the first show. We know we're better than that. We just have to make it happen. This is *not* the model for things to come.

It's only up from here." He grabbed a handful of tissues and wiped his cheek. "Boy, this stuff really runs. If we sweat like this we'll have to redo for each show."

I put a glob of albolene on my face. The grease dissolved into wet brown paste. "I'm glad we brought extra shirts." We heard cymbal crashes and cries of encouragement coming from the audience, probably Fez's table. "A fine Christian place you got me into, Cassotto."

"Yeah-yeah. Open the door. Let's listen to the tits."

Her act ended as it had begun, with Arlene ducking back into her shell and closing the top over herself as the lights dimmed to black. I couldn't tell if she had removed the pasties. With the band blaring and the stage lights up full, she arose again, now wrapped in her bathrobe. Even from the small audience, the applause was intense. After one long bow, she dashed from the stage directly into her dressing room. "We'll be back with some dance music in a few minutes, ladies and gentlemen," Tiny announced, as the house lights came on, "followed by our second show of the evening."

Then the parade began.

Larry was first. "Listen, guys, don't do too many soft ballads. This joint doesn't understand soft except when it comes to heads."

Bobby cut right to the point. "What can we do about holding the tempos down? Everything is rushing."

Indignantly, Larry pointed at me. "Hey, I'm following him. *I'm* steady as a rock. It must be him."

"It's not him. We've never had this problem before."

"Hey, wait a minute," Larry said defensively. "Didn't you say you've never worked with a band before?"

"Not with our *act*, Larry, but we've been playing in bands since we were kids. *Our* time is not the problem. You'll just have to watch Steve."

"Hey, I *was* watching him. Are you trying to tell me it's *my* time?"

"I couldn't see you during 'Rock Island,'" I said, as evenly as possible. "Len and Teddy were in the way."

"Makes no difference. I got ears. *I* wasn't rushing."

"Okay-okay, that was just the first show. We'll adjust from here. Just keep a look-out. And please ask Len and Teddy not to stand during the show. Steve'll move a little closer to center stage so you can see him."

"Oh, certainly. Whatever you say," Larry shrugged, and walked out.

Next, Tiny's huffing bulk filled the doorway, red-faced, angry, a soprano: "I *told* you, I *told* you! You better come up with some snappier tunes or you'll *die* on the weekend. There are six hundred people each show, and they ain't gonna sit for that strummy *shit*. If this crowd starts yakkin', you're *dead*. You can have another talk-through if you come up with any ideas. But if I were you, I'd be thinking hard about doing something up with the horns—we can play anything! I told you," he yapped, waddling off, "I told you!"

Next, it was Andy, who stood outside and casually lit his pipe. "Small house," he said, as if it was our fault. "Not good for pictures. Small houses don't want pictures. Big groups are more festive. Ah, it's Monday," he shrugged, and disappeared. At least he didn't say anything about our material.

While backstage opinions have the power to bruise, club owners and their hirelings have the power to fire. Next, came John, the one I really dreaded; he closed the door and leaned against the wall. "You did eighteen minutes, pally. You gotta do more time, and you gotta do something about your act." Bobby started to interrupt, but John squelched him. "Take some advice from the voice of experience," he said firmly. "Trust me, I know. I've seen 'em all. Do familiar material. You'll do much better. You got the goods, not the act."

Bobby fought back. "Our material is *fine*, John. It's fresh and original. You're just not used to it. You probably don't even listen to the radio. And, I might add, we did as much time as we had rehearsal for."

"Hey, don't get crazy with me, pally. I'm your friend. I'm on your side. Tiny told me you had full rehearsal but you got no book. Those folk things are good for television where everything's a close-up and you can hear every word. This is a *nightclub*. People are eatin', drinkin', havin' a good time. Nobody wants to pay that much attention. Once in a while? Sure. But not every song. It's a different business out here in the trenches. Ya gotta *project*. Now, I'll help you—what do you know that you can sing with the whole band?"

"Just a minute, *sir*. Before everyone rewrites my act, we're going to give it a chance. And before I make any changes—and *I* will be the *only* one to make changes—we'll wait and see what happens when the lights are right and when the tempos are together and when the audience isn't *puking*. It's tough to be a hit when your big ballad is accompanied by *retching*. *You* could do something to help out in that category, John."

"Yeah? What would you suggest, not serving? How 'bout chocolate soda? Would that make you feel better? Besides, I didn't notice a no-service clause in your contract."

"That would be ideal, of course..."

"*Ideal?*"

"Well, maybe you could control them more. If you see somebody getting laced, *cool it!* Don't serve him."

"Don't tell me my business, pally!" John snapped. "Those guys are harmless. They're nothin'! They've been coming here for years. It's too bad one of them got sick."

"And couldn't you wait until we finished before seating that last party? We were in our last song."

"I didn't know it was your last song. And even if I did, it wouldn't make no difference. Those are very important people." He un-leaned. "Now I'm telling you, this crowd is used to *up!* Don't fight the voice of experience. Start thinking about putting a little more *up* in your act. I'm your friend, pally, don't forget that. I'm trying to help you."

Bobby went back to cleaning his face. Their eyes met in the mirror. "Anything else?"

John stared at him, and then shook his head. "No." he said, opening the door, walking out.

Bobby hurled his towel on the counter. "Fuck him! The world is filled with critics and they're all here in Michigan. *Double* fuck him!"

Clipper strolled in, ending our brief privacy. "Great show, gentlemen, *great* show. Loved the part where the guy threw up. Keep that in. Gets laughs. Very human." Then he sensed our mood. "Seriously, that was not the best of all possible audiences. Don't do too many soft ballads when the house is small. In this arcade, they go right to sleep." Bobby looked at me and shook his head. "Oops. It appears that you've had your fill of advice. However, you're a big hit with the ladies. I'm with some friends who thought you were very good."

Bobby ignored the compliment. "Do you do the same material both shows?"

"No, I change a hunk or two or three or five. Second shows during the week are a good place to break in material—do what you like. And, tonight, since the house is so small, I'll do fifteen brilliant minutes and punt to you. Now, pay attention, gentlemen. After work, some of us are going to the Bagel for breakfast. It's the local greasy spoon, and they serve local grease all night long. Join us. It's a show business tradition—eggs and heartburn at two AM."

"I don't know. We'll see." Bobby turned to me as he put on his street jacket. "I'm gonna hit the head and think."

I cleaned my face as best I could, then went into the club. There was no waiting line of admirers, no adoring fans, no low-cut ladies panting for my autograph; just a big empty showroom with fewer people than before. Maybe this was better. I didn't want to have to make conversation with anyone until we had done a good show. If someone said they liked us, how could I believe them?

I went into the bar and spotted Bobby in the phone booth. The staff was taking care of their own business, not at all interested in a Bronx guitarist trying to force a smile.

"Tea, please," I said, when the bartender came over.

"Tea? Oh, you're the show. Corner table," he pointed, turning to one of the waitresses. "Martha, bring the kid here some tea."

"Two, please, with lemon. Bobby will probably want some, too.

"I spoke to George," Bobby said, sliding in.

"What did he say?" I asked, excitedly, somehow expecting that George would already have gotten a report even though the show had just ended.

"'Stick to the act and don't let anyone change anything that doesn't feel natural.' He's gonna call tomorrow after he hears from the Morris office."

"How are they going to know anything?"

"Someone'll report, dummy."

"Who?"

"Probably John."

"Oh, right."

"Who knows, maybe the drunk was an agent."

"I could always go to medical school."

"Yeah, and I'll become a barber. Mama's better, though. I called home, too."

"Hey, that's a great idea. Save my place."

Hoping a voice from home would lift my spirits, I called collect, with no phone company games. My mother accepted the charges. "The first show is over, Ma. It was unbelievable. They never saw anything like us. The crowd was small, but it's early in the week."

"Are you eating good food?"

"Yep."

"Did you wash your socks?"

"I've only been here one day, Ma. I have plenty of socks. Look, everything is fine. I just wanted you to know we opened."

"That's nice. Arthur was home for dinner tonight. He's working on pediatrics. He helped deliver twins yesterday."

I regretted the call. "I'm glad."

"Watch your money. You know what I mean."

"I know, Ma, I know."

"Don't let Bobby teach you any fancy tricks."

"I didn't call for a lecture, Ma. I just wanted to tell you that we opened, and everything is fine. Well, I have to do another show now, so I'll...I'll talk to you later...later in the week. Say 'Hi' to Pop."

"Write to us. It's cheaper."

"I will-I will." I couldn't wait to hang up.

"Remind me not to call home again," I said, back at the table. "My family has absolutely no concept of what I'm trying to do."

"Forget it—they're there, you're here. And from *here*, it's only up." He gave me the high sign with his eyebrows. "Why don't you...er...meet me in the dressing room, Curlique. I'm going to have some more tea."

I turned to see who he was looking at. One of the dancers—the last one in the line, the one who had smiled at him—was standing at the bar. She was wearing a tweed sports jacket over her costume, but it didn't take much to see that she had a great body.

He went to the service counter, poured hot water over his tea bag, then offered his hand to the bartender. "Hi, Bobby Darin."

"Jake Smith."

"I hope that you don't mind that I helped myself to tea."

"No problem."

Then he turned to the girl. He was half Gable, half Mitchum. "*Hi, I'm Bobby Darin.*"

"See you backstage," I said, unheard.

Clipper was in the dressing room, combing his hair. "Got a girl?"

"Nope."

"Got a guy?" he swished.

"Nope," I laughed.

"Ah, the single life; carefree, uninvolved. And a musician! A *guitar* player, yet! Today's magical instrument. The passport to romance. A few strums and they tear your pants off. I missed my calling. I should have been a musician—that's where the action is. You must have killed them in college."

"Never went to college. Bobby and I met in high school."

"In *high school?*"

"We played in the same band."

He squinted in the mirror, rubbing his teeth with his pinky. "See anything in the line that looks interesting?"

"They all look interesting," I smiled.

"Check 'em out, laddie. There's some nice head out there."

It was a little weird to hear Clipper talking about women in this sleazy way. I tried to be cool. "Are most of them married?"

"A few of this, a few of that," he sang. "And if you're looking for some real action, just say the word."

"Oh, no, that's okay. We just got here," I said, trying to sound mature, and at the same time wanting to duck the subject. Thankfully, Bobby walked in, carrying his teacup like an English Lord, whistling to himself, his mood changed—now very up.

Clipper noticed. "If tea would do that for me, I'd change my name to Wong."

Without a word, he took off his jacket and began smearing albolene on his forehead.

"Shouldn't we get made up later?" I asked softly.

He stopped. "You're right. I wasn't thinking."

Clipper became more formal. "Gentlemen, I do not wish to seem preachy, but I will offer one more bit of friendly advice: this show is Monday Night Bowling, and the lanes are empty. The band outnumbers the house, so keep things zipping along. There's nobody out there—only that holdover table of art lovers. So zing zing, and we're into breakfast." He stood in the doorway. "I'll leave this stuffy room to you and your patty-cake. This club is a good example of why I became a comedian: I had this burning ambition to make empty chairs laugh. Then I saw Dr. Freud. Freud was a fraud. After this engagement, I'm going back to my day job...*dentistry.*"

When neither of us reacted, he shrugged and walked away.

"What's going on?"

"What do you mean?" answered the Cheshire Cat.

"Come on, something's up. Don't bullshit me."

"I just met a nice lady in the bar."

"I saw you making a move. Tell me."

"Her name is Myra, she's from Kentucky, and she usually goes to the Bagel after work."

"Seems like a popular place," I said. "And now you have a date, right?"

"Not quite, but I allowed as how we might be a little teeny-weeny bit hungry after work."

"We?"

"Yes, we."

"And...?"

"And I was wondering if you're feeling hungry?"

"Am I *supposed* to feel hungry?"

"Well, that would depend on if you'd like to meet someone."

"Of course I'd like to meet someone! Does she have a friend?"

"Curley, not only does she have a friend, but one of the girls in the line is her *roommate*! And they're staying at that famous mecca for show-folk, the one and only Wolverine Hotel! The possibilities are endless! So, *if* you should decide to be hungry...and no one's forcing you, of course...maybe we can work out a room swap later in the week!"

"All based on my appetite?" I grabbed my stomach, "Oh, no! So it's hunger that I've been feeling! I couldn't imagine what that pain was! Listen carefully: the next sound you hear will be my appetite growing."

There was a knock on the door. "That's the best timing I've heard all night," he laughed. "Enter!"

It was Fez, fez in hand, along with Twirler, and in between them, the leather-clad Heinrich. My first instinct was that they'd decided to end their evening by breaking a few skulls—ours. Oh, God, I promise I'll never do shtick with a man in a hat!

"I'm Donny McClure," Fez began, humbly. "We just wanted to say that we enjoyed your show."

"...and I'm sorry I got sick during your song," Twirler added. His face was very pale.

Bobby flashed his compassionate numero-uno. "Oh, that's okay, my friends. Those things happen. Feeling any better?"

"Yeah, once I got rid of it."

"Where in New York you all from?" asked the leathered hunk.

"The City."

"Never been there. Hear it's quite a place."

"Yes, it is."

"We're from Big Loaf Bakery," Fez said. "I'm bread foreman; Jack and Matty are cookies and cake. Sounds funny, I know." We shook hands all around. "Big Loaf supplies the club; we come to see every new show—professional discount. We hoisted a few too many tonight, that's all. Sorry. We just wanted to tell you that you're really very good. And we *know*—we're a tough audience."

"I'll say," winked Bobby. "Only kidding-only kidding."

"You're just like Clipper, ha ha," Fez said. Then he turned to Twirler. "He's just like Clipper. You're here for two weeks, right?" Bobby nodded. "Well, we'll be back again next week for certain."

"Swell," Bobby said.

"Yeah," added Twirler, "I want to see you when I'm in better shape. I won't get blotto again. Promise. Thanks for understanding."

"Sure," Bobby said.

"If we leave before you go on, it's because we gotta get home," Fez added.

Heinrich grunted.

"We'll look forward to seeing you," Bobby called after them. "Thanks for coming by."

"Congratulations, Cassotto," I said, "you've got your first fan club. At least we'll have bread to eat."

Tiny plodded by. "Five minutes. Short show. Cut a tune. And before you get your balls in an uproar, everybody cuts second show. Weekends, you can do two full shows. Straight? Now, what'll it be?"

"Cut 'Scarlet Ribbons' and put 'Hold 'Em Joe' second instead of 'Jamaica Farewell,'" Bobby said.

"We didn't rehearse 'Hold 'Em Joe,'" Tiny squeaked.

"That wasn't my fault. Just follow Steve."

"I'll take the first four bars alone to set tempo, like this," I said, grabbing my guitar, and strumming. "Then you join me at the lyric. I'll nod to you."

He motioned me to stop. "Sounds like the others. Okay, we'll watch you."

"I thought you wanted to do the same show," I said after Tiny left.

"Clipper's right. Let's break in material. There's nobody out there except Big Tits and her goons. This'll be our rehearsal."

There was rustling and fussing in the hallway as the Cuties lined up.

"Which one's the roommate?" I asked.

"Don't know."

The Cuties did only one number. Clipper cut right to

introducing Liz. "He's calling my name," she said breathlessly, skipping by. She had changed into a tight black gown.

"You look very pretty," I said, going to the door.

"Why, thank you, Steve."

While Liz was on, I began with makeup. "Little grease, lots of powder, right?"

"Right."

"Let's get a clothing brush so we can keep the powder off our suits."

"Good idea, Curleybean."

I peeked through the pin-hole while Clipper was on. Except for a few people in the bar, Cleavage's ringside party was the only table.

Clipper struggled through one parody. Then we heard it. "Message from Garcia!" John yelled from the back of the club.

The hoods all laughed.

Clipper shook his head. "I just hate it when the audience gets a bigger laugh than I do. Only kidding-only kidding. And now, dearly departed, it's my pleasure to introduce two young men from New York. It's their first club engagement, and I know you're going to love 'em. And if you don't love 'em, at least be kind. I was talking to the boys backstage before the show, and neither one of them could explain what the hell nice kids like them were doing in a joint like this."

"Message from Garcia!" John cracked again.

"Yes, John, I got the message. Here they are, Decca recording stars...Bobby Darin...and Steve Karmen."

The only thing wrong with the second show was that there was no one to hear it. The act played better in every way—much more relaxed and unpressured. Tiny and Larry were more together, and when the band joined in for the ending of "Rock Island," even though it was still a polka, for the first time I had an inkling that our material might work. Things were starting to make sense. I could tell that Bobby was pleased, too. Cleavage continued her little game, swaying back and forth to our rhythms. But now the gorilla wasn't even paying attention; deep in conversation with another hood. We were just a harmless background annoyance. There was hardly any applause; only a smattering from the women, John, and some remaining staff. In the darkened wings, the perfumed bathrobe concealing Arlene Stevens slid by on its way to her shell.

I knew I wasn't going to leave my guitar backstage, but when the band crowded into the dressing room for their coats, I used the opportunity to smooth the subject with Bobby. "Is this room locked at night?"

"No," Len said, "but you can leave your stuff. Nobody comes back here."

"Do you guys leave your horns?"

"No," said Teddy.

"I need mine at school," said Len.

"I leave my piano," Artie said.

"I leave the drums, too, but not the sticks," Larry said.

Tiny said nothing, still clearly pissed.

It was a Marx Brother's movie—bodies struggling with garments in every direction. Clipper squeezed away. "I'm off to the Bagel, amigos. Hey, that sounds like a song."

"We'll see you there," Bobby called brightly, leaning from side to side to avoid this bumping ballet.

"Right!" I added.

"Meet me in front," Bobby said, after the room had emptied. "I'll be out in a minute."

"You okay?"

"*Just a bit tattered*," said Lawrence Olivier. "A couple of minutes of quiet. I'll be ready-Teddy veddy soon."

It was getting cold backstage. Sharon padlocked the photo lab as Andy watched, puffing his pipe. She looked about Andy's age. I wondered if they were married. Did they fool around in the lab when there were no customers? Maybe they got high first on the chemicals.

The showroom was dark. The beery smell was creeping up again between the tables. I brought our teacups to the kitchen. The men in Cleavage's party were still in the bar. Liz was at a booth, nursing a drink, talking to John. I heard laughter as the molls came out of the ladies room. Cleavage was walking a bit slower, laying back, glancing toward the backstage entrance, apparently looking for someone. Our paths crossed near the door.

Up close, she was as beautiful as she had appeared from the stage. Her rosy skin had a delicious powdery smell, and she wore just the right amount of makeup. This lady sure didn't use an albolene base. Her body radiated heat as she came closer—it almost took my breath away. I stepped out of the darkness. She must have recognized me because of the guitar.

"Oh, you're the other one," she whispered secretively, pretending to shake my hand. "Give this to your friend." Inside her deliciously warm palm was a folded piece of paper. "Tell him I'll be at that number tomorrow, after one." She turned to join her companions. "Gotta go!"

I pocketed the message and watched her glide into the bar. Every movement telegraphed sex. Hidden, quietly alone, I was amazed at how she could have such a dizzying effect on me.

Kong Carlo grumbled something about being kept waiting, but she fluffed him again, insisting he help with her coat. After they'd all gone, I walked into the bar. Liz and John seemed to be arguing. When John saw me, he moved away and began tallying the register.

"Going for breakfast?" I asked. "I'm told it's a show business tradition."

"Oh, I could never eat at this hour," Liz said softly.

I wanted to be debonair. "Staying at the Wolverine?"

"No. The Royal Palm, a few blocks away."

"Are you from Detroit?"

"Chicago."

I didn't know what else to say so I started to repeat myself. "Have you worked in this area before?"

I think she knew I felt awkward. "Oh, quite a lot. The whole circuit."

"What's the circuit?"

"The Copa in Pittsburgh, the Cabin Club in Cleveland, the Metropole in Windsor, the Purple Onion in Indianapolis..."

"Sounds like you're on the road a lot."

She smiled. "Sometimes it seems that way."

Bobby came into the bar. "*You do a fine act, Miss Lizzy, a fine act,*" said Clark Gable.

"Why, thank you, Mr. Rhett," she drawled.

"Last call," said Jake. "Want another, Liz?"

"No thanks, Jake. I'm on my way home."

"*Can we give you a lift, Miss Scarlet?*"

"Why, that would be very kind of you, Mr. Rhett, if it's not too much trouble."

"Our pleasure," he said.

"Our pleasure," I added.

While Bobby yakked with Liz, I hailed a taxi. She sat between us. There wasn't enough room in back for three people and my guitar case. Bobby insisted it be stowed in the trunk, but I put it on the front seat next to the driver. "In case it gets bumpy, I can keep an eye on it," I said, avoiding the look that I knew was on Cassotto's face.

At the Royal Palm, Bobby refused to take the money that Liz offered, and after a mild protest, she said good night. We watched her go into the lobby. "You're right, she's got a nice figure."

"*And it'll be yours if you're patient, podner,*" said John Wayne. "Now, to the Wolverine Hotel, driver. Let's change before chow time."

"Do you want the guitar now?" the cabbie asked.

I leaned forward to retrieve my instrument, but Bobby held me back. "It's only a few blocks. It'll survive. *Yes, she wants to fuck you, m' boy,*" opined W.C. Fields. "*She wants to fuck you, and she's all yours.*"

I ignored him. "I have a message for you, from the big set at ringside."

"Really?"

He opened the folded paper. "'Help, I'm a prisoner in the Big Loaf Bakery.'"

"Serious."

"Okay, it says, 'Tigers: eight, Indians: seven.'"

"Bobby!"

"'Monica. Man smart, woman smarter. Call me.' Hey, action! Monica, Myra, the week for M's! I'll call as soon as we get back."

"Don't," I cautioned. "She said after one, tomorrow. If you call tonight, I have a feeling that you might be interrupting something."

"Is that what she really said?"

"*That's correct, m' boy,*" I answered, in my best W.C. Fields. "*Call her tomorrow, m' boy, tomorrow. She certainly wants you, Roberto, certainly wants you, m' boy.*"

"407. Any messages?"

"Nope," said the grump, looking up from his magazine. He pointed at my thing again. "You're not going to play that in the room, are you?"

"You asked me that last night."

"Just checking."

"Guaranteed not. Strictly for put-away."

"Which way is the Bagel," Bobby asked.

"Out the door, turn right, up two blocks, can't miss it. You boys in a show or somethin'?"

"We opened tonight at Club Temptation."

"Oh, yeah. Some of the dancers stay here. What do you do?"

"Folk songs," Bobby answered proudly. "Have you heard 'Rock Island Line?'"

"Is that you?"

"That's Bobby!"

"Nah, never listen to the radio."

"It just came out," I said.

"Well, good luck, all that."

"Yeah, and the same to you," Bobby said, rushing me along.

The huge, white-bulbed sign that spelled BAGEL could be seen for blocks. At two AM it was the only life on Woodward Avenue. But what glowed on the outside was a dingy, depressing luncheonette on the inside. Long, grimy, florescent fixtures made everything look yellow; the lifeless food in the hot-counter looked like it had been sitting there all day. I would have expected such a shabby place to be empty, especially at this late hour—but every one of the formica tables was filled.

Clipper was seated next to a small, bronzed-skinned woman with tightly cropped blonde hair. Her spangly evening gown looked completely out of place in this funky hash house. I couldn't tell if she was white or very light Negro. She might have been in the audience at the first show.

Opposite them sat the dancer Bobby wanted to hit on, and another girl. I didn't recognize her from the Cuties. Maybe he'd gotten his signals crossed.

Clipper introduced his wife, Laurene, and pushed two cracked plastic menus across the table. "We've ordered. Proceed with caution."

Bing Crosby sat next to Myra Hilliard. "*Hi, again.*"

Myra was in her early twenties, had dark hair and hazel eyes that glowed with energy and excitement.

"Hello everybody," I smiled, sliding in next to Clipper, and across from Chris Evans. Chris had broad shoulders, a square face with high cheekbones, and a pug nose; her short blonde hair was sprayed stiff, and she was wearing "hide 'ems"— a term Bobby had invented for the outfits worn by girls who chose to keep their equipment secret. Her loose-fitting, striped shirt was buttoned up to the neck, revealing nothing. But she had sweet eyes. Chris was definitely non-show biz.

When his food arrived, Clipper turned nasty. "See here, sir, don't they ever wash the utensils? This fork is filthy! And my glass has fingerprints all over it. Not mine, I might add!"

"Eat, Clipper," Laurene said, not looking up.

"Darling, a customer has the right to expect a modicum of cleanliness. Look at those eggs! They've been fried in Mobil."

"There's nothing wrong with the eggs, Clipper," she interrupted, "except that they're getting cold." She was exceptionally rough with him.

"I was just..."

She cut him off again. "Just *eat*, Clipper."

Clipper ate. The waiter must have faced this ranting before because he paid no attention until after he had taken our order, when he brought Clipper another glass and fork without comment.

During the meal, Clipper and Bobby dueled each other about show biz trivia. I just nodded along, smiling occasionally at Chris, who smiled back, not saying much either. After the day's roller coaster of emotions and the late-night influx of food, I was tired. I really wanted to accept Clipper's offer for a ride back to our hotel, but Bobby insisted that a walk would do us good. I knew he wanted private time with Myra.

The girls were setting a brisk pace. "Go easy, ladies," he called. "I know it's cold, but not *that* cold."

He caught up to Myra, and guided her ahead, while I fell in next to Chris. Time to break the ice. "You were very quiet at the table."

"I like to listen," she said simply, even guardedly. "That's how you learn."

"Oh? What did you learn tonight?"

"To listen and watch."

"Forgive me. Bobby told me you're one of the dancers, but I honestly don't recognize you. I didn't want to seem stupid at the table, but...you *are* in the line, aren't you?"

She laughed. "It's the wig." Her voice was throaty, with a Midwestern accent.

"You don't look like you're wearing a wig."

"I'm not. But I do at work."

"Why? Your hair looks great."

"Thank you. It helps if I have to mix."

"Mix?"

She spoke quickly. "Drink with customers, socialize between shows, after work, like that. Most of the line mixes, but I don't like to so I wear a wig to change my look. Mickey's not too strict, but other club owners are. Chez Dee, in Pittsburgh, that was the worst—that's where I bought the wig. If you don't mix, you don't work. I'll never understand why customers like to drink with dancers. After all, we're just doing jobs like anyone else, like a shoemaker or a grocer. People don't want to drink with their shoemakers, but they sure want to buy us drinks." She shrugged. "I'll never understand it."

"Well, you fooled me. I'm happy to meet another performer. Where are you from?"

"Lorraine, Ohio," she said.

"That's really America out there, isn't it?"

"I guess so. It's really quite beautiful. What part of New York are you from?"

"The Bronx."

"Lorraine is smaller than the Bronx. How does it feel to be on the road?"

"A breath of fresh air—working, doing the act, being away from home. Known Myra long?"

"Four months."

"At Club T?"

"Heavens no. We've only been here four weeks. The Cuties have been on the circuit."

"Right, the circuit," I said. "How long will you be here?"

"Another four weeks on this contract, but there's rumors of an extension."

"And then?"

"Don't know. But our manager'll come up with something."

"The Cuties have a manager?"

"Why, of course we do. We're an act, you know. How do you think we got here?"

"I never really gave it any thought until now. Did you always want to be a dancer?"

"So many questions!"

"Sorry."

She was right. We walked in silence. Then she said, "I won a scholarship to a dance school when I was ten, and when I graduated from high school some of the girls formed an act. I worked with them for two years until I joined the Cuties."

"That must have hurt your parents very much."

"Why should it?"

"Didn't they want you to settle down and pursue a real career? That's what my parents want."

"Oh my, no. They encouraged me to get out on my own. Especially my Mom. She said, 'if there's a time for sowing oats, it's when you're young enough to sow them.'"

"So you're sowing?" I said, fishing.

"I'm sowing," she answered simply. "This is your first club, isn't it?"

"Could you tell?"

"No," she smiled. "Clipper told us. Well, maybe...yes."

"Our first show was a real bomb. I wondered if you...or anybody said anything, or..."

"No one said anything. I thought you were very good...the parts I saw."

"The audiences are...different here than anywhere we've worked before. We'll just have to adjust. The second show felt better, though."

"Are you a songwriter?"

"Yep."

"What kind of songs do you write?"

"Ballads, calypso, rock and roll, anything that comes to me."

"Did you write any in your act? I never heard any of your songs before."

"No. Bobby and I changed the lyrics on 'Jump Down.' And he wrote 'Limbo' himself."

"I think songwriters are so talented. Have you and Bobby known each other long?"

"Since high school. We're practically brothers."

"It shows on stage."

"I'm glad you think so."

"He knows you well."

"What do you mean?"

She stopped walking. "I don't know at all how I'm going to say this, or why I feel like saying it, but I will anyway. He...seems to get you to respond when he needs a straight man. He tells a joke or says something, and you laugh at the appropriate time, even though what he said wasn't particularly funny. It was just obvious to me."

"Wow! Really? That's...crazy. Where did you get an idea like that?"

"From listening and watching."

What a strange thing to say, I thought.

At the Wolverine, I asked, "What do you do during the day?"

"Movies, libraries, shopping, things like that."

"Maybe we'll see you tomorrow."

"That would be nice."

"Right."

Their room was on seven. We got out first. I would have preferred to watch them walk away from us. I almost fell over Bobby as I backed off the elevator.

"See you tomorrow," he winked, as the door closed.

"Now, don't tell me she wants to fuck me, okay?" I said, moving down the hallway, avoiding the look that was surely on his face. "One of those per night is enough."

He laughed. "So?" he pumped.

"She's nice. Very quiet, small town-ish. It was amazing—I didn't recognize her! She wears a wig when she dances. Do you know they have to mix?"

"No, but if you hum a few bars..." said Groucho.

"Jesus, it's like being a hooker."

"That's *hoofer*, pal, and it's standard policy for lines at most joints."

"That's what she said, too. What about Myra?"

"*If my instinct is correct, Watson,*" said Sherlock Holmes, "*a swapping of rooms will be dandy.*"

"Well, my instinct says Chris isn't that fast. But I'll do my best."

I took the first shower. While Bobby was in the bathroom I wrote down our day's expenses in the little book I had brought for keeping financial records.

He got into bed, turned out the light. "It's been quite a day," he yawned.

"Amen to that."

"And it only gets better from here. It was the beginning, Steve, the real beginning."

I was too tired to talk anymore. "Yep."

Then, he said after a long silence, "Thanks. The charts really helped."

"You were great, Bob."

"Night, Curls."

"Night, star." I rolled over, reached under the bed, checked that my guitar was still there, and immediately fell fast asleep.

Chapter 10

"COUNTING CEILING CRACKS"

The phone rang. I had been semi-awake since the blasting began, albolene crust gluing my eyes shut, reviewing yesterday's events in my mind. The phone rang again. It was the voice of velvet. "Steve? This is George Scheck. May I speak with Bobby, please?"

"Sure, George. Hang on."

He took the phone from my outstretched hand. "Yeah, George, good morning. It's still morning, isn't it? No, no, it's okay. Tell me." He bolted upright. "What!? *Not true! Not true!* That part, *not true!* George, I know what I'm doing so let's not get into that. Dirty, my ass! Who said the act was dirty?" He covered the mouthpiece. "Someone told the Morris office that I do a dirty act. It must be John." Then, back to the phone. "Yeah, that's John, the maitre d'. Yeah? Oh, *bullshit!* Everybody's a critic! That was part of my Groucho. It wasn't meant for anyone in the audience. Jesus, how dumb can he be? It was a *joke*, a simple *joke!* No, George, I don't do impressions in the act, but it was necessary to handle a heckler who'd had too many, that's all. Did they tell you about the guy who threw up in the middle of 'Scarlet Ribbons?' Ringside? In full view? Did you get a report on *that?* Do I get credit for singing through *that? What?* Since when am I the draw? George, I'm one of *four* acts, George, and they didn't even put my name in the goddamn paper! Get that, George? I'm not even in the goddamn ad! *Bowling* is in the ad! Maybe you should mention *that* to someone!" He covered up again. "They're expecting *me* to be the draw because of 'Stage Show' and the record, and they're pissed because there was no opening night business. It's that fucker, John." Back to the phone. "Yeah, George, I know-I know. Too folky, my ass! Everyone loved us. And it's folk-y, George, not folk-*see*. Right, thanks. Yeah, the second show was much better than the first. Did they mention *that* in the report?" He cooled off a little. "Yeah, I hear you, poppa George. Look, don't worry about anything, including your first comments. Everything's under control, or will be by tonight. Call Mama, please? That would be terrific. Yeah, thanks. No, I won't forget. Bye."

"Can you imagine that?" he said. "John said the act was dirty because I used the word *screw*. That schmuck! Maybe if I had said motherfucker, or something. But *screw*? It's hard to believe."

"What else?"

"Ah, same old story, too folky for the room."

"Wanna try a few standards? I can fake along..."

"No! You know I won't do that, so stop asking! I'm committed. Jesus, don't be like everybody else, rushing to change at the slightest bit of trouble. Those songs work! Let's stick with 'em!"

"Sure. I'm just worried that maybe they won't pick up the option."

"They'll pick up the option. Look at it this way, we didn't do bad with them, they did bad with us. What we have to do is stick to what we rehearsed, and do it so good that they can't help but like us." He flopped back on his bed and grabbed his crotch. "It's almost *Monica-time*."

"Monica?"

"The big set from last night."

"Oh, yeah. I forgot."

"Come on, man, how could you forget *them?*"

"Okay, I lied. Can you imagine if we have to go home early?"

"Stop it! They'll pick up the option. She said after one, right?"

"She said *call* after one, not come over after one."

"Picker, when they say *call*, it means come on over and jump on my bones. Hey, killer, you know what *always* happens. Guaranteed-*guaranteed*."

"Don't forget about Kong. Be careful."

"Done. What's the hour?"

I looked at my watch. "Eleven and a half."

"One and a half to Monica."

"Wanna eat?"

"Only mmmMMMMonica."

"No, star, *breakfast*, food, you know? Energy for mmmMMMMonica? Didn't anyone ever talk to you about not dissipating? Eat good and don't dissipate, that's what my father told me. Now, you can dissipate all you like, but if you fall asleep on stage tonight, dirty will be *mild* compared to the next report. So let's eat. Maybe we'll meet Chris and Myra."

"No, I want to see what happens with Monica first. If you're that hungry, eat alone. Sleeping is more important than eating," he said, rolling up under his covers.

"No, I'll curb my hunger. I want to see what happens, too. It doesn't matter that I won't have energy to strum," I said, covering my head with my blanket.

I must have dozed off, because the next thing I heard was Bobby giving a number to the Wolverine operator. "Hello, Monica? *Hi! This is Bobby Darin.*" He was somewhere between Gable and Flynn. His sleepy voice helped. "I was real happy to get your note, baby. You know, I don't know anyone in town, and I was wondering if you were free for late lunch this afternoon? It's really breakfast for me. Oh, you too? Hey, that would be great! I can come over anytime now. Do you live near our hotel? We're at the Wolverine. Of course, you couldn't know that. How far? Sounds delicious. Tell me the address again? Harding Place, number seventy-two? Absolutely. I can be anywhere in twenty minutes. Will a cab know where it is? Terrific! See you in twenty minutes. Bye, beautiful."

"Told ya," he winked, bouncing off the bed into the bathroom. "Monica's making breakfast at her place. Ta ta."

"I'll bet every cab in town knows the way to her place, ta ta."

A few minutes later, he was showered, dressed, reeking of Old Spice, his wet DA slicked back. "Guaranteed is guaranteed, Ringlets. I'll be back around five," he winked.

"One time for me," I called as he bolted out the door. "I'll wait to eat dinner. Good luck!"

I lay back, counting the cracks on the ceiling, smiling to myself, enjoying the privacy of the empty room, wondering what to do for the rest of the afternoon. Maybe I'll catch a movie, or just cruise the neighborhood—check it out for later. Maybe I'll just stay in and rest. I could use the rest. *I can do anything I want,* I thought deliciously.

I was too awake to rest. Maybe I'll call Chris—that would be a terrific way to spend the afternoon. But I might have to make up some excuse about where Bobby was, and that might queer it for him with Myra, so I decided not to. Maybe we'll get together tonight. Maybe I'd run into her somewhere—that would really be neat. I jumped into the shower.

Someone was rapping on the door. "Maid!" called a gruff voice.

"Can you come back later?" I yelled.

"Only 'til two on this floor. Then it'll be tomorrow."

"All right. Wait a minute!" I wrapped a towel around me, quickly checked that my guitar was safely under my bed, then opened the door.

Brunhilda, the maid, brushed past me indifferently, went straight to the bathroom, and came out with Bobby's towel, which she lobbed into a hamper in the hallway. Two points. She was a heavyset woman with big, thick hands, wearing a blue, short-sleeved uniform like a prison matron's. I sat on Bobby's bed, dripping.

"I'll take that whenever you're ready," she pointed, straightening my bed sheets. "There's clean towels in the john."

"Oh, sure." I went into the bathroom, dried quickly, pulled on my jeans, and handed her my wet towel. A one-handed jumper. Swish! Two more. "Could we have a few extra? There are two of us."

She pounded the pillows, grunting each time she bent over, a dynamo of energy. "You take care of me, I'll take care of you."

"Certainly," I smiled, removing a dollar from my wallet, handing it to her.

She rammed it into her pocket. "There's extra blankets in the closet. Don't use the covers for blankets."

"Sure, no problem."

I looked out at the construction site, trying not to be in her way.

"I'll vacuum tomorrow. You always sleep this late?"

"We work at night. We're entertainers, at Club Temptation."

"Where's that?"

"In Dearborn?"

"What do you do?"

"Have you heard the song 'Rock Island Line?'"

"What's that?"

It was pointless. "A record I made with my friend," I said, trying to dismiss the subject.

"Don't have a record player. Just be out by two, or it's next day."

"If we're not up because we've been out late *working*, could you please leave some towels outside the door?"

"You take care of me, I'll take care of you," she snorted, moving her cyclone into the hallway.

"Thanks. Message received. We will. For sure. Absolutely."

I dressed, and went down to the coffee shop. There was no one there from our world. I ordered bacon and eggs and bought the paper. There was a review of the show.

THE NIGHT SCENE by Herb Hesher

A show business minestrone opened last night at Mickey's Club Temptation, in Dearborn. The ingredients are good, some tried and true, some green and new, and it all comes together for a surprising stew.

The Cuties are held over for a fourth week, and along with Tiny Simpson's band, get the show off to a good start. Songbird Liz Carleton follows, singing standards, opening with a rousing "From This Moment On." Her audience join-ins get good exit-mitting from the happy Club T crowd.

Comedy MC, Clipper Daniel is up to his old tricks, making fun of everything and everyone in the club. His zingers are pointed and add to the flavor of the gravy.

The surprise ingredient is Bobby Davin, a quasi-folk act that is excitedly searching for direction. Davin appeared on the Jackie Gleason Stage Show a few weeks ago, and is pushing his first disk, ROCK ISLAND LINE. He sings along with guitarist sidekick Steve Carmen.

Fantasy headlines when Arlene Stevens emerges from a huge seashell and dances the imaginative "The Birth Of A Pearl." Lots of fun, and Mickey Conno's steaks are the best bargain in town.

Better than expected. Maybe Hesher was in the bar for the second show.

Was Bobby in bed with Monica yet? Nah, he's probably just gotten there. But then again, that never stopped Mr. Quick.

Back in the room, I thought about sleeping some more, or reading, or practicing guitar, or writing a song, or doing anything to pass the time. After the excitement and exhilaration of yesterday, being alone with nothing to do was beginning to bore me. I decided to go for a walk.

It was damp and sunless as I explored Woodward Avenue, gravitating toward the Bagel. Without its sign brightly lit it was lost in the grayness of everything else. I squinted through the filmy window, hoping to spot someone I knew, but the customers were all civilians; no show folk.

Again, I thought about calling Chris. I could eat with her if she wanted to. But what the hell would I say if she asked about Bobby? *Well, you see, he's out having funch. That's right, funch. Getting his webels off. That's a New York expression for connecting at the hot points. Oh, yes, we New Yorkers certainly are fast, but we're more than willing to share our expertise with all you deprived farmgirls.*

Again, I chickened out. Better wait for Bobby before making any serious moves on my own. Maybe I'll call Liz. No, that's a real fantasy—Cassotto's fantasy. She probably wouldn't even remember who I am.

After another block I spotted a movie theatre. A Glenn Ford Western, *Jubal*, was playing. I wasn't in a Western mood. A lady was in the ticket booth.

"Are there any other theatres in this area?

"Seen this picture yet?"

"No, just learning the neighborhood. It's my first time in Detroit."

"Not bad."

"It's very nice," I smiled.

"Thought you hadn't seen it."

"Oh, I meant *Detroit* is very nice."

I wondered if she gets bored just sitting in that booth all day long. It's probably the highlight of her day when someone buys a ticket. "Is the last show at eleven?"

"You read it right: matinee at two, evenings at seven, nine, and eleven."

I wondered if Bobby was performing his matinee. I resisted the impulse to ask if she'd heard "Rock Island Line" on the radio playing in the booth.

"Are there any all-night movies?"

"Try the Fine Arts, on Beau Bien."

The Fine Arts on Beau Bien was next to a White Castle Hamburger House. OPEN ALL NIGHT LATE SHOW EVERY NIGHT was crayoned on a shirt cardboard stuck in the display window. *Helen Of Troy* was playing, an Italian sword picture, the ideal diversion. The man in the cage was reading a newspaper.

"When's the next show, please?"

"Four-thirty. Half over now."

"When's the last show?"

"Two AM."

"Thanks. I'll be back."

I went into the White Castle and ate three green-meat Castleburgers with French fries. My hunger was endless. "Any museums in this neighborhood?" I asked the counterman.

"Don't know."

"Libraries?"

"Don't know."

"Famous churches?"

"Don't know."

"Synagogues?"

"What?"

"Couldn't resist."

"Huh?"

"May I have another Castleburger, please?"

"Oh, yeah, sure."

Having nothing to do was bugging me. I'd heard musicians describe being on the road as twenty-two hours of irrelevant bullshit just to have two hours of fun. And it was only my first day. I passed a newsstand and bought *Time*, *Newsweek*, and last month's *Scientific American*. Arthur and Pop were always reading *Scientific American*. Maybe the maid will give us some more towels if we make an intelligent impression.

By three-thirty I was back at the Wolverine. By four-thirty I had read everything once and looked at all the pictures twice. I should have gone to the movies, middle or not, but it was too late now. I went down to the coffee shop and gobbled some chocolate cake. Back in the room, I tried to nap, but couldn't. I practiced finger picking without interest. I tried to write a melody, but nothing came. I rehearsed some folk songs with endless choruses and tried to learn lyrics, but couldn't concentrate. I wanted something, *anything*, to consume the minutes. Next time, it'll be a room with a TV, no matter how much it costs. By five-thirty it was dark outside. Someone said that you always feel better after you take a shower, so I took a shower. I felt cleaner, but not better. Had Bobby gotten laid? He was rarely wrong. I looked at the pictures a third time, with one eye on my watch.

He staggered in at six-twenty, and hit the bed face down, still wearing his coat. "She was *unbelievable*, Curley. I came three times."

"Good for you."

"How much time do we have?" he sighed.

"If you want to be at the club an hour before, none. Take a quick shower, you'll feel better."

"Just did. That was the third time. She ate me in the shower. *Unbelievable!*"

"We were reviewed," I said. "The big time—they spelled our names wrong."

"Saw it." He lay motionless.

"If you're serious about catching a few, I'll call the club and tell them the cab broke down. I'll wake you in a half-hour."

"No, can't do that on our second night. I'll make it. Just let me wash my face." It took him a moment to move. Finally he did a slow pushup off the bed, shrugged off his coat, and shuffled into the bathroom. "What'd ya do all day?"

"Hung around, read, practiced."

"I'm telling you, Curls, she was unreal," he said, not really hearing me. "I wish you one like this. I'm gonna see her again tomorrow night. I may not make it home."

"No problem."

"I'm ready," he said grimly. "I'll catch a few in the cab."

Chapter 11

"IN THE SYSTEM"

Backstage was a delicatessen of smells: perfume and hairspray mingled with developer and fixer. I felt better just being with other people.

Tiny lumbered past our door. "Full show, first show. Same order?"

"No," Bobby said. "Put 'Limbo' second instead of 'Jamaica Farewell,' and 'Hold 'Em Joe' after 'Scarlet Ribbons.'"

"Want walk-ons?"

"No walk-ons."

"'Limbo' second, 'Hold 'Em Joe' after 'Scarlet Ribbons,' no walk-ons." It sounded military.

"Those fills were great last night, Tiny," I said. "Thanks for your help."

"Sounded just like a real arrangement, didn't it," he said, leering, disappearing toward the stage.

"You're a politician, Karmen. You belong with the U.N."

"They'll get it," I said, ever the optimist.

"Now, be sure and stop me if I make up before the line goes on."

"You look like you could use some."

"That bad?"

"I'm the only one who'd spot it."

When the dancers came out, I stood in the doorway, trying to identify Chris.

"Hi!" she said brightly, catching me in the act.

The Cutie in the black wig and stage makeup looked completely different from the girl in hide-ems I had been thinking about all day. Harder, more seasoned, but under the paint, it was Chris. "So *that's* you," I said, recovering. "I'd have known you anywhere."

"Did you have a nice day?"

"Great," I lied. "You?"

"Oh, we just kind of hung around, you know."

"Really? Me...us, too. Too bad we didn't know it. We could have gotten together."

"That would have been nice," she smiled.

Tiny was beginning the introductions. "Oops! See you," she said, quickly taking her place. When she went on, I tried to check out her artillery, but her stiff costume had a shape of its own.

Bobby was watching me in the mirror, grinning. "I'm tellin' you, Curley, that's a bang-bang. Just keep thinking about a room swap, *pally*."

"I'm thinking-I'm thinking!"

Clipper stepped smartly into the room. "Hi, fellas. Nice house for a Tuesday—about two hundred. Forget about last night. The job starts tonight. Knock 'em dead."

The specifics of the show weren't anywhere near as important as yesterday, and neither of us paid much attention. We were in the system, part of the routine. I concentrated on putting my makeup on so it wouldn't shine. I thought about the performance we were about to give. There was plenty of applause for the dancers, and Clipper got some big laughs. Liz passed by wearing her first-show dress. "Hi, fellas. House seems much better than yesterday."

Too old, I thought, as Clipper introduced her. It'll never happen.

"It'll be a contest," Bobby said, reading my mind, "which one gets to bang you first."

"Dream on, Cassotto."

"Curley, if there's one thing I know, it's women. Yes, this is going to be an interesting week."

Coming three times certainly seemed to have a positive effect on his performance. I had expected him to have no steam whatsoever, but he was as electric as I'd ever seen him—full-voiced, funny, and amazingly energetic. It was contagious—the audience felt it, too. In each song, he added a little body-bump or hand-clap, and they ate it up. The brightness of "Limbo" worked well in the second slot, and they were quiet and attentive during "Scarlet Ribbons." Also this time, no one threw up—a big plus. During "Hold 'Em Joe," Bobby roamed the stage, getting everybody to sing along. "Man Smart" got big laughs in all the right places, especially from a group of older women. When he played right to them, they cheered every punch line. Going off, the knockering lingered long enough for him to run on for an extra bow. He acknowledged me as I stuck my head out and waved.

"Great show!-*Great show*! Now *that's* show business!" he said, as we stood in the wings, soaking in every last drop of applause. "I feel like a gladiator! A Viking! A wench, I need a wench!"

My heart was pounding from the high of the performance. I too wanted a wench!

When the lights went out, almost-naked Arlene—definitely a big-time wench—slipped silently past and gently floated to the top of the stairs. *Ooh, would I like to get into that shell with you*, I thought! *I'm ready-I'm ready!*

"Hi! I'm still Bobby!" he whispered in the darkness.

Her drum roll started. "And I'm still Steve!"

"Don't ever *ever* fuck with me before I go on, you pricks!" she spat. "Stand back! Get the fuck out of my way!"

"Watch out for sharks!" Bobby said, daring the last word as she moved onto the black stage.

Then, patting each other on the back, glowing with success, not interested at all in her act, we returned to the dressing room.

Andy appeared in the doorway. "There's two tables that want pictures, Bob," he said happily, much more polite than yesterday.

Bobby winked at me. "We don't have any to give out yet. Nobody ever asked before."

It wasn't hard to smell a motive. "They don't want *your* pictures, Bob, they want pictures of you with *them*, you, too (he pointed, forgetting my name), and they want *me* to take them. Would you mind coming out into the club for a few minutes? They seem like nice people."

"Sure," Bobby said. "Soon as the show ends."

"Is this *mixing?*" I asked, after Andy had gone.

"Nah, this'll be fun. Trust me, we'll get something out of it, too."

Camera in hand, Andy was waving from the center of the room.

When we arrived, acknowledging compliments on the way, he positioned us at the end of the table and introduced us to the party of six. "Folks," he said, "meet Bobby Darin and..."

"Steve Karmen."

"*Hi, everybody,*" bassed Bing.

"Marvin Randolph," the father-type said gruffly, a cigarette clenched between his teeth, not offering his hand. "This is Mrs. Randolph...Harriet...and that's daughter Gloria...and husband, Mikie...that's Hazel, daughter...and Joe...husband. Harriet wanted to meet you boys. I suppose the other girls did, too. Pull up a chair."

"Please wait until after the photos," Andy directed pleasantly.

Marvin was about fifty, with stringy, gray hair lacquered straight back. He wore a dark suit and an expensive-looking monogrammed shirt with heavily jeweled cufflinks. There were ashes on his lapel. He looked like he had had a few.

Harriet Randolph was a middle-aged woman with a substantial chest jammed into a low-cut dress. Her face was freckled and tanned, with lots of cracks, like someone who'd been in the sun too long. "I love calypso songs," she began, "and you're real Belafonte. We always go to islands every winter, don't we Marvin. We love calypso songs. Some of them are so sexy. Belafonte came from the islands, you know, that's why he's so good."

Bobby corrected her. "I believe that Harry was born in New York City, ma'am."

Marvin jiggled his ice. "Impossible. His accent's too good. He's authentic. I know it."

Andy tried moving us along. "A whole set?"

Marvin growled at the waitress standing behind the Andy. "Yeah, an' another round. What'll it be, boys?"

"Just some tea, thanks, with lemon."

"Me, too. Thanks."

"Tea? Wait a minute. What's your name, waitress?"

"Martha."

"Okay, Mary, you bring these boys a *real* drink."

"No," Bobby insisted. "We have to do another show."

"Well, bring me another."

Andy popped a few flashbulbs while we all said cheese. "I'll be back right away," he bowed, heading for the darkroom.

"Sidown," Marvin waved. More ashes fell unnoticed. "Where ya from."

"The Bronx," Bobby said, grabbing a chair from an empty table nearby. I did the same.

Harriet twirled her ice, ala Marvin. "Well, you certainly are very good. *Real* Belafonte."

"What business are you in?" Bobby asked.

"Marvin has the biggest Chrysler dealership in the Detroit area," Harriet boasted. "Tiger-Town Chrysler. Chrysler Car Dealer Of The Month last month, nationwide."

"That's enough, Harriet," Marvin said. More ashes dropped. This time he flicked them off.

Harriet was bulletproof. "I thought you liked me to tell people what a big shot you are."

"*I'll bet you all drive Chryslers*," said Bing.

Marvin slurped his drink. "Course, we all do. Great car, Chrysler. Great car. We got one called a...called a Yew Norker...er...New Yorker. You ought to look into it." He yawned, clearing his throat at the same time. "So...where are you boys from?"

"They already told you, Marvin," Harriet sighed. "They're from New York."

The waitress brought his drink and our tea.

Marvin's eyelids were drooping. "Well...then, how'd you get started?"

"Maybe the boys don't want to talk about things like that, Daddy," said daughter Hazel.

"Oh, that's okay," Bobby said. "I don't mind at all. It's great to talk to new friends."

I couldn't imagine why he was encouraging these whackos; we were entertaining the Bickersons. But when he began, I recognized his press material—the capsulized life story he had been practicing for interviews: growing up in the tenements, living with his sister's family, our high school band, landing the Decca deal, George, "Stage Show," everything. It was another rehearsal. The Randolphs ate it up.

"That's quite a tale," Marvin slurred. "Say, what kind of money do they pay you boys to work here?"

"Marvin!" Harriet barked. "That's none of your business! How would you feel if someone asked you how much money you made? Would you give that kind of information to a stranger?"

Marvin was drifting again. "Hey, back off, okay? Only making conversation, girls. Relax, okay?"

"How did you get started, Steve?" Gloria asked, ignoring the argument.

Marvin's eyes were closing. I looked to Bobby for help.

"Tell the folks, Curley," he grinned.

"Bobby and I met in high school. We've been friends ever since. I'm *real* happy to be in Detroit."

Andy returned with the pictures, each in a neat Club Temptation folder. Marvin was with us again. "Do we pay now, or is it on the bill?"

Andy flashed the sincerest version of his insincere smile. "Now, please. That'll be thirty dollars."

"What! That's a great big bunch of money just for pictures!"

Andy oozed courtesy. "There's a full set for everyone, and a set for Bobby and Steve, too, of course. Wonderful memories. Wonderful pictures."

"Of course, thirty bucks, of course," Marvin grumbled, pulling some bills out of his pocket. "You know, I never authorized a full set for *them*," he muttered, pointing his full-fist of money at us.

"Oh, I understood a full set to mean pictures for Bobby and Steve as well. That's what most folks order."

"Yeah, well...well, someday, maybe we'll be able to say we knew you when; then maybe the pictures'll be worth thirty bucks. Write their names on the back, so we'll know who the hell they were. A lot of crap, if you ask me."

On cue, David Niven got up. "*Well, it's been fun chatting with you.*" I jumped up beside him. "We promised Andy to take some more pictures, so please excuse us. I hope you'll come back and see us again. It's been nice meeting you. Thanks for coming to the show."

Marvin was arguing with Harriet as we walked away.

As soon as we were out of earshot Bobby said, "First rule is that we never, ever sit down. Agreed?"

"Amen!"

"Never!"

"You're *real* Belafonte!"

"Ah, what do these farmers know."

Andy stopped us near the side of the room. "That couple wants to talk to you alone, Bob. They didn't mention Steve."

"Curley, I told you to take a bath!"

"That's okay. I'll meet you in the bar. Remember, don't sit down!"

John was leaning near the door. While Bobby romanced the

customers, I decided to romance the boss. I tried to be polite. "There was a review in the paper, John. Did you see it? I thought it was very good. Maybe the deejays'll read it."

Icicles. "More important that customers read it."

"Right." I wondered if anything ever made this man smile.

"Kid, you can find good in everything and bad in everything. The press can write the same story a hundred different ways. That's why you have to cultivate the reviewer. I helped with that review, kid. When Hesher left, he said you was good, but green, and that your material was too far-out for the room; a sentiment with which I heartily concur. 'That's the problem with record acts,' he says, 'they're only good for the studio. They can't make it in live performance. This isn't a folk room, but the kid's got talent.' I asked him to go easy on you. Sometimes he can be murder."

"Gee, thanks for helping, John. I'm sure Bobby will be grateful, too. He's done great everywhere else. We just have to get the kinks out and get a little more familiar with the room."

"What do you mean *everywhere else?* I thought this was your first club."

"Oh, it is. But we've done lots of school assemblies and parties. It's not like we've never worked anywhere before."

"Clubs are different from school assemblies, pally. Somethin' offbeat once in a while? Sure. But, these are *hep* people! They're sophisticated! They like the big ballads. That's why Liz does so good. She hits 'em right where they live. This ain't the room for a folk act. This is a class place! Mathis plays here, Bennett plays here. These people want to hear music, trumpets, saxophones. We turn down the hillbillies all the time, even if they have hits. Those yokels have one record, want big bucks, and when you book 'em, they're in the toilet! If you ask me, this is the wrong booking for you. You ought to be working joints like Mr. Kelly's, Gate of Horn. They like the strummy stuff. Here?" he gestured with his hands, "they want *up!*" He paused. "Also, this is not the room for an act that tells me to mind my own business."

"Bobby never...he certainly never meant...he's just..."

"Yeah? Your partner made it perfectly clear that no one tells him what to do. That attitude can only hurt him in the long run."

"I understand. Well, thanks a lot."

Bobby had a short memory. He was seated, deep in conversation with a middle aged couple, probably telling his life's story again.

Liz was alone at a rear table, sipping tea, wearing the same dark business suit she had worn at rehearsal. I was curious to learn more about my co-worker. "May I join you?"

"Certainly," she smiled. She was using her sexy voice.

"Your first show went well."

"Thanks. Yours, too."

"Well, much better than last night, anyway. The audience was better, too."

"How'd you like the review?"

"I thought it was a good one," I smiled.

"Hesher liked you."

I hesitated. "Can I ask your professional opinion?"

"Certainly."

"We feel that our material is right for the market today. It's new and different, and hasn't been done by too many other acts. But John says that we're not right for this room. What do you think?"

"John is the ruler of a very tiny kingdom. I wouldn't put much stock in anything he says. Yes, your act is unusual, that's true, but folk music seems to be the thing today, and I've always believed that if you're good, you can be good anywhere. Maybe it's just a case of him getting used to you."

"That's what Bobby said." I glanced at her hand. Bobby was right—no ring. I decided to test the waters. "Are you married?"

She seemed surprised. "Why do you ask?"

"Oh, just curious."

"I know that you're not married."

"How do you know?"

"You're not old enough."

When she focused directly on my eyes I couldn't help it, I had to look away. "I'm...almost nineteen," I said defensively. "In some places that's old enough to be more than married. How old are you?"

"Don't you know that it's not polite to ask a lady's age?"

"Sorry."

She pursed her lips. "I'm twenty-eight, and...I was married. I'm divorced."

He was right again! A divorcee! "Any kids?"

This time, a big smile. "A little girl, three years old. When I travel, she stays with my mother, in Chicago."

"How come you split up?"

"Steve, do you always ask so many questions?"

I retreated. "Sorry."

"He was a musician. We were both on the road, but not together."

"Sorry."

"Oh, it's no tragedy," she said. In fact, in some ways it was the best thing that could have happened. Show business marriages rarely work out. Do you have a girlfriend?"

"Nah, too busy for that." When I looked at her, I got fidgety again. Out of the corner of my eye I could see Bobby heading for the dressing room. "Well, I'm going to go backstage now. Thanks for the advice."

"Anytime," she smiled.

He was peering at himself in the mirror. I could tell he was wearing his businessman's hat. "That guy was Buddy Baron. He's a manager. Handles a few local acts. Interesting. Wants to talk."

"What about?"

"He didn't come right out and say it, but I think he wants to represent me in this area—for club dates, one-nighters, that kind of thing. Says details could be taken care of on a more personal basis right here in the Midwest—stuff that can't be done from New York, like spelling my name right in a review, or getting the record played before I get to town."

I was amazed. "What about George?"

"Oh, this would be completely separate from George, strictly regional. Of course, there's no one like George in the whole business."

I found myself protecting George. "Wouldn't he be pissed if you went with someone else after all he's done? What about your contract? Do you have the legal right to do that? Besides, how many percent of yourself can you give away?"

"Hey, slow down, Perry Mason. This might be a smart move. It's only five percent more, and only on jobs he gets in this area."

"Well, I think you should think it over first, okay? We've only been here two days, you know?"

"Yeah-yeah."

"Yeah-yeah!"

"Okay-okay."

"Liz is divorced. I asked. She's got a daughter, three years old."

"Told you."

"How about a movie after work?" I suggested. "There's a late show, *Helen Of Troy*, a sword picture. I thought I would ask Chris."

"Nah, I'm too tired." He paused. "Steve, you mustn't mention any of this to George, or anyone, understand? It's just something I want to think about."

"I understand completely. Your secret lives are safe with me. Come on, let's go to the movies."

"No, I'm really bushed. Go alone. Go-go. Make a move."

"Come on, come with me. Ask Myra. I have the feeling Chris'll be more receptive if Myra went along, at least to start."

He sighed. "Okay. I'll sleep in the theatre."

Clipper poked in. "Mickey's in the house with a table of hoods. Gangsters! What do they know about art? The late show at San Quentin."

"Really? Is there anything in particular that he hates?"

"Steve, how many times do I have to tell you: Pope, president, or putz, they're all just part of the crowd."

"Keep the tunes bright," Liz called when she came off. "Mickey's table isn't paying attention."

There were about thirty people left in the club, including five men in Mickey's group, thankfully seated a few rows back. Mickey Conno, our boss, was a large man with a full head of black hair and a barrel-deep voice that could be heard across the room even at normal volume. His steely eyes seemed to miss nothing and his pockmarked face was leather-tough—razorblades probably broke when he shaved. He looked like someone I didn't want to know. Three waitresses hovered attentively near his side of the table.

I recognized one of the other men from last night—Kong—the one who had been with Monica.

Bobby went straight through the act, except during "Man Smart" he jumped into the audience, sat on the lap of a grandmother type, and sang the whole song—including my parts—to her. The customers loved it.

"Don't anyone, *anyone*, ever tell me what kind of material to do!" he said later, toweling off, still glowing from the crown reaction. "John don't know shit! Small house or not, that was a tight show. Tight!"

"Shhh!" Andy hissed from the darkroom.

"Oh, stick it, Andy. People look at tits, not listen to them."

"Very funny," he said, stepping into our dressing room. "You boys want extra copies of the pictures I take? Twenty-five percent discount."

"You mean the ones with customers?"

"That's right."

"How much?"

"Normally two bucks a print, I'll give 'em to you a buck-and-a-half, the special performer rate, five-by-sevens, you can't beat the price. And, one night, we'll do the formal shots, eight-by-tens."

"Oh, yeah? What d' ya mean?" Bobby asked.

"Publicity shots. All the acts take pictures with me. You can't beat the special performer rate."

"Hey, Andy," asked my favorite Dead-End kid, *"don't you think that if we take enough pictures with customers, you should give us a few sets* free, *as a kind of a thank-you present?"*

"Well, I could ask the customers if they want to *buy* extra sets to give you, like those folks tonight, so it wouldn't cost you anything. But if I make specials or extras, you've got to pay for 'em. It's only fair," he smiled.

"Oh, okay. That's fine."

"So, what about the dupes?"

"No thanks. We don't need pictures with customers."

"Sure?"

"Yeah, sure, Maybe another time."

"Just so we understand," he said, leaving.

"Oh, we understand, all right," Bobby called after.

"What's with that guy?" I asked. "All he wants to do is hawk his pictures."

"Fuck him. When the time comes, I'll straighten him."

Fulfilling his prediction, Bobby fell asleep at the movies, and

very comfortably so. With a few snuggling moves, he had placed his face on Myra's shoulder, and was soon breathing softly into her chest. At first, I thought it was technique, just to get close, but a careful listen confirmed that he was really out. Myra seemed pleased as she held him, her own eyes closed, not paying attention to the screen.

Chris watched the movie.

When I took her hand, she squeezed mine. Feeling encouraged, I switched hands, and eased my arm along the back of her seat, not touching her, of course, but waiting for a romantic moment in the film. I had to wait fifteen minutes. My arm was killing me. Finally, when the theatre hushed as Jack Sernas was about to slip it to Rosanna Podesta, I placed my hand on her shoulder, and gently eased her toward me. She resisted when I touched her, but then gave in. I nestled my cheek into her hair.

At three-thirty there was a commotion in back of the theatre. A cleaning man was waking up the moviegoers who'd hung around to sleep (or whatever), ordering them to move to other sections while he swept the floor. With the sounds of garbage and soda bottles rolling down beneath the seats, I suggested that this might be a good time to wend our way home.

We bundled into the frosty night for the three-block walk to the Wolverine. Chris took my arm, keeping very close, avoiding the icy wind. When we got to our floor, a sleepy Bobby kissed a tired Myra's cheek. I wanted to do the same with Chris. But she just held out her hand. Rather than be rebuffed at this late hour, I took it. She squeezed my fingers, and smiled wearily. At least she gives good hand.

Bobby fell asleep without another word. I was right behind, hoping to dream about what could really happen if we did work out a room swap.

Chapter 12

"INSKY LIKE FLYNNSKY"

In the coffee shop, over a late breakfast and a shared newspaper (the club's ad now included Bobby's name), we entertained our best-case fantasy: "Rock Island Line" would zoom right to Number One—the fastest rising record in the history of the recording industry (why not?)—rewarding us with a long nightclub tour for big money and a triumphant opening night at the Copa, with our parents and friends cheering us on from the standing-room-only audience.

Back in the room, reality checked in: Bobby phoned the local Decca distributor only to learn that no one there had ever heard of either Bobby Darin or "Rock Island Line." An angry call to George Scheck didn't help much, either: "You have to be patient," George said. "Decca is setting up a whole promotion schedule; someone will call soon." Yeah, sure.

When Bobby complained that having nothing planned for the day was not a productive use of his time, I was glad that my own reactions were not unique. (I assumed, of course, that his getting laid yesterday afternoon counted as a productive use of his time.) When it became too late for a movie, we tried learning new calypsos to break in during second shows. It was fruitless effort. Even Brunhilda refused to listen (Bobby invited her in), dropping our fresh towels outside the door. When he called Myra's room, no one answered, and Casanova said it was probably just as well—he couldn't get it up anyway. Apathy won. I dozed off while rereading the paper, after which it was time to go to work.

The dinner show was the best business yet, but even though the audience was responsive, our performance was wooden. The moves were there, but not the snap. During the break we helped Andy earn his living. Whenever I saw Chris, it was all smiles. We made plans to get together later. By eleven-thirty the house had again shrunk to just a few tables—mostly men, Arlene's crowd—and Bobby zipped through our short show, wisely keeping his chatter to a minimum.

"Use the room to advantage, Curls," he said, alboloning quickly. "I won't be back tonight. If Monica's anything like Monday, I may never come home. *Never!* I told Myra that I have an important business meeting with Buddy Baron. That should keep her on ice for a while. If anyone asks, say the same. Can't service them all at once," he said, buttoning his shirt.

"Of course-of course."

"Seriously now, good luck with Chris. Maybe you'll be the first to bang a chorus girl."

"I doubt that Chris is that bangable. She thinks we're going to the Bagel."

"Just be patient. Patience is everything. *Everything*! Tell her you've never met anyone like her before. That always works. Play up to her. Be confident. Confidence is everything. *Everything*!"

"I got it. Sure you're not coming back? Better leave me a number—in case."

"In case what?"

"In case."

He scribbled on a piece of shirt cardboard. "Okay. In case I fall in."

"Don't worry, I won't use this, except in a dire emergency."

"Relax, Dire. I'll be back around five, probably before. Take advantage!" He paused. "With girls like Chris, sincerity is everything. *Everything*!"

"Get out," I waved.

He snapped his fingers. "Ah, you know what to do. One time for me."

Having the room to myself was a dream come true. All I had to do now was get Chris into it.

I hung back until the band cleared out, figuring that the fewer people who saw me with her, the better for both of us. Maybe John has a rule about acts socializing with each other. Anyway, I didn't want to get her into trouble. Also, being a little Darin-devious, if things didn't work out, then nobody would know.

There were no customers in the bar, only Chris and Myra seated with John, Liz, and a bored-looking Laurene Daniel, all listening to Clipper on the phone as he pleaded with a Chinese restaurant to stay open.

"Yesee! Have a velly bigee party. Eight pepul for House of Woo. Spend a rot o' money. Can be in ten mina. Will stay open? Plomise? Leavee veeeelly biiiigee tipee? Okay? Okay?" We waited in suspense. "Telliffic! Long live Chiang Kai-Chek. Oh, velly solly. Long live Chairman Mao. Yesee, Yesee. Long live Chairman Mao!" He hung up and clapped his hands. "Insky-like-Flynnsky!"

"Where are you going to get eight people for Chinese food at this hour?" Laurene asked.

"I had to say that to keep the kitchen open, darling. You wanted Chinese food? I'm getting you Chinese food." He turned to the bar. "Ladies? John? Liz? Steve? A bit of the Chinois?"

"People who eat at this hour are nuts," John mumbled, sipping a drink. "Wanna lift?" he asked Liz.

"No, thank you. I'll join you for tea, Clipper, if you give me a ride home."

"My pleasure. Anything for egg roll."

Myra put on her coat. "If you drop me, too…?"

"Sure." He turned to me. "How about you and Bobby?"

"He's gone. Business meeting. Count me out, too, thanks. I'm bushed."

"Christine?"

For an instant, I feared she might break our date in order to stay with Myra. But my fears were unfounded. "No thanks, Clipper," she said, with a cutesy glance. "I'll get a ride back with Steve." *She's being too obvious*, I thought.

"Oh well," Clipper said, "eight will be four. Have fun all. *Have-fun-all.* Sounds like the name of a Chinese restaurant. Only kidding."

On her way out, Myra whispered something in Chris's ear.

Chris laughed. "Oh, go on."

John was closing lights. "He's giving us a hint," I said. She was wearing a fabulous perfume. "Ready to go?"

"The Bagel?"

No, to bed, I wanted to say. "The Bagel will be all ours tonight."

"Night, John," she called.

"Yeah, 'night, kids," he grumbled.

I helped with her coat. "My goodness, a gentleman."

"Hey! There are still some of us left."

In the taxi, I asked if she wouldn't mind stopping at the hotel first so I could drop my guitar."

"Not at all," she smiled. "I'll change into something more comfortable."

Right! Something more comfortable! Now, that's how the road is supposed to be—slipping into something more comfortable.

"I'll meet you in the lobby in say, ten minutes?" she asked sweetly, in the elevator.

"Listen, why don't you knock on my door when you're ready?" I suggested. "I'd like to put a new set of strings on my guitar so they can stretch out over night. It'll only take a few minutes. That way you won't have to wait in the lobby alone at this hour."

She eyed me, too cautiously, it seemed. "Why don't you call me when you're ready? We'll meet on the elevator."

"I guess I could..." I said, innocently, "...ah, but why don't you come down? I'm not Jack the Ripper, you know."

She searched my eyes. "I'll be down in about ten minutes."

"407," I grinned as the elevator door closed.

Insky-like-Flynnsky! I hummed, rushing down the hallway. The room is mine for the whole night, the whole night, *the whole night.* If she comes to the room, she must want to be alone with me, too! *Insky-like-double-Flynnsky!*

The place was a mess. I fluffed the pillows, straightened both beds, and jammed all our loose clothing into the laundry drawer. I positioned the guitar case on my bed, de-tuned a few strings, and then spread some string wrappers out around it. Clark Kent never changed faster. I pulled off my shirt and took as thorough a sink-bath as I could, applying mucho Old Spice and making sure to rub some on the armpits of my tee shirt. I brushed my teeth. I chose my black turtleneck and black chino pants (sexy black gets 'em every time!)

The lighting was a problem. It was either the glaring brightness from the overhead fixture or the bed lamp, neither conducive to romance. The bathroom light with an almost-closed door would be perfect, but it was too soon to try that. I opted for the bed lamp.

Exactly ten minutes later, after I'd brushed again, I heard a soft knock. Filled with resolve, I opened the door.

"Hi!"

"Hi."

Chris had scrubbed too. She wore fresh lipstick that caught the light, and her hair sparkled from still-wet spray. She looked radiant. But she had dressed for ultimate protection: beneath her coat, her loose-fitting pink shirt was buttoned all the way to the neck, revealing absolutely nothing; her blue jeans were stiff, heavy, and cuffed at the bottom; an orange-and-black scarf covered whatever exposed skin remained. I locked the door behind her.

"Locking me in, or someone else out?" she asked, a bit too warily. Her jeans rubbed when she moved.

"Force of habit—apartment house living. Please take your coat off, and sit down," I said, gesturing towards Bobby's bed. "I'll only be a few minutes."

She slipped out of the coat, but held it on her arm as she looked around. She didn't sit.

A momentary setback. I quickly packed away the wrappers, sat on my bed, tuned up, finger-picked a folky rhythm, and hummed my way through "Scarlet Ribbons," stopping every so often to retune and stretch a string.

"You sing nicely, Steve. Sing something else."

That's the key! Music'll soften her up! "Do you know 'I'm Just A Country Boy?'"

"I don't think I've ever heard it."

"It's on the flip side of Belafonte's 'Hold 'Em Joe.'"

"I don't think I've heard that one, either. It's not part of your act, is it?"

"We do it sometimes, but Bobby thinks it's too identified with Belafonte to have any originality. 'Country Boy' should have been a hit on it's own. I'll sing it for you...if you sit down."

Cautiously, she sat on Bobby's bed, with her coat on her lap. I leaned over, and moved in beside her.

She smiled again.

"I ain't gonna marry in the fall
I ain't gonna marry in the spring
'Cause I'm in love with a pretty girl
Who wears a diamond ring,
And I'm just a country boy..."

"When did you start to play?"

"Last year." I began to pack.

"Oh, don't stop, please?"

Let's move it along, I thought. *This is no time to get bogged down in a concert.* "I don't want to wake anyone."

"Oh, yes, I understand."

I packed the guitar, slid it under my bed, then reached across and took her hand. She didn't stop me, but after a minute of silent gazing she stood and went to the window. "Do you have a girl in New York?" she asked, focusing on the future home of Woodward Plaza.

"Nope."

"Do you date often?"

"Not too much. Weekends, we're usually working. By the time we finish, it's too late for social life. When we played in our high school band, I watched a lot of girls that I wanted to meet dance by with other guys."

"Am I supposed to feel sorry for you?"

"Of course not. I'm just giving you an honest answer, that's all." *Sincerity is everything!* I got up, narrowing the gap between us. Carefully, I placed my hands on her arms. "I want you to know that I'm really glad that I met you and that we're working on the same show."

She backed away. "Please don't."

"What's wrong?"

"I don't...I just don't know you, that's all."

I moved closer, and smiled. "Wouldn't you like to get acquainted?"

Her tone stopped me cold. "I'm not ready to get acquainted, Steve. I have something to tell you."

Bobby had once cautioned me that when a girl says she has *something to tell you*, it only meant bad news: she's either having her period or she's missed it and was pregnant.

"Some things are very important to me," she began, "and one of them is getting to know someone in terms *other* than the physical *before* the physical starts. It's not that I don't like you. I mean, I don't *know* you, but I like you. I've just never met anyone like you before. I mean, well, you know what I mean. To put it plainly, I'm just a little old-fashioned, and that's how I feel."

"I truly mean no harm. I just wanted to see what it would be like to make a grab for your ass."

"What!!!?"

My joke was obviously ill-timed. "Only teasing-only teasing. Scout's honor. Don't lose your sense of humor. The truth is I've never met anyone like you, either," I said sincerely.

"Do you really mean that?"

"I wouldn't say it if I didn't mean it."

She searched my eyes again. "Tell me about New York girls. Do you expect them to...what do you expect from a girl on a first date? Since this is kind of our first real date, I'd like to know what you're thinking about."

"Truthfully?"

"Of course."

"Well, Bobby won't be back...for a long time, and I was hoping that we could, well...spend some time here in the room together, alone."

"You want to sleep with me, don't you?"

Her directness caught me off guard. "Well...er...no. I mean...yes...but I mean...no...not yet," I added hastily. *I shouldn't have packed my guitar so soon.*

"That's the *ultimate* commitment between two people, Steve, the *ultimate*."

Patience, Karmen! Take your time! "I think so too, Chris. Go easy on me, okay? I'm just a tourist. Let's call a truce. Shake. That's as much touching as I'll offer without written permission from the Mayor of Lorraine, Ohio. We don't have to get married tonight, okay? But, please, don't be afraid of me."

"Don't mistake resolve for fear. I'm not afraid. You certainly have a smooth line."

Time for a fresh approach. "You're right. Okay, from now on, you're under no pressure. I promise to control my instinctive desires until you allow me not to." I waited until she cracked a smile. "But it would sure be more comfortable if you sat next to me."

She moved to the bottom of the bed, her sandpaper-jeans making the only sound.

"Would it be a breach of moral standard if I held your hand while we talked?"

"Let's just talk for a while."

"Anything you say. I'm a man of my word." I stretched out behind her.

"Must you lie down?"

"Just relaxing." I snapped off the bed lamp, leaving only the bathroom light.

"Is that necessary?"

"There's an awful glare."

She turned the switch. "I don't think so."

I burned my fingers unscrewing one bulb. "Compromise?"

She nodded, reluctantly. I leaned back again. "I like the way the lady smiles."

"I'm surprised you can see my smile in the dark. You must have eyes like an owl. Now tell me."

"What?"

"How am I different from New York girls?"

"You just are, Chris..." With a feather-like touch, I ran my fingers down the back of her shirt. One pass told me she was wearing one of those very wide bras.

She tensed. "Steve..."

"...you have a certain sweetness...that's very different...from anyone...I've ever...met before."

Suddenly, she turned and looked directly into my eyes. "What are you?"

"What do you mean?"

"What's your religion? I must know. You look, well...Italian. Are you Roman Catholic?" she asked, sounding a bit too hopeful.

"No. I'm Bronx Jewish."

Did her back stiffen? "I thought that Karmen was a Jewish name, but I wasn't sure." She sounded disappointed. "You fooled me, Steve."

"Does it matter?"

"I've never dated a Jewish man."

"Vell, dere's alvays a foist time fer everting."

"Were you confirmed? What do you call it? Bar..."

"Bar Mitzvahed."

"Did you do that?"

This conversation was taking a strange turn. "Yes."

"I'm glad God is a part of your life," she said, examining me carefully. "Amazing. You certainly don't look Jewish."

"Really? What does a Jewish person look like?"

"Well, it's just generally a big-nosed look. You don't have a big nose. Not Jewish-big, anyway. Now, don't laugh when I tell you this, but until I was eleven, I believed that all Jewish people had little horns on their heads. Then I found out it wasn't true."

"Oh? How did you find that out?" I asked.

"Well...one day, when I was in seventh grade, I'll never forget it, my brother, Joseph brought a friend home from school. The kid said his name was Michael Ray, but Joseph had seen his registration card in the principal's office, and it was really Michael Rabincowitz, or something like that, obviously Jewish..."

"Obviously."

"...and when they were all playing around—John and Patrick, my other brothers were there, too, wrestling and fooling around—Joseph pinned the kid to the floor and yelled to all of us, 'Feel his head! Feel his head!' Patrick went first, and said 'Well, I'll be damned,' and then John, who said, 'there's nothing,' and then me. I didn't feel anything but dry hair."

"What were you looking for?"

"The *horns*, what do you think?"

"You're putting me on?"

"No, I'm not, honest."

"Where did you ever get a crazy idea like that?"

"My mother told us when we were very little that all Jews have horns on their heads."

"Really?"

"Of course. Well, the kid must have thought we were all crazy. 'What'd'ja do that for?' he says. 'To see if you had horns, Sheeny,' Joey says. Then, the kid starts to cry and runs out the door. It was funny in a sad kind of way, all of us feeling this poor kid's head. When we told my mother what had happened, she just said, 'Oh, well, they disappear whey they're very young, but you can see little marks on their scalps if you look close enough.'"

I took her hand and put it on my head. "Your mother was right. Wanna feel my stumps?"

"Don't tease."

"Seriously, I had a hornectomy. It's a tradition. All Jewish boys have it done when they're just a few days old, at a tribal ceremony called a 'bris.' Ever hear of a bris?"

"Yes, but I thought that's where they...well, you know."

"That, too. It's not widely known out of the faith, but it's a double-header. They get you on both ends."

"You're teasing me...aren't you?

"Of course, I'm teasing! Now, Miss Evans, your turn. You're Catholic, right?"

"Yes."

"That's where you go to church to confess all the sins that you're going to commit again anyway. Right?"

"Don't be a hypocrite, Steve. That's not what confession's about. Do you go to temple? What's the word for it?"

"Shul?"

"No."

"Synagogue?"

"That's it. Synagogue. That's where they wear those funny hats, right?"

"Yarmulkes."

"Do you go to Synagogue?"

"No."

"That's too bad. God can be a very important part of your life if you let Him in."

Maybe if I act a little more holy, she'll respond better. "I wish we had some candles. I like candles. They make me feel religious."

"God can fill your life," she said, solemnly, that walking-on-water look returning to her eyes. "I could never marry you, Steve, so all my warnings and precautions were actually unnecessary. No, I won't let you tempt me any more, even though you are very tempting. I hope you'll be able to understand what I'm about to tell you: I intend to marry a Catholic man. I have to, and I want to. I think it's important to marry someone of your own faith. Myra thought you might be Jewish, but I didn't want to believe her. I'm sorry, but I could never marry a Jewish man."

"Okay. The marriage is off. Let's practice saying goodbye." I reached for her.

She stopped me. "Please, you're only making things worse. I like you, but..."

It was now or never. "No buts," I said most sincerely, standing, lifting her into my arms, slipping my fingers into her stiff hair, closing my eyes, aiming for her mouth. Her lips were warm as I kissed her, first lightly, then harder.

She was too startled to stop me.

Or didn't want to.

Or couldn't.

Suddenly, there were willing arms tight around my neck, and the delicious taste of her lipstick in my mouth. Her tongue was plumbing my tonsils, exploring my fillings and gums. She pressed into my body. I got an instant erection. I know she felt it.

"This is *wonderful*, darling," I said too urgently, keeping us connected by grabbing her ass. My eager hands brushed up against her breasts. This courageous next-level contact sent my pulse soaring.

"Please, Steve, I don't want to start something that could never be finished."

"You never know, Chris. You never know."

"No, Steve..." She was breathless now.

"Aren't you excited...?"

"Oh, yes, but..."

"No buts..."

"Oh, Steve!"

We were kissing non-stop as she melted, straining to be closer to me. I moved us toward the bed, wanting desperately to lie down next to her.

But she pulled away, as if some higher power was forcing her to hold me off. "No," she cried. "No! I mustn't!"

"Chris, please, don't tease me. I was only responding to what I was receiving. That kiss wasn't a dream. I felt it! And I felt your body next to me. And you felt it, too. I know you did. You just can't turn it on and off like that. You're not a *tease*, are you? I was only doing what I thought you wanted me to do!"

She began to cry. "You're right. It's my fault," she said softly, dabbing her tears with her scarf.

"It's nobody's fault. It was a real emotion." I tried to kiss her again.

"No, it's late," she said, pushing me away. "I'm not hungry any more. I'll just turn in. Myra'll be home soon."

"Oh, please. Not yet. We're just beginning to get to know each other!"

"No. This has been a very unusual evening for me, and I have a lot to think about."

"Please, let's think over a bagel," I implored. *Oops. Too Jewish.* "Or, some tea and toast."

She flipped on the ceiling light, blinding me with mood-shattering brilliance. "I have to think *without* your influence distracting me."

"Don't go. It's too early."

"Bobby'll be home soon."

"No, no, not for a long time."

She put on her coat. "No, my dear, *sweet* Steve," she said sadly, dramatically, "not tonight. Be my friend and understand. You want to be my friend, don't you?"

Why is it that women are always asking for understanding? "Of course, I do," I said.

"Then, good night," she whispered, unlocking the door. "Don't be mad at me."

"I'm not mad. But please, *please* stay." She blew a kiss and walked into the hallway. I tried to salvage ground for another night. "Chris, regardless of what you think, this has been a fantastic evening."

"Tomorrow," she mouthed silently, and then disappeared into the stairway.

I closed the door.

Absolutely incredible! What the hell happened? What did I do wrong? I hardly touched her! She's a religious fanatic! Damn it! That's an excuse I'll have to add to the list: *I can't do it because you're Jewish.* Maybe I'll change my name to O'Karmen. Maybe Bobby knows a jump-in-her-pants prayer. He'll probably tell me to hang a crucifix on my dick, and bang the beJesus out of her. No, I won't share details this time.

But she had allowed those little grabs, and that was *definite* progress. And she was a great kisser! She just needs a little slowing down, that's all. But it's definite progress, religion or no religion.

I lay back on my bed trying to digest why, all of a sudden, I was alone. I stared at the ceiling, my favorite spot. This was certainly an unexpected ending to my first night with an empty room.

But I was wide awake, and didn't want the night to end.

I checked my watch.

It was two forty-five.

Only two forty-five.

It was still early!

I decided to call Liz Carleton.

Chapter 13

"HOPE I DIDN'T WAKE YOU"

Until now, the oldest girl I had ever taken a shot at was a twenty-two-year-old counselor at the summer camp where I'd worked the year before our band broke up. The only result then, after rolling around in a field one night while I tried unsuccessfully to remove her clothing, was that we both got poison ivy. I was seventeen, and she must have thought it quite amusing to go out with such a kid. However, that encounter fired my hopes of going all the way with her later in the summer. It didn't happen—the season ended before the poison ivy. So as far as age was concerned, Liz broke the record.

"Royal Palm," the groggy voice of the hotel operator answered after a volley of clanking phone equipment. Michigan switchboard operators must have all trained at the same school.

"Liz Carleton, please."

"What room?"

"Don't know, sorry."

"Carlson?"

"Carleton."

"Yes. Hold a minute."

There was more shuffling. Suddenly the phone sounded hollow, as if someone had picked up an extension.

"Operator?"

"Be patient, I'm looking for the room."

"No, not you, operator. I want the Wolverine operator. Are you still on the line?"

"You calling from the Wolverine? Yeah, Manny?"

"4:30, Sid?"

"Fine, Manny."

"Who else is on this line?" I demanded. "Will the Wolverine operator please *get off* the line?"

"4:30, Sid." The voice clicked off, improving the sound quality immediately.

"It's 312," said the Royal Palm operator. "I'll ring."

The scraping and clicking as he inserted the cable was so loud that I had to hold the phone away from my ear. I tried to be cool. "Liz? I hope I didn't wake you. This is Steve Karmen, You know, with Bobby Darin?"

She laughed. "Of course, I know. Hello, Steve. No, I'm awake. In fact, I only got in a few minutes ago. Is everything all right?"

"Everything's fine. I know it's...late, but I had a feeling that you were a late person, and I was wondering if we could get together, maybe have a cup of coffee somewhere, just talk for a while, I mean, if you're not too tired."

"I'm almost ready for bed, Steve."

"I thought that...just for a few minutes? Maybe we could go to the Bagel, or something."

"After Clipper's egg roll? Oh, I wouldn't want to go out again at this hour," she said, hesitating, "but if you'd like to come over, I can prepare tea in my room."

"Would you mind?" I asked, my voice showing more excitement than I wanted.

"That's why you called, isn't it?"

"The lady is a genius."

"Give me about ten minutes to put something on. It's room 312."

"Stay comfortable. It'll take me about that long to walk over."

"Well, not this comfortable!"

"Sure you don't mind, Liz?" *Stupid, don't give her an out!*

"No," she laughed again.

"I'm on my way."

I almost rubbed the skin off my mouth trying to remove the lipstick taste of Crazy-Catholic Chris. I could still smell her perfume on my turtleneck, so I changed it.

The night air was filled with anticipation as I loped the four blocks to the Royal Palm. The door was locked. The street was deserted. I peered inside but couldn't see anyone. There was no night bell. I tapped with my room key.

No response.

I tapped harder.

Finally, a hunched old man with stringy, mussed hair shuffled out and squinted at me through the glass. "You a guest?"

"I'm here to see Miss Carleton, room 312." His eyes narrowed. "She's expecting me," I said, mustering authority.

He unlocked the door. "Come in, come in. Have to call and check, hotel rules. Wait a minute." He relocked the door behind me, and then disappeared into a small room next to the front desk. The phone rattling that followed confirmed that this was the one-and-only Sid. "You have a visitor," I heard him grunt. "What's your name?" he called.

"Tetley."

"Petley. Name's *Petley*!"

"That's Tetley."

"Oh, it's Tetley."

"Yes," he nodded, "go up."

"Thank you." I should have used Lipton.

The elevator operator was asleep on a chair inside the car. "Three, please," I said, loudly enough to wake him.

"Guest, Willie. Get with it!" Sid barked.

Willie shifted, but didn't look up as he closed the gate.

"Three, please," I repeated.

As the car lurched upward, I was determined to do better with Liz than I had with Chris.

Her place was unbelievable. The lighting, dim and seductive,

was coming from a small, multicolored, shaded lamp on the dresser. Next to it was a one-burner hotplate and a teakettle. The windows were covered with what appeared to be crinoline petticoats, inventively placed to filter the streetlight. There were two small easy chairs facing each other, and two flickering candles set on top of her inverted music case, now serving as a cocktail table. A tiny corridor led to the bathroom. It was hard to believe that such a comfortable-feeling room could exist in such a sleazebag hotel.

"MMMmmm, beautiful!" I said, sniffing the air.

"That's jasmine tea." She hung my coat in the closet.

"It's more than tea. It's your perfume."

"Why, thank you, Steve."

But one thing was strange: there was no bed. My mind began to run: maybe the chairs rolled together to make a bed; maybe one of them opened up. Wouldn't that be some story if I made it with Liz *on a chair*? Lost in erotic thought, I must have had an intense expression on my face.

"Is something wrong?" said the breathy Marilyn voice.

"Oh, no, no, nothing," I sat in one of the chairs. It didn't seem wide enough for a bed. "Does this stuff come with every room?"

"Goodness, no. After the first few times on the road, I realized that if I ever wanted the comforts of home, I'd better bring them with me. Everything packs into one little bag: the lamp, the hotplate, teapot, everything."

"You ought to patent the kit. You'd make a fortune."

She looked different, sexier, wearing a long, lavender-colored satin robe right out of a Joan Crawford movie. I wondered what she had on under it. Her hair flowed over one eye like Veronica Lake, and her make-up looked pretty fresh. When we made eye contact, I felt the same uneasiness as I had at the club. "Do you ever drink tea with a shot of booze in it?" I asked, wondering why she had this effect on me.

"I don't keep any liquor here, if that's what you mean. Do you drink often?"

"No, not really. When I was a musician I used to a little, sometimes, but I always worked it off when I played. By the way, how did you like the Tetley bit?"

"I knew it was you, Steve. I don't often have visitors at three AM."

The kettle boiled. She filled the mugs, set them on the music case, then sat across from me. "This is a special jasmine tea called Ulalulalong. I hope you like it."

"I love it without even tasting it." I took a sip. The scalding water burned my lips. "It sure is nice to be here with you, in the middle of the night, if you know what I mean."

"Why are you out so late?"

Confidence-confidence! "Oh, this isn't late. Bobby and I were discussing the act, you know, over breakfast, and I just...well, I just thought it would be nice to get together, so I called."

"I see. So you did." She paused, looking directly into my eyes, and sipped her tea, seeming to enjoy the silence. "Now, tell me all about yourself. Do you have a sweetheart?"

"Nah, too busy for that."

"Sounds familiar."

"What do you mean?"

"Oh, nothing."

More silence. I gulped my tea. It was really hot. "I live at home," I coughed, "and this is my first time away. It's been great. Especially now."

"Now?"

"I mean, it's really great being here with you, in the middle of the night, you know what I mean." I lifted her hand and sniffed her wrist. "I just love the smell in this room. Your perfume sure smells great, Liz."

"It's called *White Shoulders*."

I don't know whether it was the perfume or the soft lights that made me do it, but I leaned forward, sniffed her neck through her curls, sighed, and planted a quick kiss.

"What are you doing?" she asked, pulling back.

"I just wanted to kiss you."

"Well, that's a surprise!"

Patience-patience! "Not to me, it isn't. I've been watching you all week."

"Have you *really?*" she asked. "All week? It's only Wednesday."

"Well, two days is a long time." I set my cup on the music case, and disregarding her puzzled look, leaned in and kissed her again, this time lightly on the mouth. She didn't kiss me back. Her lips were dry. I didn't dare try a tongue at this early stage. When I eased away, she caressed my face for an instant with her fingers. Her robe had loosened and I got a whiff of perfumed body heat. My heart was racing.

Somehow, she slipped under my arm, got up, and went to the hot plate. "I'm going to make some more tea."

"Enough for me," I said, clearing the frog in my voice. "I haven't dented the first cup."

"Tea relaxes me, it'll relax you too. You need to relax."

I stood and went to her. "I don't want to relax. This feels too nice to want to change."

"Steve..."

Ignoring her protest, I took her in my arms and kissed her again. "Isn't that nice?" I whispered, trying to nudge her toward the bulge that was bursting between my legs.

She felt it. "Tea!" she ordered, spinning away, pointing me to the chair. "I'm going to make you another cup of tea, or you'll have to leave immediately."

I sat down, caught my breath, and chugged as much of the hot liquid as I could stand. "I'd love another cup of your fabulous tea, Liz."

"Tell me about yourself. What kind of songs do you write? Did you write 'Scarlet Ribbons?'"

"Wish I had. I don't know who wrote it. It's a folk classic."

"I never heard it before. It's lovely. What kind of music do you write?"

"Ballads, rock 'n' roll, blues, just about anything. I like ballads, though."

The kettle was steaming again. "I like ballads best, too. They have emotion. People react to emotional songs."

"I guess that's so."

She topped off the mugs, and then sat across from me. *Back to square one. But, just because she's not ready now, doesn't mean she won't be later. The night is still young.*

"Tell me some of your lyrics," she said sweetly, crossing her legs. Was this a tease, too?

"Too bad I don't have my guitar here," I said.

"You don't need a guitar. Just hum softly."

"Okay." I thought for a moment. "This one is called 'Lost.'"

> *"Lost, and feeling low,*
> *I am so lost,*
> *No where to go,*
> *I need you,*
> *When I'm not with you,*
> *I am so lost."*

"I'm still working on that one."

"Sounds like a good beginning."

"I'm working on a hop tune, too. It's called 'Free Passes To The Movies.'" I began tapping my foot and beating time on my leg.

> *"I've got some free passes to the movies,*
> *And if you want to do something tonight,*
> *I've got some free passes to the movies,*
> *And you know I'm gonna treat you right..."*

She held a finger to her lips. "Maybe we should do this in the daytime. Less danger of waking someone."

"Sorry. I get carried away. My mother complains about that all the time, too. Believe me, I get the message."

I swallowed more tea. We made eye contact again. "I want to be close to you, Liz," I whispered, putting my cup down.

"Steve, please."

Jesus, how many times have I heard those words tonight!

I slipped my fingers into her hair. "You excite me, Liz. You smell so sweet and taste so good." This time, when I brought my mouth to hers, I zipped my tongue lightly across her lips. Her face was wonderfully warm. Instead of pulling away, she closed her eyes and began sucking on my lower lip. My pulse was hammering. I knelt on the floor, loosened her robe, and boldly slid my hand inside. She trembled as I touched her skin. I tried to squeeze both our bodies into her little chair. Our position could have won a prize in a contortionist contest. I searched for the clasp that held her bra. There was none. The fabric was completely smooth. It took another exploration to reconfirm that this kind of bra never went to the Bronx High School of Science. Undaunted, I slipped my hand under the silky material and began to slide around to the front.

"No! Don't," she said, breathlessly, pushing back.

She's pretending morality. She wants me, but she thinks that I won't respect her if we make it on the first date. But her desire will win out! I stretched full out on the tiny chair and maneuvered her alongside me. The robe slipped further off her shoulder. "Doesn't this feel terrific, Liz?" I sighed, sounding a little too desperate. "Isn't this marvelous?"

"Steve, let's not do something that we'll both regret."

"What's to regret about two people who have an instinctive desire for each other? It's natural! It's real! It's fantastic!"

My hands were flying frantically across her body. But just as I reached the waistband of her panties, she pushed back hard, stood up, shook her hair away from her eyes, and tightened the robe around her. "I don't know what's gotten into me," she said, half to herself. "You certainly have a very good technique. I wasn't prepared for any of this."

"That wasn't technique," I said, rising to my knees, reaching for her, "it was inspiration. Don't worry, darling, I won't make you pregnant."

"Steve, you're such a boy. That's not what I meant."

I stood, wildly wanting to bring her close again. "You *really* excite me, Liz."

"This is ridiculous."

"Why ridiculous?"

"Well, it just is! You must go now. It's late."

"Why?"

"Because I'm asking you to," she said sternly.

"Is that what you really want?"

She ran her fingers through my hair. "Yes, that's what I want. There's a quality about you that's hard not to like." She kissed my cheek ever so lightly, and stepped back.

Sometimes begging works. "You really don't want to send me out into that cold night, do you?"

"Don't make it any harder than it is."

It wasn't so hard any more. Sometimes pleading works. "How can you turn your passion off like that?"

"It wasn't easy, I promise you. Fortunately, good sense won out."

Sometimes bribery works. "How about another cup of tea?"

"No, it's late."

Sometimes appealing to the artist works. "Would you like to hear some more lyrics? I won't be loud."

"Another night."

Sometimes stalling works—give her time to change her mind. "May I wash my face before I leave?"

"Of course. I just want to make it clear that you have to leave now."

In the bathroom, I splashed cold water on my flushed cheeks. When I came out, she was holding my coat. As I put it on, I opened it wide to enclose her. She stepped close enough to kiss the tip of my nose, but that was it.

Sometimes nothing works.

"Goodnight, Steve," she said, unlocking the door. "I enjoyed our visit. Perhaps another night, at an earlier hour."

I couldn't control the big numero-uno that broke out on my face. "Sure. See you tomorrow, Liz. I mean *today*, I mean *tonight*. Thanks for letting me come by. And for the tea!"

She was grinning, too, as the door closed. I heard the double-lock engage.

Rather than deal with Willie again at this hour, I found the stairway. "Will someone let me out, please?" I called behind the desk.

Sid was still here—I guess Manny hadn't shown up yet. "Coming," he groaned, shuffling, rummaging for his key.

"Thanks," I said, not making eye contact.

Yes, this was a night of progress, *definite progress*, I thought, as I walked briskly back to the Wolverine.

I was asleep when Bobby came in. "What time is it?" I asked, startled.

"Five-thirty. Sorry to wake you."

"What happened? You okay?"

He turned on the bathroom light, and began tossing his clothes on the chair. "I couldn't stay at Monica's. The gorilla called, said he was coming over. She thought he was out of town 'til Friday, but he came back early. I had to split, mucho-el-quick-o!"

"Jesus! Thank God you weren't caught!"

"You're telling me. It wasn't easy finding a cab, either. I froze my nuggies." He pulled on his pajamas, turned off the light, and got into bed. "She's banging that goon right now," he said in the darkness. "That really bothers me. That's the power of money, all right." He was quiet for a moment. "You'll be on your own again tomorrow night, Curley."

"I thought Kong was in town?"

"He never shows up two nights in a row. Absolutely *never*. He's married; his wife thinks that he's out-of-town on business. Tomorrow, he'll have to be home. Definite-*definite*."

"You'll confirm that with Monica before..."

"Of course." He was silent again. Then, "How'd you do tonight?"

"Believe this? Chris got all upset when she found out I was Jewish. She wouldn't let me near her. That's a tough one. I don't know what'll happen there. But..." I hesitated. "I took a shot at Liz."

"Liz? *Our* Liz? Ha! I told you! Where? Here?"

"Her hotel," I said, remembering. "She carries equipment."

"Equipment?" He sounded interested. "What kind of equipment?"

"She made her room look all dreamy with colored lights and shades she hangs over the windows. She even had a hot plate to make tea. But there was no bed, so I couldn't make any really serious moves."

"No bed?"

"There's a hell of an echo in here. I looked all over. Nothing."

"Probably a Murph."

"What's that?"

"A Murphy bed. It comes out of the wall. Were there any big closet doors?"

"Yeah, right in the middle...sure, I'll bet that's it."

"When you're ready to make the big move, just open the doors and pull down the bed. Instant bango."

"Right."

He yawned. "Stick with Liz, Curleylox. She sounds like your best shot. Chris'll only happen if you lie to her. You might consider that. You'll never see her again after these two weeks—nothing to lose."

Chapter 14

"I'M NOT YOUR FATHER, I'M YOUR MANAGER"

On Thursday, right after the first show, George Scheck walked into our dressing room, puffing a cigar bigger than himself. I was so happy to see a face from home that I practically exploded with excitement.

"Wow! Oh Hi, George! Wow! What a great surprise! Did you see the show? What am I saying, of course you saw the show! That's why you're here!"

"Hiya, boys," he said evenly, examining the room.

George was short and had thin, wavy hair. Oversized, thick-framed glasses dominated his small face. A sharkskin suit and an ugly, wide-Clyde tie were his daily uniform. An ex-dancer-turned-manager, he still wore taps on his shoes—he called them "v-blocks"—so there was never any doubt when he was around—his tip-tap rhythm always preceded him.

Bobby seemed more controlled than surprised. "Hey, Poppa G, when d'ja get in?"

There was a discomforting tone in his voice. "Don't call me Poppa, Bobby. I'm not your father, I'm your manager."

"Sorry, George."

"I landed at four. I thought it would be better if you didn't know I was in the audience."

"Good thinking," I said.

"Steve," Bobby said, "how many times have I told you that it doesn't make the slightest difference who's in the house. We're pros, and we work the same regardless."

"Right," I nodded seriously.

"Looked like about three hundred tonight. How's it been since Monday's disaster?"

Bobby was Mr. Serious. "It seems to follow a pattern: good dinner show, three to four hundred, lots of club groups, private parties, that kind of crowd; second show

201

drops to forty or fifty, half holdovers. Tiny says weekends'll be full both shows—full turnover."

George closed the door and sat down. We sat across from him—the team listening to the coach. "Do you change material for the second show?"

"Yeah, we cut 'Scarlet Ribbons,' and throw in something different in the second slot. Yesterday, we did 'Matilda' instead of 'Limbo.' There were enough people for a singalong."

"And most of them were warmed up from singing along during the first show," I added.

"That's a calypso song, isn't it? One you sing together?"

"Right," Bobby nodded. "Steve strums while I cavort around pounding my meat on ringside tables. It's really effective. Will you stay for the second show? Of course, you'll stay for the second show! Then we'll go eat. There's an all-night gourmet restaurant."

"The Bagel!" I said.

"Is that greasy spoon still open? I thought the Board of Health would have closed it years ago."

"Have you been in Detroit before?" I asked.

"A long time ago, when I was a hoofer, in another life."

"Where are you staying?" Bobby asked. "I mean, you're not going back tonight? No, of course not. That's impossible." He flicked an imaginary cigar. *Say the secret woid, and a hotel room will appear. Tell the room clerk...to screw. Tell 'em Groucho sent cha!*"

"Is that the shtick they complained about? You're right, don't worry about it. Just don't talk like that in front of kids—they wouldn't make the connection. Remember," he said sharply, waggling his finger at Bobby, "they'll buy your records if they think you're clean-cut like Pat Boone. And we want to sell lots of records!"

"Right," Bobby said.

"Right!" I agreed.

George became a little less professorial. "Yes, I'm at the Wolverine, too. Talk about old memories, I thought I recognized the elevator operator. "

"When are you going back?" Bobby asked.

"First thing in the morning. When can we talk?"

"Well, I wasn't sure when you were arriving, so I had made...*other* plans for later." He winked at me. "Nothing that can't be changed."

George frowned. "I should have suspected you'd have some action lined up. Truthfully, it's just as well. I'm tired. Don't cancel on my account. I'll be going to bed anyway." He slapped his knees and stood. "Well, boys, my dinner should be about ready. I never eat during the show. It's disrespectful to the act."

"Don't look now," I quipped, "but we've been getting a lot of disrespect since we came to Detroit."

George was distant again. "Come out and join me, Bobby. Business conversation, Steve. You understand."

"Yeah, sure, no problem."

"I'll be at my table," he said, leaving.

After a silent moment, Bobby said, "He didn't like the act."

"How do you know?"

"If he did, he would've said so. His only comment was about the size of the house."

"Think it's the material again?" I asked. "Do a big ballad next show. Artie must know 'Prisoner Of Love.' Or better, do 'All Of Me.'"

"No. Let's not change." He grabbed his jacket. "I'll talk to him. Maybe he's just cranky from the trip."

Chris was waiting in the wings. "May I speak with you, privately."

"Sure," I said, "come on in."

"No, not in there. Please come out. There's no one here."

I did as she asked. Her words were studied. "I...I'd like to see you again," she began, softly. "I thought that we could go somewhere after work, and talk. I don't want you to have the wrong impression of me. I'm not a...tease."

"Forget it. I shouldn't have said it. It was dumb. I apologize."

"Steve, you know I'm torn between two conflicting voices. I was brought up to have certain standards, you know, values. I want you to believe me when I tell you that I'm punishing myself as much as I'm punishing you."

"You're not punishing me. Nothing happened. The problem is that you think that every guy is out to make you, so we all suffer from the poor behavior of a few overzealous individuals."

"Please don't have the wrong impression of me. I...think you're very special, but I'm not sure how to act with you. Could we begin again on a whole new page?"

"After work'll be fine. Bobby's manager flew in from New York and I'll probably have to meet with him, you know, about the act. But I'll call you as soon as I get back. Would that be okay?"

She smiled for the first time. "I'll be waiting."

"As soon as I get back." I kissed my finger and touched it to her nose. She smiled again.

I spotted them in the far corner of the showroom. Bobby was gesturing intently as George ate, nodding in agreement. There was something about George's attitude that was unnerving. I wondered what they were talking about. These were the conversations I longed to be a part of; the strategy sessions between manager and act. My info was always second-hand. George never included me; rightly so, I guessed—after all, I was only the accompanist—but I knew Bobby would fill me in later.

I dismissed my apprehension when I saw Liz in the bar. She was drinking tea. *Maybe she's Chinese under all that make up.* I told her that tea was now my favorite bedtime drink. I remembered her invitation.

"Can I call after I meet with Bobby's manager?"

"Not too late," she smiled.

It's perfect! If nothing happens with the Holy Roller— and it probably won't—I'll catch an encore with Liz. Maybe Cassotto won't be the only one who has to juggle ladies this week.

John came over. "That guy says he's Darin's manager. Wants to be comp'd."

I nodded. "Flew in to catch the act."

"Maybe he'll have more influence than I did."

I got up, not wanting to hear more opinions about material. "Excuse me please. I have to change a string."

When Bobby returned to the dressing room, he was oddly subdued. "I'm gonna ride back with George, then split for Monica's. Hit on Clipper. Or take a cab, okay? Same plan as last night if anyone asks."

"Everything good? What's up?"

"Business. I'll tell you later."

"Coming back tonight?"

"I hope not," he winked.

"Did you check it out first?"

"Yeah-yeah, I just called. Everything's cool."

"Sure?"

"Sure-sure."

Tiny stuck his head in. "Short show."

"Right. Short show."

I could see George out of the corner of my eye. Knowing he was in the audience made me try a little harder. Somehow I expected him to lead the applause in the small house; but he just sat there, watching intently, puffing away, showing no reaction whatsoever to our performance.

While the Pearl was still on, Bobby cleaned his face, and with no more words than "see you later," was gone. George didn't come back to say goodbye. Maybe he's pissed about something. It was a weird feeling, initially being so elated to see him, then being completely fluffed. I tried to put it out of my mind. We had done two good shows and now I had the room all to myself again.

Andy was in the doorway. "Bobby gone?"

"With his manager."

"The little guy with the cigar?"

"Yeah." I picked up my guitar, ready to leave.

"Tell Bobby that the lady he was with last night is big trouble if the wrong people find out...if you know what I mean."

I stopped. How could Andy know where Bobby had been last night. "No, what do you mean?"

He bent his ear with one index finger, and his nose with the other. "Mob. Tell him to be careful. She's not worth the problems she can cause."

"How did you know where he was?"

"Just some advice, okay? You're nice young kids."

"Thanks. I'll pass it along."

Clipper and Laurene were at the bar watching Jake put iron gratings over the liquor cabinets. Liz was in a booth talking to a man I didn't recognize. He seemed quite friendly. Everyone else had gone.

"Bobby out on business again?"

I wondered why Clipper paid such attention to everything. "Yeah, with his manager."

"All the way from New York to catch the act. Well, that's what happens when you're up and coming."

"Can I bum a ride with you?"

"What did you call me? Only kidding. Sure."

The guy with Liz was all touchy-touchy.

"May we go now?" Laurene asked, sourly.

"Whenever you're ready, my queen. Breakfast, Steve?"

"No, just the hotel, thanks. I have to meet Bobby and his manager."

The guy with Liz was really making moves. When I mouthed a silent goodnight, she smiled.

In the car, Laurene sat between us. "What's your manager's name," Clipper asked.

"George Scheck."

"Ever hear of Bullets Durgom?"

"Sure. He handles Jackie Gleason, right?"

"He's interested in signing me."

"That's great for you," I said.

"Milton Blackstone's interested too. Know him?"

"Eddie Fisher, right?

"Right. I'm thinking it over."

"What's to think about," I said. "Gee, people like that can really help an act."

"Well, I'm thinking it over."

"How do you like being on the road," Laurene asked, turning to look at me. "So far, it's great."

"I enjoyed your act," she smiled.

"Thanks. We're working on new material all the time."

When people sit next to each other—whether on a subway or bus or in a car—there's an inevitable amount body contact with no more significance than the mutual acknowledgement of the lack of space. But this was not my imagination. As she spoke, Laurene's right thigh was gently pressing into me, in and out, just the slightest bit harder than the motion of the car called for. When she looked at me, her eyes lingered just a bit longer than they should have. Maybe she's had a few. I shifted closer to my door, moving out of reach as best I could. For the rest of the ride, I kept my eyes straight ahead, listening silently as Clipper expounded on his ever-more-popular career.

Bobby was in the bathroom, dressing. "I thought you'd be gone by now," I said, surprised.

"Out in a minute. I just left George. He says goodbye."

"Thanks. Everything good?"

"You always ask that. Yeah, everything's good. They picked up the option. The second week is firm."

"Hey, that's wonderful! We've been held over!"

"He says there'll be other jobs, too. He'll know more when he gets back to New York."

"Wow, that's *great* news! That's fabulous! Did he say what he thought of the act?"

"Yeah," he replied, somberly. "He thinks audiences don't want to hear songs about mules while they're eating shrimp cocktail."

"Sounds like John. Well, we knew that before we came. That's probably why he looked so unhappy. Okay, what are we going to do?"

He was vague. "Don't know."

"I don't get it. Didn't the Decca deal happen 'cause you could sing folk?"

He stopped dressing. "No, that's not quite true. George said it was a tough sell to get them to invest in a folksinger, but he promised 'em I was just going through a phase; that I would grow into another Pat Boone—a teenage idol with a little Presley thrown in. Decca thinks there's only room for one big, authentic folk singer, and Belafonte's got the job. They want me to build an audience that won't label me as folk. The only reason they went ahead with the session was 'cause they wanted to cover 'Rock Island Line.' Gabler thought it was a cute tune that could be done cheap—kind of a steppingstone to something else. But if it doesn't get any quick action, they may not release another record."

"What happens to the other songs we did?"

"Dead. Decca owns 'em. *And*, according to George, they won't spring for a new session if I stick to folk. So he wants me to look for new material, cross-over to pop and rock, and he's pretty firm about it. He's afraid if I'm labeled *folk*, I'll be stuck when folk dies."

"Then let's do it. You can sing anything. Let's work on some pop."

"It's more than that. I can do Sinatra and Tony Bennett, even rock 'n' roll, but I can't work without real band arrangements. So, until things change, I have to stick with folk. Maybe I'll start to experiment, I don't know." He hesitated. "I might as well tell you all his comments. There's no other way to say this so I'll just lay it out there: he doesn't like the idea of us doing two out of seven tunes together. It's nothing against you. He likes you very much, personally, and he respects your talent—there's no question about that—it's just that he thinks that this is my act."

"So?"

"He says there's too much duo. He says we come off like a double."

My mouth went dry. "That's not true," I said quietly, suddenly realizing that, from George's point of view, it certainly must look that way.

"I fought him, too, but he's got a point. We walk on together, we sing the first-half closer together, we take our first bow together, we joke with each other on stage, we close the second half together, we walk off together. According to him, that's not a single, that's a double. He thinks I'm using you as a crutch."

I felt queasy. "I'll do anything I can to make the act better, you know that. I'll practice chords, and we'll try different material—more pop, more rock. I can play anything."

He continued dressing. "I know you can. I think he's wrong," he said without conviction. "It's my name on the record, and we really do work well together." Now the room became very quiet. Too quiet. I felt compelled to ask the next question, even though my intuition already knew the answer. "Wanna do those songs alone?"

He ducked it. "Don't ask me for decisions now. That's what George did all night." He paused again. "Look, Steve, no matter how I say this, it isn't going to come out right. I *have* to try those songs alone. I promised him I would. This is not a...demotion, it's an experiment."

"I understand. I'll stay at my microphone for the whole show. Do you still want me to sing the harmony parts?"

"Of course. Just don't come up to join me. And don't come off during the first bow either."

"S...sure. Got it."

"We'll talk more tomorrow after I get a chance to think. I've got to get this whole thing off my head for a while."

"Right. Everything'll be okay."

He put on his coat. "Steve, I have to try lots of things..."

"I understand. It's okay." My mind was spinning. "Wait. Um...er...Andy said something about Monica being mob. And to be careful."

He stopped. "Really? How does he know anything?"

"Don't know. I asked. He wouldn't say."

His eyes narrowed. "Thanks."

I nodded.

"Look, we'll get straight tomorrow, okay?"

"Yeah. We'll get straight tomorrow."

"Right."

I couldn't catch my breath. Maybe George told him to fire me.
He has the power to do that. Bobby is his act. Dear God, if he fires me, what will I tell my parents? What will I tell *anyone*? Gasping for air, I just made it to the toilet in time to heave up what was left of dinner.

The phone rang. It was Chris. "I was wondering if you were back yet," she began cheerily.

"Chris, I need a rain check tonight," I pleaded. "For a while, at least. Something has come up and...and I have to...be by myself for a while."

"You sound troubled. Are you alright?"

"Yes, I mean, yes, everything's fine. I just can't talk now." I lay back on my bed and closed my eyes.

"Maybe talking will help," she suggested gently.

"Not now. I...I can't. If things change, I'll call you later."

"I'm here, Steve, if you need me."

"Thanks. Please don't mention anything to Myra."

"Of course not."

I held my face in cold water, hoping to slow my galloping pulse.

The phone rang. It was Chris again. "Steve, I'm worried about you. Would you...like me to come down to your room?"

"No, not now. I'll call you later."

"Anytime. It doesn't matter how late."

I sat on my bed, numb. *Dear God, what am I going to do?* Suddenly, it was more than just the prospect of not singing or bowing together. It was my whole involvement in the act that had motivated everything. George must have been very persuasive. I was petrified. I wanted to calm down but my body wouldn't stop shaking.

I had never gone into a bar alone for a drink—just like in the movies—but at this moment, the emptiness of the room was unbearable. I grabbed my jacket, went down to the lobby, then down the steps to the Polynesian Room.

There were six people at the bar: two couples and two single men. Hawaiian music was coming from a speaker over the door. "Seven and seven," I ordered, straddling a stool.

"Got ID?" the bartender asked.

"No, but I'm over twenty-one, if that's what you mean."

"Gotta have ID."

I put a twenty-dollar bill on the bar. "I'm a guest at the hotel. I just got in and everything is upstairs. All I want is a drink."

He looked me over for a second, then poured the drink.

I took a huge slug and ordered another before I finished the first. I began to feel more stable with the second drink.

Duo, duo, duo kept ringing in my head. *We're not a duo. The act is Bobby Darin. How the hell can he say we're a duo? We're not a duo. The choice of songs, the keys, what we wear, everything is Bobby's. We're not a duo. What the fuck is George talking about? He's full of shit. Yeah, fuck George Scheck!* I ordered another drink.

I was deep in thought when I felt a presence on the stool next to me. Then, heavy perfume. "Hi," she said, sexily. "I'm Gina. Did I hear you say that you just got into town?"

"Oh…er…yeah," I said, focusing, trying to remember.

"Buy me a drink?"

"Oh, sure. B…bartender?"

The drink appeared instantly.

"What's your name?"

"Duo," I said. "S…Steve…Duo."

"Where are you from, Steve?"

"New York. Just got in." My tongue felt thick.

She moved a little too close. "It's late, Steve, and you look tired. How about taking me up to your room for a while? After that, I bet you'll sleep just fine." She fingered the twenty, still on the bar. "Another one of these would do it, Steve?"

Holy shit, she's a hooker! She's a prostitute! She wants to bang me for twenty bucks! No, Bobby would never, ever pay for it, and I'm never ever gonna pay for it either. Never!

I tried to pull myself together. "Thanks anyway, G…Gina," I said, as coolly as possible. "My sister is up in the room and…"

"For another ten, I have my own room, right here in the hotel…"

"Well, thanks, but…no thanks, no thanks, no thanks."

"Have a nice stay here in Detroit," she said graciously, and moved down the bar to another man who had just come in.

I took a deep breath, then ordered one more drink—one more for the road. I paid the tab and tipped the bartender five dollars. The liquor had done its job. I didn't realize how sloshed I was until I tried to negotiate up the stairs to the lobby. It took great effort to maintain composure in the elevator.

Back in the safety of our room, I realized that I wasn't thinking of Bobby Darin and George Scheck any more. *Fuck them both!* I was thinking of Chris! Chris! Hail-Mary Chris!

It was two-thirty. I reached for the phone. "Chris, iss me. Everythin' is fine now. Come down to my room."

"Oh, Steve, what happened? When I didn't hear from you, I was so worried that I called, but there was no answer. Are you okay?"

"It was somethin' personal that I'd rather discuss not now. Come down to my room?"

"Steve, you're drunk."

"Never!"

"You are! What happened?"

"Come down to my room, Chris. You wanted to talk, we can talk here."

"No...it's too late. I'm in bed. What happened?"

"Nothing...I had a...minor disagreement w' Bobby, an' I had'a think it out."

"Did the liquor help you think?"

I decided to ignore her very rude question. "Le's not talk about nonsense, Chris. Come to my room. I wan' you to come to my room so we can talk. Jus' what you wanted to do—talk, talk, talk, talk."

"It's late."

"Not late, *not.* Come on, change your mind. We're both awake. I know I am. Le's get together, jus' to talk, nothing more. I'll come to *your* room. How's tha'? I could take the stairs, and no one would ever spot a man dashing through the hallway seeking refuge in the room of a Club T Cutie."

"Steve, Myra's here," she whispered. "She's in bed too. Is Bobby there?"

"If he was, you think I would be askin' you to come down? He's still out with his manager." *He's really fucking his brains out like I'd like to be fucking my brains out with you!*

"Myra likes Bobby. Why has he been avoiding her?"

"He's not avoiding her, he's out on business. I think he likes her, too," I added hastily.

"I hope she's not disappointed by him."

"Come down here; le's discuss it."

"No, Bobby'll probably walk right in."

I took one more shot, in measured words. "Whatever un-Christian memories you have o' this room should be gone now. I sure would like to see you. You wouldn't have to stay too long. I'll even meet you at the elevator, or the stairs, of wherever you like. We need a make-up hug and kiss."

"Try to understand. You should go to sleep now. You'll feel better tomorrow..."

"B...but I feel fine!"

"...and we'll talk then. Definitely tomorrow. Goodnight, Steve, sweet dreams." She hung up.

Again un'erstan'ing! Why is it that women are always asking for un'erstan'ing? I'm the one who needs un'erstan'ing!

Well, if it's not that one, I thought, *it'll be the other. Plan B.*

Making every effort not to sound too zonked, I called Liz. "Hi, Liz. Iss Steve. I hope iss not too late."

"Oh, Steve, it's nearly..."

"I'm glad you're still up." I tried not to slur. "How would you like some company for a cup o' you-know-what?"

She sounded annoyed. "No, not tonight. It's too late."

I looked at my watch, but couldn't focus on the numbers. "What late? Iss early, Liz. C'mon. Lemme come over for a while."

"Have you been drinking, Steve?"

"Who me?"

"Yes..."

"Well, a little bit, but I'm not drunk, not drunk. Can I come over? Please? Please."

"Go to sleep, Steve. I'll see you at work tomorrow."

"You don' want me to come over now?"

Not a prayer. "No. Not tonight." She hung up. The click was like an explosion in my head.

I stared at the phone. "Sorry, Liz. Sorry I woke you. I'll see you a' work tomorrow. G'night." I hung up.

All women are nuts!

I lay back and closed my eyes.

When the room started to spin I held on to the bed frame. When it was moving too fast to hold on anymore, I groped my way to the bathroom and threw up again. Then I struggled out of my shoes, crawled back into bed, and passed out.

Chapter 15

"LEFTOVER HANGOVER"

A thunderous ringing shattered my stupor. When I tried to roll over, I was tangled in the bedspread, still fully dressed. My watch said eleven AM. I squinted at Bobby's bed—empty. Last night came roaring back into focus. I struggled up and grabbed the phone.

"Hey, man, is this the voice of the next number-one record in Detroit?"

Tympani were pounding in my head. "Who's this?" I croaked.

"This is Chick Farrell, man. Who's this?"

I swallowed. "Who?"

"Chick Farrell, man, Monarch Distributing. Decca Records promotion, you know, man? Who's *this*, man?"

"Oh, promotion, sorry. This is Steve Karmen. Bobby and I work together." *At least for the moment,* I thought.

"Oh, right, man. You must be the guitar player. That's you, man."

"Right, that's me."

"Can I talk to Bobby?"

"He's out. I expect him soon."

"Hey, this is *important*, man. You're doing the WKCL hop this afternoon out at Bloomfield Hills High School. There'll be five hundred kids, man, from all over. If they dig your record, man, you've just sold ten boxes! And you've got Ted McPhearson tomorrow morning at nine."

"That's awful early."

"Hey, man, Ted McPhearson is the biggest TV hop show in seven states, man. If *he* agrees to play your record, man, you're made! So we get there *any hour* the man wants us, man!"

"Great. Sounds great."

"I'll pick you up at three o'clock. Be ready. Bring your guitar. You can lip the record, but it looks great when you also pretend to play along. And the kids might ask you to do something live. Can you do live?"

"Sure. No problem. Do you want me to confirm this when Bobby gets back?"

"Nah. Just be in the lobby at three o'clock, man. I know where you are. See ya."

"Wait," I said, with effort. "Give me your number, in case there's a hitch." I scribbled on a corner of yesterday's paper. "We have to be back by six-thirty, absolutely no later than six-thirty. Will that work out?"

"Ease in the breeze, man. *I know dat youse New Yawk guys are woiking tonight.* Haw! Haw! I'll try to bring some live ones in to see you, maybe tomorrow. I'll look for you in the lobby, okay? Bye, man."

"We'll be ready."

My mouth was lined with wool. I pulled off my clothes, went to the bathroom, and gulped three aspirin. I gave the operator Monica's number. A sleepy lady answered. "This is Steve. May I speak with Bobby, please?"

"A moment," said the sultry voice. "It's Steve."

"Hey, what's up? Anybody hurt?"

"No, nothing like that. Sorry for interrupting. A record promotion guy named Chick Farrell just called. We're scheduled to do a hop at some high school at four o'clock. He's picking us up here at three. Any problems?"

"None. Say his name again?"

My head was killing me. "Uhm...Chick Farrell. Sounds like a real winner. He kept calling me 'man.' 'Hey, man' this, and 'hey, man' that. And you're doin' a TV show tomorrow morning, *man.* How about *that, man?*"

He perked up. "Really? A TV show?"

"*Right, man.* Ted somebody, *man,* a record show. Says he's watched in seven states, man."

"I'd like 'em to watch *this* in seven states."

"Spare me the details. It's eleven-thirty now. What time'll you be back?"

"As soon as I get up, I'm on my way home." I heard Monica giggle in the background. "An hour." He sounded distracted. "What you doin'?"

"Just got up."

"Yeah, I'm just getting...up, too. Have breakfast, don't wait for me."

"Okay. See you later."

At least he didn't mention anything about George.

I showered and tried to brush away the taste of last night. In the lobby, I checked for mail. Bobby had a letter from Connie Francis, with a big S.W.A.K. on the envelope, and a phone message from Buddy Baron. I must have slept through that one. I bought the paper. Chris and Myra were in the coffee shop. Chris waved me over.

"Feeling better?"

"Yeah," I said, avoiding her gaze. I wondered if I looked hung over.

"Where's Bobby?" Myra asked.

"Still asleep. We're doing record promotion this afternoon. Some high school hop."

She glanced at Chris. "Well, I guess I'll go back to the room."

"I'll stay for another cup of coffee, if Steve doesn't mind."

"Not at all."

"See you later. Say 'Hi.'"

I took Myra's place across from Chris. "Sorry about last night. If I said anything that offended you..."

She measured her words. "You didn't offend me. In fact, I was flattered that you thought about me when you were...in that kind of state of mind. You were very convincing."

"A lot of good it did me."

"Tell me what happened."

I held up my hand. "It's really nothing I'd like to talk about." The waitress took my order.

"Steve, it seems very unlike you to go out and get drunk. You don't seem like the drinking type."

"Chris, I'll only tell you if it ends the subject." She nodded. "I had an argument...no, not an argument...a deep discussion with Bobby last night. He was on his way out to see...his manager, and we hashed over a few business things, and I got a little upset, that's all. So I went downstairs and had a drink, to think about things. That's it, the whole story."

"Thank you. We won't talk about it any more. But if you ever want to...I'd be honored." There was something in the way she spoke that created the first sense of comfort I'd felt since last night. Maybe she really wants to be my friend. I never had a friend before who was also a girl.

The food arrived. I gulped the cold juice, grateful for its sweetness. "You may not believe this," she said, "but after we hung up last night, I really had the urge to come down to your room. You're making me think of things that...oh, we'd better not talk about that, either." She avoided my eyes, and changed the subject. "Have you ever been to a hop?"

"No. But we've played at lots of school dances."

"A hop is *not* a school dance. It's a place where kids go to meet each other and scream at records, and I mean *scream*. You're in for quite an experience. The girls'll love you. They're absolutely wild. Wait until you see how they act. They'll tear you apart."

"Bobby'll be happy to hear that," I said glumly.

Out of the corner of my eye I spotted him coming into the hotel. I waited until he was in the elevator. Then I glanced at my watch. I didn't want to end the conversation, but I knew I'd better face him as soon a possible. I called for the check. "I've got to get ready."

"I understand. Have a good hop."

"Thanks."

"I'll be looking forward to tonight," she said when we reached our floor.

"Me too."

He was face down on his bed—his all-banged-out-after-Monica position. "Bobby, what's going on?"

He struggled up and started to undress. "Nothing. I'm bushed. Nothing to worry about."

"I want you to know I'll do anything I can to help the act."

"I know that."

"*Talk to me!* Everything's straight between us, right?"

He continued ducking me. "Sure-sure. Look, I'm gonna hit the shower, and close my eyes for a few minutes. What do I have to know about the hop?"

"Chick said to lip the record, then plan something live if the kids react."

"Okay, 'Jump Down'..." He paused.

I understood his hesitation immediately. "Do you want to sing it alone?"

He answered without delay, but it felt like an eternity. "No. We can experiment with new directions at the club. For now, let's keep things the way they are." He paused again. "Steve, I hope you know this is all coming from George..."

"Say no more. This is why we're here, to experiment. I'll do anything I can to help."

"Thanks." He went into the bathroom and turned on the water. "Ties and jackets," he said.

"Right." I lay on my bed and began reading the paper.

"Hey, Curley," he called from the shower. "Wanna hear a good story?"

I went to the doorway. "Sure. What's up?"

"Listen to what Monica told me about the gorilla. His name is Carlo. He's married, kids, the whole thing. He's in the wholesale liquor business, sells booze to the club—he's Mickey's friend. She was waitressing at a joint in Windsor, and they started going out. Pretty soon, he offers to set her up in her own pad in return for a once-a-week. He travels a lot, she likes him, so she takes the deal. It's only supposed to be once a week, Mondays, that's why they were at the club. But lately, he's been fighting with his wife and coming around too much. He gonna be there for the whole fuckin' weekend! She can't afford that place by herself so she can't say no—you should see this joint, Curley, it's great! But it's stopping her from having her own life. Now she wants out. She wants to leave him, move in with her sister for a while...and then, when I go out on the road..." he hesitated, "...she wants to be with *me*. Believe that? She wants to come along on the road with *me*. How about *that* for a story? Right out of the movies, huh? What d'ya think of that?"

I stared at the shower curtain. "I don't believe it."

"True-true. Incredible, isn't it? If I work Pittsburgh, she'll come to Pittsburgh; Toronto, she'll come to Toronto. She's wants to be with me."

"No, I mean I don't believe you're even going to think about letting her."

"Why not? She's a fine lady who's been through some tough shit—mixed up with the wrong people. She wants out of that life; she wants a chance, and I've decided to give it to her. She's got some bucks saved, so she'll travel at her own expense. It won't cost me anything, except maybe meals."

He's replacing me with Monica. "I know this is none of my business, but shouldn't you think about it for a while before you commit yourself to traveling with someone? There's lots of ladies out there. This is only the...your first job." I was having difficulty referring to it as *our* act, or even *the* act. Now, it was *his* act. Maybe it always was and I just never saw it.

"Truthfully, Curley, I know it'll only last until we bang each other out. But for now, well, I've never met anybody like her. Everything's an education."

"What about Connie?"

"What *about* Connie?"

"Well, I thought you really liked *her*. What's gonna happen when she finds out you're meeting someone every time you go on the road."

"She'll never find out. She's not smart that way."

"You got a letter. I couldn't help noticing who it was from—it was written all over the envelope."

He stuck his head through the shower curtain. "Really? Lemme see." He grabbed a towel and dried his hands. I handed him the envelope. "Wait. Don't go," he said, glancing at the pages, then handing it back to me. "I'll read it later. Leave it on my bed." He ducked back under the water. "I want you to understand something, Steve: I like Connie, and maybe sometime there'll be a future for us. But right now, we're both into our careers, and she knows that. Besides, she's got a kid's mind when it comes to some things, and she's got to grow up more before I can think seriously about her. Anyway, I'm not ready to be tied down to one lady. I found that out this week. There's too many Monicas out there."

He put on his pajamas, got into bed, and read the letter. A page dropped as he nodded off, startling him awake again.

"I forgot. You had a phone call from Buddy Baron."

"Later. Wake me in an hour, okay? I have to shut down for a while."

"Sure."

I stretched out on my bed, leafing through the newspaper, wondering if it was George who had suggested that Bobby could travel with a lady instead of a guitar player.

Chapter 16

"AT THE HOP"

Chick Farrell was a grand blending of generations. As soon as he entered the lobby I knew it was him. Thirty-ish, tall, heavyset with a bulldog face, he was wearing a black-leather motorcycle jacket, jeans, and a white shirt and tie. This incongruity was compounded by his crew cut and jaw-length sideburns. His bouncy personality was hard not to like.

"I see two rock 'n' roll stars," he boomed, flashing a huge grin, arms spread wide, big belly advancing.

"*Hi, Chick. I'm Bobby,*" bassed Bing.

"Steve Karmen," I said, shaking his surprisingly limp hand.

"Since time is of the essence, I suggest that we shoot the shit in the car. Okay, man?"

"You got it, Chicklet."

"Just call me Chick," he laughed. "I haven't been down to a chicklet in years."

Bobby sat up front in the large Buick convertible while I crawled in back with my guitar. "Great wheels," he said, the star settling in.

"Not mine, man. Belongs to Stefano Ponte, Monarch Distributing. He's a friend of Mickey's, your club owner."

There was a telephone on the floorboard. As soon as we pulled away, Chick picked it up and waved it at Bobby. "Anybody you want to call? Anybody? Anywhere in the world? Call somebody. Make an impression."

"Who can we call that we wanted to impress?" Bobby asked.

"Why don't you call home," I suggested.

"Yeah! Let me call Charlie. This'll impress the shit out of him!"

Chick grinned. "Detroit 267 to mobile. Mobile, this is Detroit 267. Would you connect me with a number in New York City? What's the number?"

"Cypress 2-6725."

"Cypress 2-6725. Make it person to person for...?"

"Charlie. Don't worry; he'll be home. He's always home. Just Charlie."

"Charlie, operator." Chick listened attentively for the connection. "That you, Charlie? Good. Hold on a minute, man."

"Hey, Charlie, guess where I am?" he said loudly. "It's Bobby, you dunce! I'm in Detroit and...yes, I know you know that I'm in Detroit, but I'm calling you from a car phone...no, dummy, not a *bar* phone, a *car* phone...a mobile telephone. I'm driving down the street talking to you *from the car*! I'm goin' thirty miles an hour!" He turned to Chick. "This is not such a hot connection, man. Yeah, Charlie, this is your brother-in-law, Bobby. How is everything? Good. Is Mama home? Well, tell her that I called and that everything is fine, and that I spoke to you from a mobile telephone. Sure Charlie, when you're my road manager you can have a mobile phone, too. Yeah, I'm sorry I called you a dunce. Yeah, just give my love to everybody. Yeah, bye!"

Chick looked in the mirror. "Wanna call someone?"

This wasn't the moment to expose my life to a stranger. "No thanks. Another time."

"Tell us, Chickadee, what's the plan."

"Hop, and home in time for you to go to work."

"Tell about the hop. What do we do?"

"Lip the record, man. If the deejay and the kids dig you, you can do anything you want after that. I told them you can work live. Right?"

"Absolutely."

"Great, man. The PA's pretty good. You might get to do an extra tune or two. They're doing a remote. Ron Johnston is the deejay. Ron likes to have live sounds along with the records, so if an act can do it he lets them sing. He's a friend. He'll do a good interview. This is the only hop broadcast in town, so make it good, man. It goes out all over. Just work to the kids. And don't forget to mention Ron's name a lot—deejay's love that. In case he asks, how old are you?"

"Nineteen."

"Eighteen," I said.

"Great, man. Just play it by ear. These are good kids. They'll back you up with fan clubs if they dig you."

It was an incredible sight. When we arrived at Bloomfield Hills High School thirty minutes later, a tremendous crowd of kids, mostly girls, was milling around at the curb, waiting. They started screaming the minute we pulled up. (They couldn't possibly have known who we were, but they were screaming anyway. Maybe it was our suits, or the guitar, or that they recognized Chick's car, but something told them that we were show business, and they just went nuts). Girls kept shoving pieces of paper at us, screaming for autographs. Bobby obliged as we walked. I kept walking, trying to guard my guitar case and to keep smiling. Chick ran interference, swaying like an out-of-shape linebacker leading us through long hallways to a lounge area where another crowd was waiting—this time, grownups. We shook hands with at least eight beaming teachers who then escorted us through more hallways towards the gymnasium. As we got closer, I could hear very loud music. When we entered, we were confronted by a blur of swirling kids dancing.

On one side of the gym, two people were seated on a platform beneath a basketball hoop: the deejay and a technician running a small broadcast board and turntable.

Chick shouted, "I'll tell Ron you're here."

Bobby eyed the set up. "There's only one mike. Work close."

Ron Johnston was introducing the next record. When he spotted Chick, he looked up and waved. We were instantly surrounded by girls who were asking for more autographs; mine as well as Bobby's.

"Who are you?"

"I'm Steve. This is Bobby Darin."

"Where are you from?"

"What's your record?"

"'Rock Island Line,'" Bobby said.

"Never heard of it."

"Don't know it."

"How does it go?"

"Sing it for us!"

"We're gonna do it real soon," he smiled.

"Can you dance to it?"

"It's a hand-clapper," he said. "Bet you could make up a dance to it!"

"Yeah! A hand-clapper!" someone shouted, starting to clap completely out of time with the record that was playing. I wondered if these were the children of the people who use the Club T knockers.

"They'll be on the air in a few minutes," Chick said, interrupting with authority. "Give 'em some room, please." The girls stepped back a little, but not much.

"You're cute," one of them said to me. Ten more giggled.

"Oh, *Blondie*," another gasped, hiding behind the rest. They squealed like Munchkins. I moved back and unpacked my guitar.

"Go easy on the Curley-head, girls," Bobby said, taking over.

"Oooo, you're cute too," one of them said. She was about seventeen, and wearing a tight sweater (I wondered if the kerchief around her neck was hiding a hickey). With everyone watching, she wiggled up close and curled her fingers into Bobby's hair. "Dance with me?" she asked, leaning in, making contact.

"Oooo," the other girls moaned in unison.

Bobby ate it up. "Ab-so-lute-ly," he said, inviting her into his arms. There was another communal titter as they began swaying to the slow ballad being played. Bobby tried to hold her away and make polite conversation, but her full-chest press was winning out. He was talking to her hair.

While everyone's attention was on them, another girl asked me to dance. I glanced at Chick, who nodded that I should. I handed him the guitar, and the girl led me out onto the floor. Immediately, I was smothered in heavy perfume as she hit me with the Detroit Press, her chest grinding holes in my jacket. It felt absolutely great (except, of course, I couldn't possibly do anything about it here). I thought I was being saved when a different girl cut in, but this one immediately occupied the excavations left by the first, clobbering me with her own overpowering scent. The same thing was happening to Bobby. Girls in New York never danced like this—at least not in public. I became intimate with at least ten different hairsprays.

Bobby's last partner was the girl he had danced with first. When the record ended, she held on and kissed him, full on the mouth, lingering long enough to leave a red stain on his lips.

Obviously surprised, he recovered quickly. "Enthusiastic," he whispered, wiping away the lipstick as Chick lead us toward the platform.

There was a big cheer from everyone as Ron Johnston began his introduction. "They're here from New York, working at Club Temptation over in Dearborn, and they've got a great, hot, new record called 'Rock Island Line.' Let's get 'em up here with a great big WKCL Bloomfield Hills High School welcome! Meet...Bobby Darin and..." he paused, looking for my name on the record label, which, of course, wasn't there. "Well, we'll find out who this other young man is in a few minutes. But *now*! Here's Bobby *Darin*, with 'Rock Island Line!!!'"

The scream was deafening as we climbed up onto the platform. When Chick passed me the guitar, they roared even more. For an instant Ron Johnston reached to shake my hand first, thinking I was Bobby. But I hung back as he moved to the microphone.

The recorded strums of 'Rock Island Line' came booming over the speakers, and I played along while Bobby lipped the words. The kids were spellbound. When he began clapping, the whole gym joined in, destroying any chance of hearing the lyrics. It was hard to tell if I was even playing in sync with the track, but it didn't matter. Only the record was going out on the air. When the song ended, there was a another deafening ovation.

"Hey, come on over here, *big fella!*" Ron Johnston said. "Let's give a real WKCL Bloomfield Hills High School greeting to...and *you're on the air...Bobby Darin!!!*" The explosion that followed shook the platform as the girls pressed in. I was blocking the view of some of the kids crowded along the side, so I stood back against the wall.

"*Hi, Ron,*" said Bing into the mike, his voice echoing through the gym.

"Well, now, Bobby Darin! Good to have you here. That's a great record. When d'ja make it, Bobby?"

"About three weeks ago, Ron. We're really pleased with the response it's been getting. And your audience today is, well, just...gee, absolutely the best!"

The kids screamed.

"How old are you, Bobby?"

"Nineteen, Ron."

"Nineteen-year-old Bobby Darin!!!"

The girls erupted again.

"Nineteen years old, from New York, here to introduce us to his new Decca recording, 'Rock Island Line.' Do you have a fan club out here, Bob?"

"No, I don't, Ron." There were more screams. "This is my first trip to Detroit, and it's been just great. All of the people have been *so nice*."

"Well, I think I know some ladies who might be interested in starting a Bobby Darin fan club. What do you say, gang? Does Bobby Darin need a Bloomfield Hills High School fan club?"

There was a booming YYYEEESSS!!!

"Hear *that*, Bobby? I don't think you'll have any trouble establishing a chapter here. Now, you folks at home couldn't see him, but Bobby's got a handsome young guitarist strumming along with him. Why don't you introduce your friend to our listeners, Bobby."

I froze. "Come on over here, Curley," he called through clenched teeth. "Ron and everybody, this is my guitarist, and dear friend, Steve Karmen."

"Well, Hi, Steve Karmen, welcome to the WKCL Bloomfield Hills High School hop." There was a burst of applause, and a few screams when I approached the mike. "Where ya from, Steve?"

I leaned in. "New York, Ron. Bobby and I went to high school together."

"Who wants to guess how old Steve is?" Ron asked.

Kids began yelling numbers. "Sixteen, seventeen, nineteen, twenty-one." One kid in back yelled, "Sixty-three," and got a laugh.

"Tell us, Steve. How old are you?"

"I'm eighteen."

The place went absolutely berserk.

"Now, here we have two young singers—a pair of good lookers from New York—and we're only letting them *talk*. How about a song for the gang, Bobby and Steve?"

"Be glad to, Ron," Bobby said, taking over. "Hey, everybody, this is a happy folk tune called 'Jump Down, Spin Around' that needs the help of everybody out there. Squeeze in here, Curley, and strum a hand."

The kids started clapping as soon as I began playing. When we sang, every line of by-play evoked a scream. Even the holdout boys in the back of the gym drifted forward, now paying attention.

When "Jump Down" ended, they roared again, completely overwhelming us, unlike anything I'd ever felt from an audience before. It was an immediate surge of energy that we didn't get from the older nightclub crowd.

"Sing another one," someone shouted, followed by an approving cheer. "Yeah, sing a crooner!"

"'Scarlet Ribbons,'" he said.

I leaned in as close as I could, and began finger picking. The soft sound brought everyone to attention. This time he got more applause than screams, more respect than raw emotion.

"Let Steve sing one," a girl down front said, batting her lashes at me.

I shook my head.

"Come on," she yelled. "Let Steve sing. Let Steve Sing!"

Suddenly the whole place was chanting: "*Let Steve Sing! Let Steve Sing!*"

I shook my head again. But they would not be denied. "*Let Steve sing! Let Steve sing!*"

"Hey, I think that's a *great idea*," Bobby said, giving in, cornered. Then, as gracefully as possible, he introduced me. "Curley, sing one for the people. Ladies and gentlemen, Steve Karmen."

But as he backed off to the side, he whispered through a very grim numero-uno, "'Country Boy,' short! One chorus!"

Sweat was running down my face as I stepped to the microphone. My mouth was dry, my fingers wooden, trying to pick at the strings. "T...This is a folk song called 'I'm Just a Country Boy.'"

When I played the intro, they hushed again. I avoided all eye contact, not looking at anyone, focusing instead on the rear wall, afraid of anything that might break my concentration. Out of the corner of my eye, I could see Bobby standing back near the control board, arms folded, listening.

> *"I ain't gonna marry on the fall*
> *I ain't gonna marry in the spring*
> *'Cause I'm in love with a pretty girl*
> *Who wears a diamond ring..."*

As I reached the first chorus, a huge swoon from the girls in front startled me so much that I just stopped singing.

And stopped playing.

Completely.

A cold, dead stop.

The place was silent.

"I'm just not used to singing without Bobby," I said, flushing deep red. "Thank you very much." I stepped back.

"Well, you've got a wonderful voice, doesn't he, everyone?" called Ron Johnston, coming to my rescue, motioning for everyone to applaud.

The crowd roared YYYEEESSS!!!

Bobby's eyes revealed nothing; but nothing said everything.

Ron Johnston motioned to his soundman, then to Bobby. "Now, everybody, how would you all like to hear 'Rock Island Line' again?" There was a big cheer. "Well, HERE...IT...IS!!!"

When the record started, I stepped back and knelt close to the platform, grateful to hide again in my roll as accompanist. Bobby recaptured their attention immediately, moving and bopping with all his energy while I pretended to strum, silently staring at the neck of my guitar, intent on playing and nothing else. Now that the kids had heard the song once, some of them began to sing along in the chorus sections. When it ended, their reaction was, incredibly, even stronger than the first time.

"Thanks, Bobby Darin and Steve Karmen, with their Decca recording of 'Rock Island Line,'" called Ron Johnston, waving, invoking more applause.

"Thanks to everyone here," Bobby shouted. "And don't forget to watch Ted McPhearson tomorrow morning."

"Right, Bobby," Ron said, quickly adding, "right after everyone listens to WKCL radio. Now, let's say a Big WKCL Bloomfield Hills High School *thank you* to Bobby Darin and Steve Karmen!"

A sea of sweaters instantly surrounded us, their hands clutching pencils and papers. "Write *clearly*," one of them said. "No *scribbles!*" While Bobby was signing, I packed the guitar, trying to avoid everyone. After introducing the next record, Ron Johnston himself came over to pump our hands and tell us that we were one of the best new teams to come through Detroit in a long time.

I wanted to crawl under a rock.

It took fifteen minutes to autograph our way out of the building.

"Man, I've been here with lots of acts," Chick said, as we drove back to the hotel, "but none of them got anywhere *near* the reaction you guys got. Man, you were *fantastic!* I'll bet, Monday, there'll be all kinds of calls for the record. You did yourselves good today. That line about doing McPhearson didn't hurt either, even though it's a different station."

"Sorry. I didn't know," Bobby said.

Chick was completely oblivious to Bobby's black mood. "Oh, don't worry about it. The jocks like to have those things happen. It gives 'em something to talk about. You killed 'em, man."

He never showed it during the entire trip, but while Chick continued to praise the shit out of the both of us, I knew old stoneface was thinking. When we pulled up to the Wolverine, Chick said, "You're the greatest, man! And you can do yourselves more good tomorrow. Seven-thirty in the lobby. Don't be late; be *ready!*"

Bobby said nothing until we reached the room; once there, he was surprisingly calm. "George is right. I never saw it so clearly before, but George is right. You're a good singer, and you look good. It's not like you're just some old piano player in a corner. You're right up there with me."

"I know what it must look like, Bobby, but I swear I didn't intend for that to happen."

"I'm not blaming you directly. What happened couldn't really be helped. I can see that now."

"What do you mean?"

"Steve, I couldn't possibly have sung those songs today without you. I couldn't have opened in Detroit alone. I need you there playing for me. But I should have known with all that jailbait looking at your curls that you'd inspire something. It was bound to happen sooner or later. Ah, better now. George was right," he said, half to himself, "the man was right, and very smart. Now, the first thing is that tonight I'll sing all the songs alone, the whole act, no harmonies. What works, works. What doesn't, I'll deal with later. Just walk out with me and stay on 'til the end. And don't come off for the bow."

"Bobby, I'll do anything necessary to help the act. Tell me that you understand what I'm saying to you."

"I understand. Now, as far as social plans for tonight, since we have to get up early for McPhearson, I could use a good night's sleep anyway. So if you're planning any moves, don't count on the room. Okay?"

"I was thinking of not going with you tomorrow."

"Hey, just because I'm making changes in the act doesn't mean you have to spend the rest of the trip in the room. I'll do the show alone, of course. It's just lipping the record. Sit in the audience and watch. Lead the clapping. Maybe we'll meet some nymphos and bring 'em back to the hotel."

"Bobby, I didn't mean for what happened to happen."

"Stop already. Just accept the changes. That's what we're here for, right?"

"Right. Want the first shower?"

"No, you," he said closing the subject.

I could feel the tension between us growing all evening. His out-ward calm might have deceived others, but whatever he said to me about the act now sounded like an order. Directions, commands, everything had an edge. It might have been an important moment for him—the first time doing a whole show completely by himself—but for me it was a huge let-down. I felt useless, creatively abandoned—wanting to contribute but unable to provide much more to the act than Larry or Tiny.

"Jump Down" sounded empty without harmony. I dismissed this as sour grapes because I wasn't singing it with him. I got some strange looks from Tiny when I wasn't invited downstage—and more when I didn't even sing along—but I tried my best to ignore them. For the first bow, I just stood in place. He didn't acknowledge me at all. Then I thought that it might look better if I faked the bow music along with the band, so I bluffed a few chords of "Fine and Dandy," and attempted a smile that must have surely looked phony. Before "Scarlet Ribbons," he introduced me as his "dear friend and accompanist"; but when singing "Man Smart" alone provided him the freedom to roam the stage without my obstruction, I knew a bridge had been crossed. He didn't need my harmony at all.

"It might be better if you stayed on until the blackout," he said, back in the dress-ing room. "That way I could go off, or come back to do an extra song, or what-ever, without you running back and forth with me."

"I might bump into Arlene."

"That might not be too bad."

"Bobby, I'll break my neck. Or she will."

"Okay, let me think about that one."

Between shows, I hung around backstage, not wanting to face anyone or explain why I wasn't singing harmony any more. Andy tried to hit on me for his per-former-rate pictures, but I pushed any decisions off on Bobby. He might not want to take *formal shots* with a mere member of the band.

I saw Chris before the second show. "We're going to sack in early," I said, dodg-ing her invitation to the Bagel, "to be ready for Ted McPhearson."

"I was hoping..."

I avoided her eyes. "I'd like to, but, well...it's just that we're making some changes in the act...I guess you saw...kind of more of what I told you before, and...truthfully, it's getting me a little down. I wouldn't be good company."

"Steve, I'd *really* like to see you later, just for a talk. I think I know how you feel now. I'll be around all night, at any time. Please give me a call if you want to talk to someone."

"Thanks."

"I *understand*, Steve."

"That helps, Chris. It really does."

Later, I apologized to Liz for my drunkenness, but our conversation was cool and polite. The touchy-touchy guy was in the club again. I didn't care. Bobby insisted we leave as soon as we were done and cleaned up.

In the cab, I tried to iron out some of the hard feelings that had passed between us today. He seemed disinterested, listening quietly to my babble without comment. In the room, he said a fast goodnight, and was asleep practically as soon as he hit the bed.

In the darkness, my thoughts went back to the hop. This afternoon hadn't been the first time I had ever performed a song solo, but the previous audiences were made up of friends who were more accepting and familiar with our style. The kids today had no idea who the hell I was or what I was going to do, yet they reacted to me the same way as they did to Bobby.

And what I did worked—at least until I chickened out.

The Muse of Music was whispering in my ear. I began to think about what kind of presentation *I* might make in a solo club act, *my* act—what songs I could use, what I might wear. Maybe I could make a record, too.

But no matter how hard I tried to distance myself from the truth, it kept creeping back in under every excuse I could invented to dodge it—Bobby Darin was getting ready to move on without Steve Karmen.

Chapter 17

"JUST ALONG FOR THE RIDE"

I resolved to stay completely out of his way. It's his act, not mine. I must learn to accept that there will now be differences between our professional and personal lives.

But even the best-intended resolutions can be derailed by uncontrollable events.

When we arrived at WJZ at eight-thirty, Chick spoke with the lobby guard who called upstairs to announce us. A few minutes later, a pretty girl in her early twenties approached. "Hi, I'm Sherry Sorrentino, Ted's assistant. I heard you both on the radio yesterday on my way home from work. Very impressive."

Jesus, it's starting again, I thought.

"*Thank you, Sherry*," said Robert Mitchum, as she led us to the elevator. "Expecting a big audience?"

"We only hold seventy-five, but they'll sound like a thousand."

In the elevator, Chick went on and on about how important Ted McPhearson was for the record and how lucky we were to be able to be doing his terrific show. Bobby just nodded along, never taking his eyes off Sherry (or her set). When we reached the studio, I made it a point to inform everyone that I was just along for the ride and would hang out in back, which seemed to please Bobby. Maybe that's the way to handle everything: just keep a low profile. I helped myself to coffee and donuts from the crew table. Sherry and Chick led Bobby to a desk where a tall, distinguished-looking, gray-haired man was going over a script with an assistant. Ted McPhearson looked like someone's father—not at all like a top deejay. They shook hands. Then Bobby said something that broke everybody up.

At eight forty-five, Bill Haley's metronome, "Rock Around The Clock" came blaring through the ceiling speakers. The doors flew open and hordes of teens came running in; some rushing to find seats in the bleachers, others grabbing partners and dancing out on the floor with an unbelievable energy for this early hour.

When the record ended, a voice boomed over the PA: "HEY! Good morning everybody!!!"

Everyone shouted, "HELLO!!!"

"HEY! Welcome to WJZ-TV and The TED McPHEARSON SHOW!!!" There were more cheers. "We have lots of dancing this morning, and two great guests to entertain you with some wonderful music. During the entertainment, we'd like you to sit in the bleachers and give the act your complete, undivided attention. And if Ted talks to you, be natural and have fun! Okay???"

"OOOOOOKAAAAAY!!!" they cheered.

I wanted to disappear—someone still thinks that Bobby's is two people! It must be Chick. I nervously waited until he came back to the coffee table. "Chick," I blurted, "please tell whoever is in charge that the name of the act is 'Bobby Darin,' *just* 'Bobby Darin,' *only* 'Bobby Darin.' Bobby will do this show *all by himself*. See? I don't even have my guitar with me. I'm just along for the ride. I'm the accompanist. It's Bobby's record. I don't perform with Bobby."

"Hey, man, what are you talking about, man? Bobby's got it covered with Ted, man. The other act is Charlene Williams. She's got a crossover breaking in Atlanta. RCA sent her up to break it here, too."

"Oh, I'm sorry," I said, shrinking immediately, feeling like the most stupid-ass idiot in the world. "I was worried that...Ted expected *me* to perform with Bobby...and I...I didn't bring my guitar."

"Sit down, man, enjoy. Grab some coffee, man. Come on, I'll hang with you."

Relieved, I followed him up to the top row of bleachers, high out of harm's way, but with a perfect view of the dance floor. Sherry passed below, arm-in-arm with Bobby, who winked and shouted that they were headed for makeup. Chick waved. I smiled, wondering if the hop was still on his mind. Just before nine o'clock the music started again, and the unseen voice introduced Ted McPhearson to the cheering crowd. When the program went on the air, everyone was dancing, trying to look cool for the TV camera that was being pushed around the floor. After the first record, Ted McPhearson interviewed a few kids, then played another.

When the floor lights dimmed for the first commercial, the great voice requested everyone to be seated. A stage crew hastily rolled out a little railroad train set that had been concealed behind a curtain. An animated puff of smoke rose from the engine stack, and cartooned tracks headed off into a make-believe horizon. The locomotive window had a small seat behind it.

"They use that set for every choo-choo record," Chick said dryly. Then, responding to my puzzled look, "You know, anything to do with trains, travel, people coming or going somewhere."

Sherry led Bobby out from behind the bleachers. He was made up (a much better job than we had been doing each night) and wearing a big railroad engineer's cap. Bobby never wore a hat of any kind—on any occasion, in any weather—and this floppy doffer made him look ridiculous, especially in contrast to his dark suit and tie.

"What's your name?" one of the girls down front called, while seven others squirmed with delight.

"Bobby Darin," he said, winking, settling into the locomotive chair. "Do you like the hat?" he asked no one in particular.

"No," someone yelled. "Let's see your hair."

"Neither do I," he said, removing it, tossing it into the audience, shaking his waves back in place with a flick. The lucky girl who caught it proudly put it on.

"Can I have your handkerchief?"

"Can I have your comb?" called another.

"Your tie! *Puleeze* give me your tie!" gasped a third.

As the lights came up, Bobby ended the banter by putting a finger to lips for silence, pointing toward Ted McPhearson.

"Our first guest this morning is a newcomer to the Detroit area. He's appearing out at Mickey's Club Temptation in Dearborn, and he's got a great, new, unusual record happening on the Decca label. Let's all greet...Bobby Darin...and 'Rock Island Line!!!'"

As the record started, everyone turned to watch the monitors above the bleachers. When Bobby faded in, the railroad set didn't look half bad. Each time the camera moved in for a close up, he stared right into it, evoking screams. At times his lips didn't sync with the record, but when he began to clap, the kids were a hundred percent with him instantly—nothing like the coaxing he had to do every night at the club. The camera cut to a girl in the audience who pretended a swoon when she realized she was being televised. When "Rock Island Line" ended, there was a gigantic roar.

Ted McPhearson appeared from behind the locomotive. "Good morning, Bobby Darin. Welcome to the show. That certainly is a strong record."

"*Thanks, Ted,*" said Bing. "*It was lots of fun making it.*"

"And it has a great beat, doesn't it, fans?" The kids cheered. "What kind of a beat do you call that, Bobby?"

"That's a rockabilly skiffle beat, Ted."

"That's great, Bobby. Where are you from?"

"New York City, Ted. This is my first trip to Detroit, and the people at Club Temptation have been just great. Detroit sure is a swinging town!"

Some girls giggled.

"You seem to be a fine young man starting out in show business, Bobby Darin. How old are you?"

"Nineteen, Ted." There were more nervous sighs.

"Sherry Sorrentino, our production coordinator, says that she heard you on a radio show yesterday, and that you really broke it up at the Bloomfield hop."

I felt a warning chill.

It was unnecessary. Bobby was smooth as silk. "The audience was wonderful, Ted. I had a swell time with a swell bunch of teens."

"And we hope you'll continue to have a successful engagement out at Mickey's Club Temptation. How much longer will you be there, Bobby?"

"Another whole week, Ted," he said, looking directly into the camera, "so everybody come on out and see us at Club Temptation."

Ted McPhearson raised his arms, signaling for applause. "Thank you, Bobby Darin, and *good luck* with 'Rock Island Line,' on the Decca label. *Now,* let's everybody get up and dance...to the number one record in Detroit this Saturday morning, and for the last four Saturday mornings...from RCA...and he'll be in town next week...Mr. *Movement... Elvis!!!*...and...'*Heartbreak Hotel!!!*'"

With a gigantic scream, the floor flooded with kids, and Bobby was immediately besieged by dancing partners.

I felt someone tap my foot. "You with him?" a girl asked.

I nodded.

"Dance with me?"

I shook my head.

"Go on," Chick said. "It's good for business."

What the hell, I thought. Bobby's finished. What harm can it do? Besides, she was cute. Maybe he was right—maybe we will find some action here. I climbed down, and she led me to the dance floor. She was very powerful. With her head on my shoulder and her eyes closed, she moved in and started swaying and grinding until I wasn't sure who was leading. And just like at the hop, another girl cut in, gluing herself to me, then another bra-size, then another perfume. Across the room, the same thing was happening to Bobby, who winked when he spotted me, ever aware of the camera following him. I could imagine what was going through *his* mind.

When the last strums of "Heartbreak Hotel" ended, I thanked my latest partner and turned to leave the floor. But Ted McPhearson was blocking my way, standing next to a TV camera, shoving a microphone in my face. "Let's say hello to...tell us your name."

"S... Steve Karmen."

"Hello, Steve Karmen. Having a good time here this morning?"

"G...Great, Ted." I swallowed as the camera came closer. Some girls in the bleachers screamed.

"You're here with Bobby Darin, aren't you?"

I nodded, forcing a petrified smile.

"This is Bobby Darin's sidekick from New York, everybody. Meet Steve Karmen!"

There were more screams.

"What do you do, Steve?"

"I play guitar for Bobby." When I said the word *guitar*, the place erupted.

By this time, Bobby had squeezed through the crowd, and was standing next to me, a numero-uno firmly planted on his face. "And here's Bobby Darin again, having a great time dancing at the WJZ-TV hop. Judging from the crowd reaction here, you're *both* having a great time in Detroit." Someone was signaling to Ted from behind the camera. "We've got to go to a commercial now, but let's everyone wish Bobby and Steve good luck with their record, 'Rock Island Line.'"

Again Ted raised his arms, and again the kids responded with screams and applause. Mercifully, the lights went down.

Instantly, mobs of girls were demanding autographs and we had no choice but to stand back-to-back and sign every scrap of paper thrust at us. I did my best to be cordial, but my hand was shaking. Another record started, and the fans thinned out. It was my first opportunity to say something privately to Bobby. "I had no idea that that was going to happen," I whispered quickly as we walked off the floor.

He was still waving, grinning—Mr. Cool—but he was clearly pissed; his voice just loud enough for me to hear. "This is it, Steve. A hop is one thing, a TV show is another. As soon as we get back to the hotel, we have to have a meeting about what's going on. This is a *business* conference, so don't make any plans."

"I don't have any plans, you know that."

Sherry Sorrentino rushed over, followed by a tall, dazzling redhead. "You were *wonderful*, Bobby, just wonderful! Meet Charlene Williams."

"Hi, Bobby," Charlene said in the most lovely, Southern-belle accent, her bulging, ripe Georgia peaches straining to escape from her flowery Little-Bo-Peep dress. "Loved yer record. Gud luck with it."

"Well, hi, y'all Charlene, baby," Bobby drawled, off and running at the scent. "How's yer record dewin'?"

"Makin' national noise, an' bubblin' under. Are yew on a promo tour tew?"

"Sort of. We're working a club here in town."

"Oh, I'm always so jilous of a singer who kin do a act. This is my first record, and ah've never worked *innywhere*. You're so brave to dew that!"

Mr. Delightful oozed closer. "And you're just as brave, honey, coming all the way up here into the Yankee North all by your lonesome."

"Oh, I'm not alone. That's my Henry over there 'ginst the wall."

My-Henry was big enough to *be* the wall, a redneck sheriff in a plaid shirt and cowboy boots.

"Henry?" Bobby asked, retreating.

"Mah hubby. We drove all night to git here. Kids tew," she said, pointing to two toddlers near My-Henry. "That's Clovis and EulaAnn. They're so 'xcited to be in a real TV studio. Me, tew!"

"I wish you the best of luck with your record, Charlene," he said. "We'll be listening for it."

"Time to get ready," Sherry said, leading her away.

When we were alone again, I tried to speak, but he shushed me. My stomach was burning. I tried again. "I didn't want that to happen. I hope you know that."

Razors cut me off. "I told you we'll discuss it at the hotel!"

A half moon had been hung against the curtain, and I watched as Charlene lipped her way through a cling-cling-cling country ballad, while My-Henry, a child in each arm, stood off to the side, proudly beaming sunshine to her. But after her interview with Ted, it was Charlene's turn to dance with the boys in the crowd, and some of the heavily-pimpled types made a big point of holding her as close as they could—the Detroit Press-male version. My-Henry didn't look too happy during this part of the show.

I wanted desperately to leave. I even considered announcing that I would meet them at the car, but I didn't. I should have. Instead, I stood with Chick and waited while Bobby said goodbye to Ted McPhearson. When the show ended, most of the audience drifted off, except for two girls, both about eighteen, who stood near the door eyeing Bobby as he signed autographs. The taller one had tough body language, but she had a young, innocent face. She wore tight jeans, and her long, dark hair fell over her great set of bombers. She seemed to be offering words of encouragement to the other girl, a curly-haired brunette who wore a leather jacket over a loose blouse, a tight skirt, and bobby sox. This one had an absolutely great ass.

When Bobby came over, they blocked our way. "Hi, I'm Fran," the tough one said. "This is JoAnn. So you're going to be in town for another week, huh? Where are you staying?"

Chick interrupted before Bobby could answer. "We have to split now, guys. We have another radio show to do this morning."

"Yeah, let's split now," Fran said, coming on. "Take us to breakfast."

"That's the invitation I usually make the night before," Errol Flynn said, encouraging them.

Chick insisted. "Hey girls, take it easy. We have to make it to WWJ by eleven. There's no time for breakfast."

"That's okay, Chicker," Bobby said as we moved down the hallway, "I'd love to take both you ladies to breakfast..."

"You would?" Fran said, surprised.

"...but we're on our way to do some more record promotion. Maybe we can see you another time."

"Where are you staying?"

"Not too far down Woodward," he winked, "but this isn't a good time to be sociable."

Instantly Fran nodded her understanding, and they both stepped back, allowing us to move down the hall. But they stayed right behind us. "I think your record is great," Fran said to Bobby. "Sure you don't want to take us to breakfast?"

"Want to. Can't. Rain check?"

"Rain check," she answered, slyly.

In the elevator, Fran stood very close to Bobby, radiating lots of body heat. I saw their hands touching. JoAnn kept gazing into my eyes, giving me her best numero-uno, sexy look, which was not really very convincing. As much as she wanted a response from me, was as far as I was from giving one. All I could think of was our pending *business conference.*

Just before the car stopped, JoAnn glanced at Fran and got what seemed to be a nod of permission. Quickly stepping forward, she put her arms around my neck and kissed me, in front of everyone, closing her eyes, tonguing my lips. She kissed just like Chris (it must be a Midwest thing). "MMmmm," she sighed, sounding like a bad imitation of Mae West, "maybe another time, I hope."

"Hey, let the curley one be, beautiful," Bobby said, as we stepped into the lobby.

"I've got one for you, too, honey," Fran said.

But Mr. Romantic was ready, enveloping her in his arms, and delivering a major crusher that stopped traffic. When they separated from the long embrace, Fran looked a little shaken. "Sure you won't...er...breakfast?" she whispered, hoarsely.

"*Another time, baby,*" Clark Gable winked. We left them in front of the building "That's a sure thing," Bobby said, waving from the parking lot. "No doubt about it."

"Nah, they're just kids, man," Chick said. "Don't be tempted. She's probably not more than fifteen."

"Baloney."

"Absolutely, man. They dress up to look tough, but underneath they're just kids. Joe Karly, WBZB, got nailed by the father of a chick he met at a hop, man. He threatened to have him killed if he didn't stay away from his kid. Know how old she was, man? Fourteen. *Fourteen!!!* Joe thought she was twenty-two! And he couldn't report the threat because he was banging her. Don't be tempted, man. Let 'em buy your record, and leave it at that."

"Sounds like good advice," Bobby nodded.

But I didn't believe Bobby would take the advice.

It took a half an hour to get to WWJ from downtown. I sat in back, concentrating on the radio while Bobby talked to Chick about deejays, ignoring me completely. When he was on the air, I stayed in the waiting room, leafing through magazines, listening to the broadcast. He seemed happier after they'd played "Rock Island Line" and he'd done a five-minute interview. I attributed this to the fact that he had worked alone. But when the deejay came out to say goodbye during the next record, Chick felt obliged to introduce me, just because I was there, and Bobby started to look pissed again.

I followed him into the coffee shop. He waited until the waitress had taken our order.

"There's no other way to put this. You're hogging my act."

"You know it's not intentional."

"Yeah, maybe you don't mean it, or maybe you do and you don't even know it. Makes no difference. It's happening, and it has to stop. I know you, and I respect you, Steve, but this is it. It's *my* act, not a double of Darin and Karmen. It's a *solo* act. It has nothing to do with friendship or caring for each other, but what happened at Ted McPhearson can never, *ever* happen again, get it? Jesus, you had almost as much air time as I did! You've got to remove yourself from being any possible distraction."

"Distraction? It was an accident. I was just dancing. I know it's your act. I'm not trying to hog it. That's the last thing I would ever do."

"You're my *accompanist*, Steve, not my partner. You can't *ever* forget that. You're here because I knew I could count on you to help me through the beginning of my career, right?"

"Nothing has changed."

"Yes, it has, and you're not seeing it! Jesus, are you blind! Everywhere we go, it's *we*. People think of us as a team. You're attracting as much goddamn attention as I am. Your purpose here is to help get my act off the ground, not to be seen as a part of it."

"I know it's *your* act," I repeated, my pent-up frustration finding a voice. "There was never any question about that, not in *my* mind. And I'm *not* hogging it, Bobby. I'm trying my best to help you in any way I can. Maybe it's the way *you're* seeing things! But I am seeing what you think my role is. You want an appointment service—that's what you want, a flunky, not a friend. You should have brought Charlie. He's perfect for you. He'll do anything you say. You begged *me* to write charts because George wouldn't spring for arrangements like a manager's supposed to, and then all you talk about is spending money on Nelson Riddle. You know why I did all that work? Not to hog your act, *star*, but to *help* you. All you really want is someone you can order around."

"Know what? You're too damn dependent on me," he lashed back. "*I couldn't have opened without you*," he sneered. "Is that what you want to hear? Well, it seems to me that I've said that quite a few times already. And it's true. I know it, and you know it. But so what? Things are changing, and what's happening now is having an effect on the other parts of our relationship, and it's not supposed to. Did you really think we would be spending every minute together? In all the time I've known you, I've never seen this mother-hen side of you. Not only do you keep a record of every dime we spend, but you keep score on my pussy as well! Where the hell do you come off telling me how to deal with Monica? And what's it your business about my relationship with Connie? I haven't had to report to anyone since I was nine years old, and I don't intend to start now. Just accept that it's *my* act, and that everything I do is meant to protect my future."

"From *me?*"

"Yes, from you! Now, I'm going to lay out some rules, and if you follow them, we'll get along. Number one: when we're somewhere together, *anywhere*, the first thing you say is *no* to everything, and stay the hell out of the way!"

"Sure, I'll just wait in the car," I said, getting hotter. He ignored me.

"Number two: since I have no agreement from the deejays or the press...

"Oh, yeah, *the press*...

"...they're going to ask who you are just because you're with me, so from now on I'll do promotion alone."

"Fine," I shot back, "I like seeing the same movie five times in one week! Why not? I'm just a *distraction* from the great Bobby Darin anyway."

"Goddamn it, Steve. If you're my friend, you'll understand and accept that I have to set guidelines. Understanding is what friendship is all about."

"Jesus, you sound just like every girl who won't put out: 'Oh, darling, I need your understanding.' Bullshit!"

"Bullshit back! If you were in my position, you'd do the same thing."

"I would *not*! Since when am I the enemy?"

"Look, I came here for experience, we both know that. And I took you along because you know my music. Well, George and John are right: I'm an imitation of Belafonte no matter how I dress. My music has to change. I'm gonna cut back on guitar tunes, except 'Rock Island,' of course..."

"Oh, *of course!* You need a guitar on that one, don't you?" He had obviously given this some thought.

"...and do 'Funny Valentine' instead of 'Scarlet Ribbons'; try a few more up standards, maybe 'All Of Me,' or 'Lazy River'; maybe even play piano on some rockers. I'm going to ask John for another rehearsal Monday, to break in material. It'll add depth if I can do pop as well as folk."

"Depth-*this!*" I paused to catch my breath. "Want me at rehearsal? Want me to play along?"

"On the ones you can."

I was strangely calm. "You've got it all worked out, haven't you?" I sensed what was coming.

"That's right. And if you're not happy with the new arrangement, you can finish out tonight, and go back to New York tomorrow."

I looked him right in the eye. "You firing me?"

"No, just giving you an option. If you don't like the rules, now you have an out. We don't sing harmony anymore. I'll work out 'Rock Island' somehow."

I paused. "You want me to go home?"

"Up to you."

"Bobby, How many times can I tell you that what happened was not my fault."

"Not *all* your fault. It's the fault that you're here, that's all."

My breathing was getting tight again. "I don't believe what I'm hearing. I thought we were...friends."

"We are friends. But this is business. It has nothing to do with friendship. We'll be friends for the rest of our lives, although I don't know how you weren't aware that the chicks would chase you, too. You should have said *no!* A *friend* would have said *no*, and not danced. Why the hell were you dancing? This is not a party! This is business—*my* act and *my* career—not *your* pleasure. It just can't go on the way it is. It's *my* responsibility and *my* decision. You're welcome to stay, as long as you accept the rules."

"I assume that means to the end of this engagement."

"I don't have any other work at the moment."

"But you will have."

"Probably. I'll deal with that when it comes."

I waited a minute. "Mr. Darin, I agreed to come here to help the act. You'll find I'm a man of my word."

"I know you are."

The waitress delivered our food. I stood. "I'm...going to the movies. I'll be back...later...in a few hours."

Not looking up, he grabbed a fork and stabbed at his eggs. "Just let me know so I can plan accordingly. But be sure you base your decision on playing *by the rules*. Either do...or don't. Your choice."

"Go fuck yourself," I said, heading for the door, pushing past the shocked waitress, hardly able to see where I was going.

Chapter 18

"INSTANT VOLTAGE"

It was like being kicked in the balls. That had happened only once, so far, in my life. One of the Catholic kids from the next block had chased me on a Yom Kippur afternoon, and I wasn't fast enough. When he caught me, he'd managed to plant a good one between my legs. The instant voltage blinded me, but I had enough strength to squirm loose and resume running until I was out of range. Only then did I fall apart.

That's how it felt now. Kicked in the nuts. Fried by the instant voltage of Bobby Darin.

I made it to the Fine Arts on Beau Bien on automatic pilot. In the cold, depressing darkness of the mostly empty theatre I began to shake. It was more than just a decision to change the act: now he was ready to change his whole life, and had made it pretty clear about not caring if I was in it or not.

He has to replace me because I can't contribute enough musically, I thought. *It's my fault. I'm not a good enough musician. I'm not a good enough player. That's it, I'm still a beginner and he needs a pro. Nah, I was kidding myself. He sees me as a threat. His audiences were acknowledging me, and that was something he just couldn't stand.*

Was opening night really just six days ago? It seemed like forever. Amazing. In the space of six days, I'd lost my best friend to his career. Maybe I *am* too dependent on him, I never considered that before. Jesus Christ, I didn't plan to spend my life as Bobby Darin's accompanist, but I also never expected the ship to turn so drastically in such a short time.

I stared at the screen, hypnotized by the blurred images, watching nothing, hearing nothing, remembering.

I remembered how, after ignoring my parents' fears and warnings, I would take two subways to rehearse with him at his walk-up tenement in the South Bronx, where the lobby was filled with carriages and bicycles chained up to the walls and the hallways smelled of garlic and urine. I remembered the noise and bustle in his apartment, the radio blaring out loud music in the kitchen, and the kids, watching TV in the bedroom, sounding alive and vital—such a contrast to the monastic silence I lived in.

I remembered his beat-up, old set of drums and how all the differences in our backgrounds disappeared when we played together; and how easily we began to communicate through the language of music that we both used to express our feelings.

I remembered his contagious sense of freedom that not even the restrictions of his cramped environment could diminish; and his drive, and how I had become infected by it, wanting to be like him; and how even though his family was poor, they were always solidly behind him, and how it was possible to have nothing and still shoot for the moon.

I thought about the birth of our traditions, how after rehearsals, Bobby's mother would cook up a big pot of spaghetti for the band, and this had become a given— a spaghetti dinner after each job.

"Friends forever," he had declared, as I began to inch away from the narrowness that had dominated my childhood. I thought about how much I had believed in him, and how much I had *wanted* to believe in him.

"Bravo!" he had yelled after we sang together for the first time during a break at one of our band jobs. "Let's rehearse some tunes and do an act"; and then he and the act had become my passion. I remembered the look of exhilaration in his eyes when he discovered that I could accompany him on guitar and make him sound better, and it made me feel better than I had ever felt before.

Our worlds had been joined by the magic of music. My God, I realized that so much of everything I knew I had learned from Bobby.

And now it was all falling apart. And the fear was returning—the fear of being alone again. He had done so much to change my life, how could I go back to what life was before him?

But, now I had to decide if I wanted to stay in Detroit and be ruled by the dictator that he had become—or maybe was all along—or go home, tail between my legs, beaten. That's what he was *really* saying: that I have a choice of becoming a grown-up on grown-up terms—yes, *his* terms, at least for the moment, but not *kid* terms anymore—or just pack it up, and get out completely.

I surely didn't want to go home. Nothing could be worse than returning home in defeat. That victory for my parents would be intolerable. And what would I tell my friends? That Bobby fired me? How could I face anyone? Failing would mean that Arthur was right, that the civilian world was right, that nine-to-five was right, that straight-and-narrow was right. If I don't follow through on this, I'll surely be sucked back into that world, and that would be unacceptable at any price. No, I have to stay, that's all there is to it.

I couldn't help it. I started to cry. I must have been some weird sight, all right, sitting in that crummy Detroit movie theatre sobbing, blowing my nose, sniffling away like an old lady.

But whatever it looked like—and who the hell cared what it looked like—crying released some of the tension and my head cleared. *There was a little more than a week left,* I thought; *I'm going back to having a good time. I'm going to try and recapture some of the fun and excitement I felt when we flew out here. I just won't give him any reason for any encounter on the subject of the act. Whatever it takes, whatever he wants—I'll do what's necessary. I have to look at this positively, as a step to a new level, as an awakening. Was I strong enough? Dear God, just get me through the next week.*

 When the movie ended, I stepped into the brilliant afternoon, realizing that my life wasn't over. The next week might not always be as comfortable as I would like, but there'll be other things to do, like writing songs, and chasing Chris and Liz. I decided to put my energies into that.

Chapter 19

"A SIGN OF LESS TO COME"

"Yes, I do love you, baby, and I want it to work out for us, but what can I do? If you keep listening to your father, we'll *never* get to see each other. Sure, I loved your letter, and I'll write to you, too, but don't tell George you called, okay? It'll only aggravate things. Look, baby, we've been talking for over an hour now, and Steve just got back. Yes, I love you, too. Bye, baby."

He hung up. "Her goddamn father told George he's gonna beat me up if I come to the house again. Can you believe that? We have to sneak around just to see each other for *coffee!*"

"Connie?"

He shrugged. "Who else?" He picked up the paper.

I hung my coat in the closet and tried to choose my words carefully. "I thought about what we talked about. I would not like to go home. I would like to stay and help the act. I agree completely—it's your act." He said nothing. "But I want to say again that what happened wasn't my fault. It just happened."

After another deafening pause, he said, "Okay. I'm glad. I didn't want you to leave either. I had visions of lying down on the runway to stop the plane. Hey, how could I do 'Rock Island' without a guitar, right? I just couldn't help getting angry, but there was no other way to say it than the way I said it."

I stretched out on my bed. "No. There might have been a better way, but it doesn't matter now. We're in agreement."

More silence. "Your father called. He wanted to know why you haven't written. I told him you were too busy getting laid." I showed no reaction. "I told him everything was fine. He wished us both luck. I spoke to your Mom, too. I know you don't want to hear this, but she wants me to remind you to keep expense records, for taxes. So consider yourself reminded. Just don't discuss it with me 'til the end of the week."

"Did they want me to call back?"

"No."

255

"Thanks."

"Hungry?"

"No. Truthfully, I'm wiped out. I'd like to close my eyes for a while."

"Sure," he said, "I could sleep some more too. Connie wears me out sometimes."

You don't deserve someone as loving as Connie, I wanted to say. *She deserves someone who cares about her, and not just uses her.* But without another word, I closed my eyes and slipped into the black.

I passed my first Saturday night in show business trying to generate as much enthusiasm as playing on only three songs would let me. The Steve-less show structure worked well—the club was packed and they loved everything Bobby did. I took it as a sure sign of less things to come.

Near the end of Pearl's act, a huge wave of laughter suddenly rolled through the building. It was the sound of the unexpected. We charged into the wings to see what was going on. On stage, a fat drunk, waving a beer mug, was stalking her around the stage while the audience whistled encouragement. "I'll just lie here and wait for you," the drunk called, settling into the shell, while naked Arlene slinked away to safety behind the bandstand. John and Jake were there in an instant, each taking an arm and jerking the guy up, literally lifting him off his feet. But he was a really big guy, and broke away from their grasp and jumped back into the protection of the audience, just as the band segued to "There's No Business Like Show Business." I guess Tiny felt this tune was more appropriate to the moment than "Fine and Dandy."

"Arlene Stevens!!! The Birth of a Pearl!!! Ladies and gentlemen!!!" he shouted.

We moved aside to let John and Jake into the wings. Jake went back to the bar, but John stood next to us, catching his breath as Arlene took a final bow.

"Don't go way, folks," Tiny said as the house lights came up. "We'll be right back with some dance music, followed by our second show of the evening."

When she came off, roughly tying her robe with an angry tug, Miss Pearl erupted. "Don't ever let that happen again, you shithead motherfucker," she spat at John. "Never! You're supposed to control the audience, you cockless freak. You're supposed to be watching for shit like that! If that happens again, I'll cut your fucking balls off and shove 'em up your ass, get it? It'll be the last fucking thing that you ever do, you rotten motherfucker!" Then she stormed into her dressing room, loudly slamming the door behind her.

"*The lady has a unique way with words,*" Barry Fitzgerald said softly, "*and a nice, calm disposition, too, I might add.*"

"Save the humor for your act, kid," John grumbled. Then, "You did a good show. Best yet."

"Thanks. Coming from you, that means something."

"Now, take some advice: you did good 'cause there's a lot of people here. You'll do even better with more familiar material. People are more comfortable with songs they've heard before."

Bobby raised his voice as Tiny passed by. "John, you're reading my mind. I agree. I was thinking of trying some standards, following your advice about doing more familiar material, you know? How about a quickie rehearsal Monday afternoon? That way I could break in some new tunes."

"Rehearsal? Monday?" Tiny twitched, instantly a soprano. "Are you crazy? Forget it! You want to do something new? We'll fake it. Our contract calls for break time we don't get, rehearsal pay we don't get, and I can guarantee you that this band will not give up a Monday afternoon to rehearse an act that we've been playing all week that has no music to read anyway! Monday rehearsal is *out*."

"Hey, big man, did you hear the applause last show? Sounded pretty strong for an act that has no music to read."

"Listen, Darin, nobody says you're not a talented kid. You just expect everybody to break their chops for you all the time. Monday rehearsal is *out*," he gruffed, stomping away into the club.

John nodded in agreement. "No rehearsal Monday. Tiny can play anything. Just talk it down with him. With that guy, you'll find a little consideration goes a long way. That also works, I might add, with a lot of people."

Bobby was daggers again. "A little consideration? All I hear from you is *change this* and *change that*, and now when I'm ready to make changes, you tell me that I can't have a rehearsal. How about some consideration from management *to the act!*"

"Listen, Bobby, I got five hundred people to worry about tonight, not bullshit about rehearsals. There's no rehearsal on Monday, unless, of course, you want to pay for it. I can deduct it from your check, if you like."

That stopped him cold. John knew it, and walked away.

"Why are you fighting with him like that?" I asked.

"I just don't like being pushed."

"Nobody's pushing you."

"Hey, you just stay out of it, okay?"

"Yes, sir."

Andy poked his head into the dressing room, toothing phony-smile number five. "Picture time, star. There are at least eight tables that want to meet you."

"Pass," Bobby said.

"What? Why?"

"No pictures with customers. And that'll be policy for the rest of the engagement."

Andy's eyes narrowed. "What's on your mind?"

"Nothing at all."

"Don't hustle me, kid. You want something. What is it?"

"About those pictures you're going to take of us during the week? How about Friday?"

Andy was cautious. "Sure, Friday's fine."

"And just so there's no misunderstandings, those pictures'll be on you."

"Bullshit!"

"Andy, in case you're not aware of it, my contract doesn't require me to pose for pictures. If you like, I can prove the point, but then you'd have no one to take pictures with *tonight*. We've been very accommodating all week, posing with customers. I don't see crowds lining up for pictures with Clipper, or Liz, or the Pearl.

So, since we help you in *your* business, *you* help us with ours. The pictures we take on Friday will be *on you!* Get the picture?"

"I never give anyone free pictures," Andy said defiantly. "Maybe I can work out a discount."

"How much is the discount," I asked, butting in where I shouldn't, hoping that one of them would give.

Bobby cut me off. "Baloney to a discount. This is business. Either the pictures are free, or you're on your own for the rest of the engagement."

"Think you're a smart ass, huh? No pictures for free!"

"Don't be a schmuck, Andy. Tonight's your busiest night."

"Nuts!" he said, walking out.

"He'll be back. There's too much action tonight. I give him five minutes."

Two minutes later John walked in. "Andy says you want free pictures. That's out. He can't give them to you."

"Why not?"

"He makes it sound like it's his operation, but it's Mickey's. Andy gets a draw and a small piece, that's it. It ain't his decision to make, it's Mickey's. It's *policy*—no free pictures."

"So? Mickey will buy us pictures."

"It doesn't work that way, pally. There's an unwritten rule that says that acts, when requested, take pictures with customers. You've been requested."

"John, you're an intelligent man. Whoever owns the picture store is making money every time I sit at a table. What I'm asking for is not unreasonable. I need publicity pictures. It's tit for tat."

John shrugged. "I'll talk to him, but making waves is not smart. Owners are a tight bunch."

A few minutes later Andy was back. "There are some tables that want to meet you."

Bobby didn't budge.

"Friday'll be fine." Silence. "On me."

"Great! Let's go get 'em," he said, grabbing his jacket.

"I'll hang out back here," I said.

A few of the dancers were chatting in the wings. Chris wasn't with them. Liz was alone in the girls' dressing room at the long counter, legs crossed, polishing her nails; she was wearing the same style bathrobe she had worn at the Royal Palm, except this one was green. I remembered how soft it felt in my hands. I stood in the doorway, trying to rekindle a little. "Your hands are beautiful."

"Thank you. How's the songwriting coming?" She seemed friendly.

"Haven't had time. But it's coming."

"All good things take time."

"Thanks. Oops!" I moved aside to let some dancers pass. Chris and Myra were with them. I nodded to Liz, and then backed into the hallway out of her sight-line. I motioned for Chris to join me.

"How about some late dinner? Bobby's going to ask Myra."

"Bobby has already asked Myra," she smiled, "and I would be pleased. It's been a long time."

The late show was a bigger hit than the first. Sitting at the keyboard proved to be a good piece of business, giving the act a whole new dimension—he killed them with "Funny Valentine." Artie just slid over and stood against the wall, expressionless, looking like he was ready to take a leak. Having nothing to play, I stood at attention, hands resting on my guitar, trying to appear seriously interested.

"I'm sure you all know this next song, Tiny," he said, playing a Darin arpeggio, "so I know that we won't need a rehearsal. Pick up your licorice stick, Len, and wail along with me. The key is F major, or is it colonel?"

When he began "The Saints Go Marching In," the band recognized it immediately, and were up and freewheeling along, Dixieland style. I joined in, too. Now the crowd was really with him; and in the middle of the tune, Bobby brought Artie back to the piano for a solo while he improvised a soft shoe across the stage. Then he led everyone in hand-clapping, bringing his debut as a pure single to a roaring conclusion.

I felt like pure shit.

But Chris pulled me out of it.

In the taxi, going home from the House of Woo, I was in front with the driver and my guitar while Myra sat between Chris and Bobby in the back. The radio was tuned to an all-night music station. All of a sudden we heard "Rock Island Line." As the music became increasingly familiar, Bobby and I both bolted up. It was an unbelievable feeling.

"Hey, make that louder! That's me!"

That's my guitar leading the way for you, star, I wanted to say.

"This is so exciting!" Myra giggled, squeezing his arm.

As we all listened intently, Chris leaned forward and smiled. I reached over the back of the seat and took her hand. I got the feeling that she was genuinely happy for me; not just for the record or for Bobby—but for me.

"That's the first time I ever heard myself on the radio," Bobby said, after the record faded out without comment from the disc jockey, "except, of course, at a station during an interview. But that's not the same. How did you like the sound?"

"Oh, it was fabulous!" Myra said. "You're voice sounds so deep and full."

"That's what a professional recording does. I think the sound at the club is okay, but it's not like a studio."

"Oh, you sound great at the club too," Myra said.

"*I'm glad you think so, schweetheart,*" said Humphrey Bogart.

Chris squeezed my hand. "I thought the guitar sounded wonderfully, too,"

"Yeah, it did, Curley. What a great engineer that was, making that thirty-dollar guitar sound so big and full."

"Can we go to your room?" Chris asked quietly when we reached the hotel. "I told Myra that she could use our room for...some private time with Bobby. We share the room, so it's not all mine. Besides, I like Myra. She's just different from me, that's all, and...well...she's old enough to take care of herself," she added quickly.

My fires were lit. "No explanation necessary. I've been looking forward to this all evening. You'll be quite safe, and much warmer than out on this freezing street."

"See you later," Bobby winked, as we stepped off the elevator.

As soon as the gate closed, I kissed her. Not a long kiss, but not a grandma-kiss either. We walked down the hall with her head pressed tightly against my shoulder. Once in the room, I turned off all but the bathroom light. There were no objections. Wishing to avoid the issue of being on a bed together, at least for the moment, I grabbed two pillows and propped them on the floor. When she joined me without a speech, I knew that this was a very different woman than the one I had been with a few days ago. Maybe she'd taken some advice from Myra. I hoped so.

We began sharing very soft kisses. Her arms were around my neck. She didn't stop me as I gently tugged her blouse out of her skirt. "I've never done this before," she gasped.

"This is fabulous," I whispered.

"Have you done this before?"

"Never like this."

"But you have done this before. Is this like the others?" *What a time to start a conversation.* "Were there many others, Steve?"

"I'm only eighteen. How many others could there be?" I slid my hand up to her bra and fumbled with the catch. I don't know how she managed it, but all of a sudden her hand was on mine, holding me away. "Please don't," she gasped. With a mighty heave, she sat up and tucked her blouse back into her skirt. "We must stop. I thought I could, but...I just... I just can't."

"Why not?"

"I told you that I'm going to wait until I get married. It's not fair to go on like this if nothing is going to happen, and nothing is going to happen. After watching Myra, I thought that maybe I was too stuffy in my attitude. You must know that I'm attracted to you, but I just...can't go any further."

"Who's asking you for anything? We're only necking. You're wearing enough armor to protect a Sherman Tank. Come on down here. Nothing is going to happen."

"Steve, why is it that all men only want one thing: sex, sex, sex?"

"That's three things."

She turned on the dresser light. "If I stay here now, it wouldn't be fair to you."

"Chris, you're doing the same thing you did the other night!"

"I can't help it." She was moving towards the door. "I know you think I'm crazy, but Myra and Bobby will just have to find another place. I can't do this."

"Please, stay a little longer," I pleaded.

"I'm sorry."

She was gone. I checked my watch. We had been alone for a grand total of fifteen minutes. In the bathroom, I splashed cold water on my face in preparation for the return of a very unhappy Cassotto.

He walked in five minutes later—hair mussed, lipstick smudged around his mouth, angry and hostile. "Jesus, Steve, I was just about to make the big move when in pops Miss Chris! Myra said at least an hour. How come only twenty minutes?"

"Sorry. I moved too fast. It wasn't meant to be."

"You know, next time, damn it, take your time, even if you think you're going to strike out! Have some consideration for your roommate. Stretch a little!"

"There isn't gonna be a next time. I did my best, but she's unreachable, and as you can see, unpredictable. I seriously doubt she'll ever come into this room again. I don't know if I even want to ask her."

"Sure you'll ask her. You want to get laid, don't you? If you ask her right, we'll *both* get laid."

"Don't count on it."

"Well, that sure screws up my chances with Myra."

"Yeah, I guess it does," I said, undressing. "Look, I can't listen to problems about your sex life. I have my own, so I'll just say goodnight, okay? Goodnight."

I buried my head under my pillow, leaving the light for him to turn off.

Chapter 20

"JAILBAIT FROM McPHEARSON"

I heard a soft tapping. I looked at the window; it wasn't raining. Then a distant whisper. "Bobby? It's Fran." More tapping. Someone was outside our door. It was eleven AM, Sunday morning.

"Bob, you up?" I said.

"What's happening?" he mumbled.

"Listen! We've got company."

Giggles in the hallway, then a different voice. "Steve? Bobby? It's Fran and JoAnn." More tapping, then laughter.

"Holy shit! It's the jailbait from McPhearson. What'll we do?"

He sat up, and rubbed his eyes. "Invite 'em in. Let's see what they want."

"Are you nuts? This'll *end* your career! Pretend we're not here. Maybe they'll go away."

"What are you worried about?" he said, getting out of bed, running his fingers through his hair. "The Detroit police are all in church on Sunday morning. Besides, Chick is full of shit. They're older than fourteen. Maybe we'll get laid together. That would be an experience."

"Jesus! Don't...!"

Before I could finish my sentence, he was peeking out at the anxious faces of Fran and JoAnn. "*What are you doing here?*" asked Clark Gable, shooing them in. "Come on, quick, before we all get arrested." He turned the lock. Under their dripping raincoats, they were wearing very tight jeans and very tight sweaters.

"Nice Pajamas," Fran said, showing brass. "It's rain-check time." Then, as if she were reading my thoughts, "But don't worry about our ages. We're both over eighteen."

"You don't look a day over sixteen," he said, getting back under the covers.

"No really, Bobby," she said, trying to convince. "I'll be nineteen in August..."

"Yeah, and I was just eighteen," JoAnn added quickly, still standing near the door. Fran took off her coat, and sat on the end of his bed, every gesture and movement for his benefit. I was watching, too.

"How did you get in here?" I asked.

"Up the stairs," JoAnn blurted.

Both Fran and I shushed her at the same time, and we all laughed.

"Have you ever been up here before?" I wondered if they chased all the acts that appeared on Ted McPhearson.

"Never!" they answered in unison.

"We wanted to see you," Fran giggled. "For the rain check."

"Yeah, we wanted to see you," JoAnn repeated, looking at me, "for the rain check."

Bobby lifted his blanket. "Great! Come on under the covers." *He's lost his marbles! He's really going to try to bang her right here in front of us!*

"Sure," Fran said, kicking off her shoes, sliding under the covers, and putting her head on his chest. As soon as she was in place, she giggled again.

JoAnn giggled too.

Bobby tucked the blanket around them. "Hey, Curls, why don't you invite the lady to sit down?"

"Sure," I replied, unsure. This was very weird. "Come on over here," I said hesitantly, patting a spot near me.

JoAnn was hesitant too, but she inched over anyway, finally sitting on the corner of my bed.

As Bobby and Fran watched us, they started another wave of laughter. Then we all laughed. But I could tell that JoAnn wasn't having such a good time; in fact, she looked a little scared.

"So what's doin' in the funny papers, pussycat," Bobby said, rolling over on his side, ignoring us. With his back to us we were totally blocked out of the action.

When they began whispering, we couldn't make out any words, only the popping sounds of their lips. JoAnn kept staring at me, looking less brave by the minute. I smiled and tried to be reassuring. Why not, I thought? She was here, after all, and she kissed great yesterday. Suddenly, it didn't bother me at all that she might be underage—I'd never tell.

The moment our eyes made contact, hers darted away and looked out the window.

There was motion in the other bed. Bobby and Fran were already in the midst of a kiss. I could see his hand moving under the blanket. JoAnn saw what I was looking at and jerked up a little straighter. It was a Chris move.

"Is everything okay?" I mouthed, not wanting them to hear.

"Yes," she said, but then, after checking to see if they were looking, she shook her head *no*.

"What's wrong?" I asked, conscious of the moving bodies in the other bed.

"I'm just not used to such a public display," she whispered tightly.

"Me neither."

"Have coffee with me?"

"Sure." I decided to take a shot anyway. "But, let's lie down for a while. Then we'll have coffee."

"No, I want to go now. I can't stay here any more. Please. Let's talk downstairs. Please!"

"I thought that you came up here to...be close to us."

"Fran did. She's much faster than me. Please?"

I wondered if room 407 was just an unlucky room. Maybe in the entire history of the Wolverine Hotel no one had ever gotten laid in room 407. At least not on my side of the room. But there was no way I was going to pull this off anyway. "Okay, I'll get dressed."

"Thank you," she mouthed, visibly relieved.

"Hey, Bob," I said, full voice, "We're going downstairs for breakfast. Talk to each other for a minute while I put some clothes on."

I got out of bed, grabbed my chinos from the chair, and dashed to the bathroom. When I pulled them on I discovered they were Bobby's, so I put my pajamas on again, went back in the room, smiled dumbly at everyone, switched pants, then hurried back to the bathroom. Bobby and Fran had momentarily stopped. She was red in the face. "We're going down for breakfast," I repeated, running a comb through my hair. "We'll be in the coffee shop."

"*I'm not hungry at all,*" Clark Gable said.

"Me neither," Fran said, giggling.

As I unlocked the door, Fran winked at JoAnn. It was the female version of the Darin wink. I peeked down the corridor to confirm that the coast was clear.

"I'll meet you downstairs...in a little while," Fran said.

"Oh, don't worry about me. I'll probably go home," JoAnn answered quickly, sounding abandoned. "I have to meet my father, anyway. Call me later, okay?"

Fran nodded. Bobby licked her neck.

"Let's go." I felt like I was holding up the World Series.

I rang for the elevator. "Thanks for understanding," she said. Wow! Credit for *understanding* from a woman—I must be getting better. "I just couldn't do what she does."

"Then why did you come up here? You're not really eighteen, are you?"

"I'm sixteen. Fran's seventeen. We go to the same school. We just wanted to have some fun, that's all. But I had no idea that she was going to get so serious so quickly! And in front of everybody, too!"

"That's how I felt. How did you find us?"

"Oh, Bobby's clues were easy. We called a few hotels until we got the right one."

"Yeah, I guess they were."

She seemed shyly aware for the first time. "I liked kissing you yesterday."

"Yeah, I thought it was nice too."

"Do you have a girlfriend in New York?"

"No," I smiled, feeling a little sexy.

She must have sensed it, because she put her arms up around my neck and kissed me; it was the yesterday kiss—warm, juicy, and very exciting. She pressed into me. I ran my hand over her body. We were supercharged. When she began rotating against my chest, there was nothing on my mind except the wish that we had a place to continue this in private.

The elevator arrived at our floor.

We separated just as the door opened.

We were face to face with Chris and Myra!

Shit!

I nodded to both of them.

They nodded back, quickly exchanging wide-eyed glances as they examined JoAnn, who was busy adjusting herself.

I numbly mumbled a good morning, and guided JoAnn into the elevator, trying to stand erect without revealing the bulge in my pants. I was happy to face the front of the car.

Shit!

JoAnn took my arm and snuggled close. Should I introduce her? I blanked—I couldn't remember her name!

Shit!

I felt x-ray vision searing the back of my neck.

Double Shit!

After an eternity, the elevator mercifully reached the lobby. I stepped aside. Chris and Myra brushed past and walked into the coffee shop.

"Would you like to go to the Bagel?" I asked.

"Where's that?"

"Just a few blocks."

"Sure. But you'd better get your coat. It's pouring."

Shit! This would be a pretty dumb time to go back up to the room. Who knows what they'd be in the middle of. "No, that's okay. We can eat here."

"Anything wrong?"

"No, nothing. Nothing."

I led her to the farthest table away from the two Cuties. When I peeked around, neither was paying attention to us. They looked quite ordinary, just two women chattering away, but I didn't believe it for a minute. I was certain that every word they spoke was about me.

I desperately tried to concoct a plausible alibi. *She's my cousin.* No, that would never work. *She might as well be my sister*—Chris knows I don't have a sister. *She's a local guitar student wanting to learn the New York technique.* Too absurd. *She's starting a Bobby Darin fan club!* That's it! She came to see Bobby, and I'm taking her to a business breakfast while he rests. She was hugging me in the hallway out of gratitude for being the first Bobby Darin Fan Club President in Detroit. Damn! I could have introduced her—that would have been perfect!

The waitress took our order. As we ate, JoAnn told me the story of her life: how her parents were divorced and she lived with a stepfather who was always coming on to her. Then she apologized for getting me out of bed so early, and said that if I ever wanted to go out with just her—but not a repeat of the situation we'd just left, with a pre-conceived ending—she would like that. She wrote her number on a napkin. When she leaned over to kiss me goodbye, I was positive Chris and Myra were watching every move.

I was trapped. I couldn't go up to the room now anyway, so I decided to out-wait them, sipping coffee until they left. Just for an instant, Chris glanced back at my table. Her lips were tense, her eyes filled with hurt, or anger; I couldn't tell. It made me feel dumb.

But then, thankfully, they were gone. I paid my check and called Bobby on the house phone. "Sorry to interrupt. I'll be as brief as I can. I'm in the lobby, alone. JoAnn went home. It's raining and I don't have a raincoat, so I'm going to get the paper and hang out with the rest of the Detroit sleaze. When Fran leaves, tell her to find me. I'll be the third rummy from the newsstand."

"Thanks, Curley. You're the best."

"Yeah-yeah. This squares us for last night, okay? Enjoy-enjoy. One time for me."

I bought the paper, sat in one of the old, broken armchairs, and stared out at the rain.

Someone was touching my shoulder. It was Fran. I had

fallen asleep. I checked my watch—almost three o'clock. "I'm going home now, Steve. Bobby told me what a good friend you are. Don't mind JoAnn; she's just immature. Bye." I watched numbly as she skipped away, then I headed for the elevator.

Bobby was in the shower. "I'm back," I yelled, flopping on my bed.

"Only a blow job."

"Three hours for a blow job? That must have been some blow job."

"Can't hear you. These kids aren't any where near as brave as they pretend to be, especially when you separate them. She took plenty of talking-into. What happened with the other one?"

"We made it in the lobby, on the couch."

"What?" he yelled over the noise.

"Chris and Myra lent me their room. I bagged her there."

"What?" he said, turning off the water.

"She didn't like the idea of all of us together in the room. And truthfully, I don't think I could have done anything, either."

"Hey, what's the difference between a hotel room and the back of my car? I never saw anything stop you from making moves in the back seat of my car."

"That was only necking. I couldn't get laid in public."

"I'm public?"

"You're public."

"Ah, you're too inhibited, Goldilocks. You've got to go with the flow, loosey-goosey."

"You're truly amazing, Cassotto. I always knew you got laid a lot, but watching it first-hand has been quite an experience."

"Welcome to the road. You'll get yours. It's only a matter of time."

"Oh, I expect that you're right about that, but I could never handle your quantity of action. Maybe it's because I've never had a steady girlfriend, so I don't know what it's like, getting laid all the time."

"I never had anyone steady, either."

"Well, that didn't stop you."

"Right. It's rape and pillage until something changes."

"Like what?"

"Oh, one day, I'm gonna meet a girl who's so sweet and pure and unspoiled that she'll probably not want to have anything to do with me. But she'll be the one I marry. And she'll marry me too, because I'm gonna be somebody, and it's gonna be awful hard to say no to me. Until then, all of this is just rehearsal."

I was about to ask him if he thought Connie Francis fit that description, but decided against it. Connie was far above this conversation. "Yeah, well, I wish you good luck in finding her."

"Listen, I thought maybe I'd take Myra to the movies; soften her up for tonight. This is the perfect day for a room swap—we can start early. No shows, lots of time to make out. Get Chris on the phone. We'll double."

"She'll never come. She saw me in the elevator with the jailbait."

"Hey, ya never know 'til ya ask."

"Believe me, I know."

He gave the operator their room number. "Myra? Bobby. Yeah, I just got up. How about you and Chris joining us for a movie?" He nodded to me. "Oh really? Tell me." He listened. "Yes, he's here." He covered the receiver. "She says Chris is upset from your display of *insensitivity*."

"Go alone."

"Myra wants to be with Chris. It's *her* day off too, remember? Here, talk to her."

"I really don't want to deal with this now..."

"Talk to her!"

I took the phone. "Hi, Myra. May I speak with Chris?"

I heard her cover the receiver. Then, "She doesn't want to talk to you."

"Tell her she's blowing everything out of proportion. It was a kid about a Bobby Darin fan club."

She relayed the message. "She won't talk to you."

"She won't talk to me."

Bobby was scrambling. "Tell her it's Christian to be forgiving."

"I heard him," Myra said, and repeated his homily to Chris in my name.

She came to the phone. "Steve, after I saw you, I went to church, to pray for you."

"Thanks. What's wrong?"

"Going to church doesn't mean something is wrong. I needed the comfort of God. I went to confession, to confess my anger and my sins."

"Well, if you need an expert witness, I'll be happy to testify that you didn't commit any." I wanted to lighten this conversation. "Chris, please don't make more of this than it really is. That kid is starting a fan club for Bobby. She was so happy that she hugged me; that's all. Come on, go to the movies with us."

"I wish I could believe you, but I'm not that stupid. Why didn't you introduce her instead of ignoring us?"

"I was going to, but I didn't want to make a big deal out of it in a public elevator. And, honestly? I couldn't remember her name! Then, you were gone."

"Who was she?"

"I told you, some kid we met at the Ted McPhearson show who wants to form a Bobby Darin fan club. She hunted us down in the phone book. See, I didn't think that you'd understand."

"Wouldn't understand what? That you're lying to me?"

I'd had enough. "You're in the wrong business, you know? You should have been a nun. I've done everything I know how so you won't be so damn formal with me, but you don't trust anybody. So don't criticize what I do. Particularly since I was just *talking* to someone in an elevator."

"You weren't just talking! You're just an overblown New York big wind, Steve Karmen. Don't bother apologizing, it won't do you any good."

"I don't know where you got the warped Lorraine, Ohio, impression that I was going to apologize!"

"Don't blow it!" Bobby whispered, frantically. "Tell her you're sorry."

"You're an arrogant young man, with no sensitivity for anything except your own lustful desires."

"Yep. You're absolutely right, Christine. We have nothing in common. Enjoy your day." I slammed the receiver down.

"What the hell did you do that for?" he yelled.

"None of your business, okay?"

"Give me that phone," he growled, grabbing the receiver. "Room 714," he snapped at the operator. "Myra? I don't know what's going on with the lovebirds, but I sure would like to see you. Yeah, I know you don't want to leave Chris alone, but suppose I come up for a while. We can both calm her down a little; then the two of us can split, eat something, hit a movie, and be alone together. You want to be alone together, don't you baby? We have the whole day. Sure, they're old enough to work out their own problems, okay? That's great. Yeah, I'll be right up."

I found myself pleading. "Bobby, let's go to the movies, just us. Spend the afternoon with me. You can catch up with Myra later. Maybe Chris'll cool off by then and we'll all do something tonight."

"Shit no, pal, this is our day off—our first day off on the road. The sooner you and Chris get something going, the sooner we can start swapping rooms. I'll try to smooth things over for you."

"I'll do my own smoothing, thank you."

"I got it! *You* go to the movies. Then I can bring Myra down here. Later, we'll all have dinner together."

That was too much. "Absolutely not. You can change the act cause it's your act, but you don't have the right to change my life. I'm not gonna cool my heels in a movie or a lobby, waiting for you to get laid. No. The answer is no. I may not be a part of the act anymore, but as long as I'm here, half the room is mine, and I intend to stay in it. Chase your pussy someplace else."

His mouth tightened. "I misjudged you, Karmen. Keep the room. I can make out on my own."

"Oh, I'm sure you can," I said.

Part Three

DETROIT
The Second Week

Chapter 21

"THE WARNING"

In the space of one week we had become strangers sharing a room, but without the courtesy of strangers. The superiority in his voice weighted every conversation. The heaviness between us grew with each event. Things about him that I had once accepted as quirky or eccentric I found that I was now re-examining, as I was every aspect of our relationship. I began questioning his motives and calculating my potential reactions, guardedly uncertain of which Bobby Darin I would be dealing with next. Sometimes he still sounded like my best buddy—the one who always made me laugh, my mentor, my musical soulmate—but now, more often than not, he was Mr. Chameleon, his mood changing to suit the purpose of the moment.

I had spent the rest of my first day off from show business shuttling between the room and the coffee shop. I bought a book: *The Hoods* by Harry Grey, the story of boyhood friends on the Lower East Side who grew up to become gangsters, but no matter what changes took place in their lives, they always placed their friendship over any personal gain. Obviously, pure fiction.

Being alone also provided me with a chance to think—no Chris, no Bobby, no fights, no phones, no one to answer to, no required place to go or be. I even got a start on a new song: a love ballad, something that had never been easy for me to write before (I attributed this to trial by fire). Sitting alone on my bed, quietly strumming and scratching down ideas proved to be a satisfying way of facing the future. I'd always believed that the great love songs had been written by people who knew how to *feel* love and loss; not just talk about it. Maybe I was growing in that department, too.

When Bobby finally came home around midnight, he grumbled something about going as far as he could with Myra on the stairway, and then went to bed.

On Monday morning, the phone rang. I was beginning to hate the sound—each time it rang, something bad happened.

Bobby answered. "Yeah? Oh, hello, George. No, I thought it might be somebody else. No, that's all right, I always get up ten hours before I have to go to work. Know something, George? You're losing your sense of humor. Yeah? Word travels like wildfire?" He sounded pissed off. "Yes, *Mr. Scheck*, Steve is here. He sleeps in the same room with me, remember?" *You'd like to change that, wouldn't you, I thought.* "Yeah, we can talk." He paused. "Okay-okay." He covered the receiver. "Steve, George and I have to have a private conversation about a subject that you and I have already resolved. I would never throw you out of bed, honey, but would you mind going into the john and taking a shower? Or a loud dump? Sorry. He wants to be able to talk private-private."

"No problem."

I closed the bathroom door and turned on all the faucets. I flushed. Instant Niagara. The Rains of Ranchipur. Lookout, Noah! I wondered how many flushes it would take to use up all the water in Detroit. I slumped down on the closed toilet seat, enveloped by the steam from the shower. I flushed again.

I could still hear his voice over the waves. He was hot. "George, we've already discussed this. It's under control. Yeah, yeah, yeah. Look, just call Mama and tell her that you spoke to me, okay? Yes, that's all I want you to do for me at the moment! I told you I had everything under control, and I don't want to discuss it any more, okay? Yeah-yeah. George! Enough already! That's right." He slammed down the phone. "You can come out now. Sorry again."

I opened the door after one final flush. "I can always get a job doing effects for Metro."

"George heard about the hop and McPhearson. He wasn't too happy. At times like this, Buddy Baron sure sounds appealing—at least he's sympathetic to the situation." *That's me—the situation.* "Look, we're straight, aren't we? You understand the new direction, don't you?"

Is that what this is called? The New Direction? "No need to ask."

He touched all the bases. "I don't want any wars with you on *any* subject, so we're also straight about the room; it's your room, too. Jesus, I almost banged her on the stairway last night. I sure could have used..." Then he added hastily, "but I understand-I understand."

"I'm glad you do," I said, not giving an inch.

The phone rang again. He headed for the bathroom. "Answer. If it's business, I'm out. If it's pussy, I'm in."

Sure, now I'm your social secretary, too. "And that, folks, is how careers are born. Hello?"

"Hey, Man. It's Chick. We've got hops today! Is Bobby there, man?"

"Yeah, man. Hold on a minute. Hey, man, guess who's on the phone, man?"

Bobby took the receiver. "Yeah, man! What's shakin', baby? Another hop? Great, man! I love to hop-hop. Ready when you are, big C! Half an hour? Great, man! See you downstairs. Hey, wait man," he said. "If a seagull flies over the sea, what flies over the bay?" He waited. "A bagel, man. Get it? A bay-gull? Yeah-yeah. Okay, Chicker, see ya later." He hung up. "Mind if I take the first shower? He'll be here soon."

"The water's all warmed up."

I tried going back to sleep, but couldn't. It was lunchtime in

the coffee shop, and the place was a zoo. I looked for Myra and Chris, but they weren't there. I ordered a sandwich and juice to go, bought the newspaper and went back to the room. I ate. I brushed my teeth. I practiced fingerpicking. I worked on my new song until Brunhilda showed up. I brushed again while she made the bed. I now had the cleanest teeth in Michigan. I reread the newspaper. I was feeling guilt, or loneliness, or whatever. I called Chris.

Myra answered. "She's out."

"I was hoping to maybe smooth over yesterday."

"That may take some time, Steve. She likes you, but she feels hurt. She thinks you're too fast."

"Fast? Me?"

"She's angry about yesterday. I think she wants a little courtship before jumping in. She wants to trust you. It sounds funny but she's kind of old-fashioned."

"Did she ask you to tell me that?"

"No, but I can see what's happening."

"You sound just like Bobby."

"Is he there?" she asked hopefully.

"No, out doing promotion."

"Well, Chris is out and Bobby is out. How about me? Would you like to have coffee?"

"No thanks," I answered quickly. That's all I'd need, for him to find out I was talking to his girl. No, avoiding everything Darin is the smart move. "I have to practice guitar. I'll see you tonight, okay? Say, 'Hi.'"

"Sure. Say, 'Hi' to Bobby."

He was really up when he came in. "Man, the hop was fantastic! There was a piano. I did 'Saints' and 'Tutti Fruitti.' Killed 'em! Saw Ted McPhearson, too. He's got an afternoon radio show. Chick said the Decca distributor had a lot of calls this morning. A store in Windsor ordered fifty records. We're going out there Wednesday for an autograph party. I spoke to George, too, from the station. He's cooled off a lot."

I guess he thinks I should be grateful that King George has cooled off a lot. "That's nice."

"Anybody call?"

"Nope."

He began to change clothes. "What'ja do?"

"Practiced, wrote..."

"Steve, I know this is not what you expected, but I have to do promotion alone."

"I told you not to worry about it, so don't."

"Tomorrow, we'll go see Presley. There's a two-thirty show. Chick's getting tickets."

"Great. Wanna eat? I'm starved."

"Sorry. I ate with Chick. I'll sit with you, if you like."

"Nah, I'll grab something at the club."

"Chris's ass, I hope."

"Chris is a dead issue. But I spoke to Myra today. She likes you."

"Magnificent taste, the lady has," he said, now dressed. "Ready? Let's go."

There was no opening night excitement this Monday.
In most respects it was like last Monday: only three tables for the dinner show and a few strange types in the bar. I recognized our bakers, Heinrich, Fez, and Twirler, at ringside, back as promised, but this time with women (that explained why Fez wasn't wearing his fez). During the act, Clark Gable acknowledged their presence with a wink, but he seemed preoccupied, bored, strictly going through the motions. The lifeless sound of a dozen people knockering didn't help either—so different from the roars that filled the place on Saturday night. I was happy just to get through it; it was a step closer to going home. I was amazed at myself for even thinking that way.

Before Tiny introduced the Pearl, the women at Fez's table got up and went to the ladies' room. When the show ended, the three bakers were knocking on our dressing room door.

"You were absolutely wonderful, boys," Fez said. I couldn't remember their real names. "Your act has changed so *much* since last week. My wife, Rhoda, really liked the show, too."

"Were we that bad last week?" Bobby winked.

"No, of course not," Heinrich said. "It's just that you're better today, improved." Then, he added quietly, "And we drank a lot less tonight, you know, with the women and all. I didn't know you played the piano, Bobby. It added depth to the act. You're so talented. It's smart to show the audience your versatility. Take it from someone who's seen lots of acts."

"We've been experimenting with material," Bobby said smoothly, "changing things, switching songs, stuff like that."

"Well, you were both *fab*, really *fab*," Fez said. "Someday we'll be able to say we knew you when. And when is now. And now, we've gotta get back to the ladies. They would've come backstage, too, but they're still eating. Hope you'll come out to these parts again. You were really swell."

We shook hands all around.

"Sorry again about last week," Twirler said.

"Forget it. Just keep that bread baking. Thanks for coming, and for the comments." He continued toweling off after they'd gone. "Freddy Sharp really nailed it, didn't he? When it comes to show business, everyone's an expert."

"Yeah," I said. "I've gotta eat something or I'll drop. You want something?"

"No. I'm just gonna cool it. I don't have a lot of steam tonight. Food'll kill me for the second show. Eat light, and we'll Bagel later."

"Right."

From an empty table in the back of the room, everything was depressing. I gobbled a sandwich and watched as nothing went on, listening to John's gripe about the lack of business. I wanted to go for a walk, to escape, but it was raining. I was beginning to believe it rained every Monday night in Detroit. Each time I saw Chris, either backstage or in the bar, her expression was enough to frost Florida.

But when it came time for the late show, I was instantly alert. There, at the only occupied table in the house, were Monica and Carlo seated with Mickey and two other couples—different people from last week, but definitely relatives. I immediately went backstage to inform Bobby. He was alone in the dressing room with the door closed. He looked shaken.

"Monica's back."

"I know. I just met Carlo." A ludicrous vision of them shaking hands flashed through my head. *Hi, I'm Bobby. I've been fucking your girl. Hi, I'm Carlo. I'm going to kill you.* "I was taking a leak. He came in and stood next to me. When he leaned back to shake off, his jacket opened up, and I saw a great big gun in a great big holster under his great big armpit!"

"My God! What did you do?"

"Nothing. He didn't bat an eye, or even look at me. I pretended not to see. I just zipped up and left. I didn't even wash my hands."

"Didn't he say *anything?*"

"Yeah. He reminded me that employees must wash their hands before leaving the crapper. Of course not, numbskull! He didn't say anything."

"Nothing?"

"There were no words necessary, *pally.*"

"Maybe it was unintentional."

"Steve, those kind of people don't know from unintentional. It was a message, I know it."

"Did you tell anyone?"

"You're the first. Besides, who would I tell? What would I say? '*Oh, by the way, officer, while I was taking a leak, I saw a man in the crapper with a gun.*' Mickey's not going to do anything either. They're his friends. He carries a gun himself."

"How do you know that?"

"John told me."

"We're working in a shooting gallery!"

"It was a warning, all right. He knows something. Sweet Jesus, what am I gonna do?"

"First, ignore that whole table during the show."

"Steve, how can I ignore their table when it's the only table?"

"Play to the back like Liz does, and please, *please* don't come on to the broads. Do a short set and off. Avoid eye contact, especially with Monica. Then we'll disappear—nothing frantic, just a polite, hasty fade. What I don't understand is why the hell did she bring him here?"

"He brought *her* here, remember? She probably couldn't duck it."

"Let's just be out of here before the Pearl gets off. Okay?"

"No. Running is not the answer. They can always come to the hotel."

"Do you really think they would do *that?*"

"Steve, *they* would do anything! I've got to straighten it out. Do me a favor; go ask John to come back. Tell him it's important."

"On my way."

I waited in the hallway while John was in the dressing room with Bobby. Clipper came backstage. "What's up?" he asked, noting the closed door.

"Bobby and John. Business."

"Don't forget, good-looker, if you're interested in some real special action, just let me know."

He never quits. "Yeah-yeah, I'll let you know."

John came out and passed us as though we weren't there. I knew that Bobby wouldn't discuss anything in front of Clipper, but he seemed a little more relaxed.

"The hoodniks and their broads are back," Clipper blabbed, annoyed, powdering his makeup. "The same bimbo as last week. I recognized her tits." I glanced at Bobby—no reaction. "This is going to be death. We who are about to bomb, salute you."

Tiny filled the doorway. "Showtime. Short show. *Very* short show."

"How about a cancel?" Clipper pleaded. "Why do we have to do a show for eight people? Talk to Mickey. Talk to John. They'll listen to you."

"No cancel. I already asked. He wants a show. He pays the freight. Just don't do Mafia jokes."

As soon as we were alone, I asked Bobby what John had said. "He reamed me out for being so careless, but he doubts that Carlo suspects anything."

"And?"

"And nothing. That's it."

"That's it? *He doubts he suspects?*"

"If the man says everything's okay, it is. We've got a show to do."

"I hope he's right. I'm shaking so much...ever hear a guitar with vibrato?"

When the line was on, I looked through the peephole. Mickey's table was still the only one down front, but John had drafted some of the staff to sit further back, to keep things alive.

The hoods paid absolutely no attention. They ate, they drank, they smoked cigars, they talked to each other, but they didn't listen. Clipper zipped through a few parodies until there was a merciful "Message from Garcia." Then he introduced Liz, who did three tunes.

"A night to forget," she said, coming off.

"And we're about to begin," I said.

"Keep your chin up," she smiled, brushing her hand lightly across my cheek. It was the nicest thing that had happened all night.

"*Relax, Curley,*" said Robert Mitchum, stepping out of the dressing room, intruding on this moment, "I know exactly what to do."

I was sure he had lost it. As soon as we'd finished "Timber" he spoke directly to the hoods as though they were old friends. "Weren't you folks here last week?"

"Right," Carlo answered, after a long stare. "I remember you, too."

"Thanks for coming back tonight. Hey Pisane," he said to Mickey, "don't worry about anything. Your friends are safe. The parole officer just left."

Nervous laughter shot through the staff. "He's brave," said one of the hoods.

"We're all friends here. You folks just have a good time. If there's anything special you'd like to hear, let me know and I'll do my best."

"Sing a Sinatra song," Monica said. "You like Sinatra, don't you Carlo?"

Bobby must have confided his Sinatra obsession to her.

"Sure, a Sinatra song would be fine."

"How about 'My Funny Valentine?'" Bobby asked.

"No. Sing something *up*," John yelled from the back of the room, as if this was a family gathering.

Bobby turned to the band. "Okay, Tiny, let's do 'All Of Me' for the nice people, in the key of C, with a tempo like..." He snapped his fingers in rhythm. "A-one, a-two, a-three, and..."

With Len and Teddy ad-libbing behind him, Bobby began to loosen up, and pretty soon he was really singing out, pumping as though the club were packed. It seemed like every employee—Jake, the kitchen crew, the Cuties, Clipper, Liz, Andy—had taken a seat somewhere, and was watching. The only one I didn't see was the Pearl.

"Sing another one like that," John called.

"'I've Got You Under My Skin,'" he said to Tiny.

In the beginning, I tried to at least look like I was playing, but as the tunes got more and more complicated, I felt ridiculous, so I just stood next to the shell, at parade-rest, watching Bobby, trying to appear interested but wishing I was invisible. After a while, even the hoods were paying attention. Monica, whose face was only visible to the stage, appeared to be in ecstasy, batting her long eyelashes at Bobby whenever he looked at her—which was not too often.

At another table, Myra's face had a similar expression.

Chris was the only one who didn't appear thrilled by Bobby's performance. She sat attentively but unsmiling. When our eyes met, I nodded with as little head motion as possible. She turned away. The next time I looked out, she wouldn't acknowledge me at all.

He sang songs I didn't know he knew: standards, ballads, swingers, even "One For My Baby." It was Frank's act, except it wasn't Frank—it was Cassotto. The show was another milestone: there were only a handful in attendance, but he was singing to thousands. After forty-five minutes, he called for bows and received the best reaction of the entire engagement.

"Nice show," I said, joining him in the dressing room. "You really had everyone going."

He was furious. "Don't you ever make eyes at your girlfriend in the middle of my act, you hear? I won't put up with that kind of upstaging."

"What?!"

"Think I didn't notice? Just because you're not playing on every tune doesn't mean you have to upstage me."

"What the fuck are you talking about?"

"Were you or were you not making eyes at Chris?"

"She caught my eye, yes. Of course. So did Myra, and Monica, and everyone else in the room, I might add."

He was about to answer when Clipper bounced in. "Hey, Bobby, you were *fabulous*, really *sensational!*"

Switch. Mr. Cool again. "Yeah, Clips, it felt good to open up. The band wasn't half bad once they got going."

"I haven't seen a crowd react that way since I worked with Tony Bennett. You did yourself a lot of good tonight, Bob. You ought to think about including some of those songs in your regular act. Mickey was mightily impressed."

I heard Andy's voice in the quiet hallway. "Can I help you?"

"Looking for the singer," someone growled.

"Miss Carleton?"

"The kid."

I stepped to the doorway. Andy was pointing toward our dressing room. Behind him were the two other hoods with Carlo. One was tall and bulging, the other short but built like a tank. They both looked ferocious.

"You weren't too funny," the tall one said to Clipper, nearing the door.

"W...well, you know how tough it is being f...funny when there's such a small audience. But you folks were great! Just f...fabulous! What a gr...great audience!"

I instinctively took a few steps back as the Tank blocked the doorway. "Hey, Bobby Darin, you look like a smart kid," he said.

"Thanks," Bobby said politely, toweling off, not batting an eye. But they clearly had his attention.

"You do a nice show for a smart kid," the tall one added.

"Thanks," he repeated, his eyes now locked on the hood in the mirror, unable to turn away. I was quaking. *If they attack*, I thought, *I could hit them with my guitar. Then maybe Bobby would appreciate the value of always keeping it with me!*

"Be smart. Concentrate on your show. You'll go a long way if you save your energy for important things."

"You're right, sir," he said simply.

For a moment, Tank just stood there. Then he turned, and together with Lurch, walked back into the club.

Bobby was ghost white.

"What the hell was that all about?" Clipper asked, himself recovering.

"Don't know, Clipper," I said. "I guess they liked the show. You know, fans."

"With those kind of fans, you'd be a hit in Joliet."

Bobby grabbed his coat. "Steve, I'm ready to go back to the hotel," he said, avoiding everyone's eyes.

"We're going to eat. Join us?"

"Not tonight, Clipper," Bobby said quickly. "We've made other plans." He shot me a look, leaving no doubt that he expected me to go with him.

"Oh, sure, right," I said, "another night." I quickly packed my guitar.

Chris and Myra were in the bar, but he kept on walking, shaking his head, whispering *not feeling well* to Myra's questioning eyes.

"I'll try to call you later," I mouthed to puzzled Chris. She just turned away. In the taxi I wanted to calm him down. "Some food might make you feel better."

He didn't answer. Then, "Couldn't. Go without me."

"Nah, that's okay. I'm beat, too. I could use an early night. Do you really think they'll come after us?"

"Probably not. Do you realize what almost happened? My career could have been over because of a cunt, because of a goddamn cunt."

"Yeah, but it's not. And you learned."

"Yeah, I learned. Don't mess with what's theirs. Ever." He paused. "I hate those people."

He undressed as soon as we got to the room. He was short of breath, his voice weak and expressionless. "If I ever say to you that I'm going out to see Monica, you stop me, you hear?" Then, "Give me a hand, just in case." Together, we moved the dresser against the door.

He turned off the light and got into bed. "You know something? I'm glad we're sharing the room. Thanks, Curley. I knew I could count on you. I'd rather not be alone tonight."

"That's okay."

"'Night."

"'Night."

A few minutes later, I heard him pull the bedspread up over his head. He was shivering. "Jesus, I'm fucking freezing."

Chapter 22

"ELVIS IS IN THE BUILDING"

The electricity around the Fox Theatre was unlike anything I'd ever felt before. Held in check by wooden parade barriers that stretched all the way up the block and around the corner, a long line of teenagers of every shape and size stood six-deep across the sidewalk. There were thousands of them, all buzzing with a pulsating power. Clusters of squad cars, their emergency lights rotating dramatically, were triple-parked along the curb and across the street. Mounted police patrolled everywhere. Someone clearly had advance word about what kind of crowd control was necessary for an Elvis Presley concert. I'd heard about how the bobby-soxers had reacted when Sinatra was starting out, but seeing this first-hand confirmed that Presley's generation was breaking new ground.

We'd gotten some very strange looks from Brunhilda this morning as we moved the dresser back in place; but Bobby had assured me that if nothing happened last night, nothing would. I hoped he was right. I had offered to stay home, but he insisted I come along. "Presley is not business," he'd said, "it's entertainment, our entertainment. And Chick is taking us to lunch. A good way to save bucks."

The ticket-taker seemed to know Chick and handed him some stubs, letting us bypass the line. "Most of these kids are waiting for the five o'clock show. Elvis went clean for all three shows the day they announced. Thirty-five-hundred seats per. Have some hits, man, see what happens."

"Oh, I'm tryin', Chick. I'm tryin'," Bobby said, quietly impressed.

Near the roped-off section of the lobby some girls on line screamed. Thinking it was for him, Bobby turned to face his fans—but they were looking toward a side door where a few musicians were entering. "Amazing, aren't they," he said, recovering.

"Yeah," Chick said. "Especially if they buy your records."

We found seats in the center orchestra, about halfway back. By show time, the huge theatre was packed. When the houselights dimmed, there was a mammoth roar. I had no idea what to expect. The opening act was Elvis's backup band: piano, bass, drums, and three electric guitars. For twenty minutes they played loud country music with lots of amplified twang. For us, it was a whole new kind of sound.

"That picker didn't grow up on 138th street."

"That drummer never rode the D train, either."

Nobody really listened. The kids were here to see Elvis, and only Elvis. They twitched, they screamed, they yelled at each other over the music. If the backdrop stage curtain moved even slightly during a song, it meant that maybe *he* was behind it, and their reaction was deafening.

During intermission, groups of girls—thirty and forty at a time—began jamming the aisles, trying to get close to the stage. The cops were prepared and held them back. Then a stern voice announced that the show would not continue until the aisles were completely cleared. Reluctantly, the girls returned to their seats in the back of the house. But as soon as the lights dimmed, down they came again, encountering more police restraint, bringing on yet another announcement. This happened three times more.

When the curtain finally went up, the band was again in place, but this time at attention, waiting. A lone microphone stood center stage, bathed in a bright pink spotlight.

Shards of screams built and died in nervous anticipation, responding to the slightest movement on stage. I looked at the girls seated just in front of us. Their attention was so intense, so uncomfortable, so unsmiling, that each could only be absorbed in some very private and intimate fantasy. One was shuddering so hard she seemed near tears.

When, at last, Presley appeared—without an introduction, without walk-on music, just striding onstage, his guitar slung over his back—it was as if a bomb had exploded in the building. I knew then what Bobby was trying to accomplish (on a much smaller scale) with our opening—*his* opening. This kind of welcome was the dream of every performer: instant bedlam. I glanced at Bobby's face. His jaw was set, his grim eyes glued to the stage. "See? No walk-ons works," he shouted over the din, not looking at me.

Elvis was wearing a full-shouldered silver jacket that reflected the spotlight. As he prowled around, glittering with every movement, grinning at the screaming girls, I couldn't help but marvel at how his cockiness— raw and calculated at the same time—could bring on such an outpouring of passion from his audience. Each time he approached the mike to sing, the screams grew louder, more hysterical, more desperate. But this Southern hillbilly cat knew exactly what he was doing, and just to keep them guessing, he would back off again, teasing, swaggering, strutting, flashing his snarly smile, guitar still on his back, continuing his game of dare. When he leaned over to say something to someone in the first row, they went wild.

At last, with the girls in the audience literally sobbing in anticipation, he swung his guitar around and swiveled down into a performance position.

And then he sang.

"Well, since my baby left me!"

His knees exploded into a double bump as the band played two thunderous notes in sync with his movement.

Boom! Boom!

When I thought they couldn't possibly have gotten any louder, they did. He had to wait a full minute before singing again.

"I found a new place to dwell!"

Two more howitzers.

Boom! Boom!

Now the entire audience was standing, screaming at the top of their power, stomping their feet. Girls were jumping up and down, trying to see over other girls who were jumping up and down. We had to stand, too, just to see what was going on.

Bobby was watching everything through narrow slits, more observant than being absorbed by the fantastic force.

"It's down at the end of Lonely Street,
Heartbreak Hotel,
Well I feel-a so lone-ly babeh..."

It was quite impossible to hear him. When the band joined in and the tempo started, the crowd settled a little, but only until the next verse. Then it was up to thunder again. Chaos and pandemonium.

His performance never got better—it didn't have to. He had completely grabbed his audience with his first notes and then manipulated them to his will. It didn't matter that we couldn't hear much of his voice over the non-stop screaming. If we wanted to hear him sing, we could buy his records. No, we were there to *feel*, and feel we did. It was an hour of atomic energy that left us weak.

When he finally walked off, not to return, even though the kids continued to scream *moooooore* for five minutes after the house lights went up, I knew that I had been part of something very special. As we walked up the aisle, I felt alive, exhilarated, and empowered to seek new directions in my own music.

Bobby looked stunned and depressed.

In the lobby, we met Myra and Chris, coming down from the balcony. Chris looked beautiful.

"Well, this is a surprise," Bobby said without enthusiasm.

"Hi," I said to Chris.

"Hi," she nodded softly, not smiling. She sure was a master at holding a grudge.

"Wonderful, wasn't he?" Myra said, glowing.

"Yeah, great," Bobby answered, clearly envious.

"Bet you've got some new material for your act," Chris said to Bobby.

He glared at her sharply. "You never know, baby, you never know." Then he introduced Chick.

"Hi, ladies; bye, ladies. I'm gonna split, man. See ya, nine-thirty."

"Why so early?" Bobby asked.

"We do the Windsor morning shows. Don't worry, I'll get you home in time for a nap."

"Fine. And real big thanks for today."

"Me too," I added.

"Sure, man," he smiled. "Bye, everyone."

"Let's all go for coffee," Bobby ordered.

On the walk back to the Wolverine, Chris stayed by my side, but she wouldn't touch my hand. In the coffee shop, though she sat next to me, she kept to her corner of the booth, paying attention only to Bobby and Myra. Maybe she's just waiting for me to apologize—again.

All Bobby talked about was Presley, and the more he talked, the angrier he got. Everything became a comparison between the theatre and the club. He blasted the way the club ran its ads, his arrangements (*rudimentary* was today's descriptive), his stage clothing, the average age of Tiny's band, and pretty much anything else that was job-related. The bull was charging. "Did you see how the crowd reacted every time he moved his body? Fantastic! And his material was so different. Even 'Blue Suede Shoes.' He sang it like it was his own tune, not Carl Perkins's. Unbelievable!"

Myra listened, nodding along.

I said nothing.

Chris stayed out of it, too, eyeing me from time to time without revealing anything about what she was thinking, and turning away if I looked back at her.

"Working in a theatre is different than working in a club, isn't it?" Myra said, looking at me, smiling.

"Yeah. More people, more applause," I said, looking at Chris.

It was as if he had been waiting for me to say something—anything to give him a reason to release his frustration. He was at my throat instantly. "No, damn it, Karmen, it's more than that. It's *much* more! Now that kind of *jerk* remark shows just how little you know about show business. This was a *different* kind of audience than we get at the club. These are kids who buy records. They went nuts because they knew they could. They knew who they were coming to see. That's the power of a hit record and proper promotion. They loved Presley before he ever got out on stage. The club gets adults who don't even know or care who's on the show, and that's a fact of life. No, we get a *different* type of crowd and it has nothing to do with size. So why don't you talk about what you know, not what you don't?"

I got up. "I don't need a lecture just because you're not Elvis Presley, okay? I was just answering a question, just making conversation. Obviously you don't want conversation. You want a soapbox and an audience. Well, you've got one. I'm going up to change for work."

"*I'll* take the check," he snapped, with a wave of dismissal.

"Get a receipt! For taxes!" I shot back.

Chris followed me out to the elevator, and broke the ice. "Why does he treat you like that?"

"I don't know. But lately everything is a battle. And it's only getting worse. It's pretty clear how this week is going to end."

She took a deep breath. "Would you like to get together tonight?"

"Truthfully, no." She was as surprised at my answer as I was. "Chris, I'm just a little tired of trying to explain my life to everybody. You're awfully sympathetic when Bobby beats up on me, but when I look to you for understanding, if it's not exactly on your terms, you just kick me in the balls like he does."

"Well!"

"Well, what? Does the truth hurt?"

"My offer is rescinded, Mr. Karmen."

"Fine." She turned and walked briskly back to the coffee shop. *Rescind this!*

Back in the room, I stood under the shower trying to wash away my anger. He was waiting when I came out, still tense, still impatient. Without a word, he bounced off his bed, and locked the bathroom door.

"Wanna talk?" I asked when he came out.

"About what?"

"Presley was great, wasn't he?"

"We agreed on that before."

"So, I'm repeating myself. Doubles, you know? So I'm repeating myself."

"You're un-funny, Karmen."

It wasn't worth the effort. "You know something, star? You need more than new material. A new personality would be an improvement, too. You've forgotten that I'm your friend. Abuse somebody else, okay?"

"Fine," he mumbled.

"Fine," I answered.

The silent treatment continued through the cab ride and through getting made up for the first show.

When Clipper walked in, Bobby was staring at the floor, breathing deeply, psyching himself for combat.

"You all there, Bob?" he asked.

"Just warming up."

"There's a social club in the house, about fifty women. No jerking off on stage."

"No problem."

"Thanks, trouper, we're short on towels. Only kidding."

"I'm going out front," I said, not wanting to witness any more of his blackness.

Clipper stopped me in the hallway. "Don't be bashful, Steve. If you're not interested in this special action, just tell me. It won't go begging."

I was surprised at the strength of my own anger. "Goddamn it! Back off, Clipper, okay? If I want to make some moves, I'll let you know. I don't like being pressured, okay? I don't want to think about anything except the shows I have to do, okay? Get the message?"

"Hey, sure. If you want to be serious, be serious. But don't forget, there's a time for this, and there's a time for that."

"Thanks. I'll let you know," I said, heading into the club.

"Presley's killing business," John grumbled.

"Presley?"

"People watching that pervert can't be here at the same time."

"Oh, right." Bringing up the fact that most of Presley's audience was underage would have meant nothing.

We stood in silence for a moment.

"I'm going to get some tea."

"Drink booze. The bar could use the business."

Elvis was still foremost on Bobby's mind, too. He sang "Timber" with more body English than ever before, exaggerating even his normal grunts and shakes. This seriousness continued through "Rock Island Line." Then he turned to me, a look of rage on his face. "Gimme your guitar, Curley," he ordered.

I had no choice but to hand it over. I stood next to the piano, feeling naked.

"This afternoon, ladies and gentlemen, I went to the Fox and saw Mr. Hips. Know who I mean?" He held the guitar in position and rocked his legs.

A woman screamed.

"Somebody knows," he said, getting a big laugh.

"Sure, Pelvis," someone else yelled. There was applause.

"Shake 'em, honey," another lady called, breaking everyone up.

"Look out, sweetheart, here I come!" he growled, yanking off his tie and jacket, throwing them over to me, then straddling down in front of the microphone, mussing his hair, waving my guitar around like a toothpick.

My *guitar!* I winced. I couldn't watch. But I had to.

"Hey, man," he mumbled, pressing his lips directly to the mike to distort the sound. "No need to go all the way downtown. Rock 'n' roll is here at Club T." He began to mumble.

"MMMMMmmmmm, *well, since my babeh left me!*"

Bam! Bam! His legs quivered to the strum of the non-chord he played. They loved it. After two more minutes of mumbles—which even got laughs from the band—he took a deep bow, then walked off to big applause, tossing me the guitar on his way back.

I caught it just in time.

Now his entire attitude had changed; he was Bobby again. For the second half, jacketless, he sang "Funny Valentine" at the piano, "All Of Me," and "Saints," then exited to a huge hand.

"Presley stays in, it's a natural," he said, wiping his face.

"Take it easy with the guitar, okay?"

"Ah, don't worry about it. If anything happens, I'll buy you another one."

"Oh, *sure*, you'll buy me another! What the hell gives you the right to use my guitar as a prop? It's not a prop, it's a musical instrument that it took me a long time to earn the money for..."

"Yeah, *thirty bucks*," he sneered.

"Yeah, that's right, *thirty* bucks! You want to throw guitars around? Get your own!"

"How come every difference of opinion we ever have is based on something to do with money? Did you ever ask yourself that?"

"I don't have to ask myself about that. This is not about money. All I want is a little respect for my guitar."

"Bullshit! My Elvis Presley is based upon M–O–N–E–Y 'cause you're worried that I might not have the money to replace it if something happens." He paused. "What's the matter, don't you trust me?" he grinned.

"If I didn't trust you, asshole, I wouldn't let you use it".

"Yes, you would," he said quietly, looking in the mirror.

"Wanna bet? Wanna B–E–T? Wait'll you see what happens next time you ask for it onstage. You better think about what you're gonna do if I say *no*. Better think about *that*, star! Better *prepare* for it! I take a lot of pride in my instrument, regardless of what it cost, and if I let you use it, you'll have to absolutely promise to respect it. If not, strum your dick out there. That ought to get you a few laughs."

Instead of fighting back, he completely disarmed me. "What are you getting so pissed off about, Curley? Relax. Your guitar is safe. If you don't mind, I'd like to use it in the act, just for the Presley hunk, of course. I promise to take good care of it until I can get my own. Okay?"

I gave in again. "How can I say no?"

"I mean it. I'll take care of it."

Arguing was useless. "Please."

He stopped in the doorway. "Did you notice how the biggest screams tonight came when I did Presley? Maybe everyone's right: maybe I should switch to rock.

'Rock Island Line' never gets *that* kind of reaction, not in the club, not even at the hops. It's a different kind of music than what the kids are listening to."

"You wanna be a kid act, or work big clubs?"

"I've been thinking: maybe it's possible to do both. Nobody's done that yet, crossed over from rock on records to working big clubs. Maybe I'll be the first. Wasn't Presley's band great? Wouldn't it be great to travel with the same band all the time, the same rhythm section? What a great big sound! For theaters *and* clubs."

"That's 'cause everything's electric."

"Right, electric! And the volume controls the crowd better than demanding silence with soft fingerpicking." He looked at me. "Think you could handle electric? Maybe I'll write some rock songs."

"You mean after all this, you'd still want me to accompany you?"

Before he could answer, Myra walked by. "I'm going for coffee. Want to join me?"

"Sure, sugar. Think about it, Curls," he said, offering her his arm. "We'll talk more later."

I closed the door and slumped into a chair. Could I believe what I'd just heard? Does he really want me to play electric and stay with him? Or is this just his way of easing me out with an acceptable excuse? *Yeah, Karmen wouldn't go electric so I had to replace him.* No, this was the professional Bobby Darin talking. If I played electric, I might stay with the act a little longer, but the personal side wouldn't change. No, electric wasn't the answer.

He returned just before show time. "Buddy Baron's in the house. I told him I was thinking about changing directions, doing more teen tunes, and he got very excited. He wants to talk tomorrow, after promotion, so I'll be out for the afternoon. What about electric?"

"I didn't think you were serious. You've been hot and cold lately."

"Well, no need for a decision now. And speaking of hot, I won't be home tonight. Since Myra's room is unreliable, I called Monica. Carlo is out of town, for sure-for sure, and she wants me to come over. So our room is yours."

"Bobby, you're crazy! What about the goons? What about last night?"

"It's cool. Nobody'll know."

"Bobby, you told me to stop you if this ever came up again. Remember how you felt last night? Remember pushing the dresser against the door? Why risk your life when you've got a sure thing happening with Myra. Use your head. It's better; we'll swap rooms. I'll keep Chris out, I promise."

"No. Monica says it's safe, and I believe her. Use the room yourself. And think about electric. It's a serious offer."

As soon as the late show was over, I packed my guitar, said goodnight, and left while Bobby was still changing. Liz was seated at her usual table in the bar, but the touchy-touchy guy was with her again, heavy on the make. She was smiling at him. She didn't see me at all.

I was tempted to ask Chris and Myra if they wanted a ride home, but then decided this was not the night for making-up talk. Fuck everybody. They're all busy in their own worlds anyway. I hailed a cab, and was in bed twenty minutes later, longing for the sleep that would end this awful day.

Chapter 23

"PART OF THE BAND"

"I've changed my mind. I want you to sing all the songs with me, right by my side. It's more important to have fun and be friends than to fight about the act. The act works. If we change anything, we'll change it together, just like we always have. You sing the harmony; we're gonna have fun; you sing the harmony; we're gonna have fun; you sing the harmony…"*

Then I woke up.

Drenched with sweat.

Out of breath.

I glanced at his bed. Empty. I wondered if he was safe. Why do I feel this way?

I needed to talk to someone. I called Chris. Maybe she'll be more forgiving in the daylight.

"Hi, it's Steve. Did I wake you?" I asked. "Would you like to bury the hatchet and have breakfast with me?"

"No and yes," she said.

"Meaning?"

"No, you didn't wake me, and yes, I'd love to have breakfast with you."

"Great. Fifteen minutes?"

"Make it a half hour. I'm still in bed."

I resisted a corny comment. "Right. Half an hour."

As I hung up, Bobby walked in, a flurry of motion, throwing last night's clothes into the bottom drawer. "I'm gone for promo. If Buddy calls, take a message. It's for sure-for sure: he wants to manage me. Told me last night."

I stayed in bed, watching. "What about George?"

"Well, obviously nobody in the business has ever thought about regional representation before. I think it's brilliant. George is there and Buddy is here, two

305

managers; two separate people doing two separate jobs in different parts of the country. Twice as much effort. It's a smart idea."

"Yeah, at twice the price. But," I added hastily, "it's your decision."

"Correct. And just for your information, Buddy also thought there was too much of you in the act, so that's two people who had the same opinion. One confirms the other. See, it works already."

"I thought we'd settled that…"

"Yeah, but there's one more change, under the category of trying things out. Buddy insisted, and I agree: I want you on the bandstand before I'm introduced. I'll walk out alone. Makes more sense. We'll try it tonight."

I had expected this move. "Whatever you say. But, you might think twice before pissing George off. Buddy Baron may sound great for the moment, but New York is New York, and Detroit is Detroit. They build careers in New York—they build cars in Detroit."

"Take you long to think that one up?"

"Bobby, if two managers was such a great idea, other acts would have done it before. Also, if I had a manager who had gotten me a record deal and busted his ass to get me club bookings, I wouldn't be so tempted by the first fast-talker who came into the joint. Whatever happened to loyalty? You might as well make John your manager, too. I mean, Jesus, he has an opinion, too, right? Why not cut *him* in for a piece. You'll probably be the only act in America that owns two percent of himself."

"You're awfully nosy, you know? It just so happens that John DiCicci is a very knowledgeable person about show business, and he probably will help Buddy with my management. He knows every club owner in the Midwest."

"Do you realize how crazy this sounds? You're going to let a glorified bouncer manage your career?"

"He's a maitre d', not a bouncer."

I sat on the side of my bed. "Oh. Sorry. Excuse me. "

"Thanks for being so supportive," he said.

"You're right. I'm butting out. No more arguments. There's no point. It's your decision."

"Exactly." He checked his watch. "Chick'll be here any minute. Is this a good time to talk about electric?"

"Oh, sure, why not." I swallowed hard. "I've decided, when this week is over, I don't want to work with you any more. Not electric, not acoustic, not folk, not anything. I can't."

"Okay," he said, continuing to dress. "We'll always be friends."

"That answer is much too simple. Wanna listen for a minute, so I can tell you why? Or do you want to do this another time?"

He stopped dressing, took a long look at me, then sat on his bed. "Go."

"I don't think you understand what's really happened here this week. You need someone who's willing to change directions every time the wind blows a new style into your head, and that's fine; that's your call. And it's not that I can't change musically; that'll just take practice—and I don't mind the practice if I can contribute something. But my opinion has to matter. When we came here, we came *together*, with an act we'd developed *together*. Now, you're making all the decisions by yourself. You never even consider that I might not agree with you. I think I'm entitled to my opinion since we planned everything together. Without it, there's no point in my being here."

"Okay. What's your opinion?"

"Well, for one thing, I think you're antagonizing the wrong people. This business about two managers is not smart. It serves no purpose when you blow off the people who've been trying to help you."

"Like you?"

"Yeah," I said plainly, "like me. And like George."

"Screw George for this conversation. He doesn't need you to defend him. Stick to yourself. You expected to be more a part of the act, and you're sore because you're not."

"Well, maybe...I guess I *wanted* to be, or *hoped* to be, or whatever. I came out here to play on every song. I like singing harmony parts, standing next to you, it was

fun...anyway, it used to be, 'cause that's how we've always been doing it."
Amazingly, I felt very calm at this moment, speaking my mind. "But that's not
why I'm sore. And I'm really not sore anymore. We came out here to learn, and
boy, are we learning! I'm really a songwriter, anyway, at least I want to be. But, for
me, the big thing is that we came out here as *friends*. Now there's a side of you that
doesn't care about anything except climbing the ladder. I never saw it before."

"So?"

"So when my opinions don't count for anything, that's not a friendship, that's an
employer-employee relationship. I'm not your employee, Bob, I never was, I
never will be. I'm your accompanist. And I thought I was your friend."

He was speaking simply, too, without anger, just stating facts. "In the cold light
of day, Steve, in the real business world, the fact is you are my employee."

I shook my head. "Then only for this week." I waited. He said nothing. "And I
wish you the best."

The phone rang. It was Monica. "This won't be long," he said.

"Go ahead, take your time. We've said everything." I went into the bathroom
and washed my face.

His voice was cold. "Listen, baby, I have something to tell you, and I hope you
understand: we can't make plans to travel together. Yes, I know what I told you,
baby, but...well, it's impossible for now. And I can't see you anymore this trip
either. I'd rather not tell you why...Monica, after I left this morning, I stopped at
my manager's office, and he told me that somebody called him—somebody knew
I was with you last night! I know Carlo's out of town, but somebody found out!
Maybe he's having you followed, or me followed, I don't know, but I do know
that we can't see each other until this thing cools off. No, I can't call either. That
would be dumb wouldn't it, if Carlo answered? I know you are, and I'm rooting
for you to do it. I hope you can. But for now we have to cool it. I don't even like
talking on the phone. It's not good for either of us, baby. Yes, I'll write as soon as
I get back to New York. I know you do, baby, but I can't say those words; it'll only
make things worse. Please try to understand, baby. I have to go do promo now;
they're waiting. I'll write to you soon, very soon. Yes, baby, of course. Bye. Bye."

I came out of the bathroom. "I couldn't help hearing. Why didn't you tell me
that someone was watching? Jesus, what are you going to do?"

"Relax. I made it up. In fact, the story was Buddy's idea. He thinks that only bad could come of it. Besides, she was getting very clingy. This was a fast way to end it."

"You're really unbelievable."

"Look, Steve, let's not whip this one now. Let's just get through the next couple of days, then we'll have a chance to talk it out when we get back home, okay?"

"Whatever you say. But now you know where my head is."

"Right. I do."

Twenty minutes later, Chris was sitting across from me in the Wolverine coffee shop. She was all pink and shiny. Her eyes twinkled. "I was surprised to hear from you, especially in the daytime," she began.

"What's that supposed to mean?"

"Don't get mad. I thought I'd have to form a Bobby Darin fan club for you to pay attention to me."

"I told you that was nothing..."

"I know. I'm just making a joke. Skip it. I'm glad you called."

"We're past all that, right?"

"Yes," she said. "Are you okay?"

"I just needed someone to talk to."

"I'm here," she said softly.

I decided to unload everything. "I think it's pretty obvious what's happening on stage. I can't control that—it's his act. But our personal life is...well...our friendship is...it's changed. Nobody knows this, so please don't tell *anyone*, not even Myra..." She nodded, absorbing every word. "He fired me the other day."

"No!"

"I know; I couldn't believe it either. He accused me of hogging his act at the hop, and again on McPhearson. It's absolutely not true: I couldn't help what happened."

"What happened?"

"Oh, the deejays talked to me on the air, asked me to sing, and it took attention away from him. Then last night, we had another argument about him using my guitar in his Presley imitation."

"Steve, Bobby has been using you. You're just not seeing it. I wondered when it would come to a head. Do you remember the first night we met?"

"The night I didn't recognize you?"

She smiled. "Yes. I'll never forget that night. I saw it then, how you were the straight man for his jokes, laughing in all the appropriate places, exactly when you were supposed to, exactly when he wanted you to. And it's all proving itself."

"I don't get it."

"You know, for someone so talented, you're so naive. You'll have to face facts sometime. The job may have started as two friends doing an act together, but it's turned into a test of your friendship—*much* more than which songs you sing or play on. It's obvious how he feels about you by the way he introduces you for your bow. The caring and sincerity of the first few days are gone. There's a slickness to him now that I honestly don't think is attractive at all."

"You see it too! I didn't think that anyone could notice."

"Of course, I see it. You learn a great deal about people when you watch them perform every night. Myra noticed it first. She really likes Bobby. Why, I don't know. They must have things in common that... Myra says...well, that's another subject."

"You watch the act every night? I've never seen you there."

"Every show. Myra too. We watch from the side, back out of sight. Bobby has changed. And so have you. You're frowny lately; you always look worried."

"Not on stage," I said, defensively. "Well, it's been tough looking delighted when there's nothing to play."

"No, not on stage," she said, "although your smile is a little more forced than it used to be."

"I never thought things would end up this way."

"If you ask me, you'd be better off on your own. You said you might want to try it someday; maybe that someday is here. I wanted to tell you that earlier in the week but your head was too filled with...with other thoughts to want to hear it."

"What I don't get is that I've known him for years and years—all the way through high school. We've been like brothers, best friends. All of a sudden he's treating me like...like a threat."

"Maybe the friendship wasn't quite what you thought it was in the first place."

"That's impossible."

"Why?"

"It's just impossible, that's all. We've been through everything together. He's my best friend."

"Do you ever wonder if you're *his* best friend?"

I paused. "Oh, I...well...if he has a best friend, I'm it...but I don't think he has a *best* friend, not in the sense of how you mean best friend. Bobby has lots of friends."

She kept probing. "Are you just one of his friends, or do you think that you're special?"

"Of course, I'm special, I think...I know I'm...that he...if I have to answer that question, then..."

She reached across and took my hand. Her touch was warm. "You don't have to answer. It's just something to think about, that's all. You have a very tender side, if you would only show it more. Pray to God for help, Steve. He'll understand." Her sincerity was overwhelming, as though she were on a mission to help another human being in trouble. "With God's help, you'll grow through this experience."

She was gazing angelically into my eyes. I didn't want to break her mood, but I couldn't help thinking that after all this religious revealing and sharing, she might be ready for some serious moves. And there's an empty room upstairs.

"Chris," I asked as gently as I could, not wanting to scare her, "how 'bout coming up to my room? Bobby's going to be out all day, and we can continue this conversation in private."

"I'd like that..." *This is it! At last, it was all going to work!* "...but I promised to go shopping with Myra. And truthfully, I'm not sure I could resist you. I have no plans tonight, though."

Crushed and then saved. "Sure. Tonight'll be great." *There must be something wrong with me, I thought. Somehow the physical part of my relationship with Chris didn't seem so urgent anymore.*

"Tiny, I want you to set up a stool for Steve behind the piano."

"It's too tight back there."

"Steve is skinny."

"Where he is now is the best spot for him."

"I want him on the bandstand, as part of the band when I come out," Bobby ordered. "Move some things around if you have to, but make room."

"There's no room."

"And when I finish, wait a second before introducing Arlene so he can come off, unless you want him up there while she's on. He won't drool much."

"There's no place for a stool."

"It'll fit very well right next to Artie. Of course, you don't have to do it, and then I'll ask John. And if he can't get you to do it, I'll ask Mickey. So, as a wise man once told me, 'save yourself a confrontation.' Just put a stool next to the piano."

"I'll see what I can do," he said, fuming, waddling away, pissed.

"And move his microphone, too," Bobby called after him.

"There's no need to wear makeup," he said, as we dressed. I had figured that out already. When it was time to go on, we stood in the wings, together as usual, and waited as Clipper finished his last hunk. "As soon as he begins my intro, just walk out and sit down."

I put on my serious-artist face and squeezed behind Larry to get to the barstool next to the piano. Artie looked up, surprised. Tiny paid no attention, but he hadn't forgotten to move my microphone.

While Bobby was down front trying to figure out who he was, I was on the bandstand learning who I wasn't. The show was a blur as I sat quietly during the songs I didn't play. When it came time for the Presley bit, Bobby came back to the bandstand, did some shtick with Larry, and just extended his hand. I passed him the guitar without comment. The imitation killed them again. When he walked off, I waited until the blackout and then eased out, just avoiding Pearl in the darkness.

"How did that feel?" he asked in the quiet dressing room.

"Like I was part of the band. Is that what you want?"

"Yeah, much cleaner. Let's keep it that way."

"Fine."

John passed by. "Good show, Bobby. You learn fast. Come out front when you're ready. There are some people who want to meet you."

"Be right out. I appreciate your understanding, Steve. I really do. This is break-in country. I have to try new things. I promised George I would."

"Did you speak to him?"

"Yeah."

"Did you tell him about Buddy Baron?"

"Not yet. That's a face-to-facer."

"Did you tell him that I'm not going on the road with you any more?"

He paused for a moment. "Yeah. But if you change your mind, there'll always be a place for you in my show. And it doesn't change our relationship. I hope you know that."

"Sure," I said. "Seeing Myra tonight?"

"Yeah, she missed me. Absence makes the heart grow Henry."

"I'd like to use our room for a while, assuming you want to be alone with Myra, too."

"Chris?"

I nodded.

"Hey, maybe I was wrong about her. Absolutely."

I decided not to answer.

"Well, I'm off to mingle."

I changed my clothes and got some tea from the bar. Bobby was in his element, working the room, posing for snapping Andy, smiling at everyone.

Liz was talking to some customers as I headed backstage. She excused herself and followed me. "Got a minute, Steve?"

"Sure. What's up?"

"I've been wanting to talk to you, but you're always so busy." She seemed very friendly.

"I've been hitting the sack early."

"This time I'd like to ask for some of your advice," she smiled. "I thought you might be able to help me."

"If I can..." We stepped into the wings.

"I'm thinking of coming to New York to look for work. And a record deal."

"That's great. Tea bags and all?"

"Tea bags and all. I hope I'll see you there."

"I guess so," I said, hearing a warning voice in my head. Somehow, Liz belonged in Detroit, not New York.

"I don't know if I told you this the other night, but I think you're really special. It's been a great engagement watching you."

"Thanks. You'd need binoculars to see me now."

"I guess changes are natural when you work with a partner. I've always been on my own so I wouldn't know about that. Steve, what I wanted to ask you was do you think you and Bobby could introduce me to some of the agents in New York?"

"Well, I don't know many myself. I've always left that kind of stuff up to George Scheck, Bobby's manager. I guess you could call him. He was here last week. He saw your act. Maybe he could introduce you to some club date agents."

"That would be wonderful. Do you know of any reasonable places to stay? Got a friend who wants a roommate for a few weeks?"

"Gee, no. Sorry."

"Do you have room at your house?"

"Are you kidding?" I laughed, thinking of how my mother would react if I brought Liz home to live with us. "I live with my parents. Can't help you there. Sorry. Bobby lives at home, too."

"I wanted to talk to you about it because it would be nice to know someone there, you know, someone to turn to. I hope I'm not imposing..."

"No, not at all. But I have to get ready for the show," I said, looking for a polite out. "You know, Bobby's friend Donny Kirshner wants to get into personal management. He's a sharp guy. Maybe you could talk to him."

"That's a good idea."

"Well, see you later. If I can help, of course, I will."

"Thanks," she said, moving very close to me, so close that I could smell her perfume. "Would you like to come by after work and...we can have some tea and talk some more?"

Holy shit! It was a direct invitation. The groping of our first encounter flashed through my mind. Then I remembered Chris.

"Wow, Liz, that would sure be nice. Lemme see what Bobby has planned. You know, with all the changes in the act and all, we usually discuss things after the show."

"Well," she smiled again, "tea is always easy."

Wow, I thought. Wow!

"Be on guard," I said to Bobby, back in the dressing room. "Liz wants to come to New York, and she hit on me for a place to live. She wants advice—about agents and stuff like that. She'll probably hit on you, too."

"She did already."

"Oh."

"I told her to look me up when she gets to town. I guess she was probably covering herself by asking you, too."

"Oh, probably, right. Well, I thought I'd mention it. Just for information, you know."

Second show, I was a little more at ease at my new secret-service post. These are my dues, I thought. I should really follow Chris's advice, learn as much as I can, then go out on my own. I was beginning to really like her. She's got a good heart under that nun's habit.

I waited while Bobby changed, then we walked out front together. Chris and Myra were waiting in the bar.

So was Liz. A week had passed since I'd been in her room. I smiled at her as we all left. "Have a nice evening," she said, a bit coolly, I thought.

Clipper was already at the Bagel with Laurene, whom I hadn't seen in the club all week. He invited us to join them, but Bobby led us to a separate table. "Enough showbiz for one night," he said under his breath.

"Did you know Clipper before this engagement?" I asked.

"Not directly," Myra said, "But I've heard that Laurene isn't really his wife. She kind of just lives with him."

"Really?"

Chris noted my reaction, somewhat with displeasure.

"Yeah," Bobby said, taking Myra's hand, "maybe he likes to have somebody close to him when he's on the road."

Myra smiled. I looked at Chris. She was quietly shaking her head.

"I'm beginning to like you, Steve Karmen," Chris sighed as I closed the door to our room.

"It's about time," I said, turning off the light. "Look at all the good things we've been missing."

"It's very dark," she whispered.

"We'll talk in Braille."

"Could there be just a little light. I want to see your face." I opened the bathroom door a crack. "I have a big favor to ask. I want to stay here tonight. I told Myra that she could have our room for some...privacy with Bobby. Would you mind if I napped on the other bed? I don't want you to think I'm teasing you. I'll be completely dressed. I'd like to believe I can trust you, or I won't stay. Can I trust you? Really?"

"Yes, you can, Chris. I promise not to do anything that you wouldn't want me to do."

"Are you sure?"

"Yes, I'm sure. But don't sleep in that bed. Sleep here, next to me. I won't make any moves, I promise. It would just be nice to hold you."

"I've never slept with anyone before."

"Neither have I, though I wouldn't exactly call this *sleeping* with someone, not in the biblical sense anyway."

"What would you call it?"

"Two friends with an agreement. Like summer camp."

"Promise?"

"Promise."

"Will you keep your clothes on?"

"Absolutely. T-shirt and shorts. Okay?"

"Absolutely not. If we're going to do this, I want you to be fully dressed."

"You mean I have to leave my socks on?"

"You know what I mean. Dressed, at least with your pants on."

"How about pajamas?"

"Street pants, or I won't stay."

"Okay. I'll be right back."

In the bathroom, I washed my face, brushed, and then added some Old Spice for effect. I pulled on a clean t-shirt, then my jeans, which were so tight that if I did get an erection, it would probably kill me. For safety, I left them unbuttoned.

"You sleep under, I'll sleep on top," she said. "I'll use the spread as a blanket."

"But..."

"No buts. Please lie down."

I did as she directed and she tucked me in, motherly-like. Then she laid down with her back to me, covering herself with the spread.

"Good night, Steve."

"Good night, Gracie."

I turned and put my arm around her, but she moved it away. "Please relax," I said, "It'll be more comfortable for both of us. I couldn't possibly reach any part of you through all this clothing—plus the sheets, plus the blankets, plus the bedspreads."

She took a deep breath. I moved closer. We lay there, motionless, clothing-to-clothing, blanket-to-blanket. As her breathing became less guarded, mine did too. I asked what she would have done if I had said she couldn't stay.

"I knew you wouldn't say no," she laughed.

She was right. With my face nuzzled into her back, we began whispering like two kids. I told her about Arthur, and sleeping in the kitchen, and about growing up in the Bronx, and she told me about her family and her first club job.

In one respect it was time to accept the facts: any fantasies I had about her would surely remain just fantasies. Chris Evans could probably never be Mrs. Christine Karmen. There were too many distances between us—both geographically and religiously. But, she was a genuinely nice person with a good heart; and starting to be real fun to be with. As we dozed off, I thought that tonight was a step closer.

To what...I still had no idea.

Chapter 24

"BOBBY'LL BE A LITTLE LATE"

The door burst against the chain. "Hey, Steve, it's me. Lemme in."

"Just a minute," I yelled, untangling.

Chris bolted up, stood quickly, fussing frantically with her hair. I unlocked the door. "What time is it?" she asked.

"Seven-fifteen," Bobby answered before I could, looking at neither of us.

"Oh, it's late...I mean...early, I mean...I'll see you both...tonight," she said. "Thanks, Steve, for..."

"Right," I said, cutting her off, trying to ease any embarrassment.

"Good night...I mean, good morning," she said, dashing to the stairway.

"'Night," I called.

"'Night," Bobby repeated, a little too cutely, throwing his clothes on the chair. "Well? How was it?"

"Fine."

"Dressed?"

I pulled off my jeans and got back into bed. "Yeah, well..."

He went into the bathroom, took a leak, and washed his face. "Home run."

"What?"

"Myra. Home run."

"Good for you."

"She's got lots of potential."

I said nothing.

He got into bed. "Eventually they all come around, Curley. You could even make it with Chris if you did it right."

"Bullshit. You don't know anything about her. How come you always measure a girl by whether she puts out or not? Chris happens to be very nice, even though she doesn't put out. Besides, I don't think I could be involved with someone who'd just jump in the sack with me. I'll leave that kind of action to you and your road career."

He grinned. "You falling for her?"

"No. I just don't think it's necessary to knock her because she doesn't put out. You falling for Myra?"

"Think Myra's a slut?"

"Jesus, I never said that."

"You implied it."

"Well, she's a lot easier than Chris, that's for sure, assuming you're telling the truth."

"Think I'm bullshitting?"

"No, I take that back. But, if everything was so *wonderful*, why'd you leave so early?"

"Ah, she felt guilty keeping Chris out after the sun came up. But the sun did come up, and it was long enough, thank you."

"You're welcome."

"Do I detect a twinge of jealousy, ol' Picker?"

"Jealousy? God, no. I'm fucking bored—bored with your home runs."

"Yeah, well, three more days and we'll be back in New York, and you won't have to deal with this anymore."

"Sounds great. Can't wait."

"Nice rhyme," he said, turning over.

The phone rang at one-thirty.

"Yeah, Chickadee, what's up? I'm up. I'm always up, man. Sure. Half an hour? Great. Gives me enough time to get it down, ha ha. Yeah, very funny, man. Bye." Then, he announced to my rolled-up covers, as if I had to know, "I'm going to do a hop. I'll be back by six. If you're hungry, eat. I'll hit on Chick for dinner."

"Fine."

I heard him shower and dress, then Mr. Old Spice floated out of the room without another word.

A few minutes later, there was a sharp rap on the door, not with knuckles, but a broom handle. Brunhilda. "Maid," she bellowed.

"Leave some towels, please. I'm not feeling well," I yelled.

"I won't be back today," she threatened.

"That's okay."

I heard her cart rolling down the hallway. "Only bums sleep all day," she said, sounding like my mother. When I opened the door, she'd left only one towel and one washcloth. *Fuck him,* I thought, *I'll use the clean towel!*

I called Chris, hoping for breakfast company.

"She's out, Steve." Myra sounded weird, troubled.

"Know how long?"

"No. She went to church."

"Church?" I asked.

"That's what she said. Did you two have another fight last night?"

"Not at all."

"Is Bobby there?"

"No—out doing a hop."

"Oh."

"Look Myra, I probably shouldn't be saying anything to you anyway, but Bobby said he likes you, and that you might see each other after this engagement."

"Did he really say that?" she asked, sounding surprised.

"I mention it only because, well, you might want to take it with a grain of salt. I mean, he might be saying things he doesn't mean."

"I don't understand."

"Wanna have coffee?"

We sat across from each other.

"Myra, what Bobby does is none of my business, I swear, but there are things going on that...well, I know you're kind of serious about him, at least it seems that way..."

"Bobby has other girl friends," she said, "if that's what you mean. He told me."

"No, that's not it. He's got his mind on *other* things, conflicting things. This booking's been a turning point for both of us, with some big, unexpected changes. I know you can see what's happened in the act. Well, our friendship has changed too. So has he. He's just different. I thought I knew him, but I guess I don't. Nobody's ever seen the Bobby Darin that we're seeing this week, including me."

"Chris told me that you're thinking of splitting up," she said.

"Not thinking. It's a done deal. These three nights will be my last in the act."

"I'm very sorry."

"Yeah, well, thanks, so am I. But the fact is that he doesn't need me anymore. He's a solid performer on his own. My part is down to nothing. If his record wasn't a guitar tune, he wouldn't need me at all. I'm not contributing. I'm wasting time. I would have bet you a million bucks a week ago that at the end of this engagement I wouldn't be standing back with the band, hardly playing. But that's my problem. I just want you to know that everything he thinks, eats, and sleeps is the act and his career, and he's not letting anything stand in the way—not friendship, not *anything*. He's very single-minded. I hope you're getting my message. Don't be misled. I mean, he means well, but his head's someplace else."

"Thanks, Steve. I'm sorry he's hurt you so much."

"Yeah, well..."

"I know what Chris sees in you—you're nice."

"Thanks. So are you."

"Do you think you'll ever see her again?"

"I'd like to. I guess. I hope so."

"That's what Bobby said last night. I told him I didn't want to just be a memory from his first job, and I think Chris is feeling the same. She knows deep down she may never see you again."

"Maybe. You never know."

"I shouldn't tell you this, but you've been honest with me, and you probably know it anyway: I've seen lots of guys try to get to first base with her but she wouldn't even have coffee with them. You're the first; don't break her heart. It would be easy for you to do that. Don't lead her on without letting her know if you're really serious. Chris has hang-ups that way."

"Thanks for telling me." I was getting that awkward feeling. "Well, I'm glad we had a chance to talk."

"Me too. Good luck to both of you."

I paid the check. In the elevator, she kissed me on the cheek. I thanked her again and then went back to the room to spend the rest of the afternoon polishing my new song.

Bobby called at six. "I'm going to be a little late, Curley, so meet me at the club. Do me a favor: bring the white shirt in my top drawer, the one I haven't worn yet."

"Sure." I heard a woman's voice in the background. "Where are you?"

He laughed. "Somewhere in Alaska. I don't know..." Then he whispered, "I stopped at Monica's for a little while. I'll meet you at the club. Cover for me, okay?"

"Are you nuts? You'll get killed! You said it was all over..."

"Things change, Curley. I know what I'm doing."

"You're right. I'll meet you at work."

There was more laughter. "Later, gator," he giggled, hanging up. Here I go again, covering while Cassotto gets laid. He's right: Sunday can't come soon enough.

"Be ready to go on as soon as he gets here," John barked, passing the dressing room.

"I'm always ready, John." He ignored me.

Clipper came in. "Hi, big guy. Want to get something going tonight? I know a fine lady who would make you very happy. Don't pass this one up, my friend. She's really super-duper special. Tonight would be perfect, and I know the lady's available."

I thought for a moment. The days were dwindling down to a precious few. Why not give it a shot? In some cultures, losing your cherry with a professional is the way it's done. In some, even a boy's father takes him to a hooker (not in *my* father's world, of course). Oh, what the hell, why not? If I'm cool, Chris'll never find out. I might even make it back early enough to see her after I do it. I'll tell her I'm going out for a drink with Clipper to discuss his point of view about doing a single. I could always leave. Anyway, it's a shot. Something positive to go home with after all this shit. Funny, I thought, how I just wanted to get this part of my life over with, too. "You know, Clipper, maybe I will."

He was obviously pleased. "Wonderful! I'll take care of everything!"

"Great. But let's not tell anybody, okay?"

"Oh, sure. Perfect. Absolutely not!"

Tiny's melon-face appeared in the doorway. "Lots of parties tonight. Keep it clean, Clipper. Where's Darin?"

Getting laid. "He'll be a little late."

"Does John know?"

"He knows."

Half an hour later it was show time, and still no Bobby.

"He get in yet?" Tiny asked, ready to go on.

Yeah, he's getting in right now, schmuck. "Not yet."

"Well, I hope he makes it."

Oh, he's making it, all right. "Is there anything you want me to do?"

"Like what?"

"Like anything."

Tiny just walked away.

Chris was lining up. "Later?" she mouthed, hopefully, smiling.

"*Late*, later."

"Oh..."

I wanted to be as convincing as possible. "I'm going for a drink with Clipper," I whispered, "to talk business stuff, you know..."

"Oh, yes," she said, offering understanding.

"...but I won't be back too late. I'll call as soon as I get in." *Oops, poor choice of words.*

"Oh, sure..." she said.

Tiny introduced the show. While Clipper was on for his first hunk, I went to the back of the house and stood near John. "Late is late," he griped, "but this is too much. Life is too short to worry about whether acts show up or not."

"Bobby says you're going to be part of his management."

John eyed me suspiciously. "Did he say that?"

"Was it a secret? Don't worry, I won't tell anyone."

"We haven't finalized anything yet. He has to straighten himself out with George Scheck before he can announce changes. This has to be *top priority* secret. Understand?"

"Excuse me, John. Bobby's my friend. I've never betrayed his trust."

"If he doesn't get here, we'll go right to Arlene," he said, walking away. I wondered if they docked your salary when an act misses a show.

Backstage, Liz was in the wings, ready to go on. "You look worried."

"Bobby's not here yet."

"Really? What happened?" She seemed genuinely concerned.

"Out doing promotion. Probably stuck in traffic." *Yeah, stuck in Monica.*

He still hadn't arrived by the time Liz came off. Wild thoughts were zinging through my head. Maybe Carlo's hoods had found them together. Tiny glanced at me, and then eyed his watch. I shrugged.

Clipper wasn't doing well. After fifteen agonizing minutes, the restless audience was quite ready for a "Message from Garcia." Still no Darin. Maybe I should have offered to do a few folk tunes to fill the slot.

But just then Bobby and John walked into the wings.

"These things happen, John," he was saying, "don't get your balls in an uproar. I was doing record promotion, to help improve business, you know? Hey, killer, you all set?"

"Always," I said, relieved that he was alive.

"Don't ever do this again, Bobby. You'll only hurt yourself and your career. The mark of a professional is to be prompt, ready to perform."

"Here that, Steve? That's the mark. *Mark-mark.* Sounds like a dog with a hare-lip. *Mark-mark. Mark-mark.*"

"I'm telling you for your own good, Bobby! Don't be a wise ass."

"Okay-okay. Get Clipper off and we'll go out and kill 'em. I'll work in these clothes," he said, wiping his face with a towel. "I'll make up a story."

John yelled "Message From Garcia!" and Clipper segued right to Bobby's introduction.

When I took my station behind the piano, Tiny sassed, "Where the hell was he?"

"Why the hell don't you ask him yourself?"

"Don't *you* get snotty with me, kid!"

"My name is Steve!"

"...And now ladies and gentlemen, one of the bright, new stars in the celestial firmament of show business, making his first appearance in Detroit. Let's welcome, with a great big Club Temptation hand...Mister...Bobby...Darin!!!"

He looked completely out of place in jeans and a sport jacket, but getting laid proved once more to inspire his performance. After "Timber," he excused his appearance. "Sorry about my outfit, folks, not looking my best for you, but I was doing record promotion with a group of kids at a youth center, and we got to yakking about teen problems, and I completely forgot the time. But I'll do my best to make it up to you...with a song."

In the back of the room, I saw John shake his head, then walk away into the bar.

"Was he pissed?" Bobby asked later in the dressing room.

"About to have a baby."

"Yeah, well, it all worked out."

"He was going to cut to Arlene."

"Never doubt that I will be there, Curlique. I will always be there. Besides, that show was one of the best, and that ought to smooth over any ruffled feathers. Now, I don't want to see any fans yet, at least not for a while; no pictures, nothing. Would you ask Martha or somebody to make me a sandwich and bring it back here?"

"Sure."

"I'm gonna snooze in the chair 'til the next show. Maybe you could keep guard so I can catch a few. Ham, cheese, mustard would be fine," he yawned, "and a glass of milk."

"Gotcha."

"What a shitty show," he sighed after the late show. "I just couldn't get it up. Lifeless."

"I know you don't want to hear this, but maybe you're getting it up too much. You're tired."

"You're right. I don't want to hear it."

"Okay, I'll change the subject. I need some advice."

He paused in his toweling. "Lay it on me. What's up?"

"All week long Clipper's been hitting on me to set me up with somebody he thinks I can bang. What should I do?"

"What do you want to do?"

"I was thinking of taking the shot. The job is almost over, and...well...that's what the road is all about, I recall someone telling me. Besides, if I don't do it, I'll never know what I missed, right?"

"Right. Maybe you'll do better than you're doing with Chris..."

"Leave her out of this," I said.

"Hey, go easy, okay? I'm whipped. Did he say who it was?"

"No."

"If that bothers you, don't do it."

"Please, I need advice."

"Okay. What can happen? You'll get laid with strange pussy? That's one of the best parts of being on the road, Curley."

"It just doesn't feel right. It's too impersonal."

"Look, Steve, *doing* is the only way you learn. Nobody expects you to marry the bitch. People get laid for the fun of it; don't take it all so seriously. Clipper seems like an okay guy to kill an evening with. What's the worst that can happen? You'll dip it and come back to the hotel. No, that's not the worst. The worst is that Clipper'll tell jokes while you're dipping it. If that's the case, I wouldn't go either."

"Come on, it's not funny."

"Sure it is. Do it! Got for a cab?"

I nodded.

"Instant decision. Instant bango. Case closed. Enjoy-enjoy."

"I told Chris I was going with Clipper to talk showbiz. If it comes up, cover me." I hesitated. Bobby sensed it. "Go-go!" he said, reassuring me. "I'll take them both back to the hotel. One time for me."

Clipper bounced in. "Hey, guys. That was a terrific show. What enthusiasm! What reaction! What energy!"

"What bullshit," Bobby said, putting on his coat. "I'm going to hit the road. Have fun, guys."

When we walked through the bar, I felt certain that everyone knew I was going to fuck a whore.

Chapter 25

"DESPERATE ON A DARE"

Peer pressure from Darin. I should have known better. I just didn't want to listen to my instinct.

I rank this as one of the stupidest things I've ever done: the kind of desperate teenage thing you do only on a dare.

Self-conscious and scared, I asked Clipper where his car was. He said that Laurene had taken it earlier. We hailed a cab. I tried to be cool. "Fill me in on the details."

"Who needs details when de-*tail* is waiting."

Clipper instructed the driver to take us to the Starlight Motel. I started to chatter. Throughout the entire conversation he never looked at me. "Do you ever go to baseball games? I think the Tigers are in town."

"I'm not interested in professional athletics," he said.

"Have you been doing your act a long time?"

"Long enough to know better."

"How many jokes do you know?"

"Not enough."

"You do some very funny stuff."

"Sometimes, yes. In my opinion, *you* can't miss either. I'm not only talking about Bobby, I mean you, too. You've got great potential. You handle yourself well on stage. You have a special quality that can really make it."

"Thanks."

"It's a fact. I see you've been changing things around this week. Are you upset?"

"No. Why, do I seem to be?"

"No, just asking."

"No, I'm not upset. Nothing I can't handle."

With each passing minute I was becoming more anxious. Why do I let myself get talked into things like this? What the hell was wrong with sticking with Chris for the rest of the trip? Or even Liz? I'm not Bobby Darin. Maybe Clipper had hit on Bobby first. No, Bobby would have told me. I think he would have told me.

The neon sign was dark when the cab pulled up in front of the Starlight Motel— a low, characterless building somewhere in suburban Detroit. Clipper paid the fare. I asked the driver for his card.

"You won't need that," Clipper said. "I'll drive you back."

I took the card anyway, then followed him through the lobby to the rear of the building.

"This place is out of the way and very private. I like that," he said, unlocking the last door in the corridor. "You're really going to enjoy this."

A wave of nausea swept over me. I broke out in a flash sweat. There, in the small, dimly lit room, sitting up in bed, under the covers, wearing a fluffy flowery bathrobe, was Mrs. Laurene Daniels.

"Hello, Steve," she smiled sweetly.

I glanced around the room, looking for the fabulous piece that Clipper had been touting. But there was no one else. *Man, am I dumb!* "Hello, Mrs...er...Laurene. How are you?" I looked around again. Then it dawned on me how truly naïve I really was. *Holy Shit! Clipper wants me to fuck his wife!*

"Relax, Steve. There's nothing to be nervous about," Clipper said, zipping behind me to lock the door. He helped me off with my coat, which I yielded automatically, then gestured toward some whiskey bottles on top of the dresser. "Let me get you a drink. Seven and seven, right?"

"Yeah...er...sure...sure. How...how are you?" I asked, repeating myself.

She laughed softly. "I'm fine, Steve."

Clipper made drinks.

"None for me, Clipper," she purred.

There was soft music coming from the nighttable radio. I downed half the warmish fluid on the first gulp. It was strong and made me gag.

"I was telling Steve how much we both enjoyed his stage presence," Clipper said, sitting in the only chair in the room, leaving me standing between them at the foot of the bed. "Laurene enjoyed your act too, didn't you, honey?"

"Very much," she cooed, not moving.

I couldn't move either. My feet felt nailed to the floor. "I just do what Bobby wants me to do."

She gestured toward the bottom of the bed. "Sit down, Steve." I obeyed like a zombie. "Are you having fun here in Detroit?" Her voice was deep and throaty, much huskier than I remembered.

"It's been a whole b...b...bunch of new experiences," I said, gulping down the rest of my drink.

Clipper lifted the glass from my unconscious hand and refilled it. Then he nodded to Laurene. "You folks excuse me," he said, going into the bathroom, closing the door behind him.

We were alone. The music seemed to get louder as the booze took hold. I couldn't look at her. She sat up and reached out to me. "Come closer. Take your jacket off. I'll bet you didn't know that I was attracted to you from the very first time we met."

My jacket tumbled off with a mind of its own. "You were...?"

"I don't bite, you know...not unless you want me to."

I was in shock. "I...I...this is a little awkward for me. I've never...I mean...of course, I have...you know...but I've never..." I couldn't stop blabbing.

"Never what?" she said, soothingly. "Don't be afraid, Steve. Clipper must have told you how much I've liked you all week. He did, didn't he?" I wondered what he was doing in the bathroom.

My head was buzzy from the booze. "Well, he mentioned that he knew someone...someone *very nice* who he thought that...well...that...you know...but he didn't tell me that it was his w...with you."

"Come a little closer. Let me touch you," she said reassuringly, taking both my hands into hers. "Don't be afraid. Clipper and I always want to make each other happy, and if touching you makes me happy, and sharing my body with someone very special like you makes me happy, then I know he'll be happy. Clipper would never want me to be unhappy." Her robe fell open as she slipped out from under the covers. She made sure that I caught a glimpse of her breasts before she adjusted it loosely around her. Then she sat cross-legged on the bed next to me and began kissing my fingers, sucking on them, eyeing me as she slid them, one at a time, in and out of her mouth. I couldn't remember if I had washed my hands before I left the club. She never took her eyes off me, but I could smell the unmistakable scent of her body heat. "See," she said, running her fingers across my cheek, "there's nothing to be afraid of." She knelt beside me and kissed me.

I couldn't return the kiss. My lips were pasted shut. She moistened them with her warm, wet tongue. "Put your arms around me," she whispered. "Don't be afraid, don't be afraid."

I closed my eyes, blindly following directions. My face was full into her naked chest. Her skin was soft, spongy, and creamy-smooth. She pressed her breasts against my closed mouth. "Bite me," she ordered sharply.

I opened my mouth to obey, but I couldn't do it. I just couldn't do it. At the last minute, I pulled back.

"Don't be afraid, Steve," she commanded, speaking quickly, breathing deeply, reaching down between my legs to feel for the erection that wasn't there. I was shrunk so small that I don't think I could have found it myself. She groped around my crotch for a moment and then, realizing that I was not in the least aroused, backed away.

"I'm sorry...that I'm not...more responsive," I muttered. "I'm just not comfortable."

Laurene leaned back on the headboard, and left her robe open so I could see her naked body. But now her expression was changed, harder. "Would you like some more to drink?" she asked. "Maybe it'll help." Now the sensuous tone in her voice was gone. Now she sounded more like the shrew bitch that broke Clipper's balls at the Bagel each night.

"No, no more. I'm just not...I mean, I can't. I...I'm sorry."

"Clipper!" she barked. Instantly he was bouncing out of the bathroom, eyes red, smelling from cigarette smoke. But it wasn't cigarette smoke—I'd never smelled anything like it. "What's wrong?" he asked hoarsely.

"He's a dud. He can't get it up."

"I thought that you were interested in getting laid, Steve," he slurred, thick-voiced.

"Well, I thought that...that we would be...you know...alone."

"I was in the can. I wasn't bothering you. I'll lock the door if it makes you feel better?" He headed back to the bathroom.

"No! No, that's not it."

He turned. "Well?" he demanded. "Don't you like her?"

"No. I mean, yes...of course, I do...I mean...but..."

"She's the best piece of ass in the world, and you can have it *free*! Just fuck her, kid! *Fuck her*!!!"

"I...I can't. I don't know her...I don't know you. I can't get laid with...with some-one waiting in the other room."

"He's a dud, Clipper. Face it. You flunked again."

I stood quickly, grabbed my jacket, and put it on. "This is not for me. No. Sorry, folks, this is *not for me*!"

"You know, punk, you're a real disappointment. I thought you were *man* enough to want to get laid with the greatest. The *greatest*! Go on; get out of here! Go back to your chorus girls."

"That's fine with me," I said, yanking my coat from the closet.

"Just get out," he said, turning away.

I unlocked the door and charged down the hallway. In the background distance I could hear Laurene Daniel's disgusted voice. "You never come through for me, Clipper, never! You're a singles-hitter, and I want a home run!"

I desperately needed to get out into the night air. I didn't know where the hell in America I was, but I ran at top speed for a few blocks until I spotted a tele-phone booth outside a closed gas station.

"What's your address?" asked a gravelly voice.

I squinted at the street sign. "I'm at...Canfield and Nine Mile Road. I'm at the Total Gas station."

"After midnight, the rate is double the meter to go to downtown."

"No problem. How long'll it be?"

"Fifteen minutes."

"As quickly as possible, please. It's cold."

"We drive at the limit, mister, not faster."

"Okay-okay. I'll be waiting."

"How do I know you'll be there?"

"Come on, man, have a heart, I'm freezing my ass off. One of your drivers just brought me here a half an hour ago and gave me his card. I'm not going anywhere. Just hurry, please?"

"What's your name?"

"Daniel. Clipper Daniel."

"Stay put, Daniel. We're on the way."

I huddled in the gas station doorway. Even though I'd had a few drinks, my head was clear. What an ass I am! I did this just to prove that I could be as much of a swordsman as Bobby Darin. Well, I certainly proved something else, alright—I'm not Bobby Darin. Jesus! What weirdos! Sickos! I began to shiver, partly from the cold, but mostly from revulsion: I could still smell Laurene's scent.

It was two-fifteen. If I called Chris, undoubtedly the conversation would get around to where I was, where I had been, and what I had talked about with Clipper. And, of course, there was the absolute certainty that even if we slept together again, we wouldn't *sleep* together. Maybe Myra was with Bobby in our room. There were too many possibilities to consider.

No, I needed someone who wouldn't push me away, someone to talk to, and also to *not* talk to. My hands were numb as I dialed the Royal Palm. "Liz? It's Steve. Are you sleeping?"

"No. Just reading."

There was desperation in my voice. "Can I come over and read with you? Please?"

"Where are you?"

"Not far. I could be there in fifteen minutes. Less. Please? Please?"

"You sound troubled."

"Well...nothing that a good book won't cure. Come on, Liz, make us a cup of tea, and I'll help you turn the pages, okay? I really need someone to talk to. Please?"

She paused for what seemed an eternity. "I'll put the water on."

"Thank you. I'll be right there. Thank you. Thank you."

I called the taxi company. "This is Clipper Daniel. Where's my cab?"

"Be patient, he's on his way."

"How long?"

"Ten minutes."

"Well, tell him to hurry."

"How the hell can I tell him? He ain't got no phone! He's on his way. He's looking for you."

"You told me that fifteen minutes ago. I'll wait for a while. If he gets here, he gets here." I hung up, frustrated that I wasn't on my way already.

Suddenly a taxi turned the corner. I flagged him down, practically running in front of him. "Where ya goin'?" the driver asked. It wasn't the driver looking for me.

"The Royal Palm."

"Ugh. Downtown. Sorry. I'm heading home."

"How about an extra five over the meter?"

"You're on. Get in."

Ah, the power of the schmeer. That's one technique Bobby Darin taught me that really works!

Chapter 26

"ONE TIME FOR ME"

As soon as she closed the door, my arms were around her.

"Whoa, fella! You're very affectionate tonight. What's come over you?"

"Just happy to be here, that's all."

She was wearing the lavender robe. "Have some tea."

I reached for her again. "Not now."

"Now!" she ordered, backing away, searching my face. "You seem so...angry."

I slowed a little. "Sorry. I don't mean to be." I hung my coat and jacket in the closet. "Maybe I've been thinking about what's been happening all week and it's starting to show. Sorry again."

"Is that what you wanted to talk about?" I nodded. "I suppose you have a right to be upset, judging from the smaller role you're playing in the act. Personally, I liked the songs you did together much more."

"It's gotta be obvious to everyone what's going on, now that I'm just standing behind the piano..."

"Oh, that's not what I'm talking about. I'm talking about the rejection. Bobby's rejecting you." She pointed to the chairs and we sat across from each other. Full teacups were waiting.

"You're very observant, Liz."

"Did you ever think of performing on your own?"

"I've been thinking of it."

"You should. You have something very special. Maybe a record company will think so, too. If you two split up, then you'd be more than just an out-of-work *musician*, you'd be an out-of-work *performer*. Maybe if you thought of yourself that way, you might get something going."

"In the strictest confidence, I think that's what's going to happen. But I haven't discussed it with anyone yet. You're the first." *A small lie.*

"I'm sure you'll do very well. Where were you tonight?"

"Clipper and I had a sandwich."

"Clipper?"

"Yeah, show talk, stuff like that. He's a strange man."

"Yes. Where's Bobby?"

"He wasn't feeling well; went to sleep, worn out from promotion." I moved closer. "May I kiss you, Liz?"

"Is that all the conversation you want to have?"

"For the moment, if it's all right, please, I don't want to discuss the act, I don't want to talk about Bobby Darin, and I don't want to drink tea. I just want to hold you."

"You're such a sweet boy."

"What do you mean, *boy*?"

She silenced my lips with her finger and came into my arms. "Take your time, Steve. I don't have an *off* switch. I'm not going anywhere."

It was as if I had been racing out of control toward a distant finish line, staggering, stumbling, wondering if I would ever get there. But now, as uncertain as I still felt—and as excited as I had ever been—there was also a calm, inner voice telling me to just let it happen. *Just let it happen*. Liz's perfume, the warm room, the perfect lighting; it all overpowered any reason for keeping control. I had always been the logical one. Tonight, it was time to let that part of me go.

She ran her fingers through my hair, and caressed my face with her soft hands. With each touch, I felt my armor falling away.

After getting as close to her as I could on the chairs, I eased up, and went to the big closet. "It's time for Mr. Murphy," I said hoarsely.

She was watching me, smiling a wonderful smile of permission. The bed was behind the doors, just as Bobby had described. But I was too nervous. When I yanked on the strap, the frame came bumping down. "Oops. Sorry."

She laughed, then quickly covered her mouth.

I sat on the bed and kicked off my loafers.

Liz knelt on the floor next to me, brushed her hair back away from her face, took a sip of tea, and squirted it from her mouth into mine as we kissed (Bronx Science girls *never* did anything like this!).

I pulled off my clothes and threw them somewhere out in the room. My shorts came off along with my chinos. I felt embarrassed, and ducked under the covers.

"What are you doing?" she asked, with a knowing half-smile.

"Waiting for you, Liz, since the first moment I saw you at rehearsal last week."

"Steve, that's a little dramatic, isn't it?" she said. But her words were gentle.

"Yeah, I guess so," I answered. "I'm sorry." For a long moment, she just stared at me. Could it be that this was not going to happen after all? Did I say the wrong thing again? Was I too fast again? Too flip? Too anxious? Was she going to change her mind?

She sensed my uneasiness, and let her robe fall, then slid into bed next to me and cuddled close. I covered us both, then kissed her. She put her head on my chest, and we lay silently beside each other. Her hair smelled of flowers. I ran my hand along her warm back wondering what to do now.

"It's a dancer's bra," she whispered. "Just lift it up." *How did she know my thoughts?*

Magically, the bra popped up and came to rest around her neck. She raised her arms to help me remove it. When it was gone I could feel the sensation of her skin against my chest. I wanted to kiss every exposed part of her. I reached down and tugged off her panties and tossed them on the floor. I strained to reach her nipples. They jumped to attention as they entered my mouth. She pushed me back on the pillow, then rose up on top, scissoring her legs around me. When I felt the strength of her thighs surrounding my hips, I was desperate to know the feeling of being inside her. But she held me back. Silhouetted in the candlelight, she was beautiful, hair cascading around her face, covering my face with a blanket of silk.

"Slowly," she whispered, controlling me, demanding my body to take its time. "Slowly, so you'll remember forever."

Still not allowing me to move, she began to rock, leaning forward to brush her breasts up against me with each motion, releasing her thighs just long enough for me to slide a little lower on her flat stomach. When she had me exactly where she wanted, she reached down, and with one magnificent thrust, I was inside her. I couldn't help it. I began to come, exploding, cannoning into her.

As soon as she felt me throbbing, she began pulling on me, contracting, then releasing me with muscles I never knew a woman had, rocking faster and faster. "Oh, darling!" she cried, kissing me repeatedly, her wet mouth licking wherever her lips touched, digging her nails into my shoulders, the strokes between us growing wider with each pull, but never quite far enough to lose our connection. "Oh, darling Steve!" she repeated, just loud enough for my ears only. Then, at the height of the passion that was driving us both, she froze, clamping us instantly to a halt. Suspended in mid-air, she began to shudder. It would have been easy for me to close my eyes and become lost in this physical act. But Liz's face held an expression that said there was nothing else in her world at this moment but me, and that I was doing this great thing for her.

I thought I had come my last drop, but when I felt her flooding heat all over me, I began to come again. Sensing what was happening, she coaxed each new throb out of me, squeezing and releasing my body with pulls and grunts until I was drained. When it was done, she eased her body full down on top of me, and put her head on my shoulder.

"Did that feel as wonderful to you as it did to me?" she whispered.

"Yes!"

"Have you ever done this before?"

"No!"

"I didn't think so."

"May I sleep here tonight? With you?"

"Of course, my darling, of course."

When our bodies separated, she turned over, pulled up the covers, took my arm, wrapped it around her breasts, and held us tight together. I drifted, at peace in her cocoon. Whenever I focused, I wondered if this was real. But her warm body was there to reassure me that it actually was.

After a time, from a state of semi-consciousness, I felt her hand massaging me. As if in a dream, I was hard again. She turned to face me, lying on her side, and slid me into her easily; this time keeping her hand between our stomachs. In a moment, I was coming again. When my last contraction ended, I just fell out.

"Sleep, Steve," she commanded.

I obeyed.

Who knows how many minutes or years passed? With the light of dawn beginning to outline the windows, I was awakened by the movement of Liz's head under the blanket, resting on my stomach, her tongue caressing and warming me. As I got hard again, I began to ache something fierce. The more she tightened, the more I hurt. I could feel her teeth as she rose up on her knees and began sucking me deeper and deeper into her mouth.

"Gently," I said, through the pain, lifting the blanket a little so she could hear me.

"Mmmm, sorry," she mumbled, surfacing, out of breath. "Do you like that?" she asked, holding me with her hand.

"Oh, yes!"

"Would you like me to stop?"

"Oh, no, no. I've never done this before, either."

"I'm glad," she said, disappearing again under the blanket. When I was fully in her mouth, she began slowly moving her hand up and down in the opposite direction of her head. It was the most sensual feeling I had ever experienced. I had no control—absolutely none.

"Do you want me to c...come?" I asked, feeling that this special intimacy needed permission.

"Not yet," whispered the voice under the sheets. "Take your time. I've never done this before either. Think about something else, it'll help you control yourself."

"Like w...what?"

"Think about baseball!"

Wow, Joe DiMaggio. Jesus Christ, Tommy Henrich. Holy shit! Phil Rizzutto. Who won the World Series last year? Who cares! Finally, through the blissful warmth of her lips and the motion of her hand, I began to swell, and to burn, and then to finally burst into her mouth. I don't know if anything came out, but the few searing contractions felt like lightening had collided with my eyeballs. My toes curled. My legs twitched. When she emerged from under the blanket, looking triumphant, smiling, her eyes filled with happiness, I was numb, drained to the core. If there had been a fire in the hotel and I had to run, I would not have made it. She moved up to my shoulder and burrowed into my chest again. I lifted her head and kissed her. Then I fell asleep.

Where was I? I tried to concentrate. I unstuck my eyes. Daylight was blasting full through the crinolines: red near the window, blue and green on the closet wall.

I was at Liz's.

Where was she?

Right next to me, still sleeping, her makeup smeared. So what? To me, she was the most beautiful woman in the world. I kissed her cheek and nuzzled close. "I have to go."

"Not yet," she said, eyes still closed. The sheets around us were deliciously warm.

I found my watch. "It's eleven-thirty. I have to get back." I don't know why, but I felt like I wanted to run, as if I had no right to be there, as if there were another part of my life calling to me.

"Stay. We'll have breakfast. Then we can come back to bed." But my head was filling too quickly with thoughts of Bobby Darin, of Chris Evans, of Club Temptation, and of the world outside her door. "I really have to go."

"What's wrong?" she asked, her eyes fluttering open.

"Nothing. I just didn't realize what time it was."

"Do you have plans?"

"No. But Bobby might be looking for me, waiting for me, something like that."

"Steve, he's not looking for you. Stay more. Everything else can wait."

I leaned over and kissed her. "I'm too weak to talk."

"Then stay and sleep some more."

"I have to go."

"You still haven't told me why."

"I just have to. May I use your shower?"

Yes, she nodded, no longer trying to change my mind.

I let the hot water inject energy into my bones. After I'd dressed, I sat next to her. "This was the most incredible night of my life," I said humbly. "Thank you."

"Yes, it was incredible," she sighed, stretching seductively. "I'll see you tonight."

I pecked at her lips. Mine were as dry as hers. "Tea'll do it every time," she grinned, rolling back under the sheets.

I kissed her again. "I'll let myself out."

In the glaring daylight I rushed back to the Wolverine Hotel, praying that I would not run into Chris or Myra in the lobby.

Chapter 27

"WILL I EVER
SEE YOU AGAIN?"

I came four times! Four!!!! I wanted to yell as I closed the door.

But I didn't.

He was in bed, on the phone, still in his pajamas. He bid me enter as though it were okay; that I was not interrupting anything important. "Great, man, yeah, thanks for everything. I couldn't be doing any of this without you, you know, man? I'll be downstairs in twenty minutes, man." He hung up, then looked at me with a big, leering grin. "Where ya been, Curley?" he drawled.

I wanted desperately to keep it short. "With Liz."

"Liz? *Our* Liz? Hey, I called it, didn't I?"

"Yeah." *You called it, all right, motherfucker. And the last time was a blow job! A B–L–O–W job that B–L–E–W my head off, Darin*, I wanted to scream.

But I didn't.

"Was it great?"

"I can't carry on a coherent conversation right now."

"Hey, I was just asking, that's all. If I'd have known you were going to be out all night, I would have made better use of the room."

"Gotta get some sleep."

His grin grew. "Wiped, huh? Welcome to the big time. Sure, killer, hit the sack. You've earned it. You can tell me later." *You can bet that this is the last thing I will ever be telling you about later, killer.*

He headed for the john. "Sleep tight, morning glory. I'm out with Chick again. Back by dinner."

"Great," I grunted, throwing my clothes on the chair.

"Hey, Mr. Neat, don't get sloppy now," he laughed. I ignored him. "Before I go, tell me what happened with Clipper's fabulous piece?"

I pulled on my pajamas and got into bed. "He wanted me to fuck Laurene."

This seemed to catch him totally by surprise. "What? Wow! No shit! What happened? Tell-tell! Did ya do it?"

"No," I said disgustedly into my pillow, barely able to move my mouth.

"Why? She looks like a great piece to me."

"Seepy-seepy. Can't talk, tell you later." The next thing I knew he was shaking me. It was six-fifteen, time to go to work. I felt like I had gone a few rounds with Jake LaMotta. "I didn't hear you leave."

"I know. You snore, honey."

"How was promo?"

"Super. I did the Bloomfield hop again. They went crazy when I played the piano. Kids love record acts that play instruments," he announced authoritatively.

"Ever think of the tuba?" I mumbled, struggling up. "That would be original."

"Ever think of a shower? Do it," he pointed. "John says there's lots of reservations. He came with me. So did Buddy. And just for the record, I was right: having Midwest representation helps enormously. Having someone to guide me through the crowds gave the kids a real feeling of what a star is all about."

"I'm glad it's working out," I said, moving unsteadily toward the bathroom.

In the cab, he asked, "So, what happened with Clipper?"

"Promise never to tell anyone."

"Of course."

"It was weird. I really thought he had someone different lined up, but maybe I should have known better. Jesus, when he wanted me to fuck Laurene I panicked. I could never do that."

"Was he in the room?"

"In the can."

"You can be sure he wasn't taking a dump. Probably jerking off. Some guys are like that. They can't bang their chicks enough themselves, so they have to get somebody to do it for them. Turns 'em on."

"Yicch! If I'd have known beforehand, you can bet I wouldn't have gone."

"I would have fucked the shit out of her," he said quietly.

"Well, I'm sure she's still available."

"Wrong, pally. Once guys like that take their shot, they usually don't try again so close to home."

"I don't believe it. You mean you could have fucked her right in front of Clipper? Jesus, I couldn't."

"Don't you ever imagine doing kinky things like that? Banging two chicks at once?"

"Oh, I guess I've thought about it. But I don't think I could ever do it."

"Well, now that you've dunked your dickie, I suggest you think up something quick if you still want to take a shot at sinking Chris. I covered you last night, but you gotta take it from here. Unless, of course, you're planning to spend the rest of the trip with Liz. That might be interesting. Well, no matter. Congratulations. Official-*official*. Yep, I called it, didn't I?"

"Big house, tonight," Clipper said to no one in particular.

Bobby was putting on his makeup. "The bigger, the better."

"Where're you headed from here?" he asked, still not looking at either of us.

"Home to regroup. You?"

"Copa, Pittsburgh. Change of scenery. I've had enough Detroit for a while. Time for new faces."

Andy appeared in the doorway. "How about the pictures now, Bob? Okay? Let's do it quick, before it gets crazy. Friday nights, it's always crazy."

"Hey, sure, why not. Give me a minute to get dressed."

"We'll start with the individuals," Andy said. "You first, Bob, right out here. The wings'll be a perfect backdrop."

I was expecting the usual wisecrack from Clipper, but he said nothing.

Bobby stepped into the hallway and began flashing numero-unos at Flashing Andy. I tuned up, not knowing what to expect from Clipper. He broke the strained silence quietly, so only I could hear. "I'd appreciate it if you wouldn't mention last night to anybody."

I combed my hair, not looking at him. "Of course, I won't."

"I have my career to think about. Some people might not understand."

"Right."

"You left too soon," he said through gritted teeth, suddenly angry, but still not raising his voice. "You didn't give her a chance."

"It wasn't what I expected."

"What did you expect?"

"Not your wife!"

"Who then, a hooker? I'm not a pimp, you know!"

"Nobody said you were."

"Laurene has a healthy sexual appetite, that's all. If she wants to make it with somebody once in a while, it's all right with me."

"Forget it."

He got angrier. "You're just a young *putz* who doesn't know shit! She really wanted to lay you. She's *the best*! And you couldn't do it."

"Shut the fuck up, Clipper," I snapped, raising my voice, immediately quieting him down. "You wanted me to go with you? I went. It didn't work out. As far as I'm concerned, it's over. You wanna make more out of it?"

He was silent again. "Well, I just hope I can trust you to keep it to yourself," he grumbled, grabbing his tux jacket, walking out.

Contrary to Captain Kodak, it was a lousy time for pictures. The wings were bustling—the band passing by, the line getting ready to go on.

"Hey, Steverino, get your face out here," Bobby yelled. "Let's put your puss down for posterity."

I grabbed my guitar and stood next to him, facing Andy.

"Show your teeth," Larry said, pausing to watch.

"Show your ass," Bobby said, showing his teeth.

"Shake hands, boys," Andy directed, "and smile, like you mean it. No, no, Steve, you look forced. You too, Bobby. No, that doesn't look real either. Okay: Steve, meet Bobby—Bobby, meet Steve." Flash. "Okay, thanks, guys, that'll do it. I'll print 'em up later."

"Wait a minute. I want one more," Bobby said, motioning to Myra, who was standing next to Larry. "A quickie."

"Sure," Andy said, reluctantly. "But that'll be extra."

"Take the picture, clown. Never talk business in front of a lady."

I stood aside as Myra cuddled up close.

"Now one with Steve and Chris," Bobby ordered, waving for Chris to join me. I wondered if she suspected anything about last night.

"Hello stranger," she said softly.

"Hi."

"Arm in arm," Bobby said, positioning her next to me. "That's right. And smile! No, you look too forced. Chris, meet Steve—Steve, meet Chris."

"It's nice to see you," she whispered. "What happened to you last night?"

"It was late, and..."

"I was waiting for you."

"Put your guitar down," Andy directed. I obeyed.

"Would you like to get together after work?" she asked, facing the lens. Out of the corner of my eye I could see Liz in the girls' dressing room, putting on make-up, watching this whole scene in the mirror. After last night, I felt a little dumb taking pictures with Chris. I nodded to her. I don't think she saw me.

"Let's see what Bobby and Myra are going to do."

"Let me work that out," she said. "I think I know already. Tomorrow's your last day. I want to see you."

I tried to catch Liz's eye, but she was no longer watching. "Okay. Sure."

"Now one of the four of us," Bobby ordered.

"Wait a minute! That's more pictures than we agreed to." Andy was catching on.

"I said I'd straighten you later, Andy. Take the pictures. It's going to be a heavy night. I'll make it up to you between shows."

There was no way he could refuse without a war. "Okay, okay, let's do it. I gotta go back to work."

"Now, just one more of Steve, alone."

"Hey, wait a minute..."

"Friday night, Andy. Busy-busy. One shot of Steve, and that's it. Steve, stand there, put your foot on that chair. Wait! I want to brush your suit." Bobby jumped into the dressing room and came out with his clothes brush, winking at all of us so that fuming Andy couldn't see. "There, now he's ready." Andy got set. "Wait!" Bobby interrupted again. "The guitar." He handed it to me. Finally, Andy flashed.

"Two copies of everything, and four of the group shot," Bobby said. "But we don't need 'em until tomorrow, Andy. And thanks!" Andy was very pissed as he trudged away.

"And that, *pally*, is how to deal with a prick," Bobby said, leading me into the dressing room.

"He's very tee'd."

"Fuck him. I've earned those shots. John told me I had more picture requests than any act since Mathis. He owes me. I don't like it when a guy who owes tries to welch. You can use the solo shots for your own PR. When you're on your own, you'll have pictures to work with."

It was another acknowledgement of the ending. "Thanks."

While the Cuties were on, I hung around in the hallway trying to get Liz's attention. Finally, she came out of the dressing room, ready to go on. I wasn't sure how she would receive me today. "I'm having trouble walking," I said.

"I know what you mean."

"It may be corny to say thanks, Liz, but thanks. It was absolutely wonderful."

"Yes, it was." But she broke the spell quickly. "Have you decided what you're going to do?"

"It's pretty well been decided for me. Can I call you later?"

She was a little cool. "If I'm still up."

"I'll call you later," I said.

Once again, I sat across from Chris at our regular Bagel table. Bobby and Myra had already gone back to the hotel.

"Just one more night," she said.

"Yeah, one more night. What happens now? How long will you stay in Detroit?"

"We have another month on our contract. I guess I'll stick it out. Truthfully, there's no future with the Cuties. I don't like the life that much, you know, living out of a suitcase, and all that. There's nothing permanent. Oh, it's fun, and most of the girls are nice to work with. And meeting you has been, well..." She took a breath. "But I've been at it for almost two years, and its pretty much the same all over. I thought I might go back to school." I smiled. Religion aside, my parents would love her. "Maybe nursing," she continued. "I think I'm getting ready for a change. What about you and Bobby?"

"I'm going to take a shot on my own."

"Oh, Steve, that's wonderful. Maybe we'll work together sometime."

"You just made the fastest comeback in the history of show business."

"Well, if I knew you'd be coming out this way, it might keep me kicking a little longer. That would be something, wouldn't it? Both of us working on the same show again?"

"That would be nice to look forward to."

We were both quiet for a moment. "Will we ever see each other again?" she asked.

"I'd like to."

"Me too. But when?"

"Don't know."

She perked up. "I've heard rumors that the Cuties may play New York..."

"Gee, where? Wouldn't *that* be great!"

"But, it probably won't happen for six months or so, and by then, I might not..." She stopped again. "What do we do?"

"Don't know."

"Do you really think that we'll ever see each other again?"

We were repeating ourselves. "I'd like to. I guess, well...I don't know."

More silence. "I really enjoyed getting to know you. You've changed a lot since we met. You're very different...and, well, I know I've been saying it a lot, but...you're special."

"You've changed, too, Chris."

She looked away. "I might loosen up a little if I wasn't spending my time arranging my schedule to suit Myra's romance with Bobby."

"Wow, you too? I'm glad I'm not the only one who feels like a social director."

"Myra's afraid that Bobby is seeing another girl. Is he?" When I didn't answer, she said, "I think you can trust me, Steve. There have been evenings after work when we...I mean...*he*...hasn't seen Myra. It wouldn't be right if he were seeing someone behind her back."

"I can't discuss that stuff, Chris."

"Steve, it's very plain that he's slept with her..."

"And she with him..."

"Don't you think sleeping with someone deserves a little more respect? What ever happened to commitment? To being faithful? Myra would be crushed if she found out that Bobby was just playing her along."

"About what?"

"Didn't he tell you he asked her to quit the line and to travel with him when he comes out on the road again?"

"What?!!"

"He says he wants her to be with him, and he's going to invite her to New York, too, to meet his family."

Cassotto never ceases to amaze. "No, he didn't mention it. But between you and me, well...I wouldn't take it too seriously. He won't travel with anyone who can't help the act. That's why I'm leaving. If she wants to travel with him, she'd better learn to play electric guitar."

"You really mean that?"

"He's got one thing working in his head, Chris, one thing only."

"Should I tell her?"

"No. He'll do that on his own. He won't drag it out past this week."

"Oh." She became very quiet again. Our food arrived. We ate in silence. Then, "If I ask you something, will you be honest with me?"

"Chris..."

"Have you...gone out with Liz Carleton?"

"What? When? I've been with you almost every night."

"Not last week..."

"That wasn't my fault."

"...and not last night."

"Chris, she's almost old enough to be my mother," I said, sounding more defensive than I would have liked. "Well, not quite that old...but what makes you ask a question like that? You know where I was last night."

"After all this stuff about Bobby, I'd just like to know where you were. We share a dressing room, and women talk, you know. I'd just like to hear you say it."

"I don't know what you heard...but no, I didn't go out with Liz Carleton." (This was actually true; we *technically* didn't *go out*.)

She avoided my eyes. "I missed you last night, that's all, and I...I was wondering where you were. You could ask that of me? Go ahead, ask me."

"What?"

"If I've gone out with another man since I've met you. Go ahead, just ask."

"It's none of my business if you did."

"I thought that's what you'd say. That's what Bobby said to Myra when she asked him the same question. You're so...so smooth. You really have a smooth line, Mr. Karmen."

"Come on, Chris. You're sounding like the old, untrusting Chris from last week. Last night, I went out with Clipper. I told you that. Ask *him* if it'll make you believe me. When I got back, Bobby and I went at it again. After that I really didn't feel like being with anyone."

"I missed you, that's all," she said softly, looking away. "Steve, I'd like to ask that same favor again, if you don't mind, if I could...Myra wants one more night with Bobby, and..."

Carrying this amount of guilt, there was no way I could refuse.

Later, after we groped around for a while, and I agreed to sleep in my clothes again so Bobby could be without his with Myra, I couldn't help thinking what a difference there was between last night and tonight!

Chapter 28

"MESSAGE FROM GARCIA"

Again, Bobby came home just after sunrise and Chris left quickly, her modesty intact. Again, he seemed upset—about what I wasn't sure—except at this point, I didn't care. The engagement had been a success, certainly for him (he had probably gotten laid more times in two weeks than anyone in the history of getting laid), and in many ways for me too. Maybe the distance he had put between us was coming from a fear of the pending solo-ness of his professional life. That's what I wanted to think, anyway. I fell back to sleep without any conversation.

It was midday, Saturday. My open suitcase was on the closet floor. "How come you're packing?" he asked. "We don't leave 'til tomorrow."

"Just getting organized."

"Pack later. Let's talk." I closed the suitcase and sat back on my bed. "It's over between me and Myra."

"Sorry."

"Yeah, well, it was for the best. She wants to be more involved than I do. Too bad. She's really broken up. I just wanted you to know in case it comes up with Chris."

"Okay. Now, I have something to tell you, too. I've decided to take a shot on my own."

"I figured. You'll do good."

"I thought I would ask George if he'd handle me."

His tone changed immediately. "Hey, didn't we agree that George was off limits for other boy singers?"

"Well, I thought that maybe he'd feel differently after you tell him about your Detroit managers. Of course, I'll wait until you tell him. And if he's not interested, maybe he'll recommend somebody."

"Jesus, I hope you'll have the good sense not to do any of my material. That would be pretty shitty."

"You mean folk material? Why don't you say that to Freddy Sharp. He's more of a threat than me. Besides, don't you know by now that I would never do anything to hurt you?"

"Yeah-yeah. I know-I know. Well, maybe someday when we're both big stars we'll look back on this job as the start of a new life for each of us."

"I hope so. It was for me."

The phone rang. It was Myra. "Of course, sure, baby. I'll be down in five minutes." He hung up, and went into the bathroom. "She wants to talk. I'm going for breakfast."

As soon as he left, I called Chris.

"You were right," she reported. "They broke up last night."

"Yeah, the star told me."

"Now can you understand the hurt that's caused when people sleep together before they're married? Myra feels used, and truthfully I don't blame her. She just wanted Bobby to promise he wouldn't sleep with other girls until they had a chance to meet again, which incidentally, I thought was a fair request, considering what happened. But he wouldn't agree."

"At least he's honest. How about some food?"

"No, I'd better wait for Myra. She may need me. If she's all right, I'll call. If not, I'll see you at work and after work, although I don't know where. Somehow, sleeping in my own room again after sleeping with you is going to feel...lonely."

"Call me. I'll be here."

She never called. Bobby came back a half-hour later with a newspaper, a sandwich, and a container of juice. "Eat. Read. I don't want to talk."

"I thought I'd eat with Chris."

"Stick for a while, okay?" His voice was troubled. "Please? I might need a buffer."

This ends tomorrow, star; tomorrow. "Sure." I devoured the sandwich, and dozed off. When I awoke, he was getting dressed. "Ready for tonight?"

"As usual."

"It's closing night."

"Yeah, I know," I said wistfully.

"Closing night is very special, Curley. You don't seem to be interested."

"Forgive the pun, but why is this night different from all other nights?"

"Because it's closing night."

"Oh, that clears up everything."

"Steve, closing night is a grand tradition in show business. There's an extra sense of camaraderie between the acts that are all going their separate ways. The second show on closing night is very loose, filled with fun and surprises."

"I never heard that before."

"You saw Sinatra at the Copa? All that shtick wasn't part of his act. He was very loose, very ad-lib, very special. It's rock 'n' roll night!"

"Oh. Rock 'n' roll night. I see."

"Hey, Curley, it's the end of the engagement, so let's try to make it something special. No matter what's happened between us, tonight is like opening night. All hatchets are buried."

"Do we have to rehearse with Tiny again?"

"Ah, forget it."

"What's the matter? You the only one allowed to have a sense of humor?"

We bought some pound cake in the coffee shop and shared it in the cab, stopping on the way to buy a bottle of whiskey for the band. Another tradition, he said.

"Interested in knowing how much money we made?" I asked.

"You know already?"

"That's the advantage of keeping records."

"Don't tell me. I don't want to know."

"You're right—you don't want to know."

"Okay, tell me."

"If we cab-it to the airport tomorrow, we'll end up with a profit of almost a hundred and twenty dollars for the two weeks. Sixty bucks a piece," I paused, "assuming we're still splitting even."

"Of course. That was the deal. Is that before or after commissions?"

"After. I figured ten percent to George and ten to the Morris office, both off the top."

"Jesus, only thirty bucks a week. That's not going to do much at home."

"You'll make more when you're on your own."

"Nah, not likely. The only thing I'll save on is the other fare and maybe a little food. I'd probably still be eating with somebody, or have somebody with me—if not a guitarist, then a lady." He rested a beat. "I know this is not how we expected things to end, but it's for the best—for both of us. This way we can each have our careers and still be friends."

"I'd like that very much."

"No question. Friends forever."

"I mean it, Bobby."

"Me too. If I can ever help..."

"Me too."

He was silent. "Myra wanted me to agree not to bang anybody else. That's crazy, isn't it? I couldn't make a commitment like that. When I told her, she fell apart. I might see her from time to time if we cross paths, but I've changed my mind about traveling with her, or anyone for that matter. So, that's one for the Curls."

"Nobody's keeping score."

"I can't be serious about somebody at this point in my career. Besides, she's not really my type."

"I've heard that before."

"*And you probably will again,*" Groucho mugged.

"Did you tell her that?"

"No, of course not, I'm telling *you* that."

"Chris says she really fell for you."

"Yeah. And Myra says Chris really digs you, too."

I shook my head. "Only in a religious sort of way."

"Well, take some advice from the voice of experience: look out tonight, she's set to pop."

"No chance. That'll take a wedding ring."

"They're all the same, aren't they?"

"I guess so."

A photographer from a high school newspaper was waiting at the club door. I headed straight for the dressing room while Bobby played star for the camera. The joint was packed.

Clipper was changing. "Closing night, Steve. It's been."

"Thanks, Clipper. No hard feelings, I hope."

"Nope."

Bobby came in. "Well Clipperberg, it's the last night. Anybody throwing a party?"

"What for?"

"You know, closing night."

"Ha! Fat chance. You're lucky if Mickey'll cash your check. Good news: I'm off to Florida."

"Florida?"

"Yep. Club dates."

"Great. Maybe we'll run into each other sometime."

"Yeah, maybe," he said, heading into the club.

"Did I miss something?" I asked. "Yesterday, wasn't he going to Pittsburgh?"

"That's Clipper's bullshit—he's probably out of work."

"Don't look now, but after tonight, so are we."

I watched from the doorway as the Cuties lined up. Myra's eyes were puffy, even through her heavy stage makeup. She avoided mine. Chris seemed distant, too.

When Liz was ready to go on, I stepped into the wings.

"I missed you last night," she said, primping in the mirror.

"You won't believe it, it couldn't be helped."

"I believe it. What time are you leaving?" Was this a renewal, or just making chatter?

"Eleven." I hesitated. "Can I call you...later?"

"Not tonight. I'm going home early tomorrow, to see my daughter. Maybe we'll catch up in the Big Apple."

"That'll be great," I smiled.

She looked at me. "I wish you all the best, Steve. Don't be too tough on yourself. Keep showing the soft side. People like that."

"That's very profound."

"It was meant to be."

The first show was the blockbuster of the engagement. The packed house loved everything he did. But between shows was just like any other busy night—any special closing night festivities never materialized. Andy delivered the pictures while Darin was out working the room, and tried to get me to pay for the extras. I told him to deal directly with Bobby. "That's hopeless," he grumbled, and walked away.

Just before show time, John came backstage to remind the line that there was rehearsal Monday for a new routine. I felt empty; rehearsal didn't apply to us.

"Good luck to you, pally," he said. "I hear you're gonna be out on your own. Maybe we'll book you if you have a record."

Suddenly, being my own act required that I be courteous to a potential employer. "Gee, that would be great, John. I'd really like that. Thanks."

"But ya gotta have a record," he warned. "No record, no work. That's the hard reality of our business, pally." He probably doesn't even remember my name.

"I may want to fool around a little second show," Bobby said as Tiny walked by. "A little ad-lib, loose, not the written notes, you know."

"So, what's different?"

"Very good, Tiny. Very good. You know, someday, Tiny, I'll be back here as head-liner, and I'll never forget you. Hey, just for once, smile at me."

"Why the hell should I?"

"Come on, Big T, it's closing night. I made a bet with Steve that you don't have teeth. He says you do. Settle it for us, huh?"

"Go fuck yourself, Darin. You're a punk and you'll always be a punk. You'll fool a lot of people with your talent, but you don't fool me."

"Hey, Tiny," he said, as our bandleader walked on stage, "seriously, thanks for everything. I couldn't have done it without you."

"Pick up the music after Pearl," he directed, powdering before the late show. "I have a feeling that the band is going to split quick. This may be *our* closing night, but to them it's just another night before their day off."

I wondered if he really thought about it that way—our last show together. "Maybe tradition hasn't reached Dearborn yet."

"Wanna try a swap later?"

"Sure, but I thought..."

"Yeah, well, she wants to see me one more time, to *talk*. Maybe I'll dip it again, who knows."

"Whatever you like. If Myra works it out with Chris, it's okay with me. Did you see the pictures?"

"Yeah, they're great. Take yours?"

"No."

"Do. Leave a set. Take the rest. Give some to Myra and Chris. They'll have mem-ories for when their taps fall off."

By the time he had reached his second hunk, Clipper was slurring his words, visibly drunk, and not at all funny. After a few minutes of nothing, John's voice boomed out from the back of the room.

"Yesh, Yesh, *Messhage from Garshia*," Clipper muttered. "Yesh, I get the messhage. Critics! Everyone of you are God-damned critics!" This was no joke. Suddenly the whole room hushed. "Ladiesh and genelmen," he pleaded, "you don't know what ish like in my business. You think all it is is just getting up here an' bein' funny? Well, it isn'. I have to wait until the agent calls and tells me how I did before I know how I did. Did I make the customers happy? Wash I funny? Here I am, forty-five years old, asking how I did. Isn' tha' something? If there is a God, He will know that I have received little here…"

"Message from Garcia!" John snapped again. If it was quiet before, now it was deadly.

"Yesh, yesh. So now ladiesh and genemen,…"

"This is it, Curley."

"It's been great, Bob."

We shook hands. "This is the beginning, Steve, not the end. Thanks for everything. I couldn't have done it without you."

"You know I wanted to be here more than anything."

"…for his final appearanch here at Club Temptashion…"

Bobby stopped me when I began to go to my place on the bandstand. "Walk on with me for this show, Curley. Let's end the way we began. Let's go on together."

"Sure you want to do that?"

"Positive. It's my act, right?"

"It's your act, right. I'd like that."

"…and we all hope that he comsh back again, les' welcome…Bobby Darin!"

The applause was very full as I went to my harbor behind the piano. The first half of the show passed quickly. When he took his bow after "Rock Island Line," the reaction was thunderous. All the record promotion had helped—audiences were beginning to recognize the tune. Then he returned to center stage. "Ladies and gentlemen," he began, "this has been a marvelous engagement for me. It's my first major nightclub, and I want to thank everyone here at Club Temptation for all their help and support. To Mickey, your host; to John, your maitre d'; to Sharon on the lights; and to all the staff, a million thanks. To Tiny Simpson and his great band...I couldn't have done it without you all. How 'bout it, folks? Let's hear it for the band!"

When the room quieted again, he did something I'll never forget as long as I live. "Now, there's a very special person that I want to thank, and introduce to you." He paused. "I met Steve Karmen back in high school and we've been best friends ever since." My face flushed; I was glad not to be downstage at this moment. "Not only did we play in the same band when we were kids—I was the drummer and he was the lousy saxophone player (the audience laughed)—but when he learned how to play guitar, he agreed to be my accompanist, and put aside his own desires and ambitions to help me launch my career. Tonight, I have the great pleasure of being able to return some of the help he's given me over the years. I want you to be the first to know that, after this engagement, Steve Karmen is going out on his own, as a single, and I think that this wonderful audience deserves to be the first ever to hear what he's going to do. Now, he didn't know I was going to do this, but I want him to come up here and sing a song for you. Ladies and gentlemen! Please welcome Steve Karmen! Come on out here, Curley!"

My heart was pounding like crazy as I squeezed around Larry and came to center stage. Bobby had a great big numero-uno plastered all over his face. "Go get 'em, Curls! Sing 'Country Boy,'" he whispered, "the whole tune." Then he walked into the audience to stand near John at the back of the room.

I was alone. "Thank you, ladies and gentlemen. This is...a complete surprise. I want to thank my friend, my *best* friend, Bobby Darin, for sharing his stage with me. I don't have a full band to accompany me, but I'll try to make it sound full with just me and my guitar."

"Too much talk, just sing," Bobby yelled, and the audience broke up.

"You're right," I smiled, and began.

For the next three minutes, as I sang, the room was pin-drop still. It was the most incredible feeling of musical power and communication I'd ever experienced. Hearing my own voice echo through the attentive silence only made my singing emotionally stronger. I never sang "Country Boy" better. When I strummed the last chord, the applause was overwhelming.

"More...more...sing more!" a few people yelled.

I backed off. "Thank you, ladies and gentlemen, and especially thanks to Bobby Darin for giving me this chance. Bobby, come on back up here."

There was more applause as he returned. When he reached the mike, he shook my hand and patted me on the back. "You did great," he said, so only I could hear, "I knew you would. Stay here. We'll close it together."

"Ladies and gentlemen, Steve and I are going to finish this engagement with a special song that proves that women really are smarter than men." As always, I knew exactly where he was going. I played the intro and we sang "Man Smart"—trading choruses with the same bright energy as we had on opening night, and with the same love of music that had bonded us together right through high school and up to this moment. No matter what else had changed between us, music was still our glue. The audience laughed in all the right places, and when it ended, we bowed as we had rehearsed, and then walked off together, smiling, acknowledging the applause, practically falling all over each other.

"You go out," I said, wanting to stay in the wings, but when Bobby took his bow, he yelled for me to join him.

I took a few steps out, waved, and walked off again, appropriately leaving the last applause for him. We met in the sanctuary of the dressing room. "I've seen you do a lot of things this week that I couldn't predict, but that takes the cake. I don't know what to say."

"Nothing to say, Curls. You earned it. It was my way of saying thanks, and wishing you luck."

While the Pearl was on, Clipper came in. "A lil' drama, I shee. I knew you had it in you, Steve, I told you so. Well, congratulations and goo' luck. I hope that your trip home is...in a plane. Only kiddin'-only...oh, what the hell." He shoveled his makeup into his garment bag. "Remember, never sit directly on a toilet seat," he said to himself, "always spread out paper." We both smiled. "We'll meet again," he said, offering his hand to both of us.

"I'm sure of it," Bobby said.

"Goo' luck-goo' luck."

"You too, Clipper Daniel."

He stopped in the doorway. "Tha's the name my parents gave me." Then, without looking back, "Goo' luck, fellas. Goo' luck, 'n' goo' bye."

When the show ended, some of the Cuties passed by, wishing luck; then John, who told Bobby that he would call next week; then Andy, who mumbled something unintelligible about extra pictures; and then, finally, Liz, dressed in street clothes.

"It's been great working with both of you," she said. "I hope our paths cross again, somewhere. Maybe in New York. I'll be rooting for big things."

"*Thanks, Scarlet*," Gable said.

"You're the best," I whispered when my turn came to hug.

"Good luck to both of you."

The band came off last, and the goodbyes moved into the wings. We shook hands with everyone, including Tiny. Larry brought our music folders into the dressing room. "Here are your charts, guys. Next time we meet, maybe there'll be notes on 'em."

"There's a bottle of hooch for you all," Bobby announced grandly. "I hope you enjoy it with my thanks for helping us out so much. It's corny, but we really couldn't have done it without you."

"Yeah, well, see ya," Tiny said, leaving, not caring to participate in tradition.

Artie found cups, and in a few minutes we were all toasting each other.

"Here's to the next time we meet," said Bobby.

"I hope we're making more money," Larry said.

"And getting laid regular," Artie said.

"Drink up," said Teddy. "To everyone's health."

"To health," said Len, as we all drank.

"See you, good luck, bye," they said as they walked out of our lives.

Backstage became very quiet. It was really over. I could hear the last customers leaving. The Pearl came out of her dressing room counting her music parts. She was wearing a tweed business suit that completely disguised her fabulous body. "Bye, fellows," she said, moving quickly into the showroom. "Have a happy life." She was gone before we could respond.

"It's absolutely amazing that neither of us ever spoke to her during the entire engagement."

"I still want to *speak* to her," Bobby said, leering. "Well, maybe someday." He picked up his clothing bag. "Ready, Teddy?"

I hoisted my guitar case and stuck the music envelope under my arm. "Right behind you." I glanced around.

"It'll never be like this again, Curley."

"You're probably right."

"It was great, wasn't it?"

"Yes, it was."

"Thanks, club," he yelled to the stage.

"Yeah, thanks club," I repeated softly.

We met Chris and Myra in the bar, and then, for the last time, I walked through the doors of Mickey's Club Temptation.

"Does anyone have déjà vu?" Myra asked, as we finished our farewell bacon-and-grease breakfast at the Bagel. She looked as though she might break down at any time. "Doesn't this remind you of a night two weeks ago when we all sat here for the *first* time? It seems so long ago, doesn't it? So much has happened."

"Sure has," Bobby said. "What was just a dream two weeks ago has become a reality. The first club job is history—we did it."

"Yes, you did it," Chris said, squeezing my hand under the table.

"Being back home is sure going to feel different," Bobby said. "Of course, I'm sad about leaving this place and all its memories, but moving on is what life is all about."

"What about you, Steve?" Myra asked. I could feel Chris's hand tighten.

"This has been the best two weeks of my whole life."

"Me too," Chris said.

"Practically speaking," Bobby went on, "I think that someone on the road shouldn't expect to establish lasting personal relationships. The life is too transient. Look at Clipper and Mrs. Clipper." He glanced at me, almost winking. "They're not happy. The entire concept of the road is contrary to having relationships. You have to settle down to make it work. Acts on the road are not settled." Myra began to cry. "Hey, baby, don't start again. I was just making conversation."

"I can't help it," she said.

"Are you packed?" Chris asked.

"Steve is. I'm not."

"Hoping for a fast getaway?" she asked, eyebrows raised.

"No, just an old habit of being prepared," I said.

"How are you getting to the airport?" Myra sniffled.

"Taxi," said Bobby.

"Too bad we don't have a car. We'd drive you."

"Yeah, too bad," I said.

Bobby got up. "Ready to walk back?"

"Sure, let's not postpone the inevitable," Myra said.

He motioned that I take the check. "Enough already. Let's not spoil the last night."

When we reached the hotel, Myra kissed my cheek. "Good luck, Steve. I hope we'll meet again someday, and that things go well for you."

"Thanks, Myra, and for you, too," I said, hugging her.

"Could we postpone our goodbye for a little, Chris?" Bobby asked. "If you don't mind, I'd like to talk to Myra privately, up in your room. Just for a few minutes."

"Okay with you?" she asked.

Myra nodded. "Just for a few minutes."

"I bought you a gift," Chris said, opening her purse in the privacy of our room. "I saw it yesterday, and thought of you immediately. I hope you like it," she smiled bravely, her eyes tearing.

I unwrapped the small jewelry box. It contained a silver medal on a chain.

"It's a St. Christopher's medal. He's the Saint for people who travel. I had it engraved."

I turned it over. *To Steve, from Chris. 4-30-56* "Thank you. I've never had anything like this. "

"Let me help you put it on." I felt her warm hands fasten the chain around my neck. "I hope that you'll wear it sometimes, and...think about me."

"I'll never forget you, you know that."

"There's something else I want you to know," she said, looking into my eyes with utmost sincerity. "I want you to know that...when I have my first baby, if it's a boy, I'm going to name him after you. I'm going to call him Steve—either his first name or his middle name."

"Suppose your husband objects?"

"Oh, he won't know the reason I want the name Steve, and I won't tell him. The mother is entitled to a say in choosing the name, you know."

"Suppose it's a girl?"

She kissed my cheek softly. "In that case, you're out of luck."

"Thank you. It's a wonderful gift." I put my arms around her. I could feel her body tremble as we kissed.

"I really hope I'll see you again."

"Me too." I meant it.

"I'd better go now. I don't want to leave Myra for too long." She stepped back. "I'll write to you, Steve. Thank you for two wonderful weeks."

"You've just said everything that I was going to say."

"Then...there's nothing more to say."

She opened the door, but came back into my arms for one more kiss. "You were terrific tonight. I was so very proud of you."

I smiled weakly, feeling abandoned. "Bye, Chris."

She backed down the hallway. We couldn't take our eyes off each other. She blew a kiss as she stepped into the elevator.

Five minutes later, Bobby walked in. I was folding clothes into my suitcase. He put his suitcase on his bed and we packed in unison. "Myra was really a ping-pong, back and forth between tears and passion. She'll get over it."

"Chris gave me a St. Christopher's medal."

He glanced at my neck. "That's a very special gift. Know what it means?"

"She told me."

"Going to wear it?"

"I don't know."

"Did she tell you it gives all Jews the right to make it with the goyim?"

"Put in a wake-up call, will you?" I said, not wanting to talk.

"What time's our flight?"

"Eleven."

"Eight's early enough. I'll finish in the morning. I'm bushed."

"Me too," I said, moving my suitcase onto the floor, undressing, and getting into bed. "I'm looking forward to going home."

"Yeah," he sighed, turning out the light. "It's been great, Curley. Thanks."

"Thanks to you, again, Bobby," I answered in the darkness, thinking about Chris giving in someday to her Catholic dream man. And naming her son Steve.

Chapter 29

"HOME"

This time, I knew when the plane began to move. I had flown before.

This time, there was no need to run the act. I wasn't part of it any more.

This time, there was no excitement about what it would be like to be in show business. I was in show business—officially, a veteran of my first campaign, a professional. And an adolescent no longer.

During the flight, I sat quietly, deep in numbed thought, my guitar clenched tightly between my knees, only toying with the free lunch. Bobby woofed his down and then ate most of mine. From time to time we made eye contact, nodding at each other in silent understanding, in acceptance, in resignation. There were no words necessary. The end was just a few hours away, and we both knew it.

At LaGuardia, Nina and her kids were waiting, but no Charlie. When I saw Pop, his warm smile was almost enough to make me feel good about being home. Then I saw Arthur with him and I deflated immediately His expression held contempt for this obvious waste of his valuable time. I guessed Pop had dragged him along for the ride—no one in New York must be sick today.

The moment of truth came at curbside. When all our bags were loaded, and with everyone watching, Bobby put his arms around me and spoke softly in my ear. "Thanks, Steve. I couldn't have done it without you."

Smiling as best I could, I returned his embrace. "Good luck, Bobby."

"We'll talk," he said.

"Right. We'll talk."

Soon we were on the Major Deegan Expressway, heading home. Arthur was driving. I was in back with my guitar.

"Did everything go well?" Pop asked.

"Everything was fine."

"You seem very quiet."

"It's nothing."

"He's probably in love," Arthur laughed.

"You'll never know, brother, you'll never know."

Mom had prepared a Sunday chicken. "How was the food in Detroit," she asked. "I'll bet that you ate spaghetti every day, right?"

"Right."

"It's good to eat your cooking, Mom," Arthur said, digging in. "The food at the hospital stinks."

"It's a shame that they don't feed their young doctors better. Pretty soon, they'll be eating like entertainers. How do they expect doctors to be energetic when they don't feed them properly?"

"Their energy comes from being young," Pop said. "So tell us about show business, son. How was it? Really."

"It was a great experience, Pop, I learned a lot."

"Yeah? What'dja learn, sonny-bucko" Arthur grinned, "as if I didn't know."

"Hey brother, go stuff your face, okay? God protect your future patients."

But the needle kept coming. "Meet any cute girls out there?"

"None of your business, okay? Cure any interesting diseases lately, Doctor Pasteur?"

"There's no need to be snippy," Mom said. "Arthur was just asking a question."

"Did the club attract big audiences?" Pop asked.

"Weekends, it was jammed—five hundred people each show. We did two shows every night. The first one was usually pretty full, except Mondays. That's a slow night."

"Were there other acts?"

"Yeah. A line of dancers, a girl singer, a comic, us, and a stripper."

Mom's eyebrows went up. "My son worked with a stripteaser?"

"So? Was it one of the chorus girls" Arthur drooled between bites, "or was it the stripper?"

"Hey, you're not as smart as everyone thinks you are, pill pusher. And if you don't change the tone of your questions, you're going to find your stethoscope shoved up your ass!"

"Don't use that kind of language in this house," my mother said.

"Relax," Arthur sneered. "You've lost your sense of humor, boy."

"You never had one, *Tarzan*."

"Was the hotel clean?" Pop asked, trying to mediate.

"Yeah. There was maid service every day."

"Let's hope you didn't learn any bad habits," my mother warned. "There's no maid service here, you know. Did you get paid yet?"

"No. Bobby'll work it out with George. We'll settle up next week."

"What are you going to do now?" Arthur asked. I wondered if he had been prompted by my parents to pursue this third degree. "Is Bobby booked on the road again?"

"Probably." Another moment of truth. "But I won't be going with him."

"I thought there was something funny going on at the airport," Pop said, seriously. "What happened, son? Did the two of you have a fight?"

"No. Nothing like that. I've just decided...to take a shot on my own. So I won't be working with Bobby any more."

"What do you mean? *You're* going to be an act?" Arthur asked, grinning at the impossibility of it all.

"That's right."

"That's crazy," my mother said. "You have no experience..."

"As much as Bobby."

"He's different."

"Why?"

"Because he's a *bum* from a *bum* family. *Bums* become entertainers."

"Bob Hope is not a bum, Mom. Frank Sinatra is not a bum, Jack Benny is not a bum..."

"Correct! And Frank Sinatra and Bob Hope and Jack Benny are not spending their time with chorus girls and stripteasers!"

"Everybody has to start somewhere," I said quietly.

"How are you going to do it?" Pop asked. "You'll need help."

"Well, I thought that I would talk to George first, to see if he's interested in managing me. But if not, then I'll make some rounds, and try to get work."

This was all beyond my mother's comprehension. "You're making us so miserable with all these crazy ideas! Why can't you just be something normal?"

"I expected this reaction," I said simply. "But I'm doing it anyway, so save your breath. And, if you don't mind, I'd prefer not to argue on my first day home. At least give me a few days to get my guard up."

On Monday, I hung around the house, making lists of material for a potential act, listening to records, playing guitar, renewing my relationship with Mr. Raymond-downstairs, and getting hoarse from singing; but not calling anyone. There was just no one to talk to who would understand. I felt like calling Chris, but that would cost a fortune. I wanted to hide. No, I *was* hiding. I didn't know what else to do.

On Tuesday, I went into the city, but couldn't bring myself to go to George's office. Instead, I stopped at Hansen's.

Freddy Sharp was there. "So, who else was on the show with you?" asked the voice of Mr. Know-Everything.

"A line, a comic, Clipper Daniel..."

"Oh, yeah, a weirdo of the first order," he said. "Worked Cleveland with him..."

"...a girl singer, Liz Carleton..."

"Oh, sure! Chicago! The tea lady! Shitty act, but a great piece of ass. Gave *great* head. Hey, did you make it?"

For an instant I couldn't breathe. I was crushed. Freddy and Liz! My Liz! The vision of Liz doing to Freddy Sharp what she did to me was so appalling that I almost gagged. "No, I didn't. But there was a stripper," I said, "Arlene Stevens, the Birth of a Pearl?"

"Don't know her."

"A terrific act. Talk about action, man, the *best!*"

"How's the record doing?"

"Still moving up."

"Yeah, I've been hearing it. So, where're you guys going next?"

"Not sure," I said. "By the way, where did you have your calypso shirts made?"

Three nights later, Bobby called. "I wanted you to hear this directly from me," he said, all business. "I'm taking Eric Ferrante on the road as my guitarist and road manager. George wouldn't let me take you with me even if you wanted to go, and since you want to be on your own anyway, this was bound to happen."

I tried to sound cheerful. "Good for you."

"Yeah, he'll be great. He's got his own electric and amp, and he plays folk, too." He paused. "You doin' good?"

"Great, working on material, you know."

"Yeah, I know." He paused. "Called him yet?" he asked, an edge of warning coloring his voice, probably knowing that I hadn't.

"No. I will when I'm ready."

"Well, a word of advice: don't push too hard. He's very busy working on me and Connie."

"Say, 'Hello' to her for me."

"I will. Things are good here, too. Mickey picked up the second option; believe that? I'm booked back in Club T in July, maybe as *headliner*. 'Rock Island''s forty-one next week, but no bullet. It's still being played some places, but it seems to be slowing. Donnegan's getting all the airplay. It's tough not being out there to do promotion. Well, at least some of the deejays'll know who I am for next time. Decca wants to talk about another session, more rock material, so that's good, too."

"Great."

"And just so it doesn't go any further, I want you to know that the whole thing with Buddy and John is over. So don't ever mention it anywhere."

"Of course not. What happened?"

"Another one for the Curls. George convinced me that a New York manager is the only way to go, so I called Buddy and killed the deal. But I expect that I'll stay at his house the next time I play Detroit. A good way to save money."

"Oh? What happens if you want to get laid?"

"There's always a way, killer, you know that. Well, I guess that's it...except I need a favor."

"Sure, if I can."

"Would you write out the horn licks on 'Rock Island?' I'm doing a one-nighter in Washington next weekend, and I won't have time to teach the band."

"Sure. I can do that."

"Just leave the parts at George's when you finish. Leave a bill, too."

"No, Bob. I agreed to do your charts before we left. We'll call it square after this."

"Thanks, Curley. Someday, I'll return the favor. Promise. Oh, one more thing: you didn't do too well with your addition," he laughed, not without a little dig. "You forgot to include George's travel expenses for when he came to see us. Sorry, but we only made twenty-two bucks each. He's mailing you a check."

"That's okay. It could be worse."

"Yeah, it could be twenty-one bucks."

"If you see Chris, say, 'Hi' for me."

"I will. We'll talk."

"Yeah, we'll talk."

But we didn't talk.

Not for years.

And by then, everything was different.

Backstage at the Club

My first record

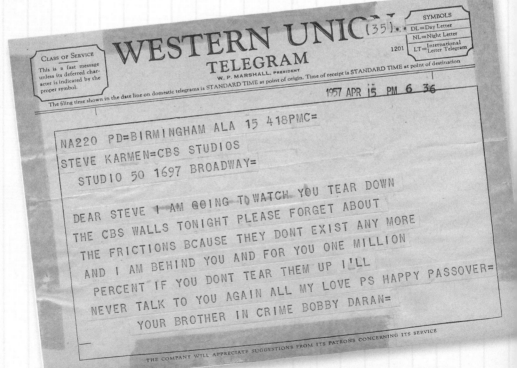

Bobby's telegram from Birmingham —
Western Union misspelled his name

My first acting composite

My Harry Belafonte look

My Tony Curtis look

My James Dean look

My Frank Sinatra look

My Teenage Idol look

On the Job

Some things never change
(They got the marquee right)

At the Roxy Theatre

SPECIAL FOR TODAY

A—COMPLETE SANDWICH LUNCHEON:
BAKED MEAT LOAF ON A TOASTED BUN
served with Free Heinz Baked Beans,
plus DESSERT: Jello, Rice Pudding, Ice Cream or Brown Betty,
plus BEVERAGE: Coffee, Tea or Coca Cola .... **ALL FOR 99**

•

B—CHOPPED EGG SALAD with Filet of Anchovies
on Thin Rye Bread, plus a Slice of Cantaloupe
with Vanilla Ice Cream .... **ALL FOR 98**

•

C—INDIVIDUAL CONTAINER OF SOUR CREAM
WITH COTTAGE CHEESE (or) VEGETABLES 85
WITH PEACH HALVES (or) SLICED BANANAS 85
WITH FRESH BLUEBERRIES 85

•

D—SCRAMBLED EGGS and Smoked Nova Scotia Salmon,
plus a Green Tossed Salad with Special Dressing,
plus Home Baked Rolls and Creamy Butter 99

•

E—ROAST BARBECUED BEEF ON A TOASTED BUN
with New Orleans Barbecue Sauce and a Tossed Green Salad
with Our Special Dressing 99

F—FIFTH AVENUE DELIGHT:
Choice of Chilled Sacramento Tomato Juice or Cup of Soup,
FRESH SHRIMP SALAD on Rye Bread
with Creamy Cole Slaw and Pickle 85

G—STEVE KARMEN CALYPSO SALAD:
Half Cantaloupe with a Large Scoop of
Borden's Creamy Cottage Cheese,
plus Fresh Jamaican Fruit, Saltine Crackers ...... **ALL FOR 89**

H—TO-DAY'S HI-LITE:
CHOPPED CHICKEN LIVERS with Crisp Bacon
and Crisp Lettuce on Thin Rye Bread,
plus a Devil's Food Ice Cream Cake Roll
with Chocolate Sauce 97

Uncle Jack's menu
(Better billing than
Chopped Chicken Livers)

"Steve, meet Bobby — Bobby, meet Steve."

Part Four

NEW YORK CITY
1956-1972

Chapter 30

"DARK DAYS"

America's brilliant playwright, Neil Simon, has written that "the ends of friendships just don't happen: the estrangement has to be fed and nurtured by large doses of insensitivities." Man, was he right. I just didn't see it coming.

I spent that first weekend trying to accurately notate the polka licks that Tiny Simpson's band had ad-libbed on "Rock Island Line." It was a struggle. I followed Teddy's technical instructions as best I could (trumpet written up a tone; tenor sax up a tone, but sounds an octave lower; alto sax down a minor third, sounds an octave higher), but my enthusiasm was non-existent. In case my harmonies were incorrect, I left Bobby instructions to tell the band to play the tenor sax part in unison. At first, I considered rewriting the rhythm parts too, so it all would match and look nice. Then, I thought: *if I wasn't going to play it, why should I give a shit? Would Eric Ferrante be playing folk guitar or electric? Ah, it didn't matter.* No, it did. Cassotto was counting on me and I wanted to do the best I could. I rescored everything, completing a whole new arrangement. On the bottom of each front page I wrote (in *very* small letters): *arranged and copied by Steve Karmen*. At least I'd be there on paper.

Writing the chart was the easy part; trying to explain to my parents why I was still doing work for Bobby was another subject. My mother's constant hovering was painful.

"Why are you...?"

"I promised him I would do this. There's no one else he can call."

"Are you...?"

"No! I'm not getting paid. Must everything be measured in money?"

"Why do you...?"

"He's not taking advantage. I have to finish the job I started. What's so hard to understand about that?"

On Monday afternoon, I brought the music to George Scheck's office. I wasn't planning to ask him until after I had my own act a little more together, but he was alone in his inner sanctum and it kind of just...came out. "I'm going out on my own, George—I guess you knew that—and I was wondering if you'd be interested in being my manager?"

He seemed prepared with his answer. "Oh, that would never work out, Steve," he said dryly, with absolute finality, cutting me off with a shake of his head and a wave of his wet, chewed-up cigar. "In my judgment..." he paused to puff, "your style would be *much* too similar to Bobby's."

"Well, the reason I'm asking *you*, George, *first*, of course, is that I think you're a *terrific* manager, and I know that Bobby is switching to a more *pop* approach, more *rock*, you know, and that *folk* is still real hot, and *calypso*, too, and well...I thought that maybe you'd be interested in having *another* boy singer, a *pure* folk singer, with a completely different approach than Bobby, of course...and that maybe you could help get me a record deal. I've been writing songs, and my material is much more like what we were doing in the act up 'til now—but not what Bobby's going to do *from now on*, of course. You know what I mean?"

"It's more than material, Steve," said the voice of velvet, sounding fatherly (I *hated* it when George sounded fatherly). "You're a talented young man, and I know that you and Bobby are good friends; but he expects me to devote most of my energies to him, and to Connie, and experience has taught that if there's competition between two acts in the same office, it's not healthy for either one of them."

"But, I wouldn't be competing..."

"You may not think so, Steve, but when Bobby has his first hit, and he'll have one soon, he'll need even more of my time than I have to spare for him now, and you'll start feeling left out..."

"But other managers handle more than one act, more than one boy singer," I said, starting to plead (even though I had promised myself that I wouldn't). "Why couldn't you do it for just a little while, maybe just until I got a few jobs? You could get me auditions for...*starter* jobs...you know what I mean."

"No, Steve, it's really impossible. I'm flattered that you'd think enough of me to ask, but Bobby's going to need every minute I can spare. Decca is not happy with the sales figures on 'Rock Island Line.'" He glared at me, and for an instant I felt like it was my fault. "And we have to be thinking of what to record next."

"Oh, I see…"

"If I change my mind," he said, dismissing me, "I'll call you."

I took one more shot. "Do you know anyone else who might be interested? You know, another manager who might be looking for new acts?"

"No. Helping you that way would only create more friction with Bobby. I hope you understand. And in the future, Steve, I think it would be better if you didn't show up here without an appointment. Business procedures, you understand. And I wish you the best of luck."

"Thanks, George."

Leaving George's office was my personal low: my family, particularly my mother, was offering zero encouragement for my new career direction; my once-best friend had moved on without me, both in his act and in his life; and the only show business manager I knew in any position to help me, wouldn't.

The days ran into each other as I moped around the apartment, with no energy for practicing guitar or flying around the room in Pop's hat like Sinatra. My lethargy became the focus of everyone's attention; every conversation carried an undertone of conflict. Arthur, at home for a mid-week meal, speculated that I had met a girl for whom I was now pining. Pop thought I might be sick, but later agreed with Arthur. "Don't worry, son," he had said, "there are lots of fish in the sea." My mother wanted to know if she was Jewish. I was glad I had decided not to wear my St. Christopher's medal around the house.

To avoid their endless prying, I began taking a late-afternoon subway into town to hang around and eat at Hansen's, hoping that being with other people would provide refuge from the confusion and depression of going through Darin-withdrawal cold turkey. When Mr. Hansen told me that Bobby had yet to pay for our stage makeup, I decided to do it myself—after all, I'd used half of it. It was just another sign that it was over—official-official. "Seen Bobby?" Woody Harris asked? "Doing record promotion," I lied, hoping the standard excuse would still work. Did Woody know we had split up? Did Freddy Sharp? Did everyone? We talked of other things: the *Billboard* charts; theories on what makes a hit; who was recording that week; which acts were looking for material; who the new hot arrangers were; everything and anything but *Darin*. If anyone had shown real interest, I had planned to explain away our split-up by saying that I had decided to go out on my own.

No one asked.

Slowly, the idea that I was turning the control of my life over to someone *who wasn't even there* became so strong that I forced myself to develop a discipline— *my* new rules—that I hoped would pull me out of my funk and put some fun back into my life.

Each day, I scheduled specific times to practice and write songs. At first, my creative head was seriously twisted. My piano playing was funereal. All I felt like doing was just sitting there, striking chords over and over, listening to their long fade-out into nothing. My strumming wasn't much better. Tempos that I tried at ramming speed had no energy. Nor did I have the vocal power to sustain a real *DAAAAAAAAAA-YOH!* It was easier and more comfortable to rest my cheek on the top of my guitar, my face so close to the strings that I could feel the vibration on my skin, just close my eyes, and pick away softly in minor keys. My emotions were all over the place. I drifted with them. Any lyrics that I scribbled were plaintive and filled with hurt and longing. And I was also filled with rage. Alone in our living room, sometimes I would startle myself, realizing I was shouting, *yelling* at the top of my voice, screaming at that fucking motherfucker who wasn't there, but who had clearly claimed a home in my brain.

Getting out of the house became an important part of my ritual. My new rules brought me to the public library (first in the Bronx, then in Manhattan) where I researched early American folk music—looking for that unusual, undiscovered idea that might work well in a live performance. I sought out any calypso record I could find to learn songs that I could sing in an act—*my* act. When I felt I had enough material together, I began traipsing up and down Seventh Avenue making endless rounds to club-date agents—just walking into their offices, always carrying my guitar, begging for work, offering to do an audition right on the spot. It was as if someone had told me that I didn't have the ability to make it—I only worked harder. *Oh yeah? Just watch me!* I became the king of *I'll show you!*

My perseverance finally paid off. In August of 1956, after four months of pounding on doors, I landed my first job: on the Saturday night cruise of the Hudson River Dayliner—a ferry that sailed around Manhattan. A belly dancer was the other act (I told my parents it was a comedian). I opened with "Day-O"; then sang "Jamaica Farewell," "Man Smart," "The Man Piaba," "Mama Look A Boo Boo"—all familiar Harry Belafonte hits—as well as the more risqué "The Lost Watch" and "The Big Bamboo"—songs I'd learned from records. I thought about including "Country Boy," my favorite ballad, but had been warned by the booker to keep things lively, so I left it out. I closed with a long version of "Matilda," Harry's classic; and amazingly, when I shouted "*Eve-ry-bod-y!*" the whole crowd sang along. It was a great feeling. I had sketched out some rhythm charts for the five-piece band, ala Club Temptation, but these New York musicians were already familiar with most of my calypso material. *Plus* the sax man also played flute, which really made things sound good. I could see the headline in *Variety*:

Karmen a Hit on the River! Parents Underwhelmed!

Part of my deal with the Dayliner was that I had to stroll the deck for an hour after the show, singing to customers. This time I had trouble keeping attention: under the moonlit sky most of the guys were more intent on putting the make on their dates; so no one really listened.

It didn't matter: I was now officially a working performer on my own.

I earned twenty-five dollars that night (less ten percent commission to the agent, of course) and when he got a good report, he began booking me, on the river again, and at private parties, and on local industrial shows that wanted a few minutes of "something different." (Oh, how I thought of Clipper Daniel, living each day wondering if he'd received a good report after some remote job somewhere. What a trapped life it was to be dependent on someone else's opinion of your worth.)

Calypso music was hotter than ever, and as my repertoire grew, I got my first nightclub job—and from a surprising source.

Late one Monday morning, the phone rang.

"Steve, this is George Scheck."

"Oh, hi, George," I answered brightly. "What's new?" Had word of my successes reached his exalted level of show business?

"A very dear friend," he began smoothly, "is the maitre d' of a small East Side bistro, the Living Room. Do you know the club?"

"No, sorry, I don't, George."

"In any event, their folk singer just called in sick, and they need a quickie substitute, for one night only, to fill in. Can you do it?"

"Tonight?"

"That's right, tonight."

"Of course I can, George," I said as confidently as my shakes would allow.

"Do you have enough material? They need a half-hour show."

I had twenty solid minutes, and knew I could stretch for ten more. "Absolutely. I don't know if you were aware of it, George, but I've been singing on the Hudson River Dayliner, and doing lots of one-nighters, at the Mark Cross industrial show, and…"

"That's nice, Steve. The club is on Forty-ninth Street and Second Avenue. It doesn't pay a lot—twenty dollars, less my commission of twenty percent, for a one-nighter, you understand."

"Of course, George."

"Be there by eight-thirty. You go on at nine."

"Great! I'll call you tomorrow to let you know how I did!"

"That's not necessary, Steve. Just send a check for the commission."

"Oh, sure, George. And thanks! Thanks a lot!"

"Happy to help," he said, hanging up.

With my new red-striped calypso shirt tucked under my arm, I arrived at the Living Room early. The club seated about 125 people and offered a different kind of atmosphere to its patrons: instead of tables and chairs there were plush couches with candles flickering on little end tables. The lights were very dim; it was all very intimate and cozy. The piano, in one corner, was lit only by a tiny ceiling spotlight, and shared its microphone with a small stand-up space next to it.

I was told to change clothes upstairs, in the back of the kitchen, next to the men's room. *Since I had slept in a kitchen as a kid,* I thought, *changing in one would be easy.*

The other act, a young black pianist, went on first. His name was Willie Treat; he wore a gray satin tuxedo and had slicked-back hair and bright, shiny eyes. Willie sang standards—particularly soft, dreamy ballads—and sounded exactly (and I mean *exactly*) like Nat King Cole. But Willie had a slight speech impediment. As he sustained each note—beautifully and on pitch—he also added the letter "M" to the end of every word. He sang, *"I'm in the mood for luuuuummmmm-mm, simply because you're near meeeeeem"; "Unforgettableeeeeem…that's what you areeeeeem"; "They tried to tell us we're too younmmmmm"*; and *"Mona Lisa, Mona Lisa, men have named youummm."* No one seemed to notice but me.

When Willie finished his set, he simply walked off, and I went on and did my show. The small, Monday-night crowd was receptive and I thought I did okay. When Willie returned for his next set, I began packing.

"Where are you going, kid?" the maitre d' asked.

"Home," I said. "I'm done, right?"

"Not if you want to get paid, you're not. It's half-on half-off until four AM. Seven shows."

Seven shows?

That night, I sang every song I had ever heard in my entire life, every calypso from "Matilda" to "Nora" to "Hold 'Em Joe"; every folk song from "Jimmy Crack Corn" to "My Grandfather's Clock" to "On Top Of Old Smokey." But after the last show, the maitre d' bought me a steak diner and offered me a full week's job—alternating with the folk singer I had substituted for. Two weeks later, I replaced him, and then stayed at the Living Room for fifteen weeks more. (I paid George commission for the first two weeks only. Since he wasn't my official manager, I figured I had earned the rest of the engagement on my own. He didn't complain.)

When the Yankees were in town, the Living Room was a favorite watering hole for Mickey Mantle and his drinking buddy, Billy Martin. As the 1956 season neared an end, Mantle was keeping pace with Babe Ruth's home record, and after night games, the gang at the club would expect the two of them to show up late in the evening, just to hoist a few. Billy Martin was always very friendly and rooting for Mickey to do well. Occasionally, we were able to chat between shows in the hallway outside the john next to my *dressing room*. Mickey usually stayed at the bar, talking softly in his Oklahoma drawl, to one of the beautiful ladies of the evening who frequented the club. I never got to meet him directly, but he always paid attention during my act. The Mick hit fifty-four homers that year (the record then was sixty), but my fondest memory of him is that he laughed in all the right places during "Mama Look A Boo Boo."

Bookings in other nightclubs followed: Martha Kaye's Velvet Club and the Spotlight Bar, small rooms that would hire a self-contained act; especially one that could sing calypso and was willing to do seven shows a night, seven nights a week. In November 1956, I moved up a slot and opened for the legendary Ethel Waters at Le Ruban Bleu in New York.

Sometimes, on weekends, when I could work out the timing between shows, I was booked as a novelty act on the Art D'Lugoff Saturday Night Calypso Concerts at Carnegie Hall. Art always got a laugh when he introduced me as "the most authentic of the non-authentic calypso singers." (How do you get to *Carnegie Hall?* You practice, mon, you practice!) I shared the stage with some of the great calypsonians—the Duke of Iron, Lord Burgess, Lloyd Thomas—island legends whose songs I'd learned from records. But no matter how friendly and respectful I tried to be, I always sensed an anger and resentment from them because I was nothing more than a smart-ass imitation from the Bronx using their bread-and-butter material, getting the job because I was white. (I always tried to find out beforehand who was going to be on the show so I could steer clear of doing any of their material.)

Watching the greats from the wings, I came to believe that my calypso successes were due more to the fact that I was *not* the real thing. Harry Belafonte had found a way of making calypso music easily understood, and fun for a universal audience. When the *authentic* calypsonians sang about sex, marriage, and infidelity, their thinly disguised risqué lyrics made everyone laugh. But when their songs were about the real-life issues and day-to-day problems of Caribbean life, the attention span of a New York drinking crowd wore thin quickly. (I realized that the *presentation* of material was equally as important as the subject matter.

Learning that an audience must understand and identify with the lyrics was an especially valuable lesson that served me well in later years, when I began to write advertising jingles.)

On the occasions when I had these doubles, Pop would pick me up outside wherever I was appearing and drive me to Carnegie Hall, where he and my mother would wait in the car while I performed, ready to shuttle me back to the club in time for my next show. Though I had made arrangements for them to do so many times, they never came in to see me work. I think they were torn between wanting to help me and having their help perceived as an endorsement of what I was doing. I know they constantly hoped I would straighten out and become a *professional*.

During the day, I kept composing, practicing, and making demos, with the goal of finding a record company that would invest in a session.

In February 1957, a small independent label, Eldorado Records, took interest in one of my calypso songs, "Gotta Have Love." The two young hustlers who owned Eldorado—Bill Buchanan and Dick Goodman—had recently created a hit of their own; an ingenious novelty record they called "The Flying Saucer."

On "The Flying Saucer," a narrator would ask simple questions: *"Sir, a spaceman has just landed on earth. What are you going to do when you see him?"* And Little Richard's voice would answer: *"Jump back in the alley!"* (borrowing a two-second piece lifted directly from his record of "Long Tall Sally"). Then the narrator would ask: *"But where will all the spacemen live?"* And Elvis Presley would cry out: *"Down at the end of Lonely Street..."* (borrowed from "Heartbreak Hotel").

Borrowing pieces of someone else's hit record is a legal no-no, and naturally, the entire music industry immediately sued Buchanan and Goodman. They were, however, able to settle the suit by giving each of the music publishers and record companies small percentages of "The Flying Saucer" income. Now fancying themselves as industry moguls, Buchanan and Goodman formed Eldorado Records, my first label. Believing that there was still a market for a white Harry Belafonte, they agreed to release the demo of "Gotta Have Love" (my own composition), but only after first signing me to one of those multipage, multiyear, imprisonment contracts.

Rock 'n' roll had created a category of greed that was limited only by how much a sharp businessman could get away with. In return for that first head-spinning shot at fame and fortune, a new artist was always signed to a record company for a minimum of a year, plus four one-year options—the company's *exclusive* option, of course. Details like the choice of material, how many recordings would be made, release dates, even what the artist would wear on tour—all belonged *exclusively* to the record company. If the singer was also the songwriter, then any original material had to be published by the record company's music publishing division (and *every* record label had one!) The artist's royalty rate was always microscopic, and everything and anything imaginable was charged to the artist as production expense to be recouped by the company *before* any royalty payments were ever made. The cost of musicians, studio, tapes, sound engineers, background vocalists, arrangers, copyists, you name it (and often any *personal* perk that a company exec wanted to bury somewhere), always found its way into the singer's red ink. Royalty statements—if any were actually sent—kept the concept of honesty at a long, arms-length distance. One-hit-wonders *never* got paid. The opportunity to take advantage of talented innocence was irresistible, and kids with stars in their eyes who had formed street-corner bands and doo–wop groups were signing anything put in front of them just to hear their songs on the radio; *thrilled* to be part of it all. Everyone was having a ball *onstage*, and getting screwed *backstage*. (The standing joke—not so funny—was that record companies controlled *everything* an artist could do, including when they were allowed to go to the bathroom.)

Of course, I signed my Eldorado Records contract without reading it, and certainly without showing it to my parents.

"Gotta Have Love" didn't sell. I never heard it on the radio or had any idea if Eldorado had even distributed it nationally. But as my act improved, I worked steadily through that winter; until, in April, 1957, an agent from General Artists Corporation (GAC), a hot talent agency competing with the William Morris Agency, heard me sing at a club, and got me an audition for "Arthur Godfrey's Talent Scouts" TV program. This Monday night network show on CBS featured new talent in a competitive format. Pat Boone, the McGuire Sisters, Anita Bryant, Carmel Quinn, Holly Loke, and other top recording acts had all gotten their starts on "Talent Scouts." (My Muse had a hand in this, too—the show was broadcast from CBS Studio 50, the same theatre that "Stage Show" had come from exactly a year earlier.)

I don't know how he found out I was going to be on, but my appearance brought about my next contact with Bobby Darin.

"Telegrams, Mr. Karmen," the CBS page said after rehearsal, thrusting a fistful of yellow paper at me—from family, friends, and one from Bobby. He was in Birmingham, Alabama, doing record promotion.

> *Dear Steve,* it read, *I'm going to watch you tear down the CBS walls tonight. Please forget about the frictions because they don't exist anymore and I am behind you and for you one million percent. If you don't tear them up I'll never talk to you again. All my love. PS Happy Passover. Your brother in crime, Bobby Daran* (Western Union misspelled his name).

On April 15, 1957, I made my debut on national television. Even though it was the first night of Passover, my parents came to the show. Pop promised to whistle loudly at the end when the audience's applause was measured to determine the winner. Later, he told me that he was so excited and proud to see me on TV that he completely forgot to whistle. There were two other contestants: a young Canadian girl who sang in French; and the eventual winner, a soldier just home from duty in Korea, who dressed in full army uniform—medals, ribbons, shiny shoes, the works—and sang a medley of "America The Beautiful," "You're A Grand Old Flag," and "God Bless America." "Mama Look A Boo Boo" didn't stand a chance. But even though I lost, Godfrey thought enough of my performance to invite me to appear on his morning TV show for the rest of that week—the standard reward to the winner of the Monday talent contest.

Each morning throughout that week, I wondered if Bobby was watching. Sometimes I felt like I was singing just for him: *Look at me, Cassotto! Look where I am! Look at where I got to on my own!!!*

Finally, on Friday afternoon, with five days of addictive applause pumping up my bravado, I decided to call him to thank him for the wire. No, that's not true: I just really needed a Darin-fix, and now I had a legitimate excuse to make contact. He was at home. I hadn't heard his voice in a year.

"Bobby, it's Steve. Thanks for the wire. It meant a lot."

"Hey, Curley, how are you?" He sounded distant, removed. "I caught the show. Ya did good."

"Thanks. See any of the morning shows?"

"No. How'd they go?"

"Great-great. There's a seven-piece band, and they do arrangements for you over night, believe that? You sing the tune you want to do to a staff arranger, and he does a chart and gets it copied *over night!*" Suddenly, I felt like I was bragging.

"Big time, huh?"

That's not how I wanted this to go. I tried a softer approach. "A little, I guess. How's your Mom doing?"

"Chugging along, but not good. She coughs a lot at night."

"I'm sorry."

"Look, I can't really yak now. Gotta pack. I'm going to Philly for the weekend."

'Work?'

"No, there's a lady I met on tour, and..."

"Say no more. I understand."

"I'm movin' out next week. Behrke and I are going to share an apartment on Seventy-first Street."

"Really." Now *I* sounded jealous.

"Nina's a killer. All she does is bug me for rent money. If I have to pay it, at least it'll be for my own pad. Should have done it a year ago. Next time we catch up, I get you the number."

"Great. Well...I just wanted to say thanks for the wire. And wish you good luck, Bobby. I hope things are going the way you want them to."

For a moment he was lost in thought. "Ah, Decca's a pain in the ass. They sprung for another session, but now they don't want to release it. I'm trying to break the deal. You know."

"Yeah. Eldorado's no picnic, either. They're all the same, aren't they?" I didn't want to let him off. "How's George?"

"He spends most of his time with Connie—Listen, I really gotta go. Maybe we'll hook up on the road somewhere. This "Godfrey" shit should keep you busy for a while."

"I hope so." We were done. "Well, give my best to your mom."

"Same here. Good luck, Curley," he said, hanging up.

It was only after this painful contact that I began to fully understand how deeply I missed him as part of my life.

To my parents, the "Godfrey" appearances gave my pursuit of show business a temporary air of legitimacy. Everyone in our building had seen the program, and now at least there was some tangible evidence for the neighbors that I had the potential to make a living. One neighbor even started pestering me to buy mutual funds—a sure sign that I was earning respect. The ultimate *family* compliment, however, came from Uncle Jack (of the transparent corned-beef fame). He named the Tuesday special at his luncheonette after me—**The Steve Karmen Calypso Salad: Half Cantaloupe with a Large Scoop of Borden's Creamy Cottage Cheese, plus Fresh Jamaician Fruit, and Saltine Crackers**, all for eighty-nine cents. (The menu misspelled *Jamaican*.) Unlike keeping track of record sale figures, I never asked how well my salad sold. But, to me, this kind of acknowledgement was definitely *big time*.

The dark side of all this was Arthur Godfrey's anti-Semitic reputation. He owned a hotel in Florida, the Kenilworth, which was reputed to be *restricted*, and my mother was ever wary. "Don't let him find out you're Jewish," she warned, "or he'll fire you." And sure enough, one morning, after I'd sung my song, he asked me right on the air: "Tell me, Steve, what kind of name is *Karmen?*" Only he spoke it: "KARRRRRMEN." I fumfered around and mumbled that, "To the best of my knowledge both my parents were born in America," perhaps not the answer he was expecting, but the only one my inbred caution was capable of giving. Being put on the spot reminded me of my first encounter with Chris, who could never really overlook my religion—horns or no horns.

Ignoring any thoughts he might have had about my heritage, Godfrey kept me on his weekly show for five more weeks. I even outlasted the soldier who'd won the "Talent Scouts" competition.

One of the joys of appearing on network television each morning was the fan mail that began to arrive at the studio. Almost all of it was from teenage girls, wanting to know anything they could about me. Did I have fan clubs? Did I have a girl friend? Did I live at home with my parents? Did I have my own room? What movies did I like? What was it like to grow up in New York? Had I ever been on a farm? Did I have a dog? A cat? Had I ever milked a cow? One asked: "Would you come to Colorado and be my date for the senior prom?" Another, from a girl in Georgia, wanted to know if I was "fixin' to get married." I had some personalized stationery printed up and tried to answer every letter. It was all wonderfully innocent.

One morning, Mr. G. read a telegram to me on the air:

> "Would Steve Karmen want to sail as paid entertainer May 17th, Moore McCormack Lines SS Brazil, to Barbados, Brazil, Argentina, etc. Disembarking North Bound at Trinidad June 29th where he can learn more calypso. Eleanor Britton, Director Of Entertainment."

Godfrey was immediately in favor of this adventure for a young man, and urged me to go. "You can come back and tell us all about it," he said, "and make us all jealous." That night, I discussed it with my parents. South America sounded like the moon. My only other lone pioneering trip, a year ago, had been to the Wolverine Hotel in Detroit, with Bobby.

"Talk to Godfrey," Pop urged. "Keep him on your side. See what he thinks."

The next day, I requested a meeting, and when I was escorted into his huge CBS office at 485 Madison Avenue, I tried to be very humble. Godfrey demanded humility from his acts. He had fired singer Julius LaRosa right on the air a few years earlier for pushing his latest record on the show, thus not being *humble* enough.

"Sir," I began, "I'm really grateful for everything you've done for me during the past weeks, and I would like to ask your advice: my agents think that I should turn down the trip to South America because I could earn more by staying here and working in clubs. Would you please give me some guidance?"

"All agents want to do is earn money," he grumbled. "If I were you, boy. I'd go."

I went.

While I was off cruising to Brazil and Argentina, my Eldorado record label owners, Buchanan and Goodman, had spent themselves into bankruptcy. In need of quick cash, they tried to sell my recording contract.

Mercury Records, a major label, was interested and offered ten thousand dollars. (A year earlier, in 1956, RCA had paid forty thousand dollars to Sun Records to buy the rights to Elvis Presley's recordings.) Mercury's logic was if I were only one quarter as good as Elvis, they'd earn back their investment on my first release. Because I was under twenty-one—a fact that Buchanan and Goodman had overlooked in their first contract with me—by law, a parent was required to approve the deal.

Pop gave them a hard time. I later learned that he had gone to their offices and faced off with Dick Goodman's father, an experienced lawyer, and had kept them there for ten hours straight—reading every clause and demanding simple layman explanations for everything he didn't understand. My tough little immigrant Pop was *great*. Eventually, he wore them down, and was able to eliminate many of the horrible terms I had naively agreed to on my own. However, one *un*changeable part of the deal was that ten percent of my income above a certain level was to be paid to a powerful Cleveland disk jockey in return for his playing my records—a kind of payola not uncommon in those years. The deal was signed, with payments, if any, to be made out in the name of the disc jockey's cousin.

In order to prove that I had actually learned enough material on the South American trip to deserve a return appearance on Godfrey's show, I had done some serious homework. In Buenos Aires, Argentina, I bought a gaucho outfit; in Montevideo, Uruguay, I purchased a cheap, but authentic-looking Spanish Guitar; in Rio de Janeiro, I bought a native Brazilian straw hat, neckerchief and shirt; in Port of Spain, Trinidad, I paid the leader of a street corner band five American dollars to sell me his steel-drum (and I painted the notes on it, so I could play it easily). I bought records in every country, and when I found songs I thought I could sing, I got friendly crewmembers to teach me the foreign words phonetically.

I returned home in June, called Godfrey's producer, and set up another audition—this time with all the props and costumes and souvenirs I had accumulated. Once again I was booked on the show. I had enough material for two more weeks, and my "Godfrey" stint ended when he went off the air for summer vacation.

In August 1957, I cut my first record for Mercury, a hard rocker called "She Had Wild Eyes And Tender Lips," for which Hal Mooney did the chart and produced the session. It was released in September, and Mercury sent me on a promotional tour to Philadelphia, where I appeared on Dick Clark's "American Bandstand" show. I spent the next day visiting all the local radio stations, along with ex-heavyweight champ Joe Louis, whom Mercury had hired as a goodwill ambassador for their label. (I guess they thought it would help sales.) At every stop, the deejays were thrilled:

"Ladies and gentlemen, we have a very special guest with us this afternoon, the former heavyweight boxing champion of the world, Joe Louis! The one and only Joe Louis! Welcome Joe, welcome!"

"Thanks," Joe would say softly.

"Joe Louis, the champ! Who could ever forget those memorable fights with Billy Conn? And with Max Schmeling? And with Jersey Joe Walcott? Tell us, Joe Louis, what's it feels like to be retired now, Joe?"

"Good," Joe would answer softly.

"What do you think of the current champ, Floyd Patterson, Joe? Think you could have beaten him when you were in your prime? Think you could teach him a thing or two, Joe Louis, former heavyweight champ?"

"He's a real good fighter," Joe would say softly.

"But not like you, Joe, right?"

"I guess," Joe would sigh softly.

"What are you doing in town now, Joe? To what do we owe the honor of this very special visit from Joe Louis, the Brown Bomber, the former heavyweight boxing champion of the world?"

"This kid's got a new record," Joe would say, and then squint at the label. "His name is Steve Krama. It's a nice song."

Then, the deejay would finally introduce me, ask how it felt to be in the same room as "Joe Louis, the former heavyweight boxing champion of the world," and then we would be out of time. "Let's thank Joe Louis and Steve Krama..."

"Karmen," I whispered to the first deejay, trying to salvage something.

"We'll play Steve's new record a bit later, but after the commercial we'll spend some more time with Joe Louis, the former heavyweight boxing champion of the world!"

On the strength of the Godfrey Show, GAC was able

to book me into nightclubs around the country. I appeared at the Copa in Pittsburgh; the Metropole in Windsor, Ontario; the Cabin Club in Cleveland; and at Woody's Purple Onion in Indianapolis—the *circuit*—always as the opening act. I worked alone at the Poodle Lounge in Cleveland, Ohio, where I'm proud to say that I set the box office record for great business. It stands to this day—the club closed a week after I did.

Along the way, I had opportunities to apply what I'd learned from working with Bobby.

Once, at a county fair in Ohio, I was booked in along with an animal act, Montana Mike and his Wonder Horse, Cupie Doll. Being a TV veteran with a Mercury recording contract had obviously blown my sense of self way out of proportion, and like an idiot, I insisted that "the singer always close the show." The booker pleaded with me to let Montana Mike close, but I was adamant. I guess Cupie Doll was sensitive about her billing, too, because on opening night, right near the end of her act—and probably after some unseen cue from Montana Mike—she crapped on the stage, leaving little, moist marbles of dump in her wake. An assistant came out between acts to quickly shovel up. I could have gotten a roar if my opener had been "Tiptoe Through The Tulips." For that show, instead of roving the stage as I had learned to do—à la Darin—I performed my entire act from a delicately stationary position at my microphone.

But my Mama didn't raise no dummies: for the rest of the engagement, I wisely let Cupie Doll close.

Doing one-nighters, I opened for Little Anthony and the Imperials at a dance party in Buffalo, New York. By this time I had abandoned the calypso shirt approach and was now working in a suit, sometimes a tuxedo, though still singing folk songs. But the change of outfit didn't help. It was a battle of folk against rock. Rock won. Easily.

I spent ten days as the opening act for Jackie Mason at Hugo's Lake Club in Springfield Illinois. Each show he did was different, and funnier than the last. But booking a Jewish comedian into this Bible-belt town was a mistake—there was absolutely no business. We stayed at the same motel, with nothing to do during the daytime; so after making the required visit to Abe Lincoln's tomb, we would hang around in the coffee shop, and I would listen to him complain, hilariously, in his thick Yiddish accent, about everything that was wrong with the world—social observations which later became the material that made Jackie Mason a major Broadway comedy star.

There was a newer circuit, too: the Playboy Clubs in Chicago, Kansas City, St. Louis, Miami, New Orleans, Baltimore, and New York, where acts were booked for two or three weeks at a time. Amply endowed young women waitressed, dressed as Playboy Bunnies, and many aspired to become centerfolds in *Playboy Magazine*. They wore costumes as skimpy as the ones worn by the Cuties; but Bunnies were required to do the "Bunny Dip:" kneeling down in a certain way when they served drinks so that their breasts were at the customer's eye level. These watering holes charged a buck-and-a-half for everything—food, drinks, and cover charge. (Comedian Jackie Gayle always got a big laugh when he explained that *almost* everything costs a buck-and-a-half.)

Of all the unexpected places, I learned the basics of conducting an orchestra at the Baltimore Playboy Club. My back-up band was the standard trio—piano, bass, and drums. Between shows one evening, I found the bass player backstage (standing in the stairwell), studying a Beethoven score and waving a baton at an imaginary orchestra. He had been taking a course at a music school in classical conducting, and this was his only time to practice. I became a willing pupil. He showed me the correct way to hold a baton, how a conductor never lifts his shoulders when he moves his arms, how to stand properly, and how to be broad enough with movement to be seen by the rear of the orchestra without looking like an orangutan. He clarified where the bottom of each the beat lies, and how to do separate things with each arm.

In later years, I conducted the New York Philharmonic Orchestra (110 players) in my own arrangement of "I Love New York," and while it was a humbling experience to repeat thirty seconds of music over and over with an orchestra used to playing two-hour Mahler symphonies, at least I know I looked *professional* when I faced them.

I was booked for three weeks at PJ's, a small club on the Sunset Strip in Los Angeles that hired only one act per engagement. Pianist Matt Dennis preceded me. During the day, construction had been going on to expand the tiny show-room, which was scheduled for completion after my engagement. Things went faster than planned. On the Tuesday of my final week, I arrived at work to learn I had been fired. The new room—at least three times the size of the old one—

was now open; and instead of my intimate folk act, PJ's had hired an electric guitar player who also worked alone, but did a more rock-type act. Trini Lopez went on to have many hit records and achieve stardom in movies. It was a sign.

One of my few chances to perform as the headliner happened at the Junior Room of the Black Orchid in Chicago. My opening act, then just starting out, was a trio of college-age musicians who played back-up for their younger sister (not only was she a terrific singer and performer, but a knockout to look at). She sang standards in a whole new, fresh way and she killed 'em—I didn't. I had great difficulty following her with my simple folk songs. Later, when this great talent dropped her last name, Ann-Margaret Olsen became a major movie star and top nightclub entertainer. It's nice to think that at one time she opened for *me*.

The New York highlight of my performing career came when I was booked into the Roxy Theatre for three weeks, as one of the acts between showings of the latest Tony Curtis movie, *The Perfect Furlough*. The Roxy ran four shows a day, five on weekends, and played to 5,500 people when it was full. But the Monday morning, eleven AM show was not unlike Mondays at Club Temptation—lots of empty. My best memories were not of the great orchestra or the huge weekend crowds, but of Joe the Barber, who came to my dressing room once a week to give me a trim; and of Uncle Jack, who brought me a giant sandwich for dinner each night before my last show. That was really *big*-big time.

Wherever I worked I did record promotion, but my few releases never sold, and Mercury finally gave up. I signed with MGM for a short time, but the results were the same.

My income never reached the level of requiring a payment to the deejay's cousin, and I never made it back to Club Temptation. And I never saw Chris again, or Liz, or Clipper, or anyone from my first fantasy-come-true. I had especially hoped to run into Liz somewhere, to take another shot; this time with the benefit of some new experiences that I had gained through my own travels on the road. But this, too, was not to be. (Liz never came to New York to look for work—at least if she did, she never called *me*.)

Chris and I exchanged letters for a few months until she wrote that she had quit the Cuties and gone back home to Lorraine, Ohio. She concluded with the news that she had met someone she was serious about, and didn't think it would be fair to him if she wrote to me anymore. But she reassured me that she would never forget her promise to name her first son after me.

GAC tried to redirect my career, and a young agent, Steve

Blauner, was put in charge. Steve was a dynamo: one of the most dedicated people I'd ever met; unstoppable when he believed in someone. There was no door that was closed to his tireless energy, and he was assigned to steer me towards becoming a movie star. Blauner set up a meeting with Joyce Selznick, the talent agent at Columbia Pictures who had discovered Tony Curtis and James Darren. She offered to do a screen test that might lead to a seven-year deal as a contract player with Columbia.

After both sides signed the agreement, Blauner sent out a proud announcement to all his colleagues at GAC:

> Steve Karmen will not be available for bookings until further notice. He is leaving for California, Sunday, to take a screen test for Columbia Pictures. If the screen test is successful, Steve will be located in Hollywood for at least six months and in all likelihood for a period longer than that.

Other agents at GAC sent me congratulatory letters.

But a week later, Harry Cohn, the boss of Columbia Pictures, died suddenly, and the new management at Columbia refused to honor the deal. Blauner threatened to sue. In response, Columbia said that they would send someone around with a Brownie camera to snap my picture—my *screen test*—thereby legally fulfilling their contractual obligations. So much for my career as a Hollywood movie actor.

One day, in spring 1958, Blauner called and invited me to accompany him to Connecticut to see a rock act that someone at the agency had recommended. The act was Bobby Darin. "Had I ever heard of him?" I briefly described how we had met in high school and worked together in Detroit, and that Bobby was a terrific performer. I didn't go that night, but their meeting became the stuff of legend.

Blauner and Bobby were a perfect match. Steve had the chutzpah to promise anything, and Bobby had the ability to deliver it. When Blauner quit GAC to become Bobby's manager, the rumor was that Bobby had to give up a big portion of his future income to George Scheck as the price for his freedom.

After Decca had dropped Bobby, Blauner got Ahmet Ertegun and Jerry Wexler of Atlantic Records to record Bobby's rock version of "I Found A Million Dollar Baby" on their Atco label, and this first release sold more than any of his earlier records. In April 1958, Bobby recorded "Splish Splash," and that summer he had his first real hit. ("Splish Splash" lists Jean Murray, deejay Murray Kaufman's mother, as Bobby's co-author. Some things never change.) Many people thought that, because of the way he phrased the lyrics, Bobby was black, and he was booked on the rock 'n' roll shows at the Brooklyn Paramount along with Fats Domino and Little Richard. But wherever he worked, he built a reputation as a solid performer. "Splish Splash" was followed by "Queen Of The Hop" (Bobby had finally gotten together to write a song with Woody Harris), and then "Dream Lover"—all Top 40 records, but nonetheless still keeping Bobby in the kid-record market.

In 1959, Blauner convinced Atlantic to take a chance and let Bobby record an album of Sinatra-style, grown-up songs. They released the first cut on the album as a single, and "Mack The Knife" became the huge hit Bobby had always dreamed of: making it all the way to Number One and winning two Grammys— for the Best Record of the Year, as well as Best New Artist.

At first they called him the brash, cocky kid who had made the transition from folk to rock to nightclubs. But when he worked around the country and in Las Vegas with George Burns, he showed that he wasn't a fluke, setting attendance records everywhere and always getting great reviews. With his first album a smash, and "Beyond The Sea," the follow-up single to "Mack The Knife" a solid hit, in 1960 he was booked into New York's Copacabana. The conquering hero was returning home.

The publicity was enormous (I even read a blurb in one of the papers that he had made a three-thousand dollar settlement to New York City for all those ancient, unpaid parking tickets that had filled the glove compartment of his old Dodge). Every radio station played his records (one did a Darin retrospective, even playing "Rock Island Line," jogging some not-so-very-deeply-buried memories). Walter Winchell wrote an entire column about the great quintet of musicians that Bobby carried with him everywhere, and although I knew that he was doing it *big time*, now the memories became even more bittersweet.

I was surprised when someone from his management office called and invited me *and* my parents, as well as all the members of our old high school band, to attend opening night at the Copa *as the guests of Bobby Darin*. By this time, my mother's rage had solidified to the point where she was calling him a "bum" whenever she heard his records or saw him on TV. In some ways, I think it was a parental expression of anger to protect her wounded son, venting the hurt I was incapable of expressing myself.

My own reactions to his successes were mixed. I could never feel comfortable enough to allow myself to be captured by his magic while he was capturing everyone else; but I also couldn't help but respect and admire what he had grown to be. It was all a product of hard work; he had earned every accolade he was receiving. I guess I just wanted to be up there with him, to be a part of what we had begun together. But that was impossible. I guess I was just jealous.

But we accepted the invitation.

On his triumphant night of nights, he was simply marvelous—dressed in a perfectly tailored tuxedo, his music played by a huge orchestra. I hadn't seen him work, except on television, since I'd stood behind him at Club Temptation, and I watched with pain and pride at how he had become the consummate performer. This was his night to show off for the old crowd as well as the new, and he killed everyone; playing piano, drums, dancing, singing all of his hit records, and finally walking off to a roaring standing ovation—when a standing ovation really meant something—leaving us all limp.

After the show, I guided my parents up to his dressing room in the Hotel Fourteen next door. We waded through the mob of admirers and finally squeezed into his suite. Nina and Charlie were there, as were Blauner and Dick Behrke, who was now Bobby's conductor; everyone was staying as close to Bobby as possible, wanting the excitement to rub off.

When he saw us, he beamed and came over, first embracing me, then my mother and father.

"I'm so glad you could come Mrs. K. You too, Mr. K. It wouldn't be my first opening in New York without you being here."

"You were wonderful, Bobby," Pop said. "It's a long way since Science High school. You were just terrific. And you didn't need the words written on your hand, either!"

"Yes, you were *wonderful*, Bobby," my mother repeated, smiling her best.

"Great show, Cassotto," I said. "Your music sounded fantastic. The big time."

"Thanks, Curley," he said. "Thanks for everything."

He spotted someone behind us, and broke into a huge grin. After another brief moment of polite conversation, he winked and melted back into his new life, enjoying the glow of every minute of it, absorbed by the adoring crowd.

As we left, in truth, I couldn't help but feel abandoned again.

Chapter 31

"ANOTHER PHONE CALL"

For many years, Bobby Darin played no direct role in my life.

By the early '60s, the novelty of calypso music had worn thin, and I worked less and less. The Beatles and their brethren had conquered the music industry, and after finally accepting that my voice wasn't strong enough to make the transition from folk to rock the way Bobby had, I decided to hedge my career options by also becoming an actor. I enrolled in a six-month course taught by director Gene Frankel at The American Theatre Wing. Then I joined the Lane Theatre Workshop, run by Burt Lane (father of actress Diane Lane).

Now, in addition to composing, practicing my guitar, and trying to improve my piano technique, I added the dimension of *emoting*—strutting around our apartment wrapped in a white sheet as my toga, my hair combed forward, shouting the "Friends, Romans, and Countrymen" speech from *Julius Caesar*. If my parents were against my singing direction, this new wrinkle drove them nuts altogether. My Shakespearean accent also brought the percussive morning comments from Mr. Raymond-downstairs to a whole new level of critique.

I took the required head-shot photos and started making rounds. I immediately learned that young actors gain experience by padding their resumes with names and details of fictitious parts they had supposedly played in out-of-town stock companies. Equipped with a list that included my real "Godfrey Show" singing credits together with some enhanced acting jobs, I joined the endless lines of hopefuls at the open casting calls that were listed each week in *Backstage*, the unemployed-actor's bible. But when, at last, my turn would come, and I was invited by the stage manager to walk on to the empty stage (as *dramatically* as I could, of course), and speak my name (as *loudly* as I could, of course), I always heard that distant "thank you" from a tired voice somewhere out in the darkened theatre. The constant rejection was made somewhat easier knowing that I was sharing the same fate as those who preceded me in the line. A few times, I actually got to read some dialogue before the guillotine fell.

Once, I was asked by an agent who'd heard that I had a musical background if I could handle the understudy role for comedian/actor Dudley Moore, who was staring in *Beyond The Fringe*, a hit British comedy that had been running on

Broadway for a few years. I'm not sure who was more desperate—the agent who put me up for the part or me, the smart-ass idiot kid from the Bronx who agreed to take the audition—but this was clearly going to be a *major* stretch in type-casting. Dudley Moore was about five-foot-four, impish, decidedly British in sound and manner, and a masterful pianist. I was six-feet tall, skinny, decidedly New York in sound and manner, and a masterful faker.

Could I read piano music? asked the agent. *"Bu' a course, Guvna!"* I said in me best Cockney. Could I speak with a British accent? *"Nu, vu den?"* I answered, in my best Yiddish. The agent laughed, got me a ticket to see the show, and told me to pick up the sheet music at his office.

One of Mr. Moore's routines, and the material that would be my audition, was a hilarious, non-ending piano romp of the "Colonel Bogey March," the theme from *The Bridge Over The River Kwai*. When I looked at the music, it was black with notes, and I mean black. Someone had taken the tedious time to transcribe every single grace note, nuance, humorous trill, arpeggio, and ad-lib that Dudley Moore played each night (even Tiny Simpson's band would have had a hard time cutting *this* chart).

On the morning of the audition, I *ambled* on to the stage, full of *here-I-am, mumbled* something in Brit-speak about my theatrical background to the faceless producers in the back of the theatre, and then proceed to fake a few bars of the music—stopping with the courageous, but sorry, excuse that I hadn't had enough time to practice the part.

Their response was also decidedly British: *"Theeeeenk yew veddy much."*

I never heard from that agent again, and I was too embarrassed to ever go back to his office.

Another time, a new musical was casting for singers who could play the guitar. This was a natural for me, I thought, and I wore my Club Temptation dark suit and light tie to the audition; I looked *very* professional. After responding to a few questions about my background, the voice in the dark asked me to sing something. I chose "Country Boy," my favorite soft, plaintive, finger-picking folk ballad. As I was walking off after the inevitable "thank you," the voice asked: "By the way, do you dance?" "Absolutely," I lied. I certainly wasn't the type to get the part of Conrad Birdie in *Bye Bye Birdie*, but for years after, I received postcards from director Gower Champion, inviting me to open calls for chorus dancers and singers. I never went to those. Faking goes only so far.

Finally, I landed a job as an understudy in a Broadway play. *The Devil's Advocate* was a World War II drama, adapted from a best-selling novel by Morris West, and directed by Hollywood legend Dore Schary. It starred Sam Levene (who had originated the role of Nathan Detroit in *Guys and Dolls*), Leo Genn (Bill Sykes in the movie *Oliver Twist*), Eduardo Ciannelli (a kind, gentle man who had played the evil sheik in *Gunga Din*), and Edward Mulhare in his first role since replacing Rex Harrison in *My Fair Lady*. The female lead was played by British actress Olive Deering, a favorite of Director Cecil B. DeMille, who had cast her as Moses' sister in *The Ten Commandments* and Sampson's sister in *Sampson and Delilah*. It was all very upscale show biz.

I joined Actors Equity, and followed the traditional tryout routine for a Broadway-bound drama: four weeks of rehearsal in New York, then off to Boston for two weeks of break-in, then on to Philadelphia for two more. In Philadelphia, I was offered the job of assistant stage manager; I learned how to *run the show*, call all the lighting cues, and direct the scene changes. One memorable night, I was invited to play poker and pass around a bottle of bourbon with Jason Robards and Martin Gabel, who were appearing down the street in *Big Fish, Little Fish*. These two theatrical giants had resonant voices made of leather, and their slight-est whispers could be heard in the second balcony (I think the Old Granddad added a little something to their ability to project).

When *The Devil's Advocate* opened on Broadway in March 1961, the reviews were good, but not good enough. After limping along for three months, the show closed. The character I understudied—a seventeen-year-old Italian boy orphaned during the war—was played by an actor who unfortunately never got sick or missed a performance, so I never got on. (Years later, I met him in an elevator. He told me he was painting for a living. Walls, not canvases. Yet another sign.)

I never developed the freedom as an actor that I saw in others, and my second and final role was a bit part in a cheapie, non-union movie. But once again, in a moment of divine intervention, my Muse took charge. After overhearing the producer of the film discussing his need for a background music score, I played him some of the songs I'd written and offered to write the score for free if he would pay for the band and the studio, and let me own the copyrights—a bar-gaining chip I'd learned from my first experiences with George Scheck.

This became my first real job as a composer, and I dropped out of the Hansen's scene completely. During the next four years, though I would occasionally go on the road for a singing date, it was song writing, producing, and conducting the scores for exploitation and soft-core porn movies that generated my main source of income. In my own small world, I was competing with Henry Mancini and Alex North: once, I had six films playing on Forty-second Street at the same time: *The Twisted Sex*; *The Girl On A Chain Gang*; *Miss Conduct*; *Hot Nights On The Campus*; *Nudes on Tyger Reef*; and *The Beautiful, The Bloody and The Bare* (a horror porno). It was the perfect place to make mistakes and grow (no one ever listens to the music in a porno film). I learned how to arrange, and to orchestrate, and conduct; and these fledgling first steps pointed my life in a whole new direction.

But old ambitions die hard. In 1963, when writer/comedian Allan Sherman cracked the record charts with comedy folk-song parodies like "Hello Mudda, Hello Fadda," a friend, Bob Arutt, and I jumped on the bandwagon and wrote a bunch of our own funny parodies about the problems of urban life. Jubilee Records released them in an album called *This Is A City?* True to form, the album didn't sell. But I brought the songs to the "Soupy Sales" TV show, and for years after I was the voice of Pooky the Lion, as he lip-synced my recordings of "Gimme That Old Unemployment," and "Sam McDonald Sells Used Cars, Don't Pay Now, You'll Owe!"

And old emotions don't simply evaporate, either. Whenever Bobby would return to the Copa for another record-setting engagement, the pangs of loneliness would start again, and I would slump around until his booking ended, unable to explain my gloom to anyone, burying myself in work. And each year I successfully fought down the urge to call him, accepting that he was in his own world: a world I was no longer a part of.

Just one time did I give in. I was unknown to his road managers, but when his secretary returned my call, I was instructed that Mr. Darin would see me in his suite at the Drake Hotel at noon a few days later—"but only for a half-hour," she emphasized, before he went to rehearse for the Bob Crosby TV Show. It was the first time we had been together, alone in a room, since the Wolverine Hotel. When I arrived, he broke the ice by giving me a back-slapping hug. He had been practicing twirling two Colt .45 cowboy revolvers given to him by his new friend, "Duke" Wayne.

"Listen to how the gun clicks when you pull back the hammer, Curley," he said counting along with each click. "C–O–L–T. That's how you know it's a *Colt*, by the four clicks. I want you to know that I've renamed the gun," he continued, flashing his now famous numero-uno. "It's my C–U–N–T gun."

I smiled. "You may be a big star, Cassotto, but some things never change."

"Better believe it," he said proudly. I glanced at his scalp, dotted with small bloody scabs. He had lost much of his thin hair. "Don't let it scare you, Curley, *and you're lucky that you can still be called Curley, Curley*," said Groucho. "It's a new restoration technique: live hair is implanted in your skull and it grows there. It looks terrible now, but in two months I'll be combing my own again."

"Well, the rest of you really looks terrific. I'm happy for your successes, Bob."

"Thanks." Then his tone changed. "Now, Steve, I know you want to tell me about your own career," he said gravely, "but I must make it very clear beforehand that you're not to ask me for anything. People are always asking me for things, and I've delegated all of my business decisions to my managers. I don't even know my own phone number. I hope you understand that we travel on different levels now."

"Of course, I understand that. I don't want anything from you, Bobby. I didn't come here to ask you for anything. I came to say hello to an old friend, that's all. And to say that I'm proud of you."

"Well, I appreciate that, Steve, I really do. Life is really amazing, isn't it? After Crosby, I'm on my way to Europe to make another flick. Can you believe it?"

"Sure, I can believe it."

"Here's the plot." He took the half-hour to tell me the story and read lines from the screenplay. Then his secretary interrupted to announce that it was time to go to rehearsal. "Wanna come watch?" he asked, without real enthusiasm.

I got the message. "No, thanks. I have another appointment. It's been really great seeing you."

We hugged again, and went back into our own lives.

As usual, he was right. We lived in two different worlds, and it
was time for me to accept that the only part of his that I would ever be in was as
a memory from our high school band and a footnote from our first club job.

Although I tried to pay less attention to his doings, I could never block him out
completely.

When Connie Francis was riding high on the charts with "Who's Sorry Now,"
"Stupid Cupid," and "Lipstick On Your Collar," she and Bobby would often be
teamed up as a musical couple on Dick Clark's "American Bandstand" and "The
Ed Sullivan Show." In 1959, they were chosen as the King and Queen of Hearts
for the American Heart Fund Campaign. But sharing music onstage was as far as
their romance would go. No matter how much Connie wanted it to work out, she
wasn't strong enough to stand up to her domineering father. Not even the
rewards and fame of "Mack The Knife" earned Bobby any respect from Mr.
Franconero, who would forever consider him a lowlife street kid unfit for his only
daughter. (Once, when Connie was appearing on the "Jackie Gleason" TV show,
Bobby showed up at rehearsal; legend has it that Papa pulled a gun and made
Bobby run for his life. After that, Bobby gave up.)

In 1960, it was impossible to avoid the publicity surrounding his elopement with
Sandra Dee, Hollywood's top young starlet. They had met on location in Rome
while filming Come September with Rock Hudson and Gina Lollobrigida. In
many ways, Sandra Dee was just like Connie Francis, perfectly fitting the cut-out
that Bobby always claimed he wanted for his ideal wife: beautiful, immature,
pure, and innocent; a pushover for a fast-talker from the Bronx.

Connie wrote in her autobiography, Who's Sorry Now?, that hearing on the radio
that Bobby had married Sandra Dee was a crushing moment for her. Her father's
reaction was: "It looks like that bastard is finally out of my hair."

Connie carried her demons for a long time. Years later, when the Biography TV
series was preparing an episode about her life, she called and asked if I would
appear on the show. "Tell them Bobby and I were very much in love." Of course,
I did as my first star asked, but the line never made the cut. Instead, I'm seen
describing how I occupied her father with small talk while Connie and Bobby
necked in the rehearsal studio next to George Scheck's office. The caption under
my interview reads: Steve Karmen, friend of Bobby Darin.

In the early years of their marriage, Bobby Darin and Sandra Dee were America's happy, bubbly, young couple—the Eddie Fisher-Debbie Reynolds of that era; the Sean Penn-Madonna of a later time. The fan magazines were filled with photos and articles about "Bobby and Sandy" and their idyllic life; their move into a new Hollywood home, how they managed their separate careers; and later, in 1961, all about the birth of their son, Dodd. When Sandy wasn't making a movie, she would often accompany Bobby to his nightclub engagements, sit in the audience, and be introduced during his act. Then, I began to hear stories from other acts about the yelling and screaming that went on backstage—mainly her complaints about his entourage: his band, road managers, PR reps, and his *inner circle* of pals who were always hanging around in his dressing room, his hotel suite, and at their home in L.A. Bobby demanded a life with his friends apart from his marriage, and Sandy's resentment of their lack of privacy became public knowledge.

Sandra Dee was an established movie star and Bobby was a wannabe. Steve Blauner did everything he could to correct this—getting Bobby roles in the film musical *State Fair*, and in *Pressure Point* with Sidney Poitier. In 1963, he earned an Academy Award nomination for his work with Gregory Peck in *Captain Newman, MD*. But his acting career never really took off, and although he and Sandy even made a few movies together—*If A Man Answers* and *That Funny Feeling*—their separate worlds were more than their marriage could stand. One day, in 1967, the press carried the story of their divorce. He had simply walked out, telling Sandy, "I just don't want to be married anymore."

Along with his personal troubles came a professional reputation for arrogance—at a time when arrogance was acceptable and cute. Musician friends described how Bobby might walk into a recording session where a big orchestra had been booked, only to announce that he just didn't "feel like singing," and would then turn on his heel and walk out. When he was booked at a club, and became moody or bugged about something, he could refuse to do a late show.

His arrogance took on a personal sting. To his inner circle of friends, Bobby always declared "you are my family, and I couldn't do it without you; and I love you and we'll be friends forever." The punch line, always omitted was: "as long as you do things my way." Dick Behrke, our kid-band trumpeter, had worked hard through the years to become a skilled arranger, and Bobby hired him to be his musical conductor. But they fought constantly—Behrke expecting a friendship greater than an employer-employee relationship. When he could no longer take

Me and Bobby D. – A Memoir

the bickering, he quit. Bobby forced the same result with another of our band-era friends, Dick Lord, our substitute drummer from the old days. Lord had grown into a successful comedian, and Bobby promised to protect him and help his career. He hired Lord, first to open for him in Las Vegas, and later to be a writer and performer on a Darin summer TV show. But as soon as the ratings suffered, or some joke didn't get the expected laugh, Lord was the first to be dropped. It was easier to blame someone he knew rather than someone he didn't. When it suited him, Bobby also ended his relationship with his manager, Steve Blauner, and then with Don Kirshner, another "old friend." We were no longer the kids in the band, swapping songs at Vinnie's, with only the glow of making music in our eyes. The old adage is true: *never, ever do business with family or friends.*

I saw every film he made, but always alone on some afternoon, not wishing to share my feelings with anyone, and wondering why I still needed these one-sided visits. But whatever role he portrayed on the screen, to me he was always Cassotto, his eyes ablaze with that same cocky Bronx attitude, and I could never fully believe his characterizations.

For a long while I was haunted by the part he had played in my youth. But slowly and finally, I began to put things into perspective.

My own career was changing. The day came when I decided
to turn down all performing work. I guess I was an example of the old show business adage about being so out-of-demand that when I quit, nobody knew it. I mark in my memory refusing an appearance on the annual Dean Martin City of Hope charity telethon as the official end of my singing career. Lenny Ditson, the kindly agent who handled this event each year, had booked me on it several times in the past—not so much for the exposure it offered, but primarily because he knew it would provide a payday for a struggling act ($104.00, I think it was, the required AFTRA union scale), and allow me to earn a much needed month's rent. Each year, I had made the hopeful phone calls, asking agents, family, and friends to watch, but they never did. I was usually on around five AM, a filler act between Billy the Balloon Blower and the Paramus, New Jersey High School Marching Band. The prospect of prolonging my career at that hour was pretty bleak. It was another sign. It really was time to get out.

There were many other hungry, young people moonlighting in the low-budget movie business—cameramen, musicians, sound engineers—people who worked on Madison Avenue during the day, in the advertising world. When one of them asked me to write the music and produce the background score for a Girl Scout commercial, this opened up a whole new field. Ever the negotiator, I agreed to provide the arrangement for free, in exchange for a small residual payment if the commercial ran for any length of time, as well as the right to own the copyright and control all *non*-advertising uses of my music.

After composing a sixty-five to seventy *minute* motion picture background score—music by the pound—writing sixty *seconds* of music for a commercial seemed like a snap. I put together a presentation tape reel—leading off with my Girl Scout commercial, followed by the best of my porno film music—and began looking for work at ad agencies.

In that first year, 1966, I wrote jingles and background tracks for Johnson's Baby Oil, Score Hair Cream, Devil Shake Chocolate Drink, Halo Shampoo, Lucky Whip, Fina Gasoline, Krueger Pilsner Beer, and Circus Peanut Butter.

Now, wearing several new hats, I was building a solid reputation as a jingle composer and arranger; as a business man, I was learning the value of being a music publisher and producer—always behind the scenes, but with enough input to make a difference in the final product.

I had several offers to form joint ventures with others, but I was never able to chase away that deep-rooted insecurity of not trusting someone again in a partnership, and I remained on my own. The single exception was the girl I met and fell in love with at acting school, someone not unlike Chris—a Catholic from the Midwest with small-town values—but someone I could talk to without the fear of being judged and abandoned again. And unlike Chris, our religious differences were of no importance to her; we found common ground together, and were married in 1961 in a simple ceremony at City Hall.

I took the challenge of becoming an arranger and orchestrator quite seriously, determined never to allow what happened at Club Temptation to happen again. At first, I wrote only for small groups—five, six, or seven players—but as my confidence grew, I began to add full sections—eight brass, five saxophones, and that greatest pleasure of all, a fifteen-player string section. I bought books on orchestration and became a royal pain in the ass to several musician-friends whom I would call to seek enlightenment about chord puzzles and harmonies I couldn't figure out on my own.

I also studied the politics and intrigue of the advertising business, where the simple approval of an agency producer or account supervisor could give me the means to hire a thirty-five-piece orchestra to play my music. Always anxious to please, I began adding back-up musical ideas into each arrangement, plotting in advance in case someone from the agency wanted to change something. Instead of orchestrating, say, for only the trumpets, I would also prepare something to be played by the flutes, or trombones, or French horns, or a different rhythm pattern for the drums. And I would mark all the *extra* parts *"DO NOT PLAY"*—that way, if I, or my client, was unhappy with a certain portion of the chart, I was always ready with a quick fix. (Of course, I never revealed this built-in flexibility to anyone.)

On the business side, after watching my jingle colleagues sell all their rights to their creative work in the one-sided standard contract that every ad agency used (not unlike the record business), with the help of Peter Kelley of the William Morris Agency, I developed my own contract form to *license* the uses of my music. I know that the advertising agency business managers hated dealing with me, and that I pushed the envelope pretty far. (Peter Bart, the editor-in-chief of Variety, has written: "In business, you don't get what's fair. You get what you negotiate.") Fortunately, I could back up my Darin-style chutzpah with my music, and I found the fulfillment of Pop's belief in the promise of America in the open marketplace, where value can be determined *fairly* between *both* the buyer and the seller.

Looking back, I placed my desire to have my music sound *original* as my prime motivator. In 1969, when asked to compose for Hershey's Chocolate, instead of working in a real studio, I chose to record "The Great American Chocolate Bar" in my basement, on a cheap, low-fidelity Wollensak tape-recording machine. I reasoned that everyone else was using slick, big-band tracks, and that my solo voice and guitar would sound different when recorded at home. (The popularity of my hit Hershey commercial earned me some publicity, and when I was interviewed on the "Barry Gray Radio Show," I told the story of how I got started scoring porno films. During the call-in segment that followed, one listener declared that she was never going to buy another Hershey product because "their music was being written by an immoral man." Another caller really made me laugh:

"Stevie, it's Uncle Jack. How come you never call the family?" Always the bigtime.)

I used a tuba for Budweiser and a Flüegelhorn for Salem Cigarettes. I recorded without echo or reverb for Plymouth, and tried every imaginable trick and technique to make my songs sound distinctive and different.

When I had scored my nudie-movies, the music was recorded *non*-union. I paid my players in cash, and insisted that my employer come up with the green at least forty-eight hours before the session (Producers of exploitation films had a well-earned reputation of promising the moon, and then disappearing as soon as the sun went down).

On my first *union* session, for Maxwell House coffee, Bernie Leighton played the harpsichord and the great Milt Hinton played the bass part. I soon discovered that the musician's union scale for jingles was the highest of all, and that the top players were always anxious to work because there were *residuals*, that irresistible magnet of endless ongoing income.

Composing jingles allowed me to record with some wonderfully talented big stars. In 1971, the Chrysler-Plymouth song was called "Comin' Through," and I wrote arrangements for Louis Armstrong, Ella Fitzgerald, The Everly Brothers, Bobby Goldsboro, and Mark Lindsey of Paul Revere and the Raiders.

Recording with Louis Armstrong was a particular high. Although this musical legend had recently been seriously ill and had not played his trumpet in over two years, his instantly recognizable, gravely voice was still in great shape. I was quite nervous when I called his house in Queens to pick the correct key for him to sing. But Louis put me at ease immediately, assuring me that he had listened to the demo tape I had sent, that he loved the song, and that we would have great fun working together. For the session, I booked trumpeter Burt Collins, one of New York's top studio musicians, to play a sound-alike version of that distinctive Armstrong trumpet style. When Louis arrived to overdub his vocal part, we all posed for pictures, and Burt and I each got a special glow from standing next to this unique icon.

But to my advertising client, a young agency producer who had flown in from California to oversee the session, Mr. Armstrong was nothing more than a hired hand. "Tell him to go 'VA VOO VA VOO VA' in the spaces," she briskly instructed me as Louis warmed up.

"We really don't need anything *extra* in there," I tried gently to convince her in the privacy of the control booth. "Louis is a master and his instinct is the best. Let's let him do it his way."

"No, no, no. No! Tell him we want to him to scat, the client wants him to scat, to sound like Louieeee Armstrong, you know, to go 'VA VOO VA VOO VA.'" (I had been instructed to call him either "Pops" or "Louis," but never "Louieeee" or "SatchMo.") I had no choice.

I decided not to give vocal direction to the great Louis Armstrong over the talk-back system, but knew I had to at least *attempt* to placate my client. Diplomacy 101. I headed into the studio and stood next to Louis while we both listened to the playback on headphones. "Pops," I began softly, "I think what you're doing is great, but the client wants you to scat in the open spaces. Of course, I'll take your best advice on whether it works or not, but for them, please consider it." (His microphone was open and we both knew everyone in the control booth was eagerly listening.) Louis nodded along patiently as the track was played again, and then said, "You really don't need nothin' else in there, man. The trumpet fills those holes up great, and that's exactly how I would have played it. And the lyric's right where it should be, and it feels right, so that's how I'm gonna sing it." Then he looked at me, with a knowing glance, raising his eyebrows, privately, so only I could see: the classic Louis Armstrong look. He had clearly suffered agency producers on other commercials in the past, and knew exactly how to handle this one. I returned to the booth. "I told him," I said, smiling to myself. "Okay, let's try it." After a few run-throughs, my client got used to the way Louis was singing it—the correct way—and didn't push to get her VA VOO VA VOO VAs in the final track. It was a big lesson: when you hire a star, let them do what you hired them for. A few weeks later, an envelope arrived containing an autographed picture of Louis playing his horn, along with an extra gift that confirmed his fabulous sense of humor: it was the famous Armstrong photo, taken through a key hole, of Louis sitting on a toilet bowl, with his pants down around his ankles. Stapled to the picture was a small package of Swiss Criss, a particularly powerful laxative. The caption under the photo said SATCHMO SLOGAN: *Leave It All Behind Ya!* That man's joy for life was endless.

Ella Fitzgerald was another one-of-a-kind artist who sang for Chrysler that year. Although she was nearly blind from complications of her diabetes, she had done her homework—the ultimate mark of a pro—and never missed a word or note.

But she was nervous and asked if I would stand next to her while she sang. Leaving a client alone in the control booth is always a dangerous thing, but on that special day, I decided to trust my engineer. I took the hand that this great lady extended to me, and we squeezed each other's fingers like two children while she performed. She didn't need my encouragement. This kid from the Bronx was very proud that day.

Jerry Lewis sang on my jingle for the Great Adventure Amusement Park. When he arrived for the session, chewing a wad of gum, he took it out of his mouth, stuck it on the glass that separated the control room from the studio, and then said: "Steve, on a film set, I'm the director and I'm the boss. This is *your* set, and *you're* the boss. Show me what you want and I'll do it." And he did. Perfectly. Twenty minutes later, he shook my hand, plucked the gum off the glass, popped it back into his mouth and left. Talk about *professional*.

Memorable jobs came from unusual sources.

Robert Evans, the Hollywood producer of *The Godfather*, *Rosemary's Baby*, *Love Story*, and *Chinatown*, and former head of Paramount Pictures, had recently been arrested for purchasing a large amount of cocaine. But instead of sending him to jail, the Los Angeles judge had sentenced him to use his ability and contacts in the film community to deliver a strong anti-drug message to teenagers.

"I could make a twenty-minute training film, and be done with it," Evans said to me, "but I want to do something of real impact. I want to produce a series of commercials to be aired on national television—no copy, just a song—and I want you to write it."

Over the next month, we met several times in New York, as I developed the lyric for "Being Yourself," the theme for his *Get High On Yourself* idea.

> YOU CAN BE SOMEBODY WITH A PLAN OF YOUR OWN
> YOU CAN SAY NO, AND YOU WON'T BE ALONE
> YOU CAN MAKE YOURSELF GET HIGHER
> THAN YOU HAVE EVER KNOWN
> WHEN YOU'RE MAKING UP YOUR OWN MIND
> DOING THINGS YOUR OWN WAY
> SETTING UP YOUR OWN STYLE
> BEING YOURSELF

YOU CAN BE SOMEBODY WITH YOUR OWN POINT OF VIEW
JUST BY ACTING YOURSELF IN WHATEVER YOU DO
YOU CAN BE SOMEBODY
AND THE CHOICE IS UP TO YOU
WHEN YOU'RE MAKING UP YOUR OWN MIND
DOING THINGS YOUR OWN WAY
SETTING UP YOUR OWN STYLE
BEING YOURSELF

After recording the music tracks in New York with a thirty-piece orchestra, the production moved to California, and I watched the power of big-time Hollywood at work. Over a long weekend on a sound stage at Paramount, we rehearsed the song with a group of one-hundred Los Angeles grade school and high school students.

On Monday afternoon, I taught the song to Evans's friends from the entertainment world: Carol Burnett, Cathy Lee Crosby, John Davidson, Linda Gray, Mark Hamill, Bob Hope, Kate Jackson, Cheryl Ladd, Paul Newman, Victoria Principal, John Schneider, Cheryl Tiegs, Herve Villachaize, and Henry Winkler; and from the sporting world, Muhammad Ali, Tracey Austin, Rod Carew, Julius Erving (Dr. J.), Rosie Grier, Ron Guidry, Dorothy Hamil, Magic Johnson, Carlos Palomino, and Willie Stargell.

(Know how you teach Muhammad Ali to sing? Verrrry carefully.)

That night, the stars and the kids got together, and sang the song over and over for five hours, while director N. Lee Lacy filmed thirty different commercials, each focusing on a separate group of stars and kids. Years later, Quincy Jones used this same technique for Michael Jackson and Lionel Ritchie's composition, "We Are The World."

That fall, NBC aired a one-hour special about the creation of the campaign, and broadcast a different commercial at the beginning of every prime time program as part of *Get High On Yourself* week.

The story of this production has been preserved in the film *The Kid Stays In The Picture*, taken from Robert Evans's autobiography. I enjoy four seconds of fame as I'm seen conducting the singers during the filming. Only my kids would recognize me.

I wrote for many top products: "When You Say Budweiser, You've Said It All," "Weekends Were Made for Michelob," "Here Comes The King—The Clydesdale Theme," "For All You Do, This Bud's For You," "Sooner or Later You'll Own General Tires," "We Build Excitement—Pontiac," "Quality Is Job One—Ford," "At Beneficial (Doot Doot!) You're Good For More," "Trust The Midas Touch," "Carry The Big Fresh Flavor of Wrigley Spearmint Gum," "Pick A Pack Of Juicy Fruit Gum," "Doublemint Will Do It!" "Hertz, We're America's Wheels," "A Taste Of Europe—TWA," "You Can't Beat The Experience—Pan Am."

While I was selling everything from cars to beers to colas to candy, Bobby was looking for that ever-elusive, next hit record. At Atco, he recorded a swing album with songwriter Johnny Mercer, *Two Of A Kind*; then a rhythm-and-blues tribute to Ray Charles, *Bobby Darin Sings Ray Charles*. In 1963, he switched from Atco to Capital Records and cut a folk album, *Golden Folk Hits*, and a Broadway album, *In A Broadway Bag*. In 1966, he moved back to Atlantic, where he had his last chart single, a folk song, "If I Were A Carpenter." For a while he recorded for his own label, Direction Records. In 1970, he switched again, this time to Motown. His records were always well-produced, but they were never *hit*-hits, earning airplay mainly on the easy-listening stations—an industry acknowledgement of someone who was once "The New," but who wasn't anymore. Lost somewhere in the cracks between the hip swing of "Mack The Knife" and the soft rock rhythms of "Dream Lover," he was always respected as a fabulous onstage performer, but had no real marketable record identity. The kids who had bought "Splish Splash" and "Queen Of The Hop" were all grown up, and the new teens were hooked on the British invasion and flower-power. The record business just passed him by. He tried many styles, but nothing stuck. He must have been furiously frustrated.

In 1971, I'd heard that he had undergone open-heart surgery. The old rheumatic fever of his childhood had finally caught up with him. But incredibly, after only a few months of recuperation, he was playing Las Vegas again. The press didn't treat it as the same thrilling, industry-shaking event as when Sammy Davis, Jr. had returned to the stage after losing an eye in a car crash; but the reviews were good, and I was glad to hear that he was strong enough to go back to work.

That's when he called.

417

I was in my office when my secretary announced in a thrilled voice that "Bobby Darin was on the phone!"

"Hey, Killer! How are you?"

I was instinctively cautious. "Great, Bob, and you?"

"Good-good."

"Still doing doubles?"

"Yeah-yeah. Right-right."

I waited, on guard. "So, my old friend, what's new?"

"Well, the first thing is that I hear you all over the tube. I'm proud of you, Curley. Some of those commercials are really terrific. You've come a long way."

"Yeah-yeah, I guess I have. And so have you, Bob. I've followed everything you've done. You did it all the right way, just like you said you would."

"Yeah, I tried-I tried." Then he dropped his bombshell. "Let me cut right to the chase: how would you like to produce my next movie?"

"Why me?" I asked, stunned, feeling the bubble of the old excitement. *Had he called five other guys before me?* I wondered instantly.

"Simple. I have a hunch that you'd be a great film producer—I saw *The Locusts*— and I always surround myself with the best people. That's why I'm calling *you*."

"Well, I'm truly flattered."

Earlier that year, I had taken a month off from the advertising world to try a new dream: I produced and directed a movie. *The Locusts* was a short film about a man driving down the parkway in his new Cadillac, who has engine trouble, and pulls over to seek help. In the space of ten hilarious minutes, his car is stripped down to the frame by passers-by—joggers, men in a golf cart, thugs in a moving van, a cripple in a wheelchair, an old lady with a shopping bag—everyone swipes a piece of the car, and finally leaves the poor guy sitting on the frame only. Then a cop pulls up and gives him a ticket for littering the highway. I finished the film without dialogue, just a music track, and it opened at Radio City Music Hall with Jack Lemmon's latest feature, *The War Between The Men And The Women*. *The Locusts* got great reviews, and won the 1972 Atlanta Film Festival Gold Medal

Special Jury Award as the best short subject of the year. So I had some small experience working in film, and I knew that it was an all-consuming occupation.

"I'm going to send you a script I own called *The Bells*," Bobby said confidently. "If you like it, think about producing it. Maybe I'll direct, I don't know yet. But I am going to play the lead. It might be fun to work together again. Will you read it, and consider it?"

"Of course, I will," I said as calmly as possible, attempting to control the sudden dizziness I was feeling.

"Call me-call me. Soon-soon."

"I will-I will."

Talk about a bolt from the blue. After I hung up, I sat there, motionless, amazed at how, with just a few words, he was able to nudge the rudder of my life again, to bridge years of separation in seconds, and still make my head spin. Was working together again really a possibility? And, after all these years, did I really want to? And what was his definition of *together*? Did he call because I had made it on my own, because he could now relate to me as an equal? Or was that just my rationalization for the painful fact that he still knew how to push my buttons and manipulate my world?

In spite of the complexities of my own life, I found myself wanting very much to be involved with him again.

The script arrived by messenger the next day. I postponed all other work to read it. It was a period western that took place entirely in the desert, and it was soon obvious that involvement in this major production would require spending a great deal of time in California, away from my growing family—something that I didn't want to do. Also, the scope of the picture was much greater than my limited film experience could handle without someone's help—most certainly, his. Quickly and gratefully, I realized that as much as my *emotions* wanted to work with him again—and just be with him again, and perhaps to foolishly join our worlds again—that I could never again put myself into the position of being his employee, regardless of title.

But I very much wanted to see him.

So I sent a telegram, Darin-style, saying without commitment of any kind, that I was prepared to come to Las Vegas to discuss the script.

When his secretary called the next day to confirm a date, I began to feel queasy about turning him down.

But this was a one-time-only opportunity.

And, this time, I knew had to do it.

Chapter 32

"REUNION IN VEGAS"

He looked terribly thin, gaunt, sickly, and he was heavily made up. Without the toupe that looked so real in his publicity pictures, the spotlight on his head showed lots of skin. He had clearly been through an ordeal and was not well. He was wearing a denim suit, undoubtedly custom-made, and a string tie—a far cry from the magnificent tuxedos he had always worn. Now I understood why the marquee of the Desert Inn had spelled his name *BOB DARIN.* Bobby was doing Bob Dylan, cashing in on the current renewed folk music craze.

His opening song was about love and peace—I had never heard it before. Then he sang James Taylor's "Fire and Rain," another folk approach. When it ended, someone in the audience yelled out, "Sing 'Mack The Knife,'" and there was a ripple of excited applause.

"I'm going to do that real soon," he said, "but first I want to sing a song that I heard on the anti-nuke march last fall..."

And that's how it continued: message-song after message-song. Mostly, the audience listened respectfully, but sometimes the sounds of eating and quiet chatter could be heard over the soft, folky ballads. They were not a particularly unfriendly crowd, but nothing knocked them out. His dynamic stage presence came through in short spurts between songs, when he clowned with ringside tables, but the otherwise heavyish material was mostly unfamiliar, requiring attention to every word. His once vibrant, electrifying trademark movement was now limited to an occasional stroll around the stage. He spent much of the show sitting on a stool, strumming his guitar and playing harmonica. A medley of "Splish Splash," "Queen Of The Hop," and "Dream Lover," treated as a tribute to the past, brought them up a bit, but when he followed it with another unknown, they settled back again into passive attention.

He had been on for about forty-five minutes. "Folks, I want to introduce someone to you. You won't know his name because you haven't heard it before...*in fact, sometimes <u>he</u> doesn't know his name, even when he knows the secret woid. Right, Fennemen?"* The audience, desperate for a laugh, responded to Groucho. "He's a wonderful composer of advertising music, and I know you've heard...," and he

421

sang the tag line to four of my most recognizable jingles. I couldn't imagine what would motivate him to do this.

"But before I introduce him, I want to tell you a story. Years and years ago, in another life, when we were kids in high school, Steve and I played in a band together. And when I went on the road for the first time as an entertainer, he came along as my accompanist, and more importantly, as my friend. He was there, helping me at the beginning when I really needed it, and I've never forgotten it. Ladies and gentlemen, put your hands together, and meet my dear friend and a big talent, Steve Karmen."

He pointed to my table. Suddenly I was bathed in white light. I stood, acknowledged the polite applause, and waved to him, mouthing a "thank you."

"And now, ladies and gentlemen, I'm going to do a song that I recorded a little bit after Steve's time, but it's one that I hope you'll remember and enjoy."

It was his Grammy winner, "Mack The Knife," and the energy and power he put into it earned him the strongest applause of the night.

When he came off and the house lights went up, a burly man with long hippy hair and wearing a real denim suit appeared at the table, and asked that I follow backstage.

His dressing room was a three-room suite, beautifully furnished, with a bar and a full kitchen.

"Hiya, Curley," he said brightly, as we embraced. He was wearing a bathrobe with a towel around his neck. His body felt bony. Without makeup his skin looked wasted.

"You were terrific, Bob, never better."

"Thanks. It was a good audience. Jimmy, get the man a drink."

"Just soda, please." We sat on the couch. "This is a great dressing room."

"Yeah, they take care of me pretty good here."

There was a framed picture on the table of a young boy, about eight years old. "Your son?"

"Dodd. Greatest kid in the world. He lives with Sandy. I gave her the house when we split up."

"I was sorry to hear about that."

"Ah, no regrets; all part of living. I gave her most of everything—the house, the cars, the money—they're only material things. There's no room in my life for material things any more. In fact, not many people know this, but I've been living in a trailer in the woods near Big Sur. God's country. Really beautiful, quiet. I keep just enough to get by and pay my band."

"I'd heard you'd remarried," I said, risking banter.

"Yep. Andrea. Greatest lady in the world to put up with me."

"I don't remember that being too hard to do. How are you feeling?"

"Never better, Curley. They rebuild you in surgery until you're brand new. Never felt better."

"Well, it was nice to hear from you after all these years." I tried to lead the conversation. "I was flattered to think that you might want to work together again."

"It's been a long time, hasn't it? Down different roads." But he took control. "Tell me about your family."

"I have three wonderful daughters and a wife who puts up with me. Business is good so I can't complain."

"I'll bet. I keep hearing you all over the place. You're a musical force in America, Karmen. I hope you work on commission."

"Not quite," I laughed, "but I'm doing okay. How come you never did a jingle? I don't think I've ever heard you on anything?"

"Don't believe in it, Steve, nothing personal. A star is a star is a star, if you know what I mean."

"And you certainly are. But some very big people have sung jingles. I recently did some spots for Chrysler with Louis Armstrong and Ella Fitzgerald. It's another way of being in front of the public. If I write one in the right situation, would you consider it?" It was a slip. I shouldn't have asked.

"That might be fun, in the right situation," he answered. But he didn't mean it. "Who does your arranging?"

"Me."

"Really? The huge orchestras, too?" I nodded. "Bravo-*bravo*! Some of them are really great, Curley. Where'd you learn how to do that?"

"Asking the right people the right questions." I hesitated, but jumped in again. "Remember my first rhythm charts? We both had big balls in those days."

"I remember-I remember. How many years has it been?"

"Sixteen," I answered, much too quickly.

"Sixteen years! Jesus, *forever*. You have no idea how many times I've thought about calling you." I smiled. "No bullshit, I mean it. Something always came up, you know. Hey, what can I say?"

"Say nothing. I understand. The important thing is that we're still here. That's something."

"That's so right," he said earnestly.

Go *slow, Karmen*. "Who do you record for these days?" I asked.

"About to sign a deal in England for independent production."

"You've made some great records, Bob. Classics. They'll live forever. I was always proud of you."

Jimmy brought my drink. "Greatest road manager in the world. More than a road manager, Jim is my best friend. Excuse yourself for a while, Jimbo—Steve and I are going to reminisce."

"Right boss," he smiled. "If you need anything, I'll be next door."

I had the feeling that the time for chit-chat was over. "Okay, tell me, did you read *The Bells?*"

"As soon as I got it. It's a wonderful script. But it's not for me."

He was surprised. "Why not?"

"Truthfully, it's unrealistic to think that I could do the kind of job you want done effectively from New York. And I can't live on the Coast, Bobby, that's out. My kids are in school, and my life is in New York."

He seemed confident of convincing me. "Well, I thought you might say that. I think I can help you with that part. A lot of this could be done from New York until we got into pre-production."

I wanted not to weaken. "How so?"

"I want you to be *executive* producer. To raise the money. That's a New York job: mostly on the phone, a few lunches, that kind of stuff. I'm sure you know other investor-types in the advertising business who'd be interested in backing a picture. You shouldn't have any trouble at all."

"Bobby, if I understand you correctly, you would like me to raise the money for a movie that you want to star in and direct."

"Bingo! Producer, points, credit, everything."

There was no hesitation in my answer. "I could never do that, Bob. I've made it a policy never to ask my clients for anything. It's not good for business."

"Well, then maybe you'd want to finance it yourself, at least in the preliminary stages. You'll get it back on the other end. You'd be full producer, you know."

I smiled and shook my head. "You're a tough guy to say no to, but I have to say no. I'm good at my own business because that's all I do, and I do it all the time. I don't want to be in the movie business."

"What about *The Locusts?*"

"Just a weekend fantasy."

He was quiet. Then he said, with uncharacteristic acceptance, at least for the Bobby Darin I used to know, "Too bad. It would have been fun working together again."

In that instant, my anger was gone. It was truly over. Done. I was no longer a pathetic kid feeling sorry for myself. It was an astounding moment. "Yeah, it would have been real nice. But it's not in the cards, at least not now, at this time in my life. But maybe another time."

"So you came all the way out here to tell me *no* to my face," he smiled coyly. "Is that it?"

"No, Bobby. That's not it. You know I could never say no to you. I came out here because you called me, and because I wanted very much to see my dear old friend again. This is just not the right time for me to get into the movie business."

Again, he was silent. He seemed defeated, resigned, with no spunk to try and change my mind. I suddenly felt very sad, almost to the point of tears.

"We always had a good time, didn't we?" he asked quietly.

"No, we always had a *great* time! A *great* time."

He looked into my eyes, and then winked at me. "Let's order before it's gets too late," he said, breaking the mood.

"Not good to eat too close to a show," we both said in unison, joking together at last.

"Hey, Jim! Bring a few menus, please?"

"Comin' up," answered the voice in the other room.

"Maybe we should go out to the Bagel," I said, trying to be light.

"Jesus, how do you remember all that stuff? Well, you always were a man for detail. What a greasy spoon! Ah, those were the days, weren't they? When we did things just for the fun and happiness of doing them. Do you remember any of those people?"

"Well, I know that you went back to Club T. Did you ever see Myra again?"

"Good-good, boychick! I didn't remember her name. No, I never did. If I recall correctly, the line had closed by the time I got there. Who was the other one? The roommate."

"Chris Evans," I said, a little wistfully.

"Yeah, Chris, the blonde, with the short hair, right? You never banged her, right?"

"Not that one," I grinned.

"Right, it was the other one. What was her name?"

"Liz Carleton."

He thought for a minute. "I remember the show, but I can't remember her face. Jesus, sometimes it's all such a blur."

I paused. "I remember her very well. Remember the Pearl? I wonder what ever happened to her."

"Gone into stripper history. But here's a piece of trivia for your files: I worked with the comic again. What was his name?"

"Clipper Daniel."

"No. Clipper Daniel was his name when *we* knew him, but when he worked with me a few years later at Ben Maxik's in Brooklyn his name was...damn, I can't remember...Burt something...Gordon! That's it! Burt Gordon was Clipper Daniel. I guess he thought changing his name would help his act."

"Did it?"

"No. I fired him after two days. Had to. He just wasn't funny. Very bitter, very angry."

"Too bad. He wasn't really funny in Detroit either. Remember 'Message From Garcia'?"

"Who could forget?" he said softly.

For a moment we were silent. "Yeah, who could forget." Then I asked, "What about Charlie? What's he doing?"

"Don't know. He and Nina got divorced a couple of years ago. I haven't seen him since. We had a fight about money, so he doesn't call. He thinks the world owes him. I don't know who's better off, he or she. She's not easy either. How're your folks doin'?"

"Good-good."

"Still want you to become a doctor?"

"Maybe in their dreams," I laughed, "but I think they're satisfied with the way things worked out. I know I am."

"Good for you."

Throughout dinner, we talked about our high school band days, the fun days, the young days, the paths we had both taken to this night. When it came time for the second show, he asked if I wanted to sit through it again.

"I wouldn't miss it for all the jingles in the world. But, would you mind if I watched from backstage?"

"Like the old days?"

"Yeah, like the old days. I'd like to see how it's done in the big time."

"Not at all. Jim'll set you up in the wings. I duck out quick after the show, so I'll say my formal goodbye now, before I get made up. Believe it or not, even after all these years, makeup is still messy." He opened his arms to me.

"It was just wonderful to see you again," I said as we hugged and kissed each others cheeks. "I hope you understand about the movie. I know I'm repeating myself, but I'm proud of you."

"It means a lot to hear you say it. I'm proud of you too, Curls. It was great to see you. I'll call when I get to New York. Promise. We'll get together. It's time for old friends to get together." Then, "Keep him happy, Jim," he said, disappearing into the other room.

I waited in his dressing room, listening on the small cue-speaker as the show went on. The separation had truly been made; the old days had become the gone days. About the time the comic was wrapping up, Bobby came out, and we walked silently into the wings together—I didn't want to break his concentration. His overture had already begun. Jim pointed to a stool near the huge lighting panel.

I watched from the side as he made his entrance. This show, some of the material was different, but the audience's reaction was pretty much the same as earlier: responding well to the oldies but poorly to the new songs.

When he came off for his first bow, I wanted to say a word of encouragement; but he passed me without notice, oblivious to anyone who was there, quickly going into a corner of the wings where Jim was waiting with a face mask attached to a portable oxygen tank.

I watched and heard him sucking in huge breaths. Then he quickly combed his hair and went back out again.

I looked behind me. There were two other oxygen tanks against the wall where Jim stood watching the stage, intensely guarding with devotion, following Bobby's every move with his eyes. His expression broke my heart.

When the show ended with "Mack The Knife," Jim was waiting: this time with an open bathrobe to receive Bobby's sweating body. And with his arms around for support, he led my boyhood friend, now huddled up and shivering, back to the dressing room.

I was riveted to my spot.

Just as the door was about to close, Bobby must have sensed that I was still there. He turned for an instant, flashed a numero-uno, and winked at me.

A year later he was gone.

1973 was not a good year for me.

In April, my father, aged 73, whose soft yet unswerving support had championed my cause as a teenager, died unexpectedly of a heart attack. Years later, when "I Love New York," a jingle I composed for the New York State Tourism account, was proclaimed as the Official State Song, I dedicated it in his memory.

In October, my wife, Sandy, aged 35, died expectedly after a devastating year-and-a-half battle with colon cancer. Raising my three daughters, then ten, eight, and seven, brought new focus to what was most important in my life.

And in December, Bobby Darin, aged 37, died on the operating table in the midst of a second open-heart surgery; that one last, futile attempt to improve his life for a few more years. His machinery had worn out, and it just stopped. The papers said he had left instructions that his body be donated to science, and that he requested no funeral or memorial service of any kind. They just took him away somewhere to become a learning tool for medical students.

Soon, Darin stories began leaking into the press. One told that just before his death, Nina had informed him that she was not his *sister* at all, but actually his *mother*. Nina supposedly refused to reveal whom his real father was, except that it wasn't Charlie Maffia. She told Bobby that Polly Cassotto was really his *grand-mother*, who had pretended to be his mother in order to shield her daughter's teenage indiscretion. Whether this was true or not, I don't know; but I cannot imagine anything but a self-serving motive for Nina to leave this sick man with this kind of deep torment. Perhaps she thought it would improve her financial standing in his pending estate. The image I carry of Bobby and his mother, the mother that we all knew, was at her funeral in 1959—all the members of our high school band attended—where I watched my friend kneel at Polly's grave, weeping uncontrollably at his terrible loss. He certainly never had that depth of feeling for Nina, regardless of which title she chose to wear.

There was also the tale of his Last Will, wherein he reportedly left all of his music business assets to his son, Dodd, but only to be distributed in dribs and drabs until Dodd reached the age of sixty-five. (Since Bobby had nothing when *he* started out, perhaps he reasoned that Dodd would be better off if he made it on his own, too, before being allowed to participate in whatever financial benefits remained from his father's career.) If this, too, was true, it felt to me like Bobby's unfair attempt to stay in the spotlight, typically keeping control, even from the great beyond. Some things never change.

After that triple-whammy year, my hope, supported by a lot of prayer, was that I'd stay alive long enough for my children to have at least *one* parent until they were old enough to take care of themselves. If I were that blessed (in this case, *lucky* is too ungrateful a word), I would have accomplished something truly wonderful with my life. Of course, things of that nature are far beyond any mortal's control, but I like to believe that events happen for a reason.

In some positive ways, the tragedy of Sandy's death opened horizons to me that I might never have seen had she lived. My children and I share a rare father/daughter closeness. As a single parent working for myself, I was able to schedule time-off during school vacations, and we traveled to as many places in the world as my successes could afford. Most of my clients accepted my priorities and were willing to postpone jobs until vacations were over.

Sometimes, I think this all happened to somebody else. I'm a vastly different person than when Sandy died, but I believe she would be pleased to see how well her children grew up. On the twenty-fifth anniversary of her death, we gathered for a celebration/memorial dinner, just the four of us. As we sat at our table, and without plan, there was a moment of silence as we looked into each other's eyes. Then Abbe, my middle daughter, expressed so eloquently what we were all feeling: "Well, we made it." No four words have ever meant more to me.

Sometimes, as the guy who never gives up, I still dream of winning some level of approval from my parents. I think they'd be proud of what I've accomplished with my career, even though I don't wear a stethoscope. My Mom got to see some of my achievements, and we reached an acceptable truce before she died, at age ninety-two, while still stubbornly living in the depressing West Bronx apartment where I was born and grew up.

As for my brother, he's still fishing under another tree, in another boat. Some things *really* never change.

And sometimes, when I think about Bobby, I wish he were here, too. I'd like to see him once more from my current perspective. I'm certain he would have found some positive outlet for his enormous talents, and be a force somewhere in the entertainment world. I know I could still learn things from him. Maybe we would be friends. Maybe time would have softened him, too.

Bobby's legacy to the music business is undeniable: he was the first singer from the rock era to make a successful crossover to the nightclub world. He proved that with hard work and a clear dream anything is possible. Who knows, if time had been on his side, perhaps he could have reinvented himself again and gotten a little closer to his goal of being as famous as Frank Sinatra.

Bobby's legacy to me is a bit more complicated.

In the beginning, he was the real-life embodiment of my Muse. Without him, my mother might have prevailed, and I might well have caved and become a very competent, very frustrated dermatologist living somewhere out in Massapequa, wondering what the hell happened to my life.

But he also left me with a never-ending distrust of partnerships.

Even today, whenever I hear his records or catch his movies on the late show, I still get that sudden, sinking feeling in the pit of my stomach. But before I force it back into the bottom drawer, my mind sometimes speculates about that last wink, that last flash of pure Cassotto.

On good days, I read it as a thanks for my being there when he needed me, when he sang the melody and I sang the harmony. *Sorry it worked out this way, Curls. Maybe we can still be friends.*

On bad days, it's just still slick Darin, who had only made contact to use me, and didn't succeed.

I know there are many people like myself, people who have been touched in some profound way by an early relationship that left a lifelong, emotional tattoo: *I went to grade school with Frank Sinatra and we sang in the chorus together; I knew Marilyn Monroe in high school, and she was built then! Mickey Mantle lived on my street, and we played catch when we were kids.* And when I hear people mention Bobby's name, I have often been tempted to say, "we grew up together, we played in the same band in high school, I did his first arrangements, I was his accompanist on his very first job, we were best friends..."

But I don't. Until now, my memories have remained too private for casual conversation.

Yet the years have given my spirit a measure of peace, with the certainty that we did share a deep friendship once—one that was real and important to both of us.

His gift to me was much more than my music. He was there when I needed him, too. He believed in me and in my talent when no one else would. He saved me. He toughened my confidence and taught me a new way of living—full out—and to be unafraid of risk. So much of his go-for-broke, spend-the-whole-paycheck attitude rubbed off on me. He unlocked my imagination. He's a part of every song that I write. I know that Bobby and I will be attached forever, the Bronx Corsican Brothers.

So, mostly, I try not to think about that last moment. Instead, I like to think about the first, that magical one, the one that changed my life forever, when he stopped me on the stairway of the Bronx High School of Science, and said, "Hey, you, with the curly hair. Wanna be in a band?"

I did.

I do.

I always will.